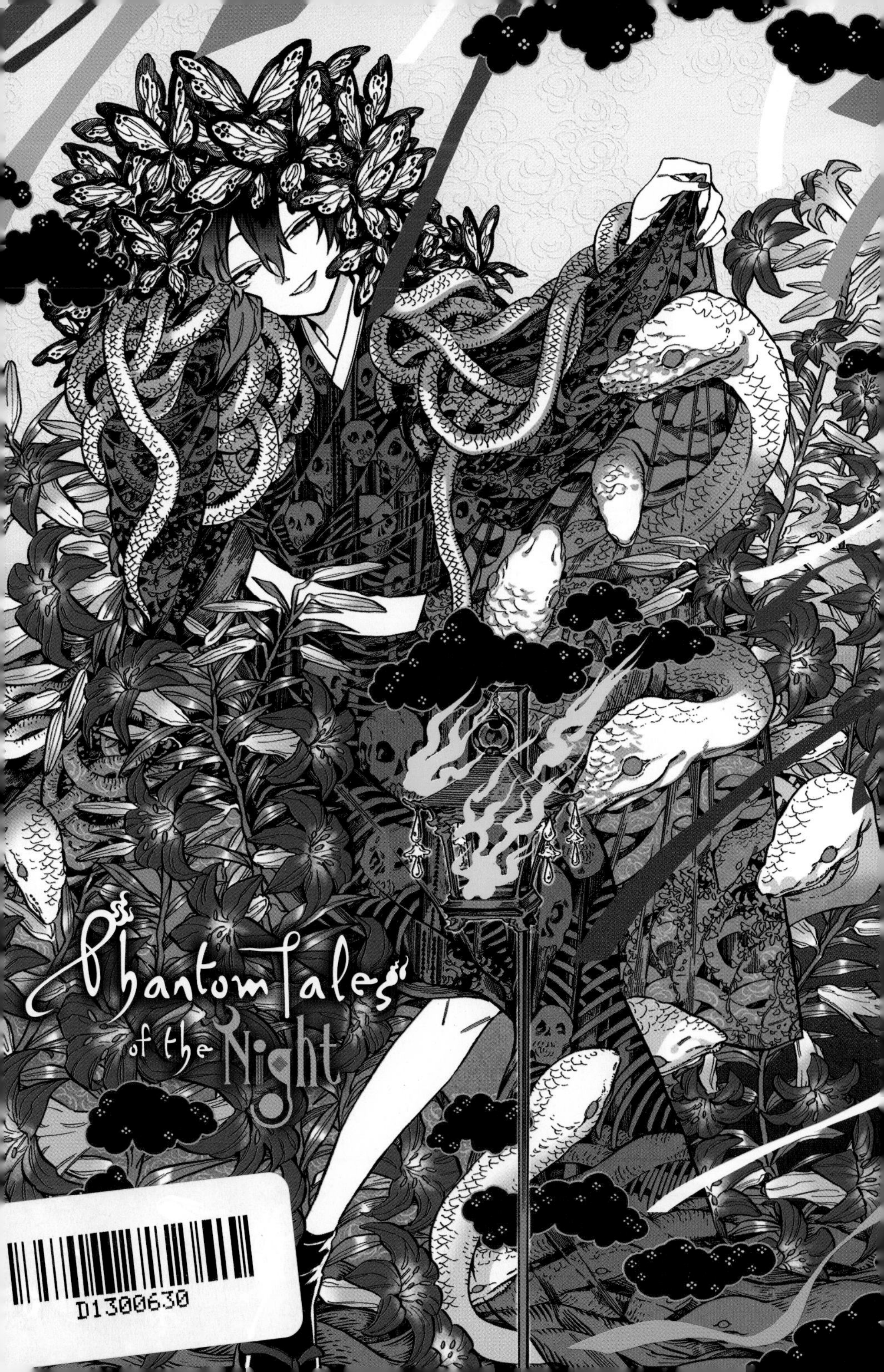
Phantom Tales
of the Night

CONTENTS

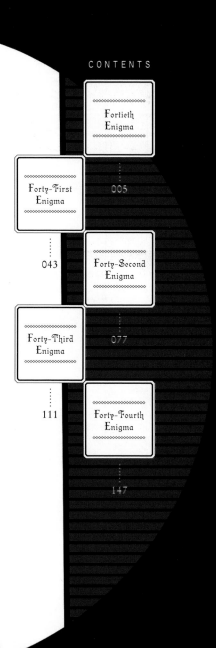

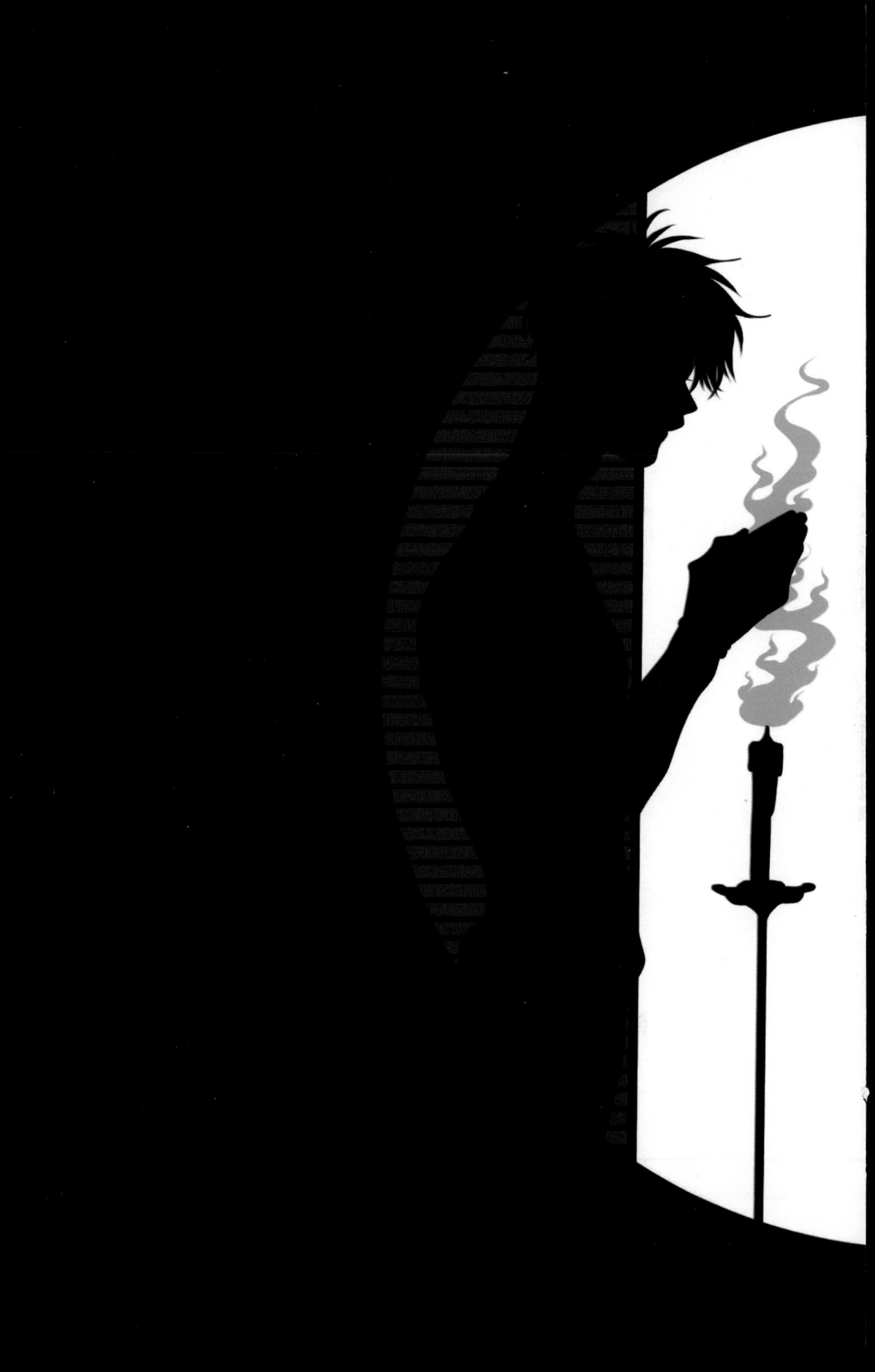

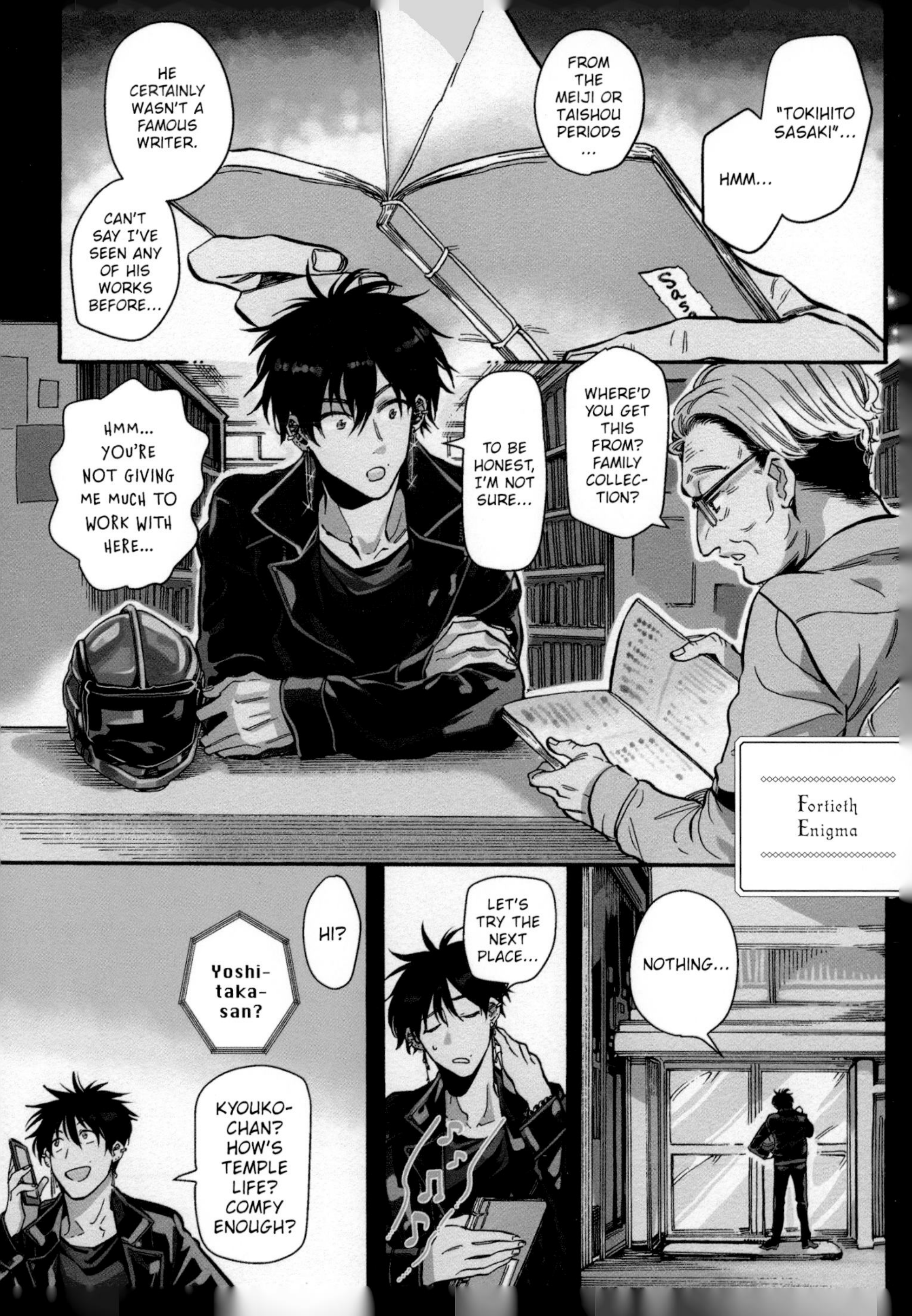
"TOKIHITO SASAKI"... HMM...
FROM THE MEIJI OR TAISHOU PERIODS...
HE CERTAINLY WASN'T A FAMOUS WRITER.
CAN'T SAY I'VE SEEN ANY OF HIS WORKS BEFORE...
WHERE'D YOU GET THIS FROM? FAMILY COLLEC-TION?
TO BE HONEST, I'M NOT SURE...
HMM... YOU'RE NOT GIVING ME MUCH TO WORK WITH HERE...
Fortieth Enigma
NOTHING...
LET'S TRY THE NEXT PLACE...
HI?
Yoshi-taka-san?
KYOUKO-CHAN? HOW'S TEMPLE LIFE? COMFY ENOUGH?

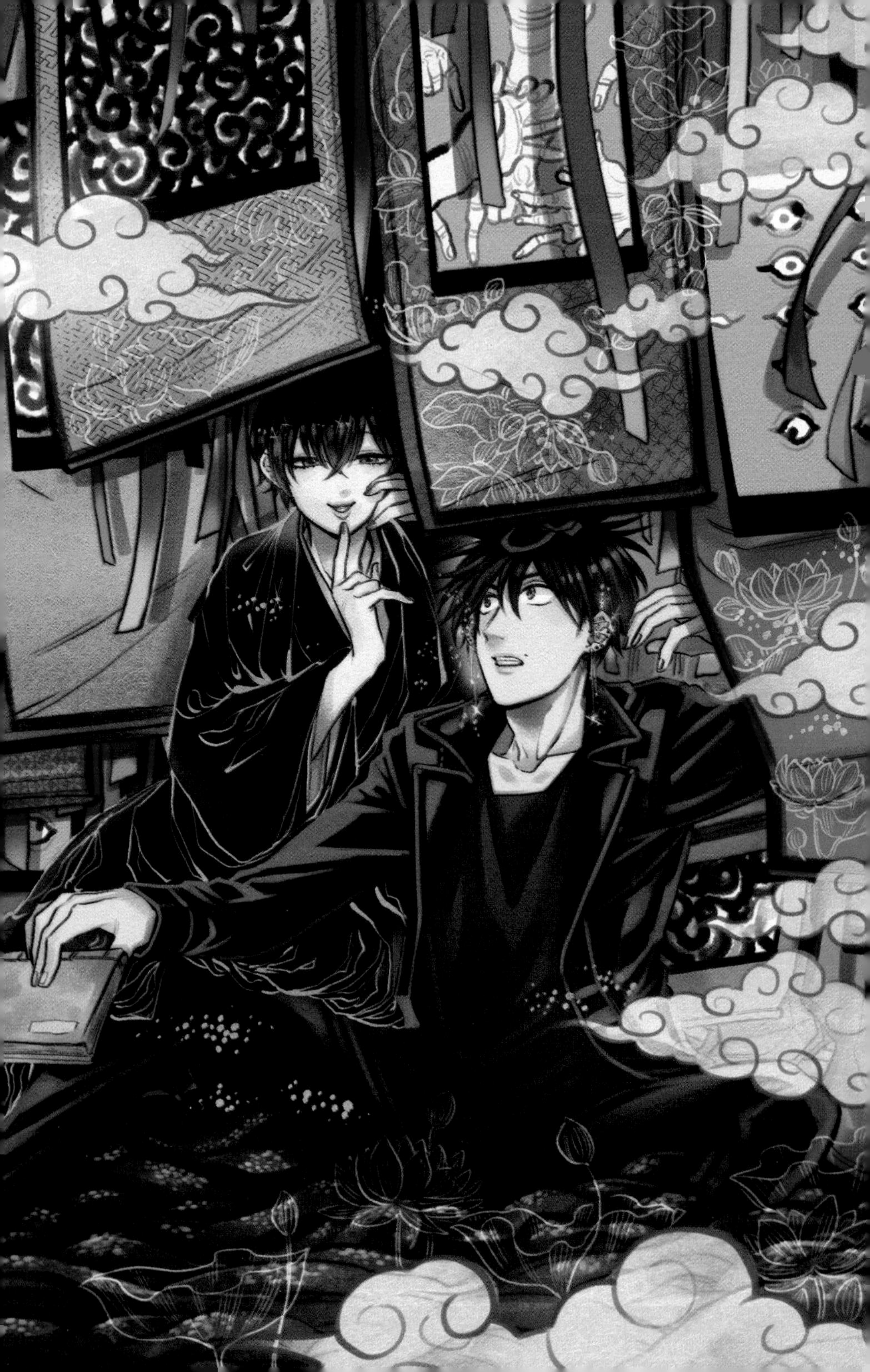

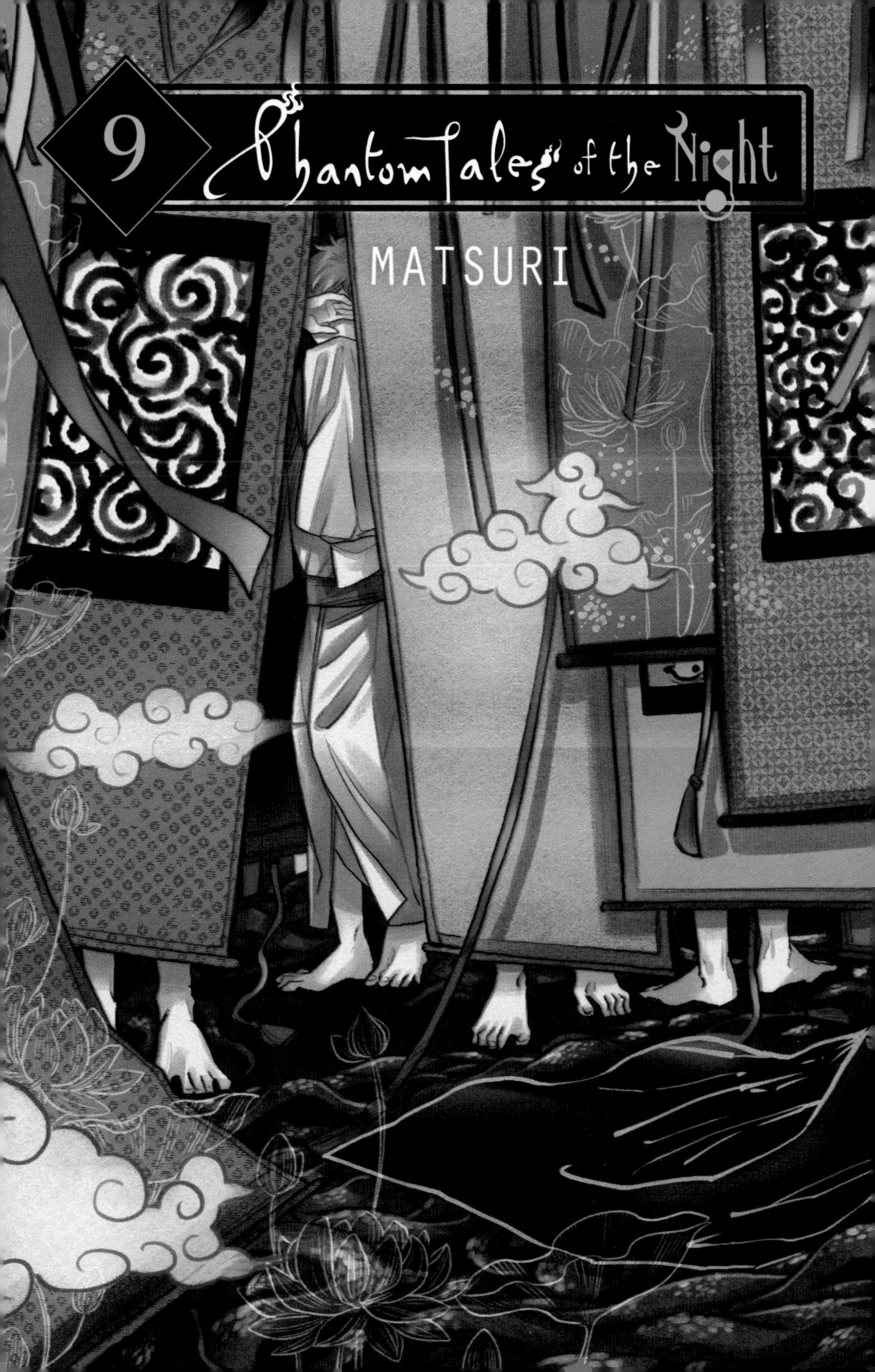
9
Phantom Tales of the Night
MATSURI

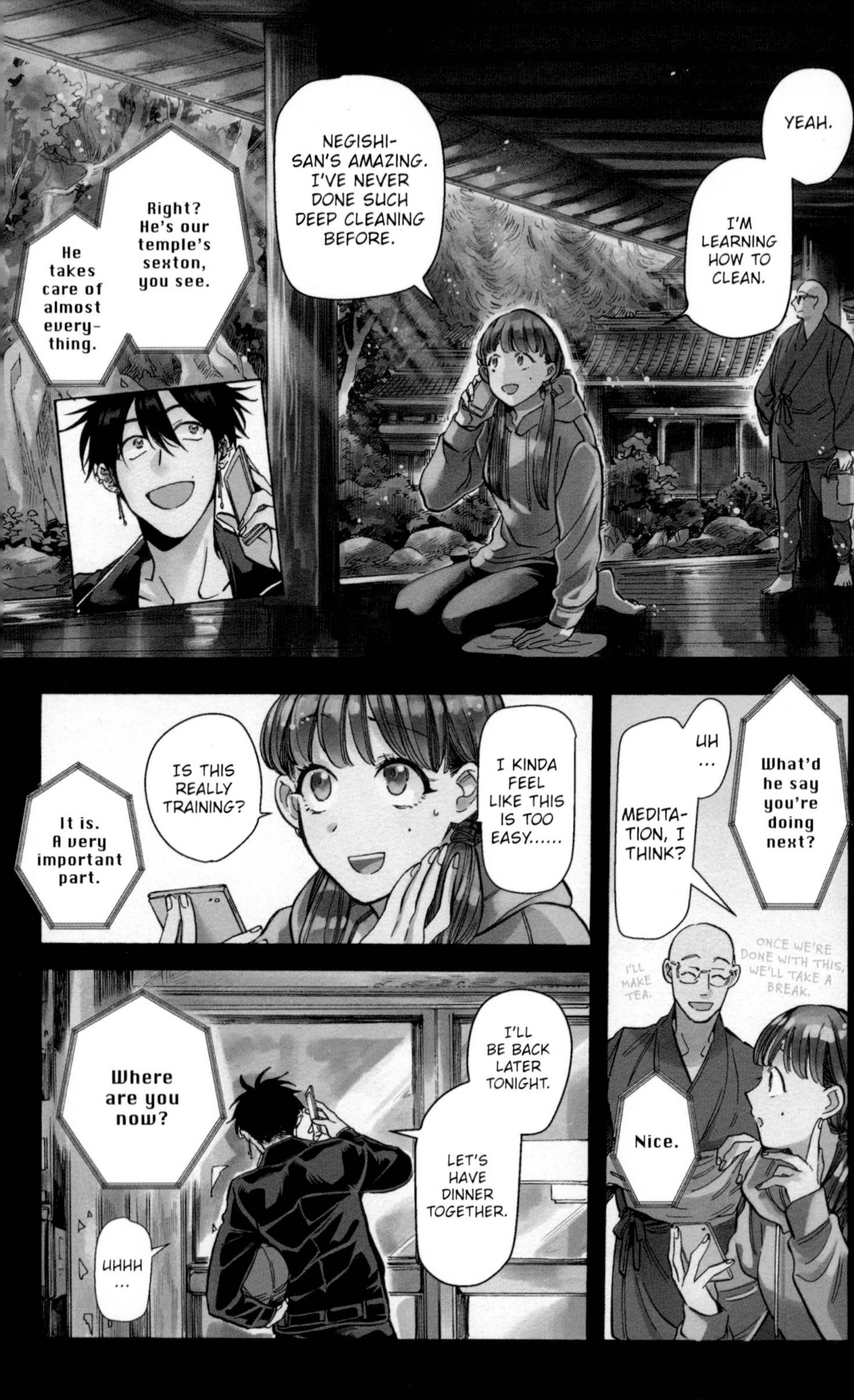
YEAH.
I'M LEARNING HOW TO CLEAN.
NEGISHI-SAN'S AMAZING. I'VE NEVER DONE SUCH DEEP CLEANING BEFORE.
Right? He's our temple's sexton, you see.
He takes care of almost every-thing.
What'd he say you're doing next?
UH...
MEDITA-TION, I THINK?
ONCE WE'RE DONE WITH THIS, WE'LL TAKE A BREAK.
I'LL MAKE TEA.
Nice.
I KINDA FEEL LIKE THIS IS TOO EASY......
IS THIS REALLY TRAINING?
It is. A very important part.
I'LL BE BACK LATER TONIGHT.
LET'S HAVE DINNER TOGETHER.
Where are you now?
UHHH...

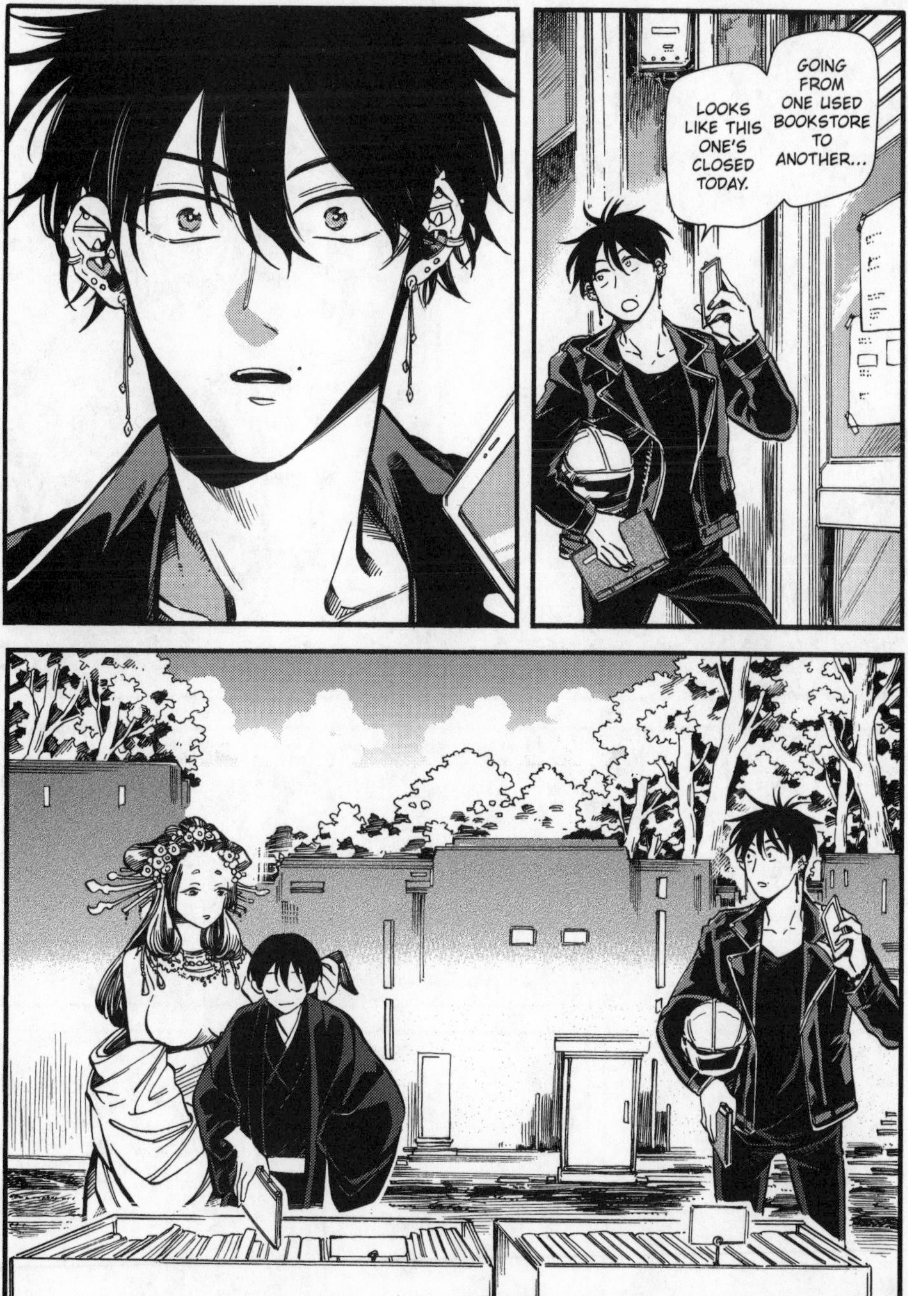
GOING FROM ONE USED BOOKSTORE TO ANOTHER...
LOOKS LIKE THIS ONE'S CLOSED TODAY.

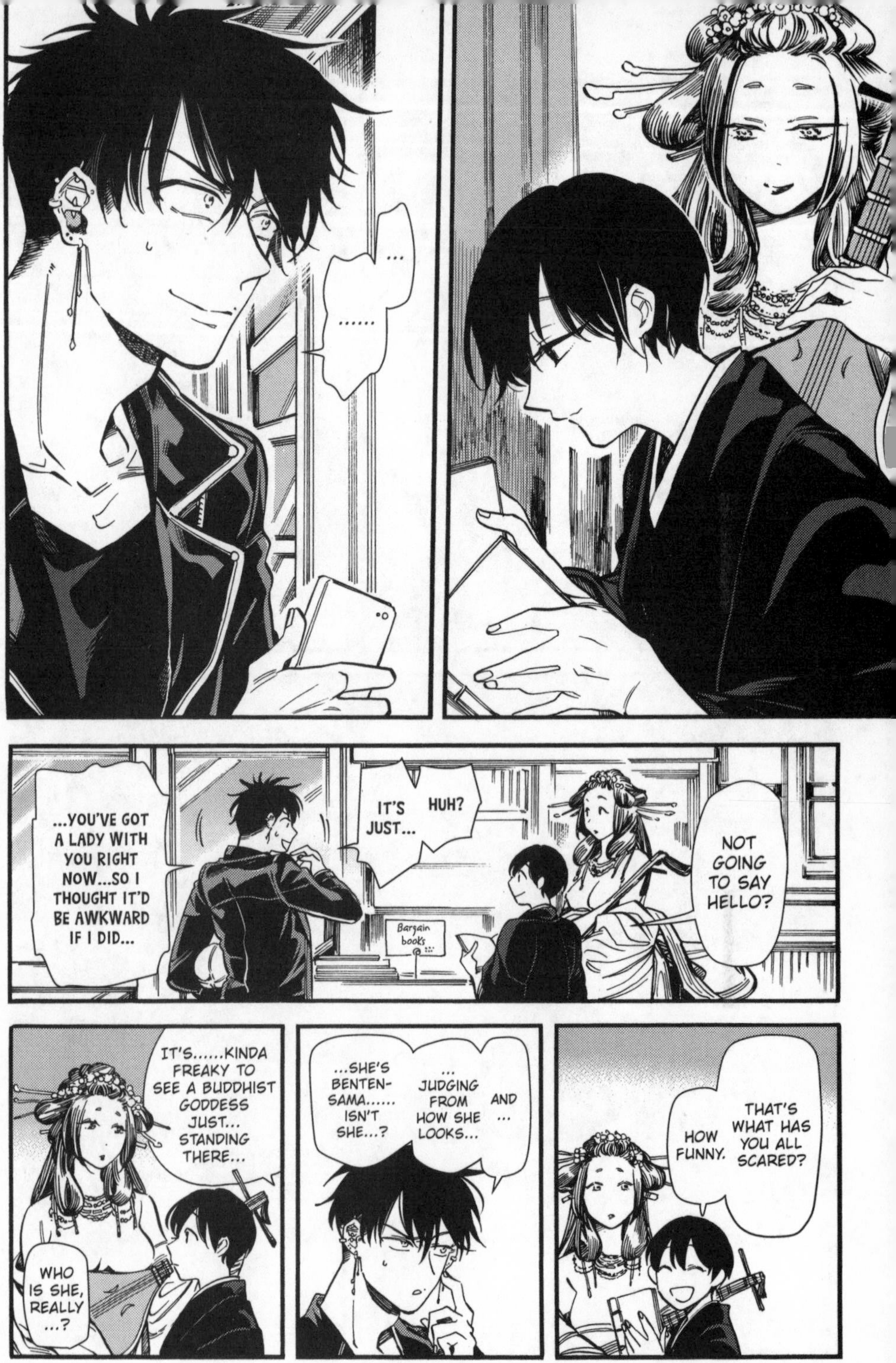
...
......
NOT GOING TO SAY HELLO?
HUH?
IT'S JUST...
...YOU'VE GOT A LADY WITH YOU RIGHT NOW...SO I THOUGHT IT'D BE AWKWARD IF I DID...
Bargain books
THAT'S WHAT HAS YOU ALL SCARED?
HOW FUNNY.
AND ...
... JUDGING FROM HOW SHE LOOKS...
...SHE'S BENTEN-SAMA...... ISN'T SHE...?
IT'S......KINDA FREAKY TO SEE A BUDDHIST GODDESS JUST... STANDING THERE...
WHO IS SHE, REALLY ...?

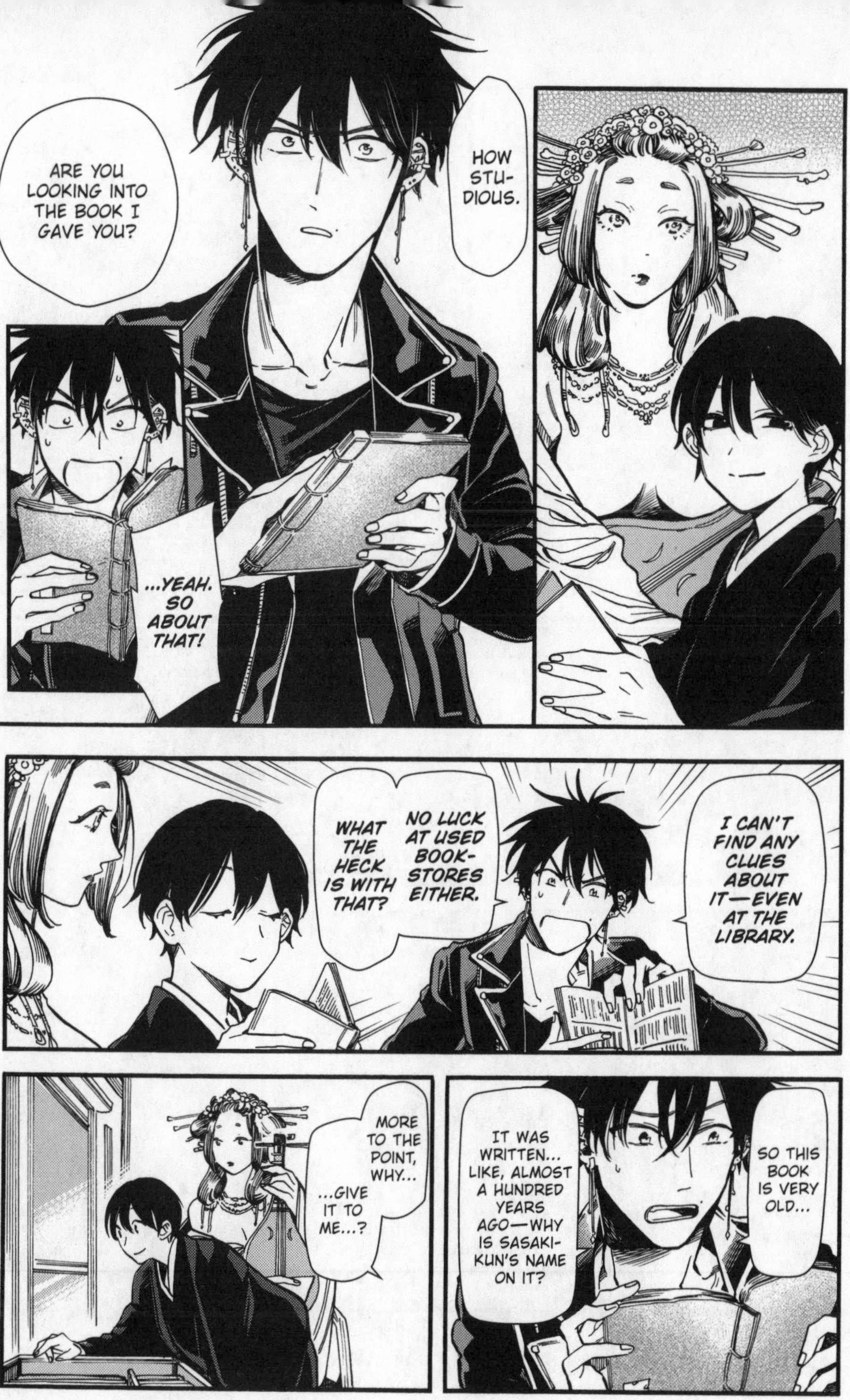
HOW STU-DIOUS.
ARE YOU LOOKING INTO THE BOOK I GAVE YOU?
...YEAH. SO ABOUT THAT!
I CAN'T FIND ANY CLUES ABOUT IT—EVEN AT THE LIBRARY.
NO LUCK AT USED BOOK-STORES EITHER.
WHAT THE HECK IS WITH THAT?
SO THIS BOOK IS VERY OLD...
IT WAS WRITTEN... LIKE, ALMOST A HUNDRED YEARS AGO—WHY IS SASAKI-KUN'S NAME ON IT?
MORE TO THE POINT, WHY...
...GIVE IT TO ME...?

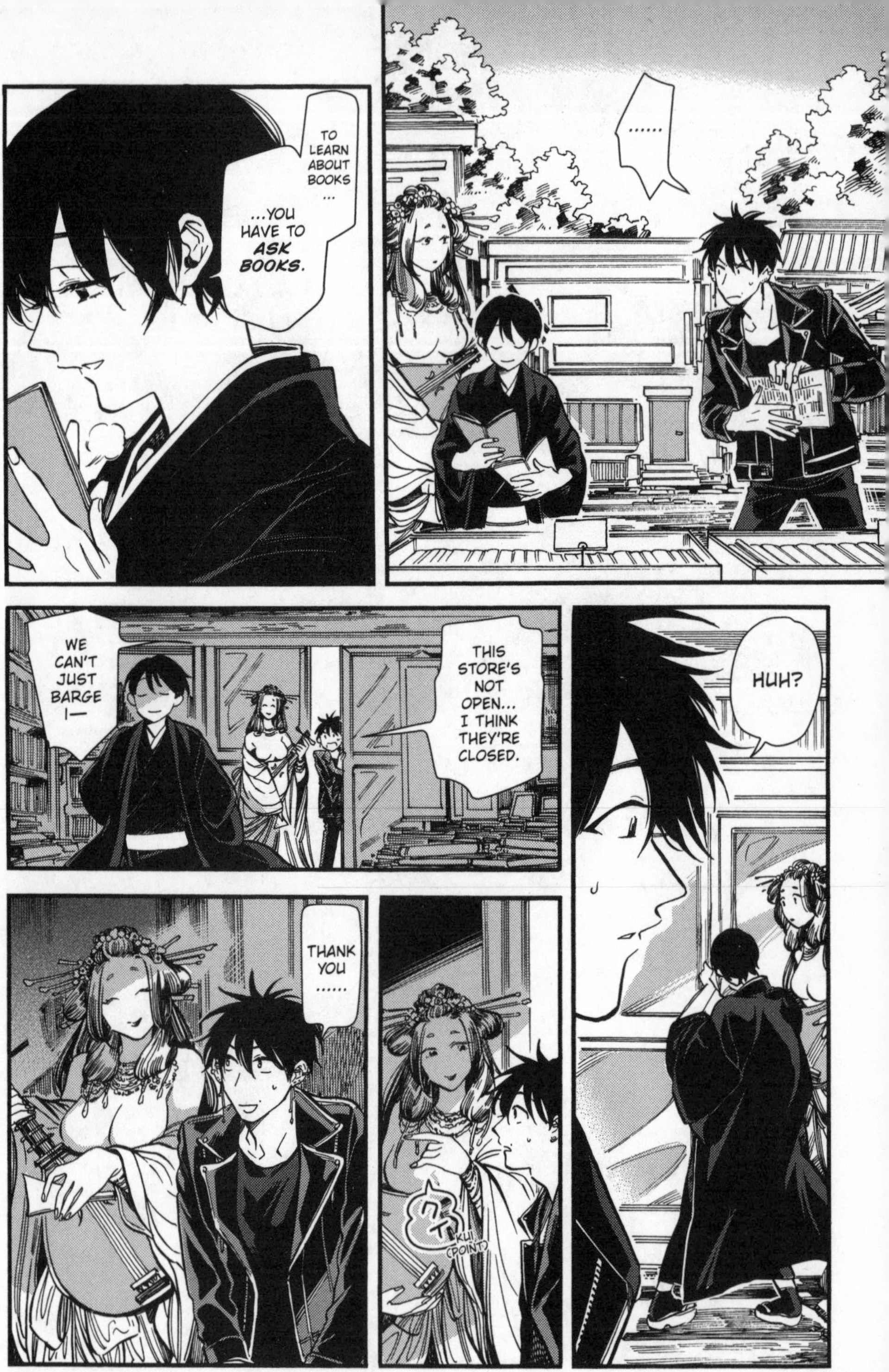
......
TO LEARN ABOUT BOOKS ...
...YOU HAVE TO ASK BOOKS.
HUH?
THIS STORE'S NOT OPEN... I THINK THEY'RE CLOSED.
WE CAN'T JUST BARGE I—
KUI (POINT)
THANK YOU ......

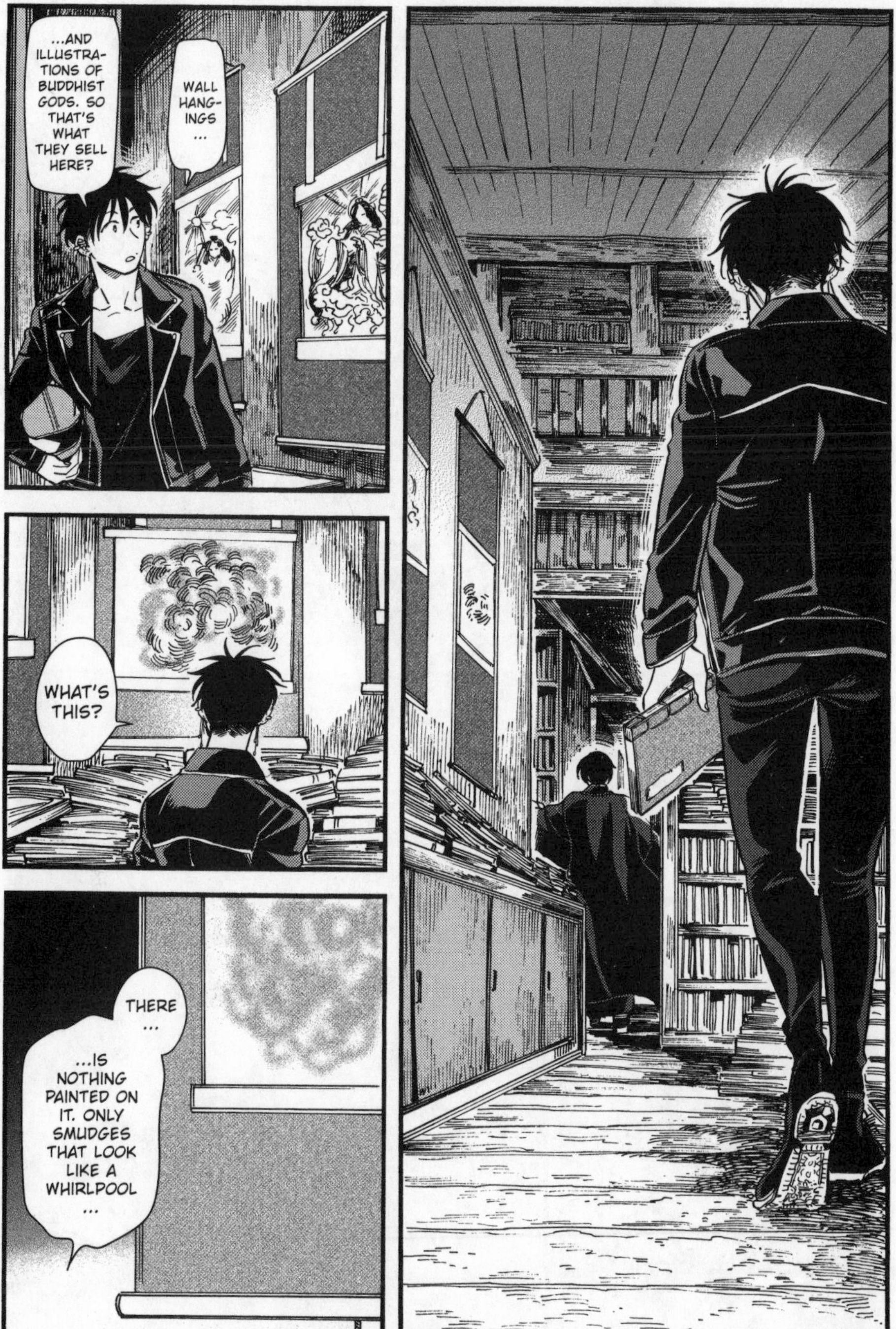
WALL HANGINGS ...
...AND ILLUSTRATIONS OF BUDDHIST GODS. SO THAT'S WHAT THEY SELL HERE?
WHAT'S THIS?
THERE ...
...IS NOTHING PAINTED ON IT. ONLY SMUDGES THAT LOOK LIKE A WHIRLPOOL ...

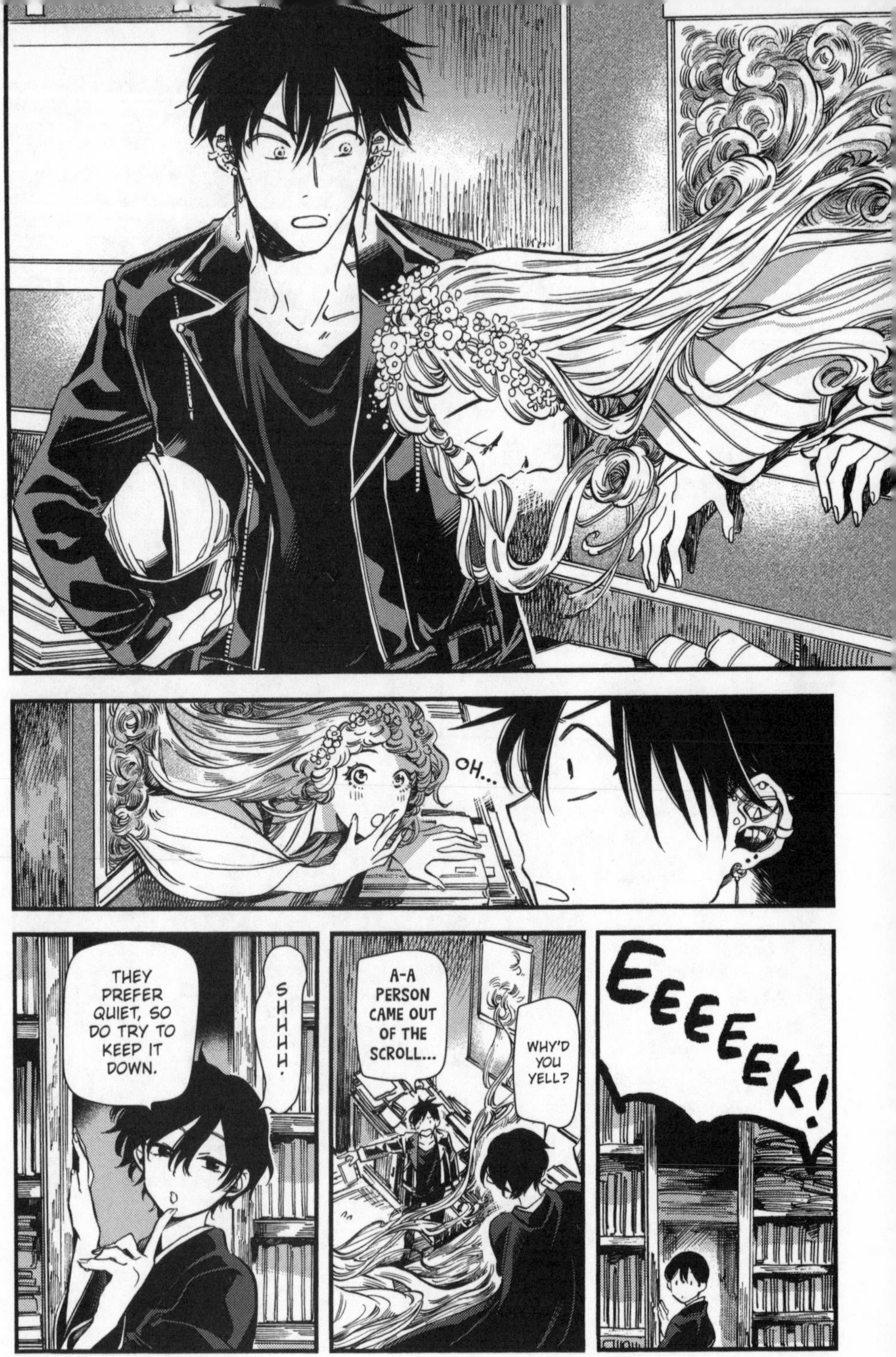
OH...
EEEEEK!
WHY'D YOU YELL?
A-A PERSON CAME OUT OF THE SCROLL...
SHHHH.
THEY PREFER QUIET, SO DO TRY TO KEEP IT DOWN.

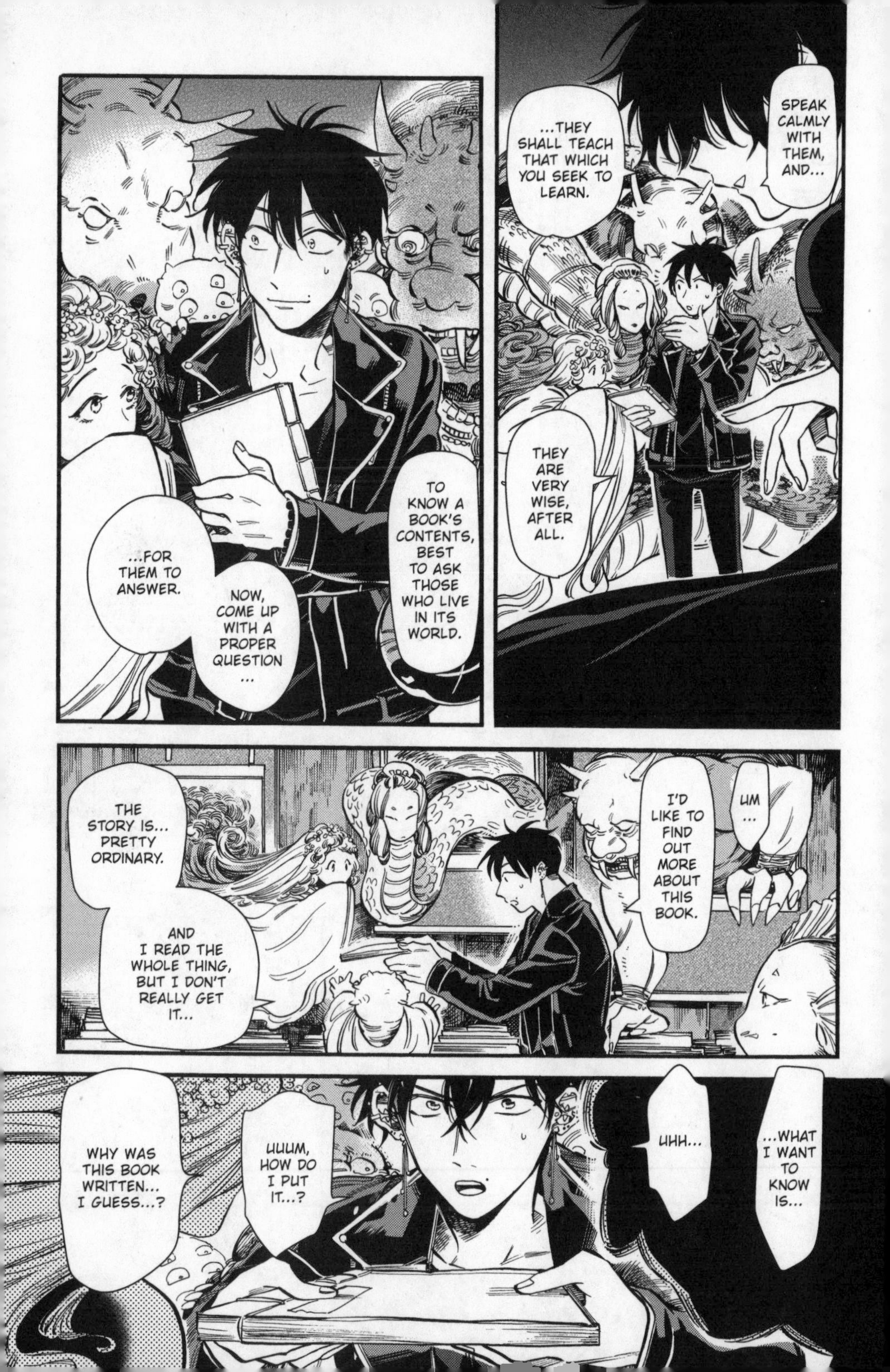
SPEAK CALMLY WITH THEM, AND...
...THEY SHALL TEACH THAT WHICH YOU SEEK TO LEARN.
THEY ARE VERY WISE, AFTER ALL.
TO KNOW A BOOK'S CONTENTS, BEST TO ASK THOSE WHO LIVE IN ITS WORLD.
NOW, COME UP WITH A PROPER QUESTION ...
...FOR THEM TO ANSWER.
UM ...
I'D LIKE TO FIND OUT MORE ABOUT THIS BOOK.
THE STORY IS... PRETTY ORDINARY.
AND I READ THE WHOLE THING, BUT I DON'T REALLY GET IT...
...WHAT I WANT TO KNOW IS...
UHH...
UUUM, HOW DO I PUT IT...?
WHY WAS THIS BOOK WRITTEN... I GUESS...?

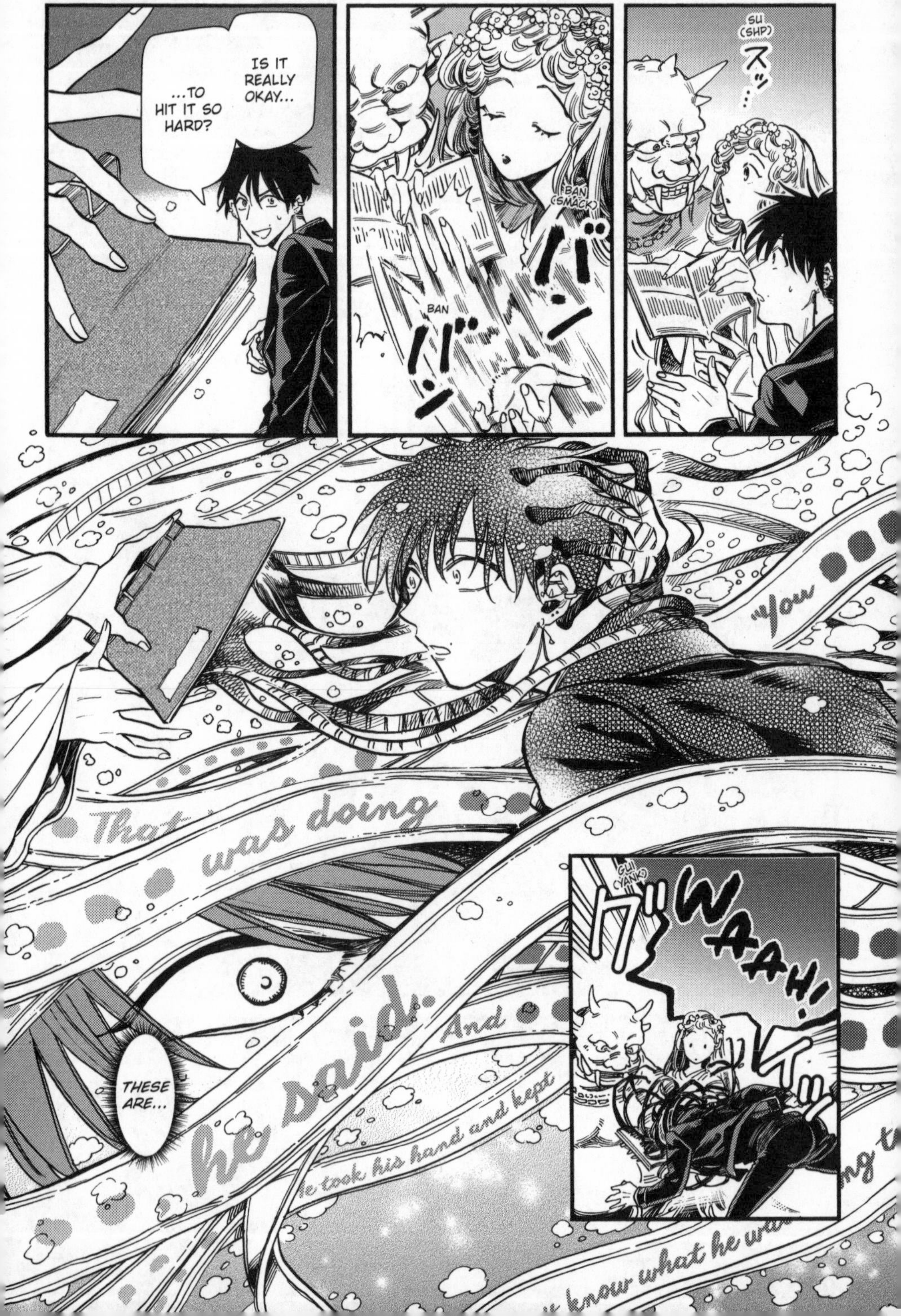
SU (SHP)
スッ…
BAN (SMACK)
バン
BAN
バン
IS IT REALLY OKAY...
...TO HIT IT SO HARD?
"You
That
was doing
he said.
And
he took his hand and kept
know what he wa
THESE ARE...
GUI (YANK)
グ
WAAAH!

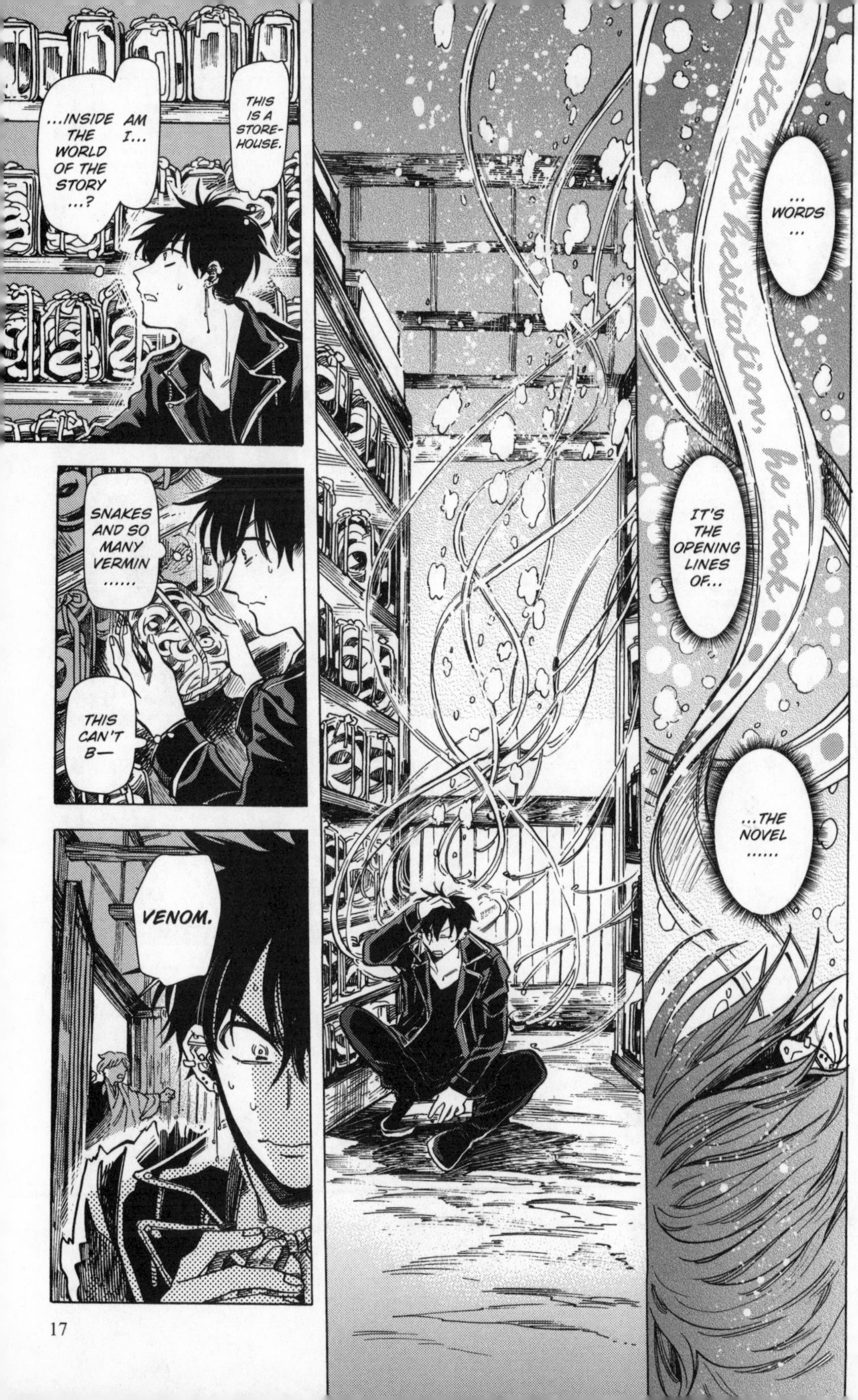
...WORDS...
his hesitation, he took
IT'S THE OPENING LINES OF...
...THE NOVEL ......
THIS IS A STORE-HOUSE.
AM I...
...INSIDE THE WORLD OF THE STORY ...?
SNAKES AND SO MANY VERMIN ......
THIS CAN'T B—
VENOM.

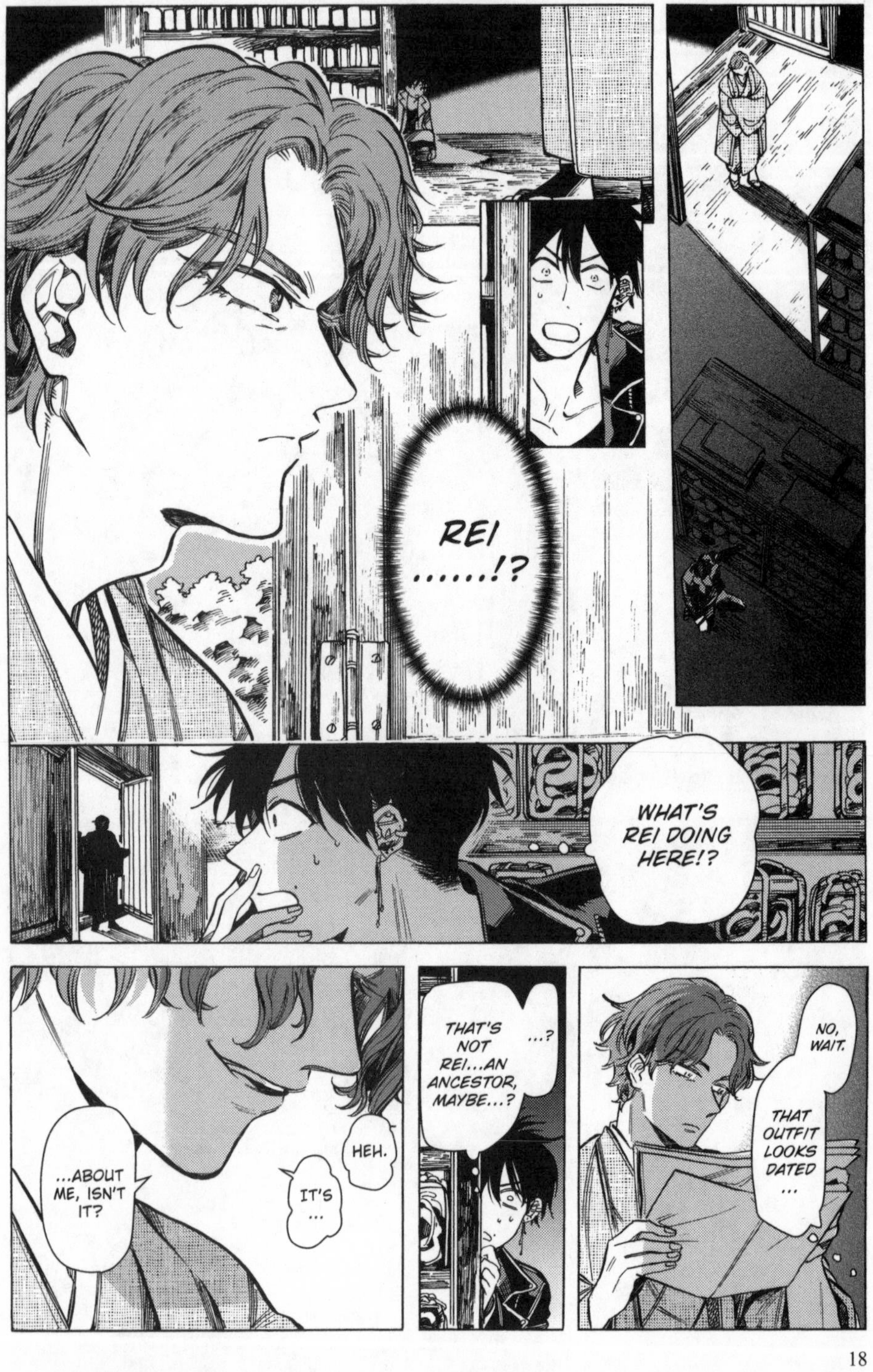
REI ......!?
WHAT'S REI DOING HERE!?
NO, WAIT.
THAT OUTFIT LOOKS DATED ...
...?
THAT'S NOT REI...AN ANCESTOR, MAYBE...?
HEH.
IT'S ...
...ABOUT ME, ISN'T IT?

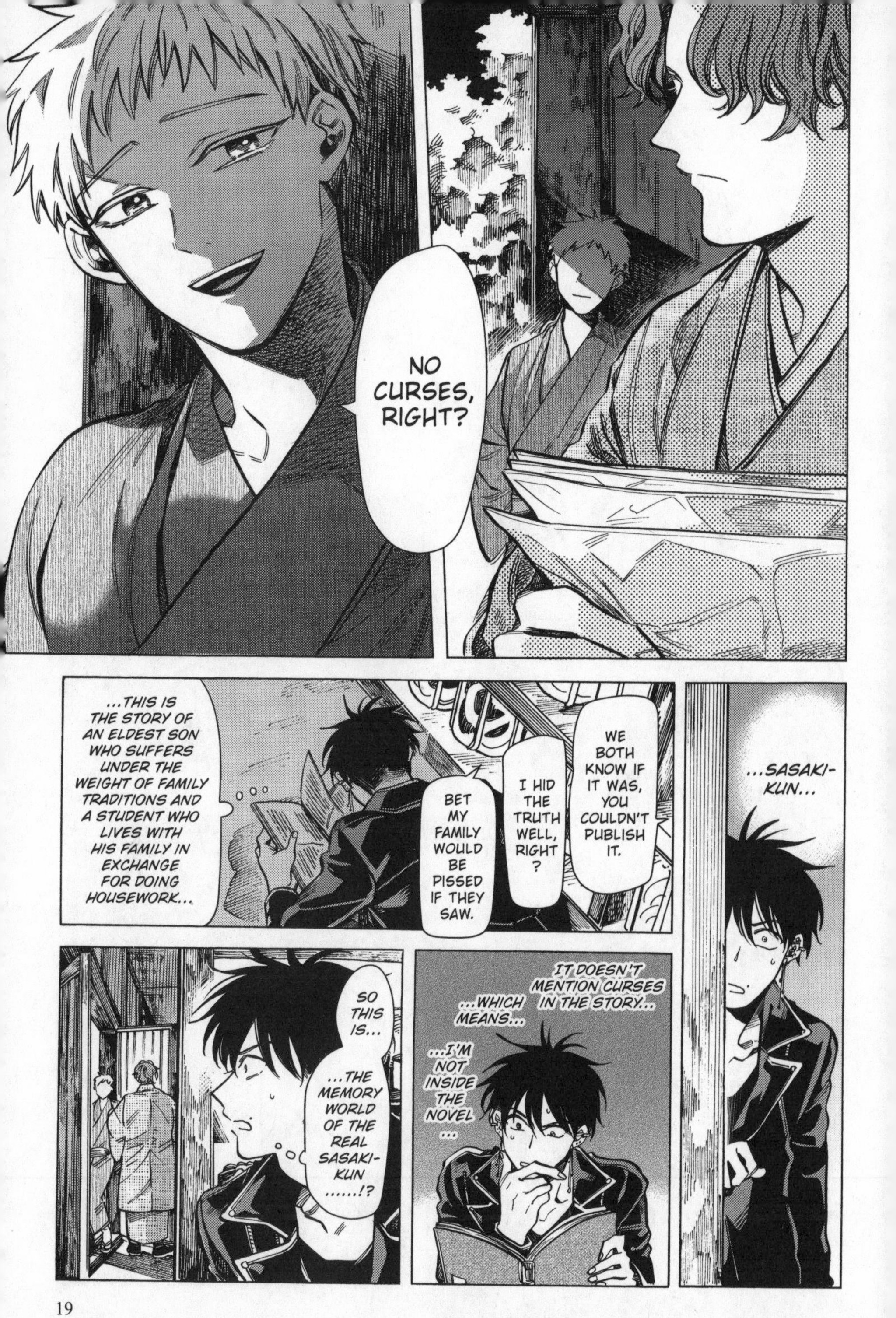
NO CURSES, RIGHT?
...SASAKI-KUN...
WE BOTH KNOW IF IT WAS, YOU COULDN'T PUBLISH IT.
I HID THE TRUTH WELL, RIGHT?
BET MY FAMILY WOULD BE PISSED IF THEY SAW.
...THIS IS THE STORY OF AN ELDEST SON WHO SUFFERS UNDER THE WEIGHT OF FAMILY TRADITIONS AND A STUDENT WHO LIVES WITH HIS FAMILY IN EXCHANGE FOR DOING HOUSEWORK...
IT DOESN'T MENTION CURSES IN THE STORY...
...WHICH MEANS...
...I'M NOT INSIDE THE NOVEL...
SO THIS IS...
...THE MEMORY WORLD OF THE REAL SASAKI-KUN ......!?

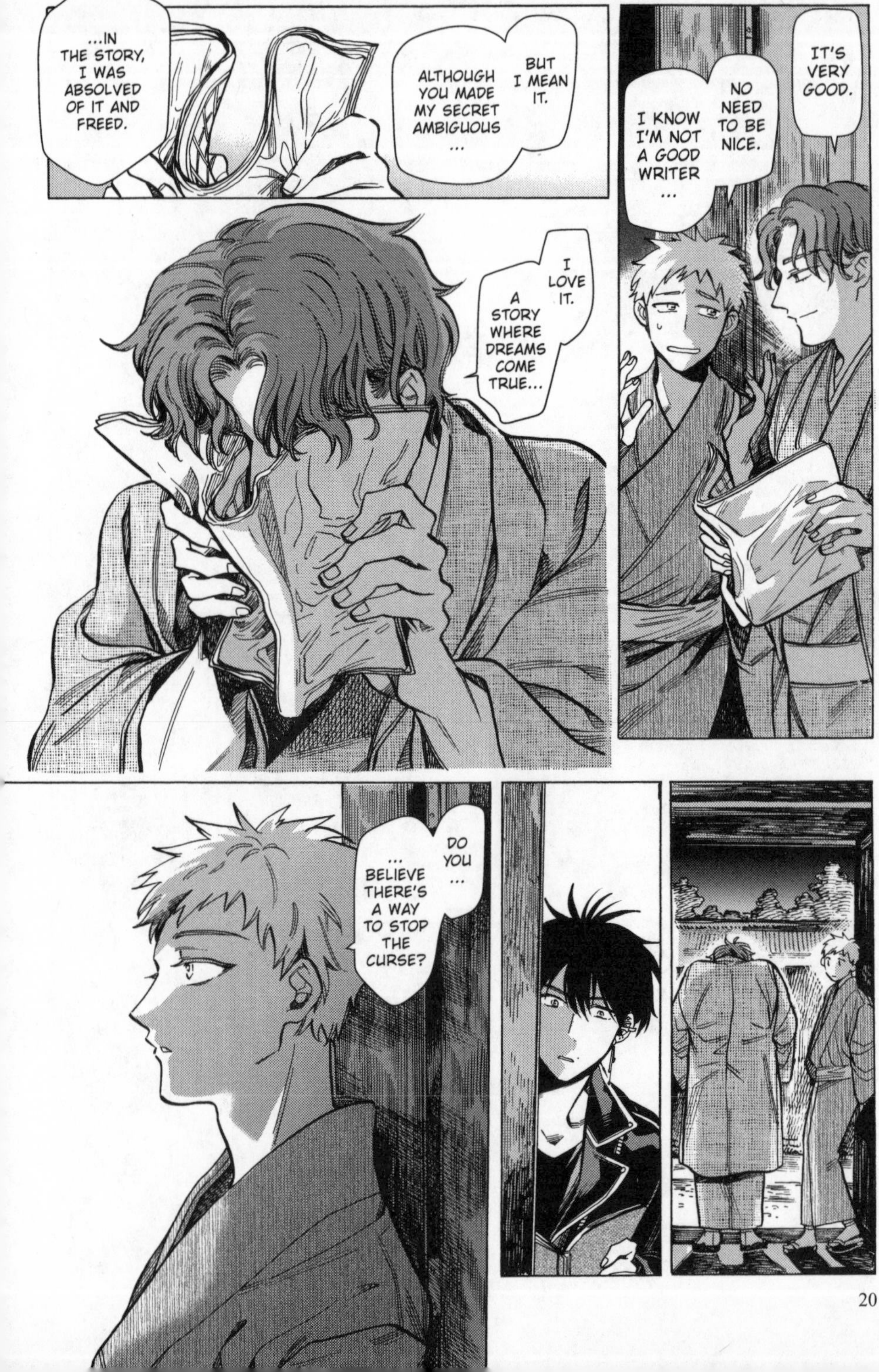
IT'S VERY GOOD.
NO NEED TO BE NICE.
I KNOW I'M NOT A GOOD WRITER ...
BUT I MEAN IT.
ALTHOUGH YOU MADE MY SECRET AMBIGUOUS ...
...IN THE STORY, I WAS ABSOLVED OF IT AND FREED.
I LOVE IT.
A STORY WHERE DREAMS COME TRUE...
DO YOU ...
... BELIEVE THERE'S A WAY TO STOP THE CURSE?

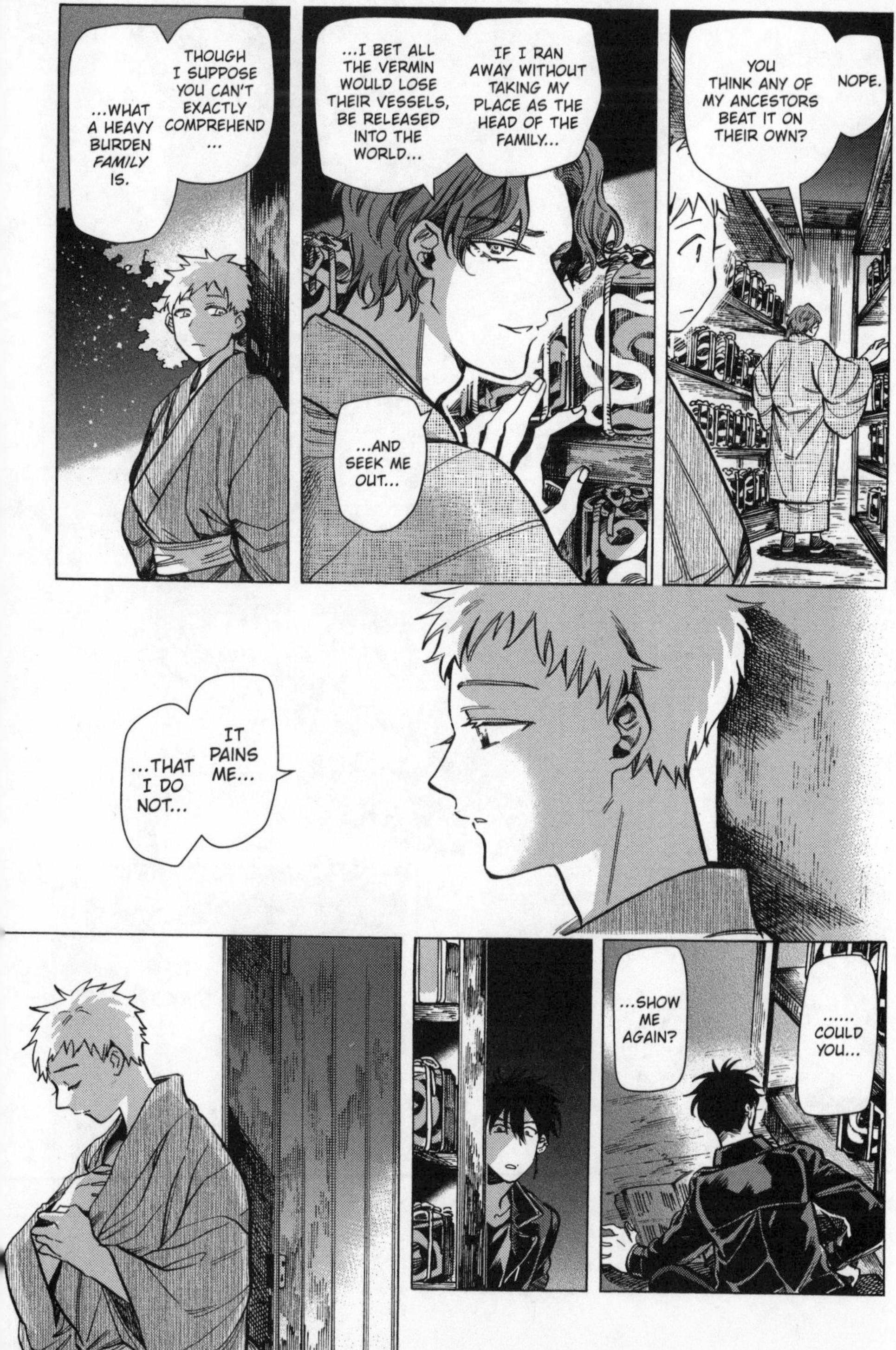
NOPE.
YOU THINK ANY OF MY ANCESTORS BEAT IT ON THEIR OWN?
IF I RAN AWAY WITHOUT TAKING MY PLACE AS THE HEAD OF THE FAMILY...
...I BET ALL THE VERMIN WOULD LOSE THEIR VESSELS, BE RELEASED INTO THE WORLD...
...AND SEEK ME OUT...
THOUGH I SUPPOSE YOU CAN'T EXACTLY COMPREHEND...
...WHAT A HEAVY BURDEN *FAMILY* IS.
IT PAINS ME...
...THAT I DO NOT...
......COULD YOU...
...SHOW ME AGAIN?

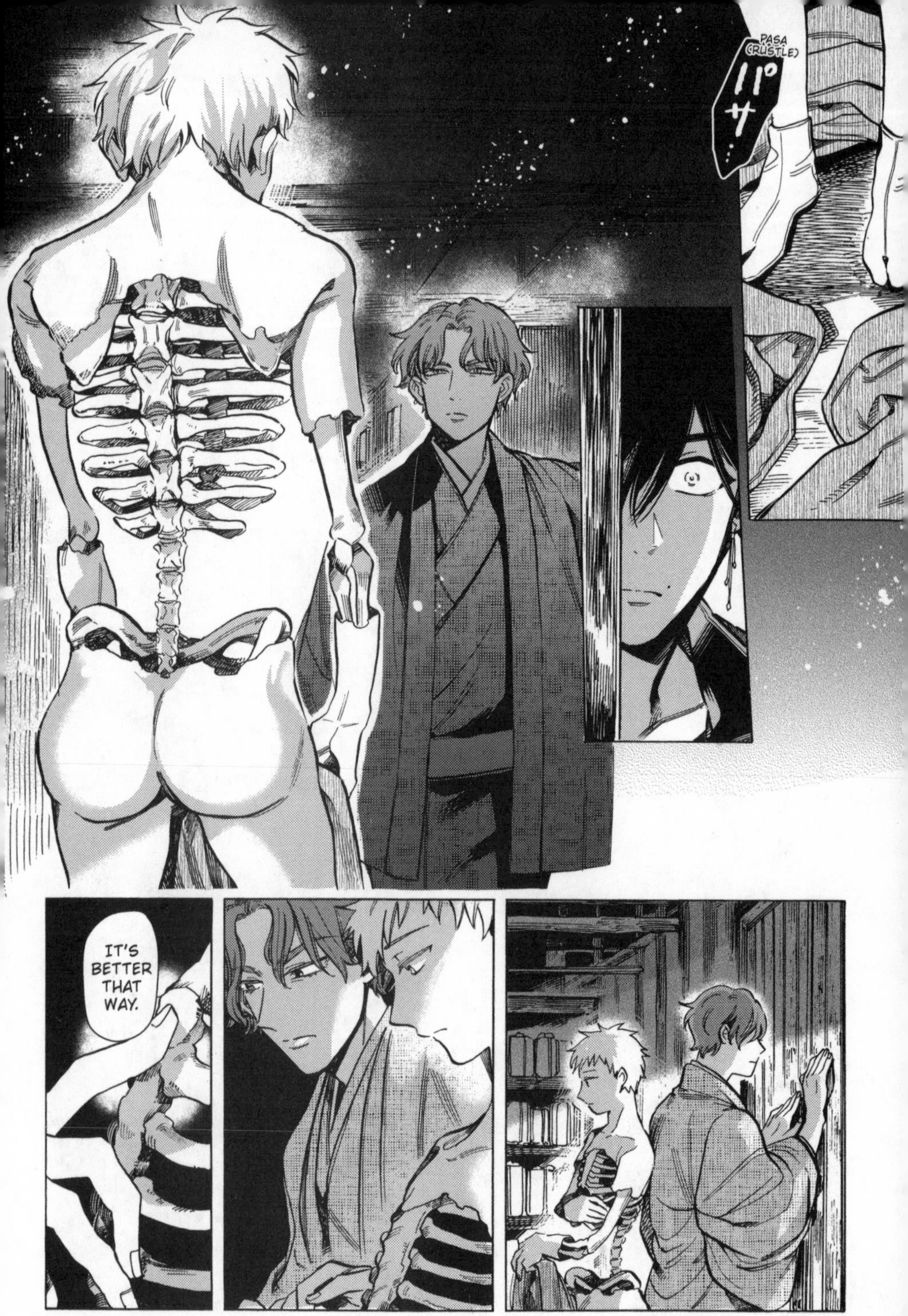
PASA (RUSTLE)
パサ
IT'S BETTER THAT WAY.

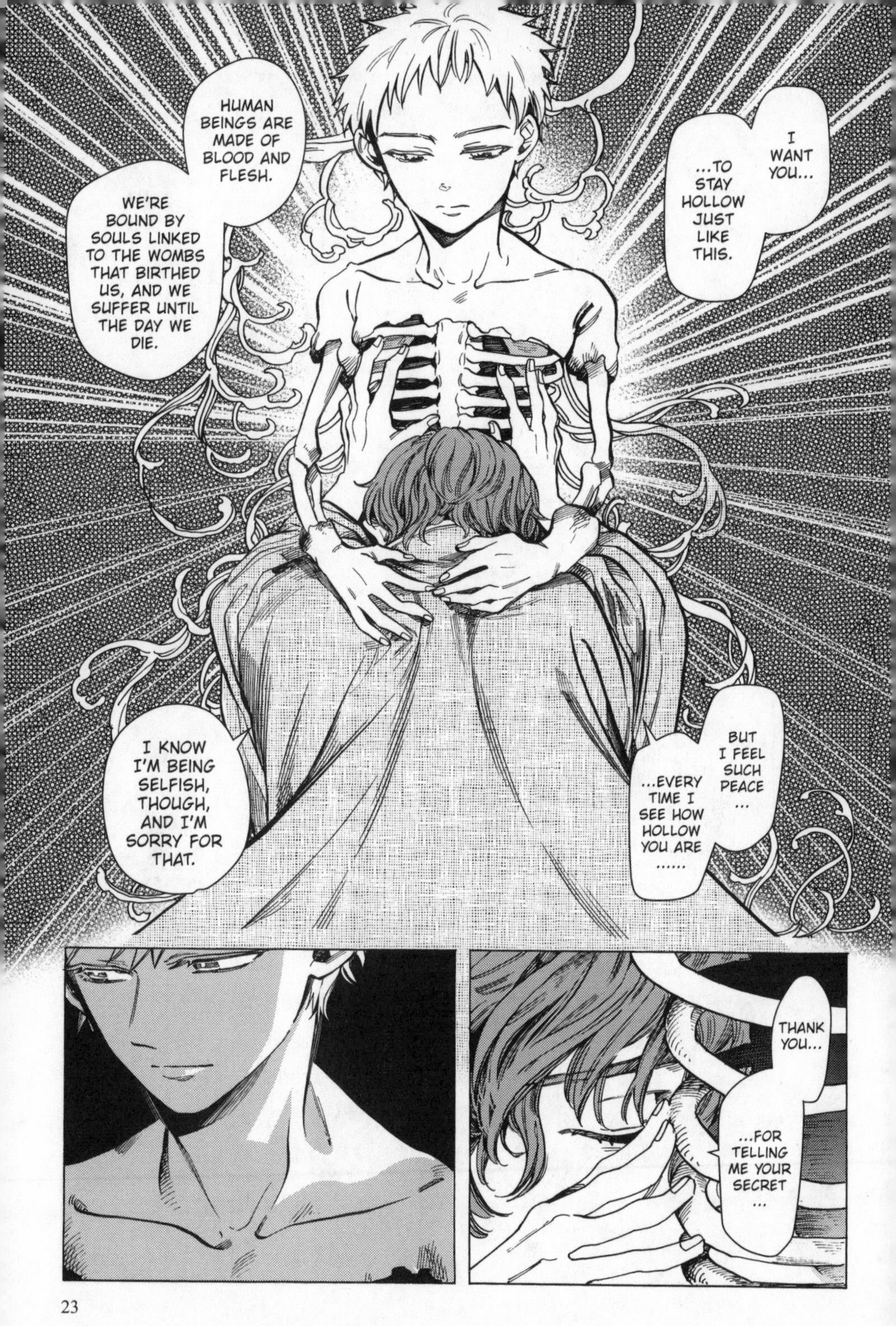
I WANT YOU...
...TO STAY HOLLOW JUST LIKE THIS.
HUMAN BEINGS ARE MADE OF BLOOD AND FLESH.
WE'RE BOUND BY SOULS LINKED TO THE WOMBS THAT BIRTHED US, AND WE SUFFER UNTIL THE DAY WE DIE.
BUT I FEEL SUCH PEACE ...
...EVERY TIME I SEE HOW HOLLOW YOU ARE ......
I KNOW I'M BEING SELFISH, THOUGH, AND I'M SORRY FOR THAT.
THANK YOU...
...FOR TELLING ME YOUR SECRET ...

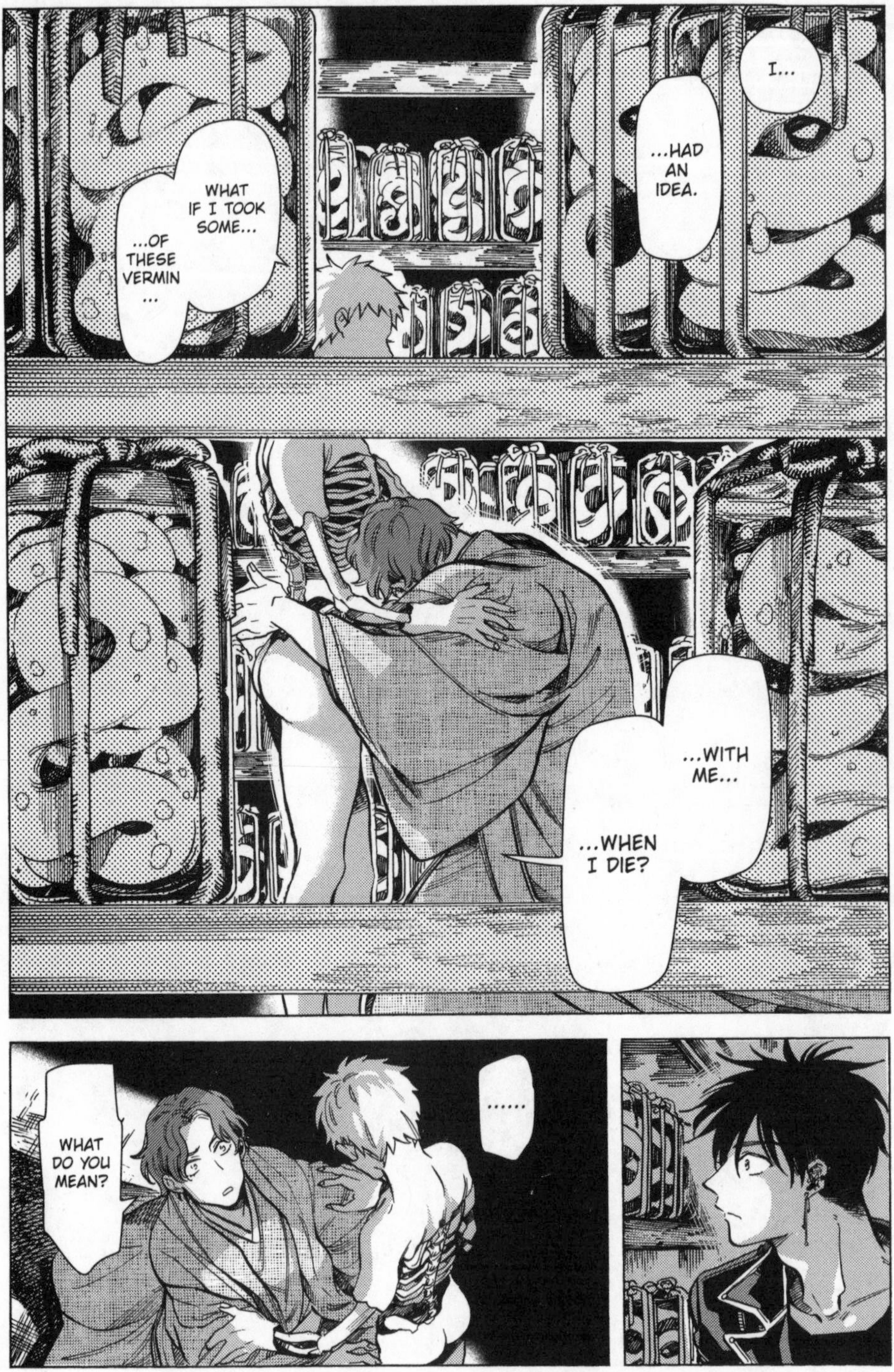
I...
...HAD AN IDEA.
WHAT IF I TOOK SOME...
...OF THESE VERMIN...
...WITH ME...
...WHEN I DIE?
......
WHAT DO YOU MEAN?

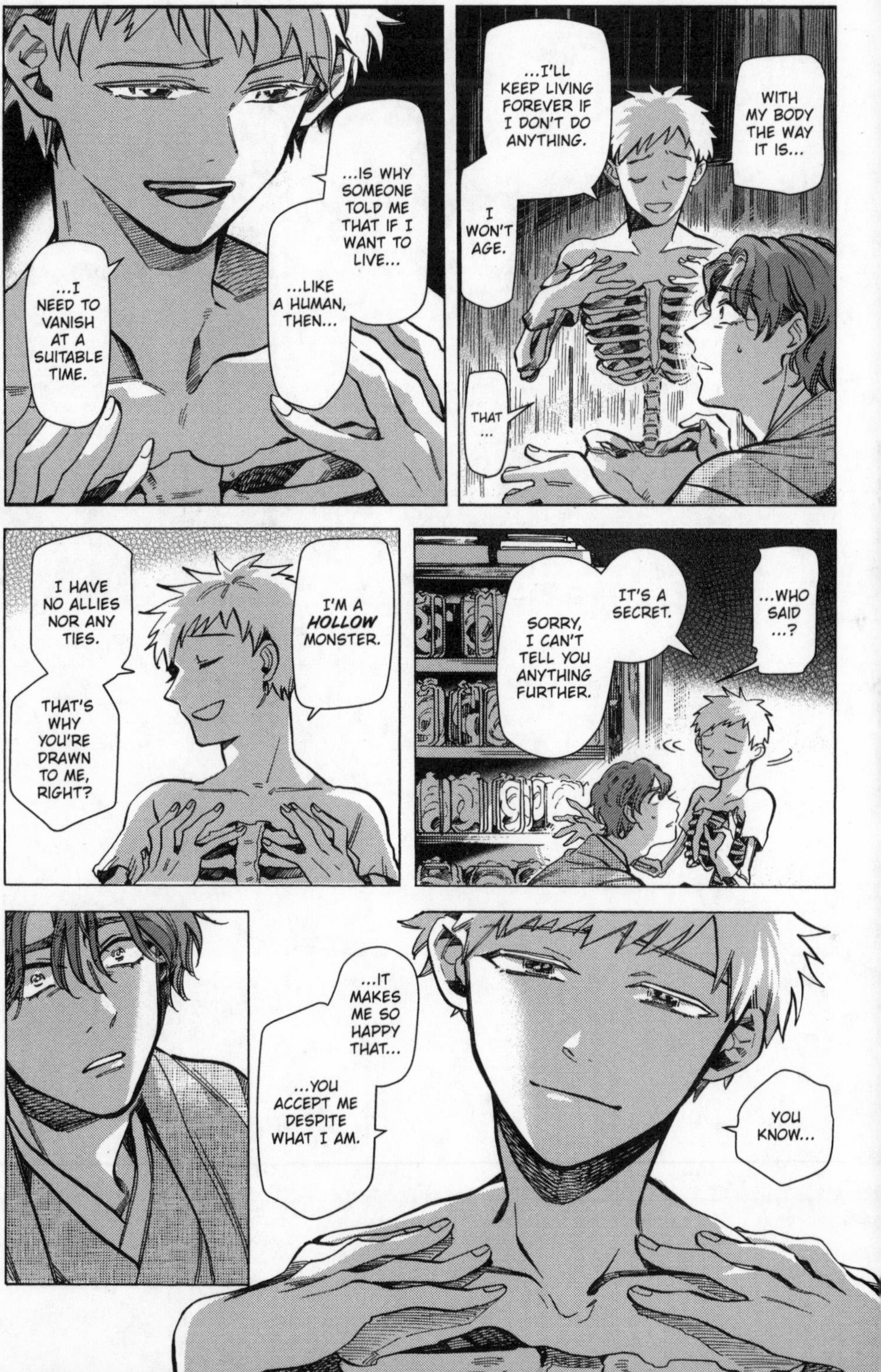
WITH MY BODY THE WAY IT IS...
...I'LL KEEP LIVING FOREVER IF I DON'T DO ANYTHING.
I WON'T AGE.
THAT ...
...IS WHY SOMEONE TOLD ME THAT IF I WANT TO LIVE...
...LIKE A HUMAN, THEN...
...I NEED TO VANISH AT A SUITABLE TIME.
...WHO SAID ...?
IT'S A SECRET.
SORRY, I CAN'T TELL YOU ANYTHING FURTHER.
I'M A *HOLLOW* MONSTER.
I HAVE NO ALLIES NOR ANY TIES.
THAT'S WHY YOU'RE DRAWN TO ME, RIGHT?
YOU KNOW...
...IT MAKES ME SO HAPPY THAT...
...YOU ACCEPT ME DESPITE WHAT I AM.

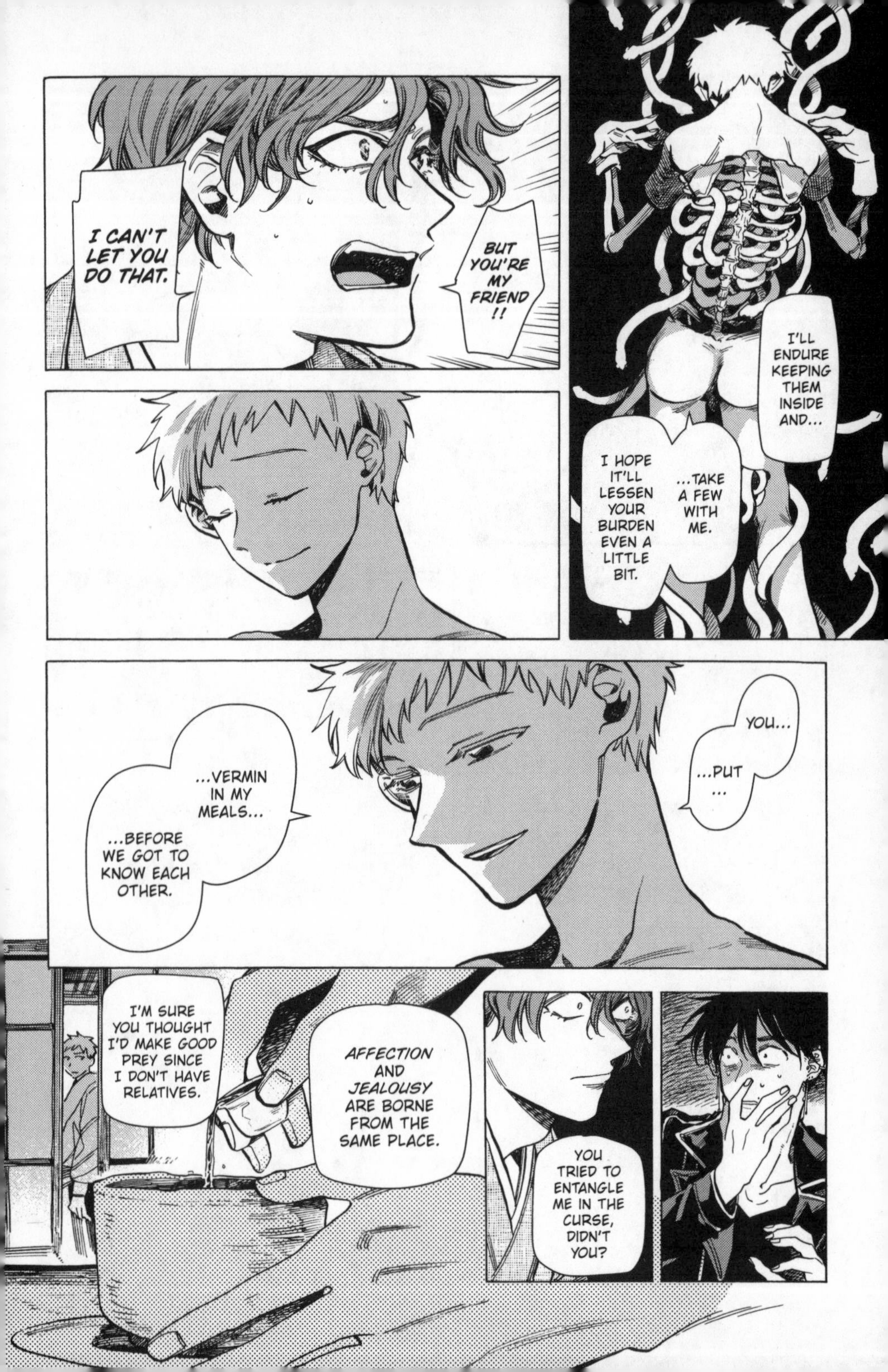
I'LL ENDURE KEEPING THEM INSIDE AND...
...TAKE A FEW WITH ME.
I HOPE IT'LL LESSEN YOUR BURDEN EVEN A LITTLE BIT.
BUT YOU'RE MY FRIEND!!
I CAN'T LET YOU DO THAT.
YOU...
...PUT ...
...VERMIN IN MY MEALS...
...BEFORE WE GOT TO KNOW EACH OTHER.
YOU TRIED TO ENTANGLE ME IN THE CURSE, DIDN'T YOU?
AFFECTION AND JEALOUSY ARE BORNE FROM THE SAME PLACE.
I'M SURE YOU THOUGHT I'D MAKE GOOD PREY SINCE I DON'T HAVE RELATIVES.

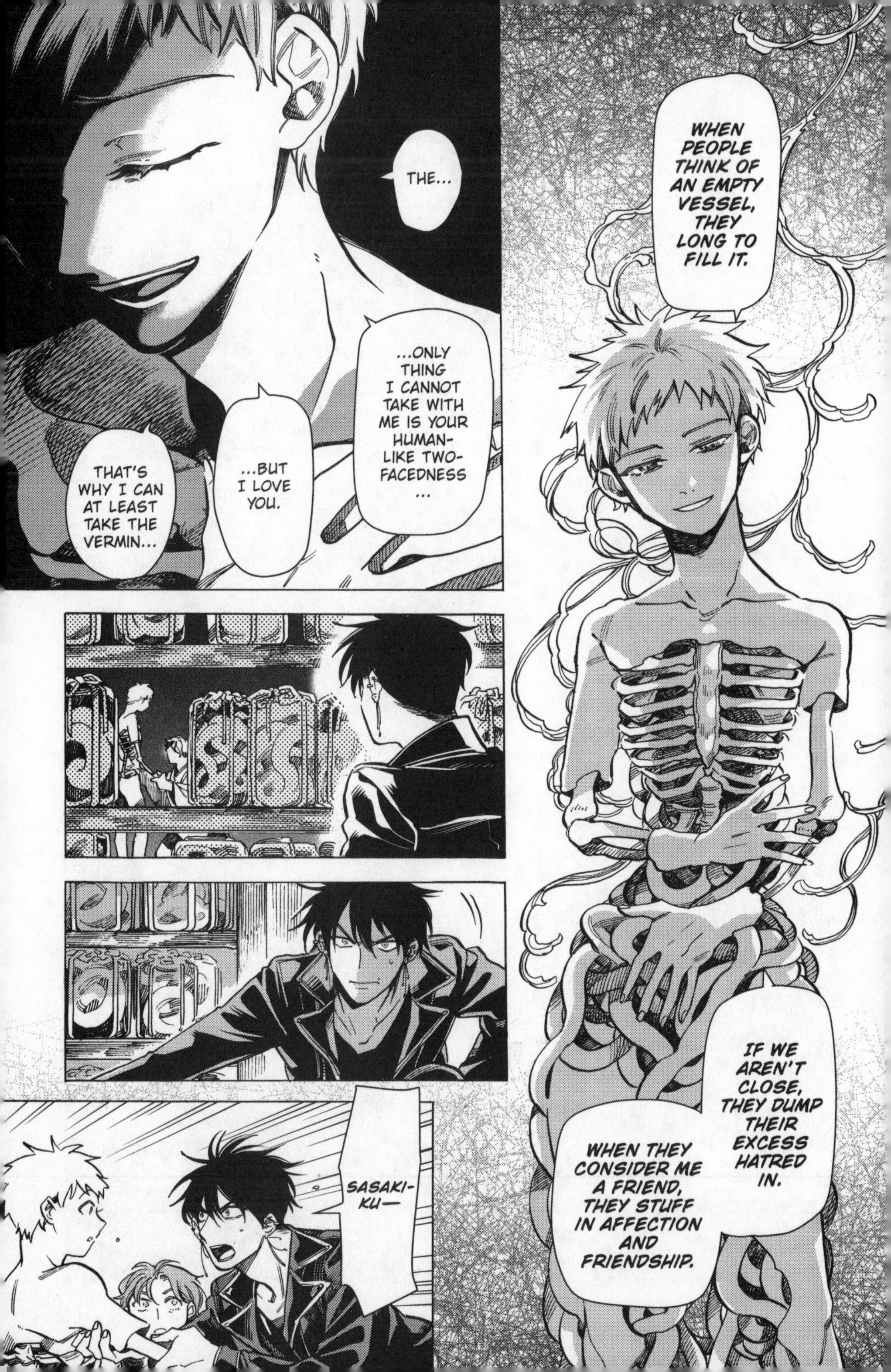
WHEN PEOPLE THINK OF AN EMPTY VESSEL, THEY LONG TO FILL IT.
IF WE AREN'T CLOSE, THEY DUMP THEIR EXCESS HATRED IN.
WHEN THEY CONSIDER ME A FRIEND, THEY STUFF IN AFFECTION AND FRIENDSHIP.
THE...
...ONLY THING I CANNOT TAKE WITH ME IS YOUR HUMAN-LIKE TWO-FACEDNESS ...
...BUT I LOVE YOU.
THAT'S WHY I CAN AT LEAST TAKE THE VERMIN...
SASAKI-KU—

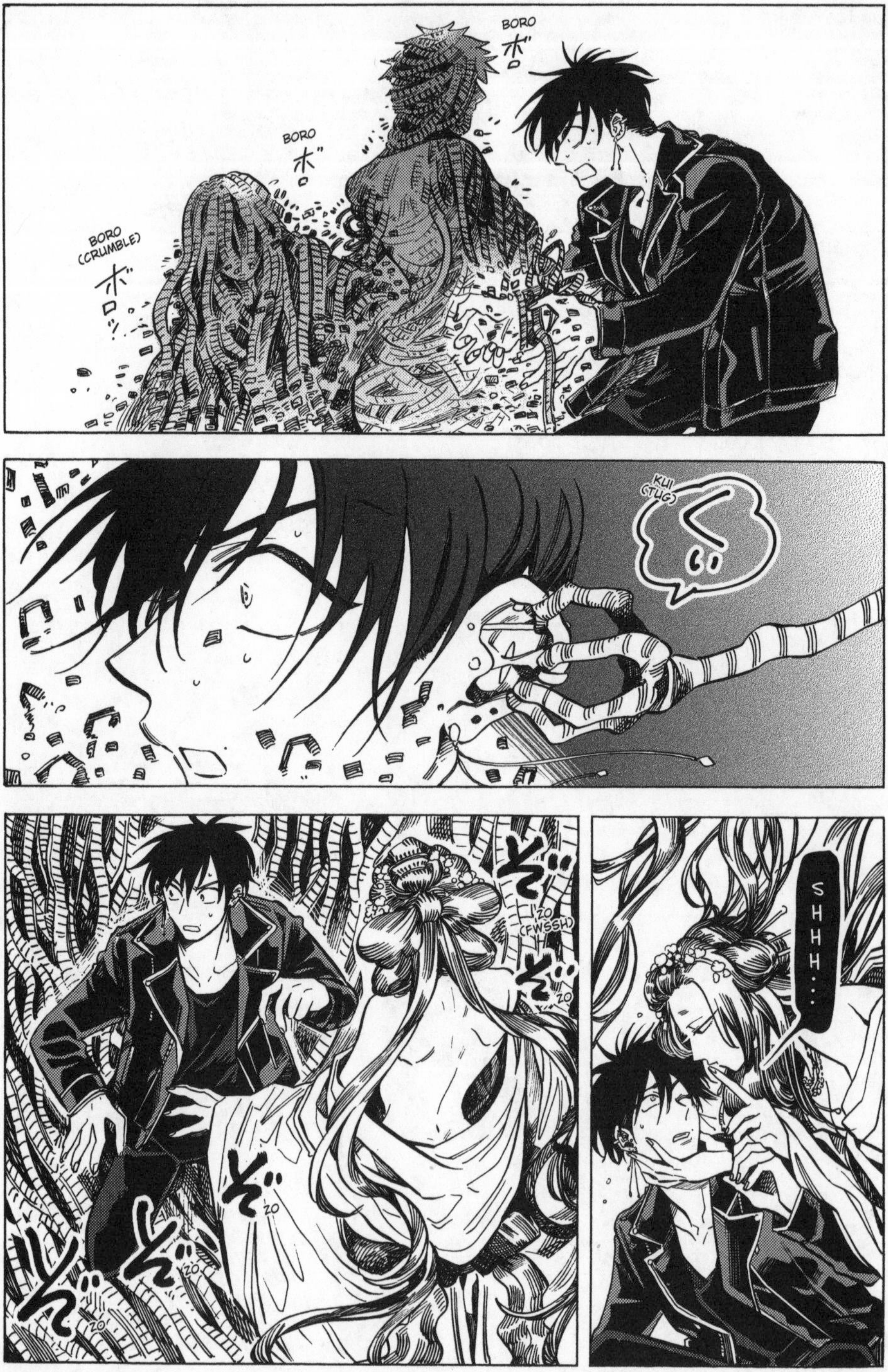
BORO
ボ
BORO
ボ
BORO (CRUMBLE)
ボロッ
KUI (TUG)
くい
SHHH...
ZO (FWSSH)
ぞ
ぞ
ZO
ぞ
ZO
ど
ZO
ん
ZO

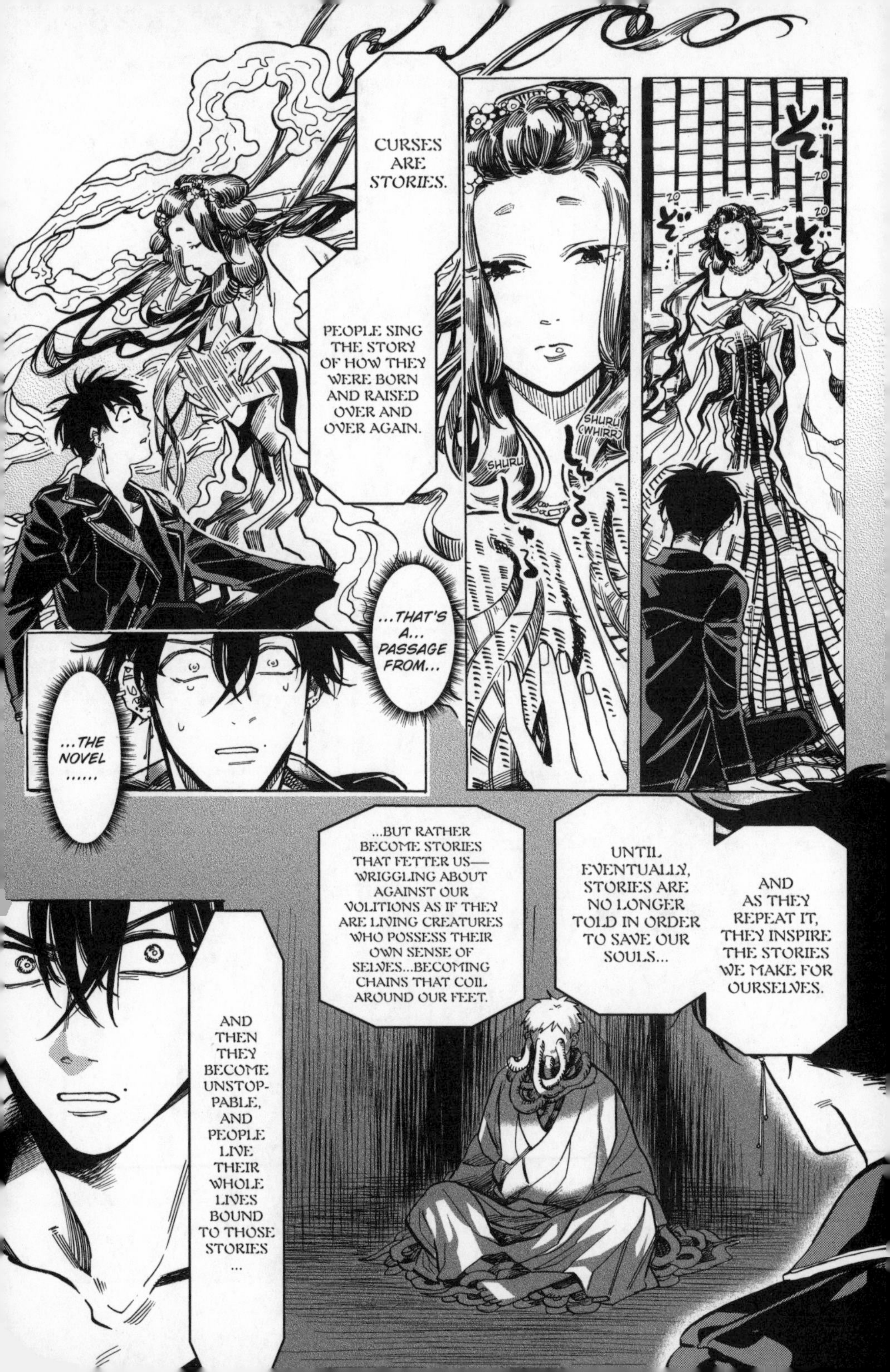
ZO
ZO
ZO
SHURU (WHIRR)
SHURU
CURSES ARE STORIES.
PEOPLE SING THE STORY OF HOW THEY WERE BORN AND RAISED OVER AND OVER AGAIN.
...THAT'S A... PASSAGE FROM...
...THE NOVEL......
AND AS THEY REPEAT IT, THEY INSPIRE THE STORIES WE MAKE FOR OURSELVES.
UNTIL EVENTUALLY, STORIES ARE NO LONGER TOLD IN ORDER TO SAVE OUR SOULS...
...BUT RATHER BECOME STORIES THAT FETTER US—WRIGGLING ABOUT AGAINST OUR VOLITIONS AS IF THEY ARE LIVING CREATURES WHO POSSESS THEIR OWN SENSE OF SELVES...BECOMING CHAINS THAT COIL AROUND OUR FEET.
AND THEN THEY BECOME UNSTOP-PABLE, AND PEOPLE LIVE THEIR WHOLE LIVES BOUND TO THOSE STORIES ...

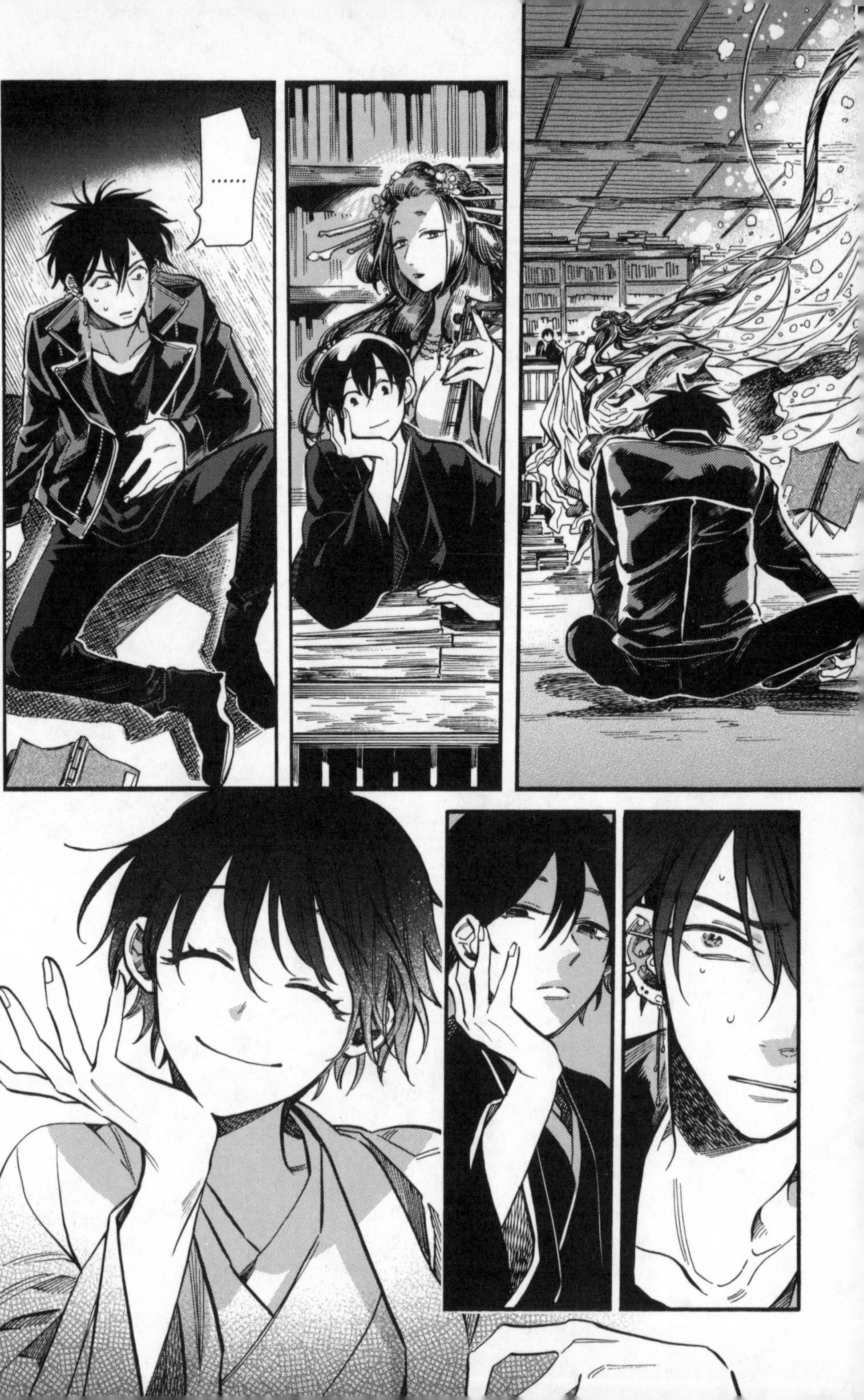
……

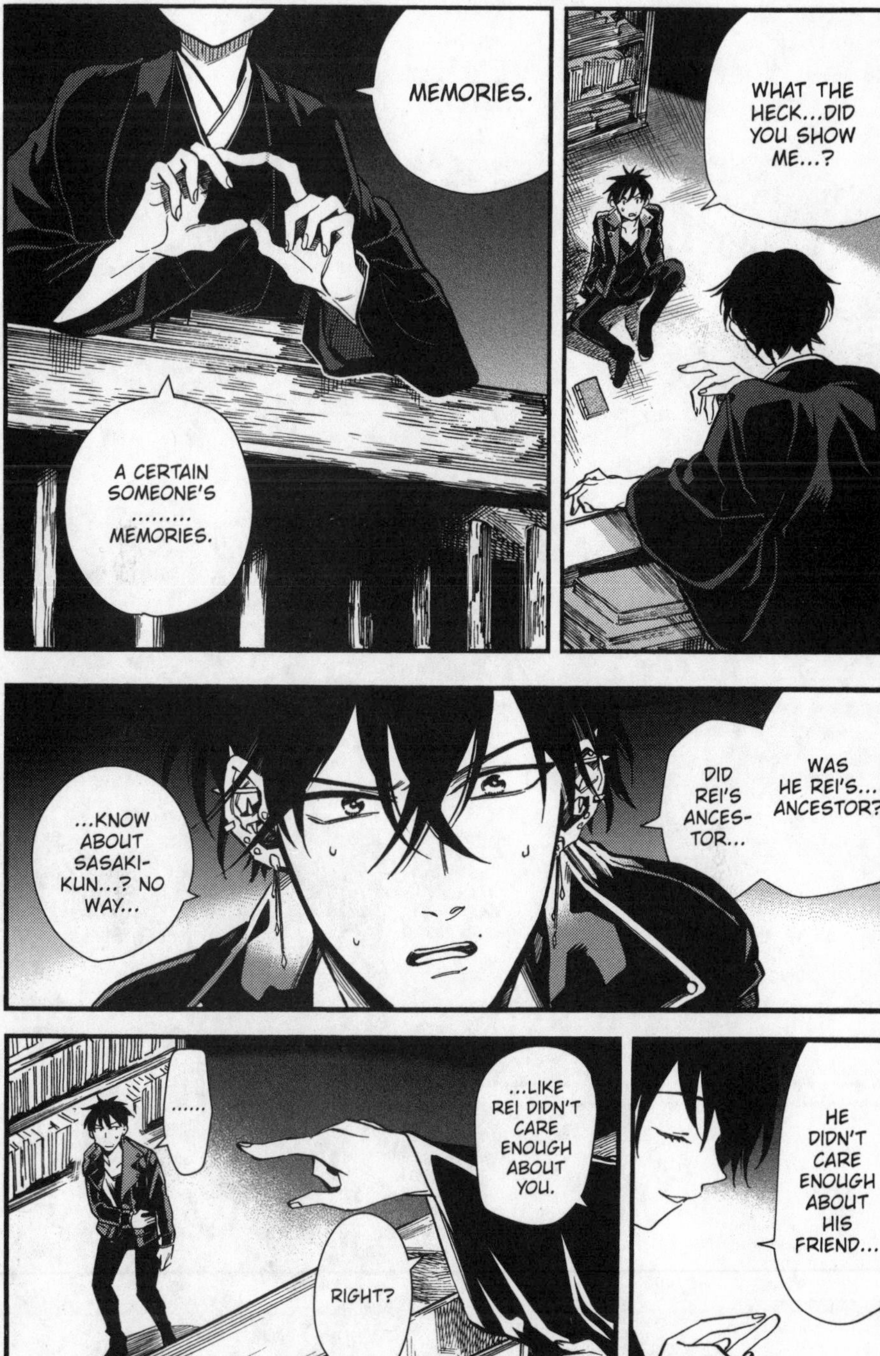
WHAT THE HECK...DID YOU SHOW ME...?
MEMORIES.
A CERTAIN SOMEONE'S .... MEMORIES.
WAS HE REI'S... ANCESTOR?
DID REI'S ANCES-TOR...
...KNOW ABOUT SASAKI-KUN...? NO WAY...
HE DIDN'T CARE ENOUGH ABOUT HIS FRIEND...
...LIKE REI DIDN'T CARE ENOUGH ABOUT YOU.
RIGHT?
......

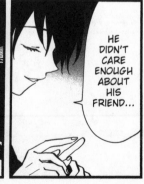

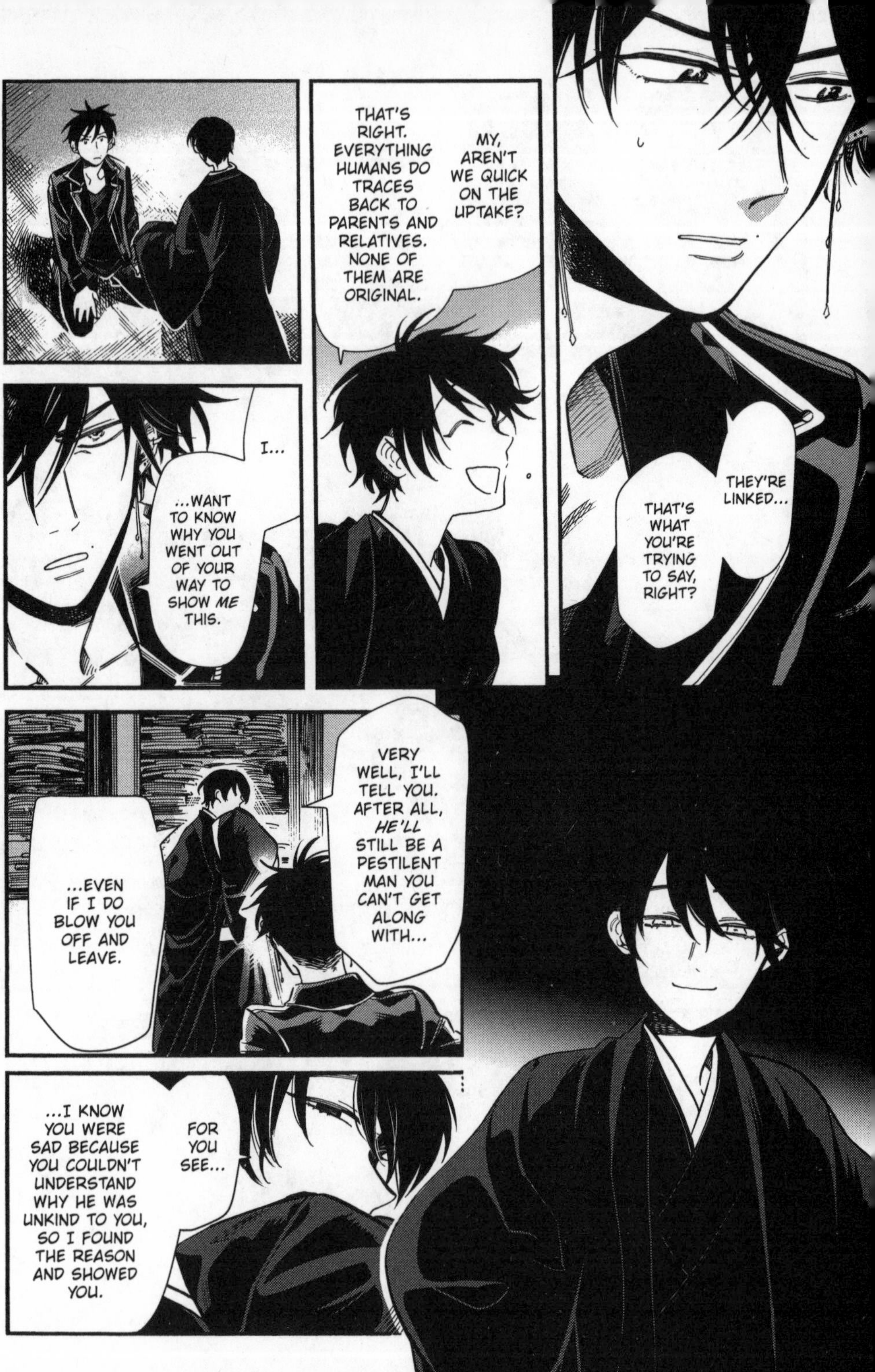
THEY'RE LINKED...
THAT'S WHAT YOU'RE TRYING TO SAY, RIGHT?
MY, AREN'T WE QUICK ON THE UPTAKE?
THAT'S RIGHT. EVERYTHING HUMANS DO TRACES BACK TO PARENTS AND RELATIVES. NONE OF THEM ARE ORIGINAL.
I...
...WANT TO KNOW WHY YOU WENT OUT OF YOUR WAY TO SHOW *ME* THIS.
VERY WELL, I'LL TELL YOU. AFTER ALL, *HE'LL* STILL BE A PESTILENT MAN YOU CAN'T GET ALONG WITH...
...EVEN IF I DO BLOW YOU OFF AND LEAVE.
FOR YOU SEE...
...I KNOW YOU WERE SAD BECAUSE YOU COULDN'T UNDERSTAND WHY HE WAS UNKIND TO YOU, SO I FOUND THE REASON AND SHOWED YOU.

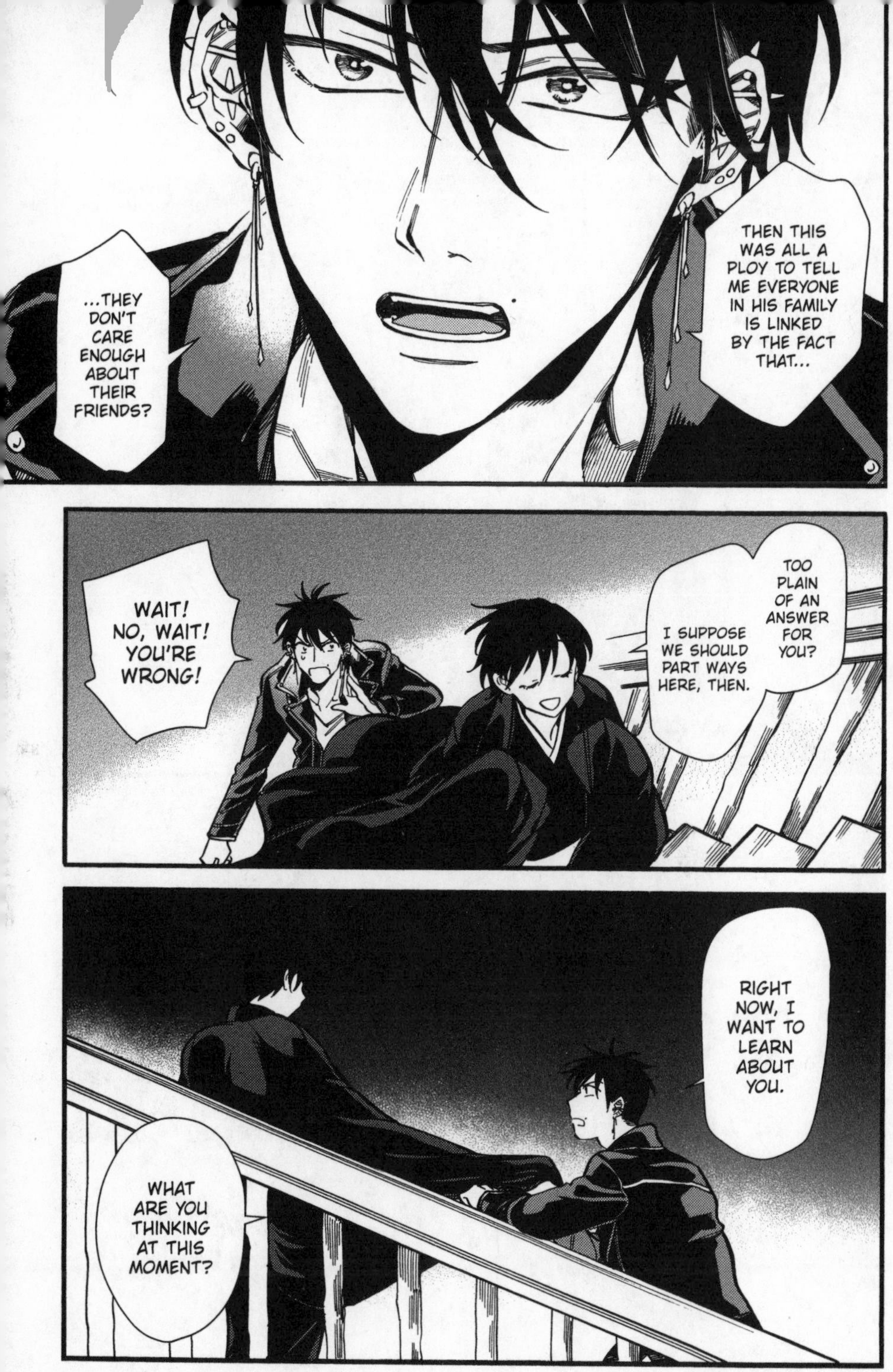
THEN THIS WAS ALL A PLOY TO TELL ME EVERYONE IN HIS FAMILY IS LINKED BY THE FACT THAT...
...THEY DON'T CARE ENOUGH ABOUT THEIR FRIENDS?
TOO PLAIN OF AN ANSWER FOR YOU?
I SUPPOSE WE SHOULD PART WAYS HERE, THEN.
WAIT! NO, WAIT! YOU'RE WRONG!
RIGHT NOW, I WANT TO LEARN ABOUT YOU.
WHAT ARE YOU THINKING AT THIS MOMENT?

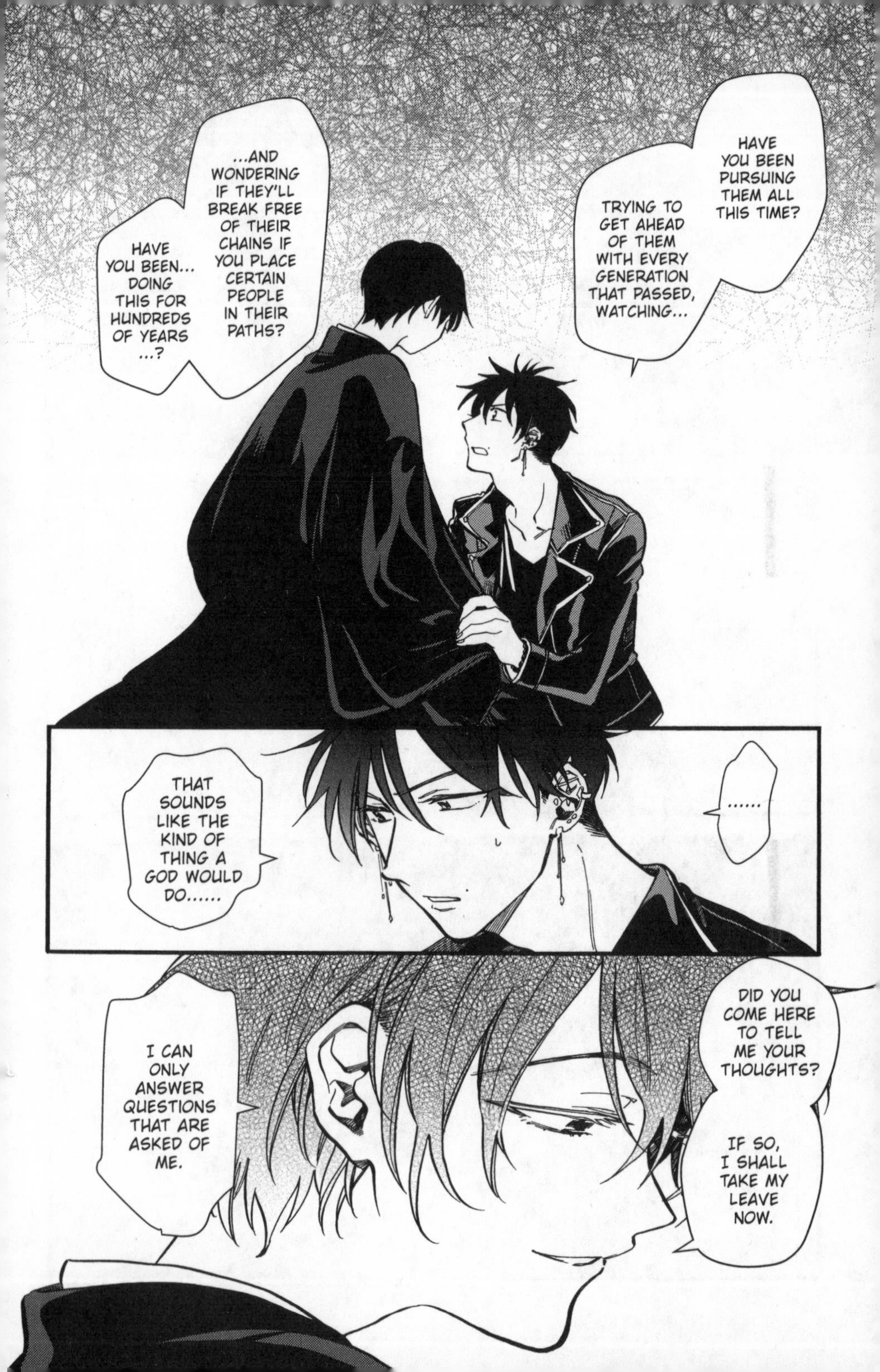
HAVE YOU BEEN PURSUING THEM ALL THIS TIME?
TRYING TO GET AHEAD OF THEM WITH EVERY GENERATION THAT PASSED, WATCHING...
...AND WONDERING IF THEY'LL BREAK FREE OF THEIR CHAINS IF YOU PLACE CERTAIN PEOPLE IN THEIR PATHS?
HAVE YOU BEEN... DOING THIS FOR HUNDREDS OF YEARS ...?
......
THAT SOUNDS LIKE THE KIND OF THING A GOD WOULD DO......
DID YOU COME HERE TO TELL ME YOUR THOUGHTS?
IF SO, I SHALL TAKE MY LEAVE NOW.
I CAN ONLY ANSWER QUESTIONS THAT ARE ASKED OF ME.

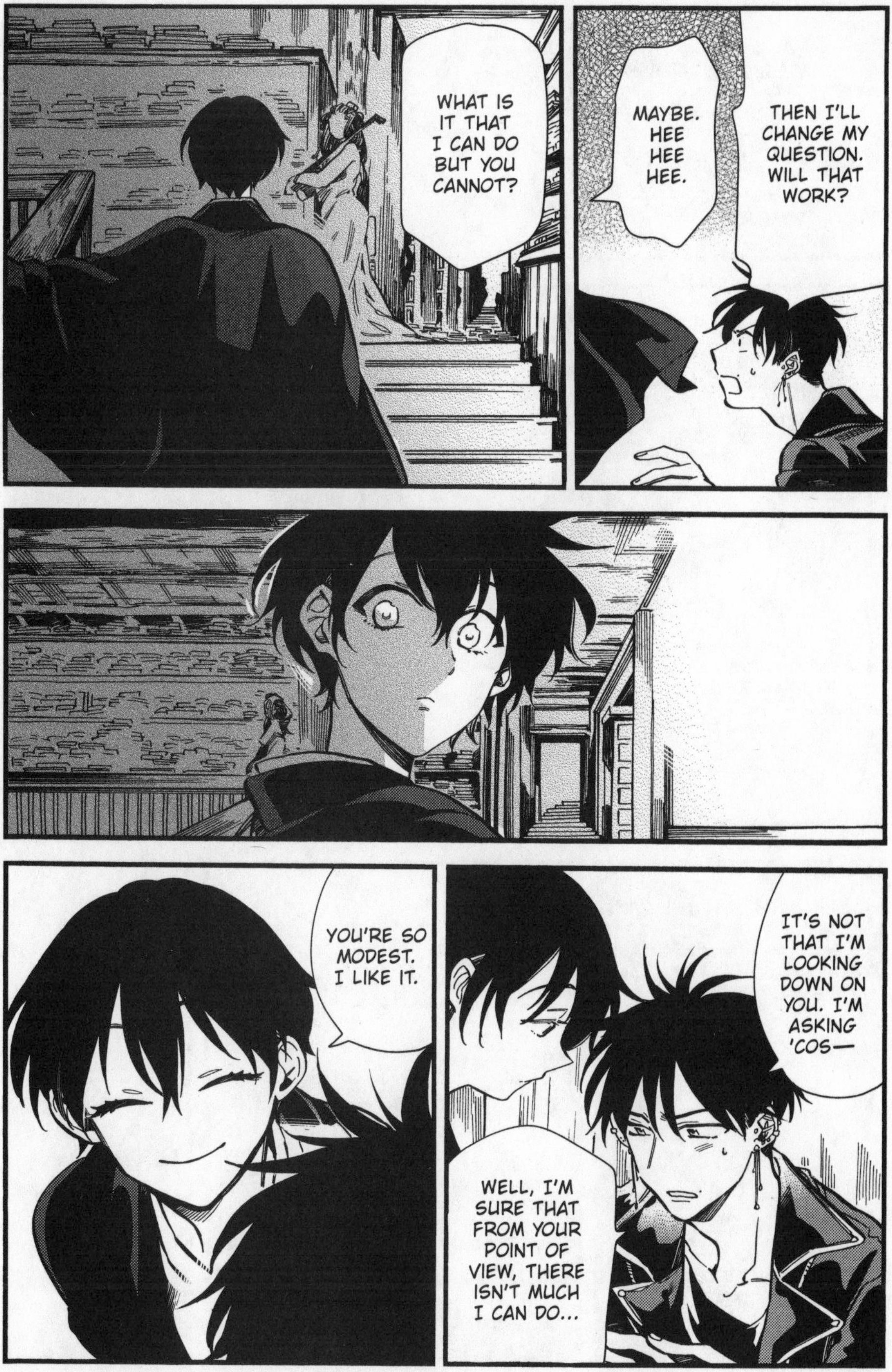
THEN I'LL CHANGE MY QUESTION. WILL THAT WORK?
MAYBE. HEE HEE HEE.
WHAT IS IT THAT I CAN DO BUT YOU CANNOT?
IT'S NOT THAT I'M LOOKING DOWN ON YOU. I'M ASKING 'COS—
WELL, I'M SURE THAT FROM YOUR POINT OF VIEW, THERE ISN'T MUCH I CAN DO...
YOU'RE SO MODEST. I LIKE IT.

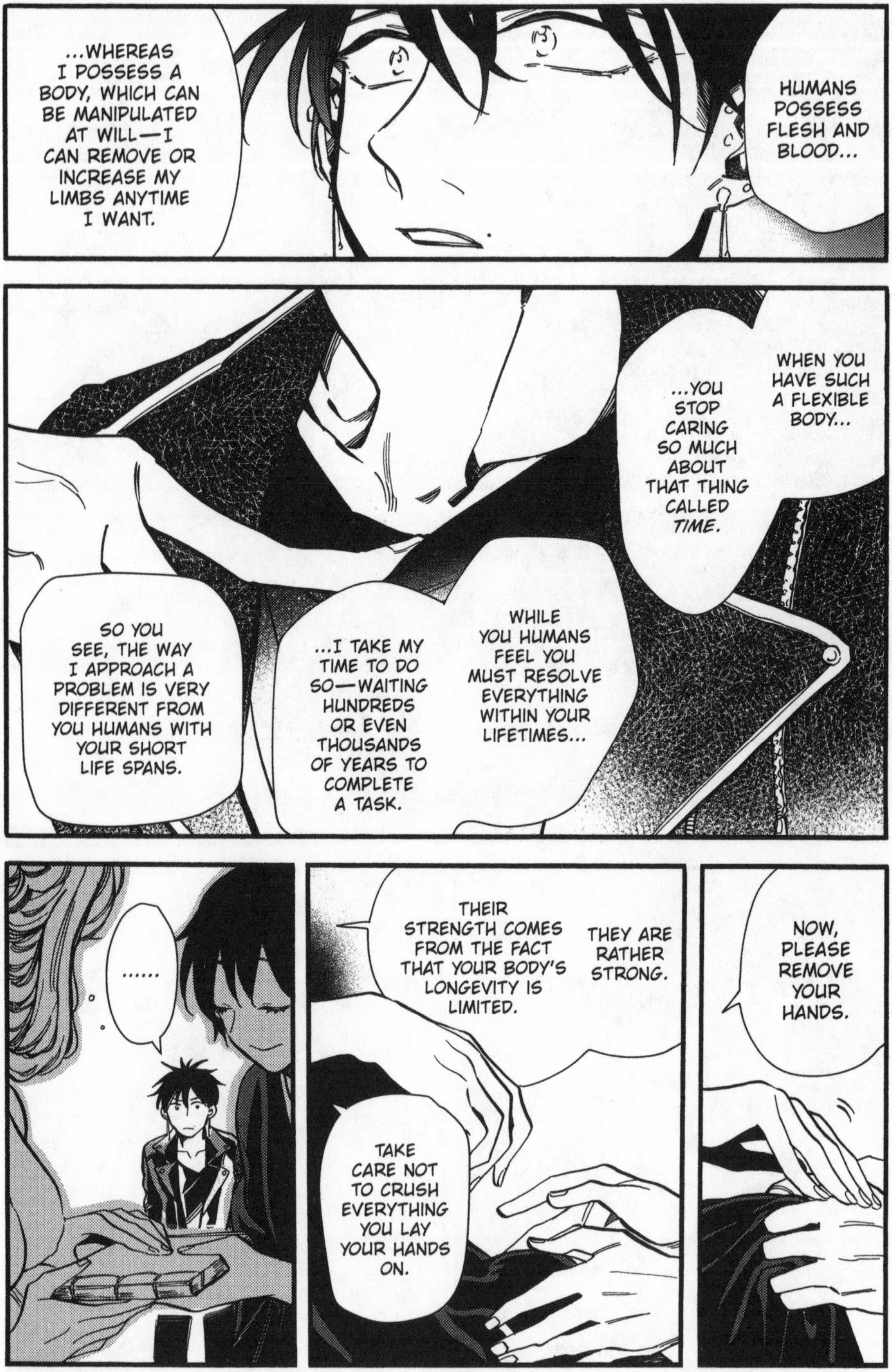
HUMANS POSSESS FLESH AND BLOOD...
...WHEREAS I POSSESS A BODY, WHICH CAN BE MANIPULATED AT WILL—I CAN REMOVE OR INCREASE MY LIMBS ANYTIME I WANT.
WHEN YOU HAVE SUCH A FLEXIBLE BODY...
...YOU STOP CARING SO MUCH ABOUT THAT THING CALLED *TIME.*
WHILE YOU HUMANS FEEL YOU MUST RESOLVE EVERYTHING WITHIN YOUR LIFETIMES...
...I TAKE MY TIME TO DO SO—WAITING HUNDREDS OR EVEN THOUSANDS OF YEARS TO COMPLETE A TASK.
SO YOU SEE, THE WAY I APPROACH A PROBLEM IS VERY DIFFERENT FROM YOU HUMANS WITH YOUR SHORT LIFE SPANS.
NOW, PLEASE REMOVE YOUR HANDS.
THEY ARE RATHER STRONG.
THEIR STRENGTH COMES FROM THE FACT THAT YOUR BODY'S LONGEVITY IS LIMITED.
TAKE CARE NOT TO CRUSH EVERYTHING YOU LAY YOUR HANDS ON.
......

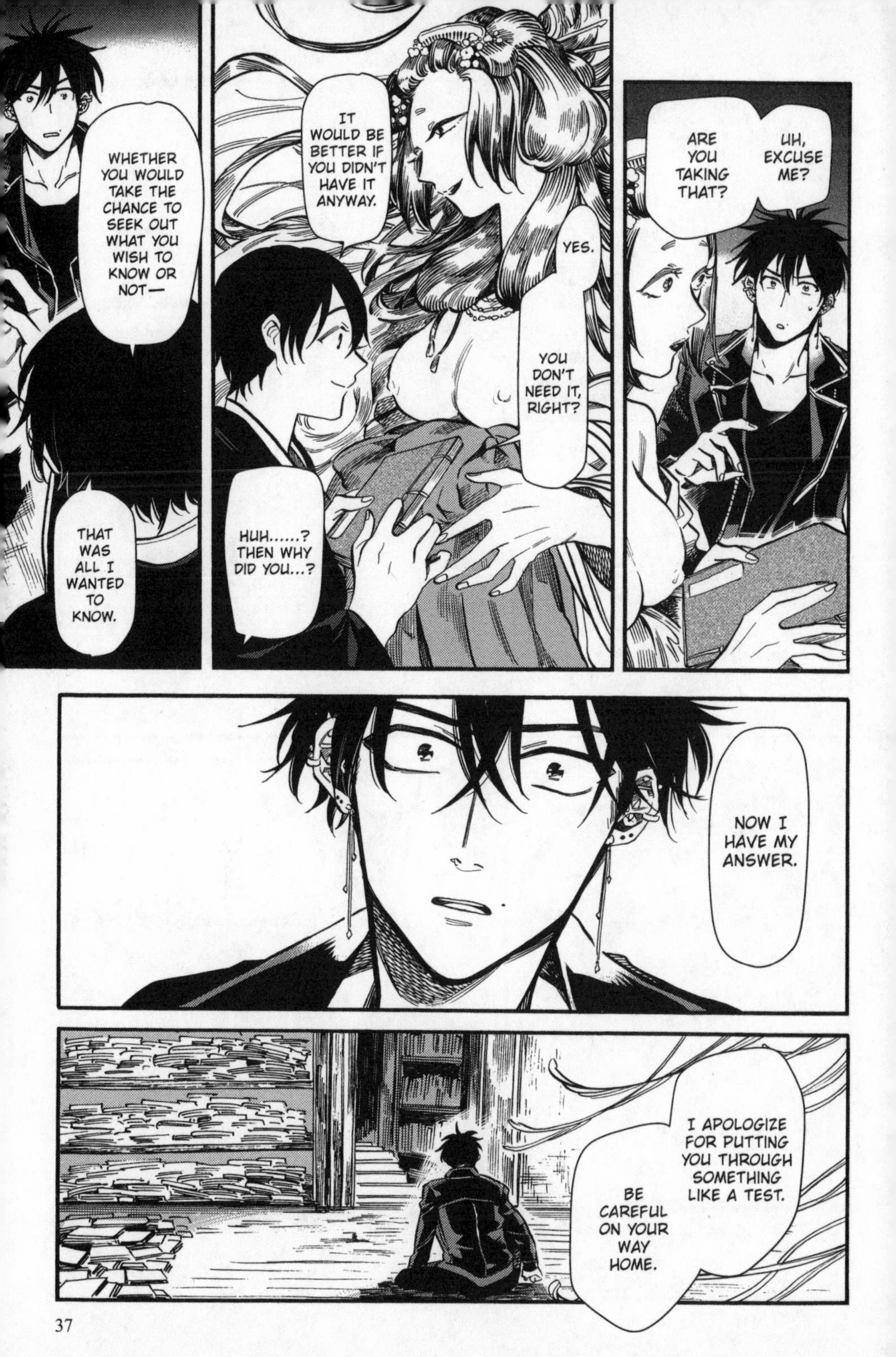
UH, EXCUSE ME?
ARE YOU TAKING THAT?
YES.
YOU DON'T NEED IT, RIGHT?
IT WOULD BE BETTER IF YOU DIDN'T HAVE IT ANYWAY.
HUH......? THEN WHY DID YOU...?
WHETHER YOU WOULD TAKE THE CHANCE TO SEEK OUT WHAT YOU WISH TO KNOW OR NOT—
THAT WAS ALL I WANTED TO KNOW.
NOW I HAVE MY ANSWER.
I APOLOGIZE FOR PUTTING YOU THROUGH SOMETHING LIKE A TEST.
BE CAREFUL ON YOUR WAY HOME.

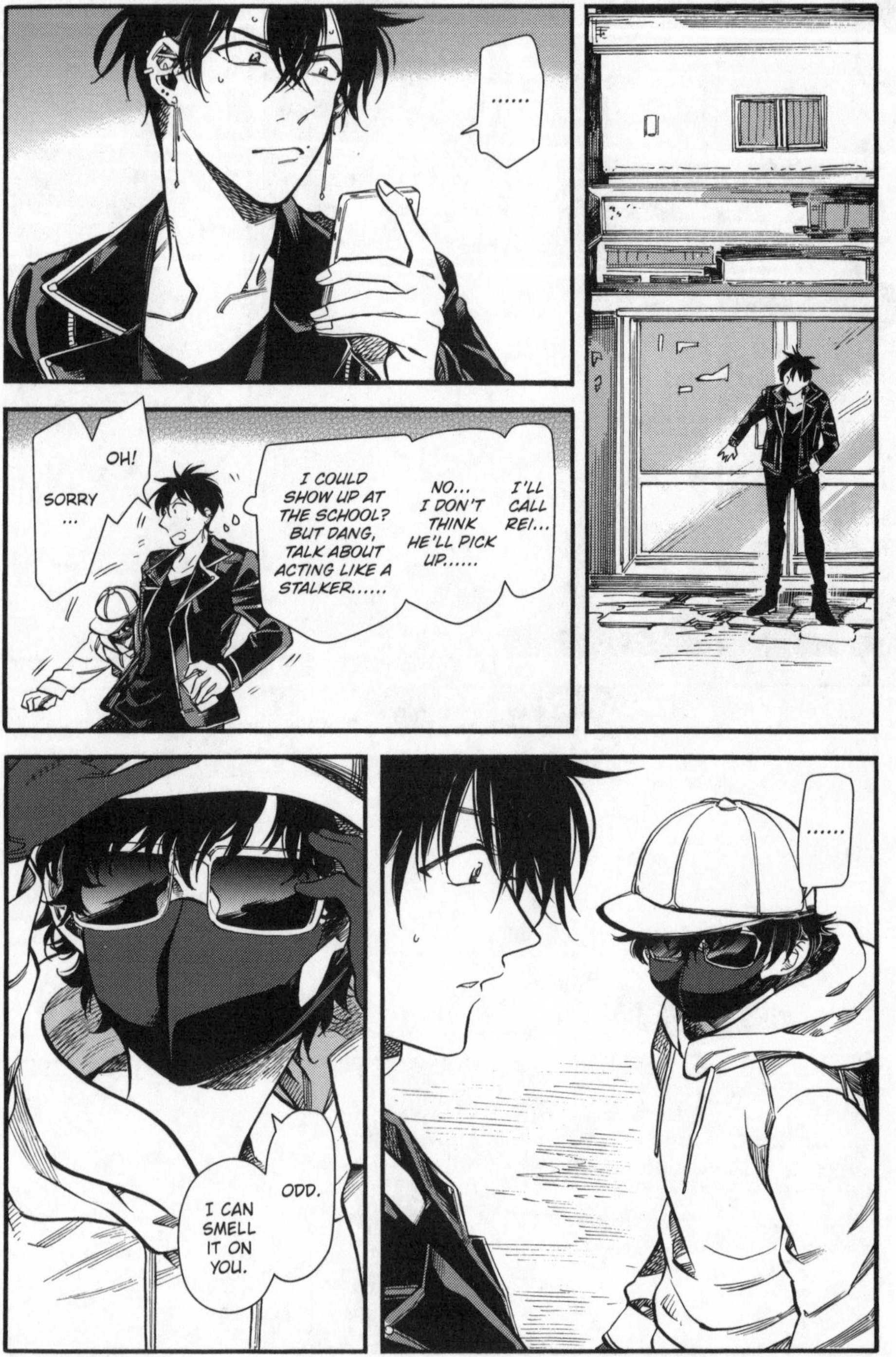
......
I'LL CALL REI...
NO... I DON'T THINK HE'LL PICK UP......
I COULD SHOW UP AT THE SCHOOL? BUT DANG, TALK ABOUT ACTING LIKE A STALKER......
OH! SORRY ...
......
ODD. I CAN SMELL IT ON YOU.

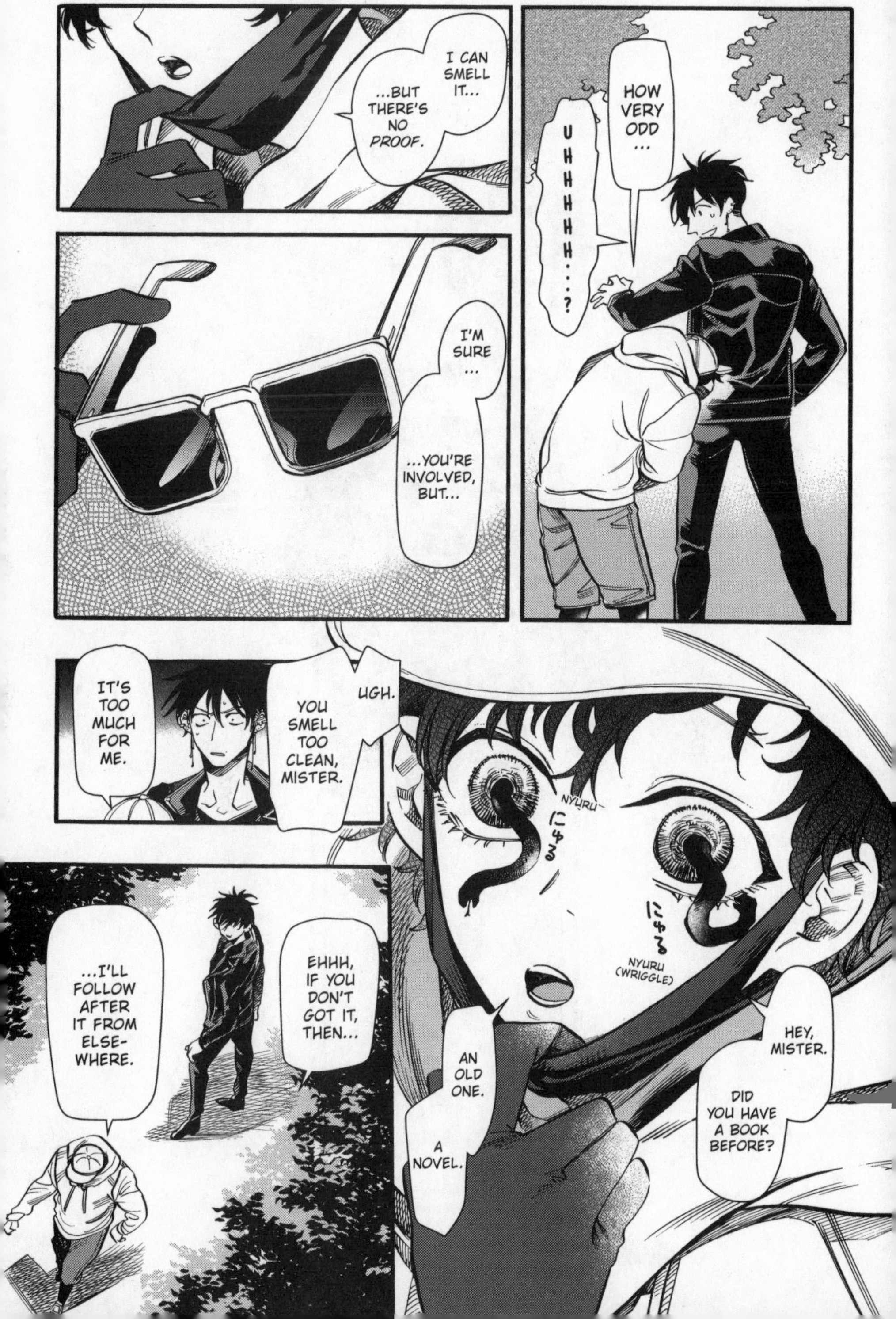
HOW VERY ODD...
UHHHHH...?
I CAN SMELL IT...
...BUT THERE'S NO *PROOF*.
I'M SURE...
...YOU'RE INVOLVED, BUT...
にゅる
NYURU
にゅる
NYURU (WRIGGLE)
HEY, MISTER.
DID YOU HAVE A BOOK BEFORE?
AN OLD ONE.
A NOVEL.
UGH.
YOU SMELL TOO CLEAN, MISTER.
IT'S TOO MUCH FOR ME.
EHHH, IF YOU DON'T GOT IT, THEN...
...I'LL FOLLOW AFTER IT FROM ELSEWHERE.

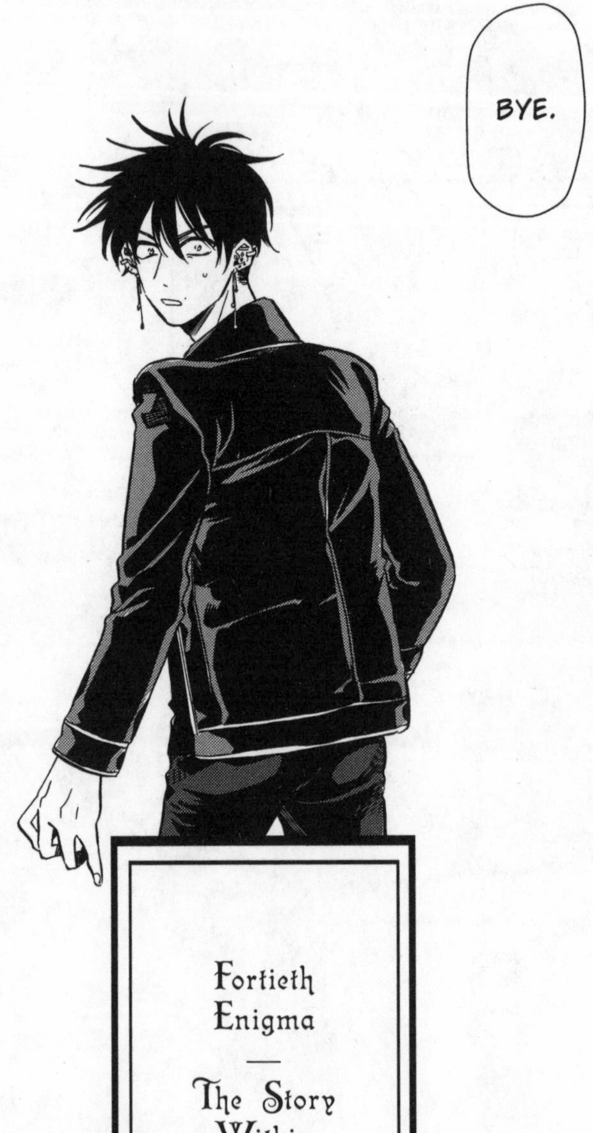
BYE.
Fortieth Enigma
—
The Story Within the Story

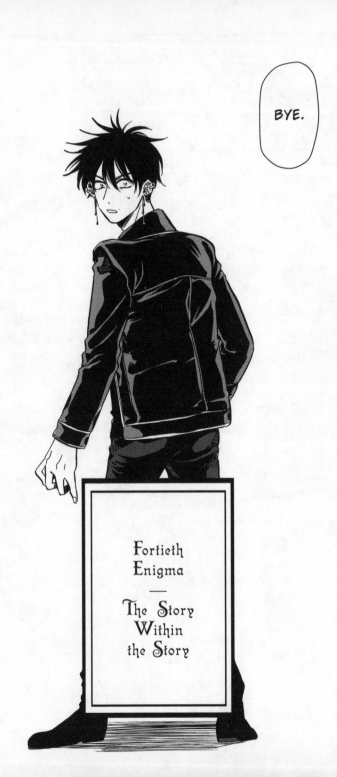

Phantom Tales of the Night

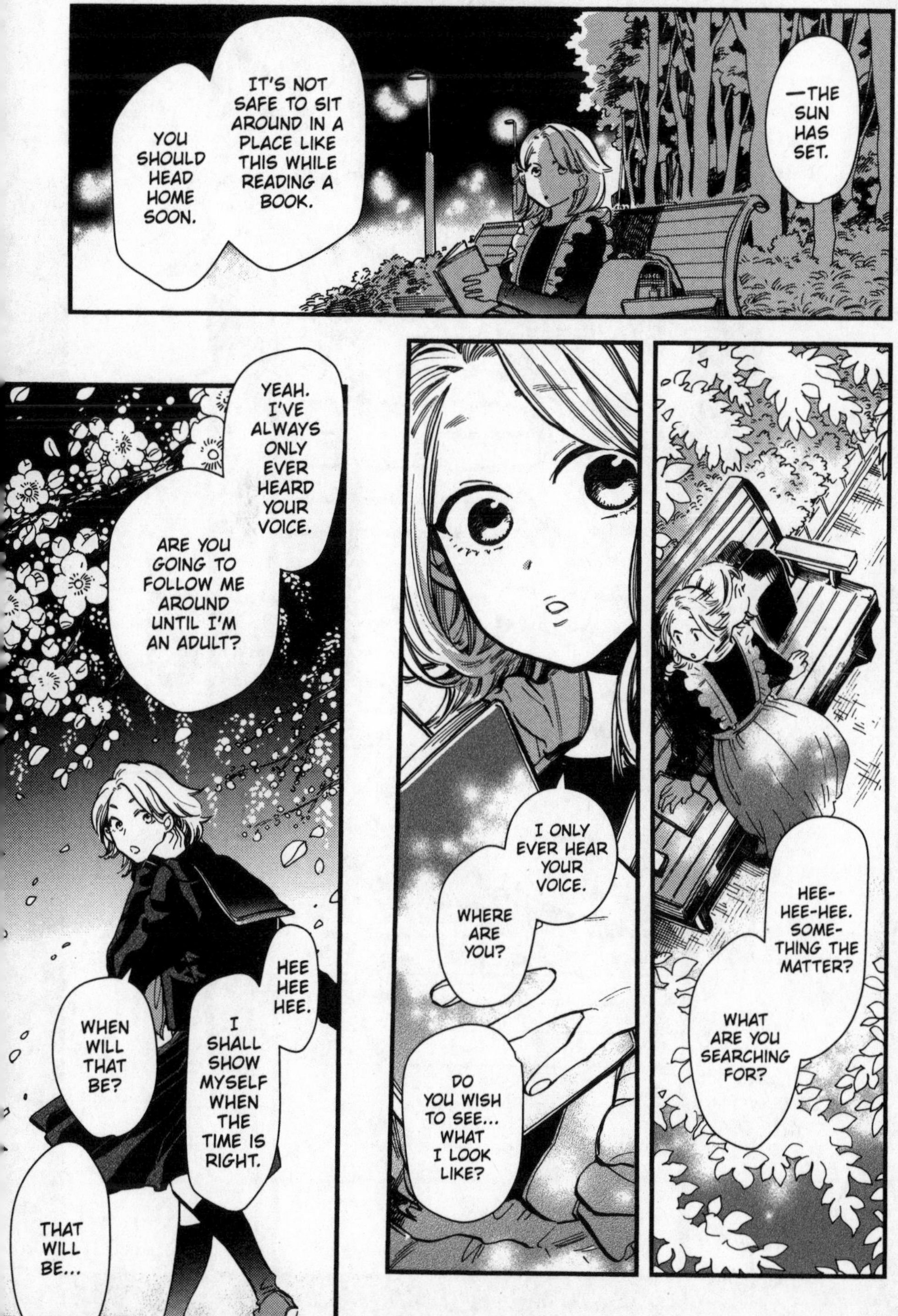
—THE SUN HAS SET.
IT'S NOT SAFE TO SIT AROUND IN A PLACE LIKE THIS WHILE READING A BOOK.
YOU SHOULD HEAD HOME SOON.
HEE-HEE-HEE. SOME-THING THE MATTER?
WHAT ARE YOU SEARCHING FOR?
I ONLY EVER HEAR YOUR VOICE.
WHERE ARE YOU?
DO YOU WISH TO SEE... WHAT I LOOK LIKE?
YEAH. I'VE ALWAYS ONLY EVER HEARD YOUR VOICE.
ARE YOU GOING TO FOLLOW ME AROUND UNTIL I'M AN ADULT?
HEE HEE HEE.
I SHALL SHOW MYSELF WHEN THE TIME IS RIGHT.
WHEN WILL THAT BE?
THAT WILL BE...

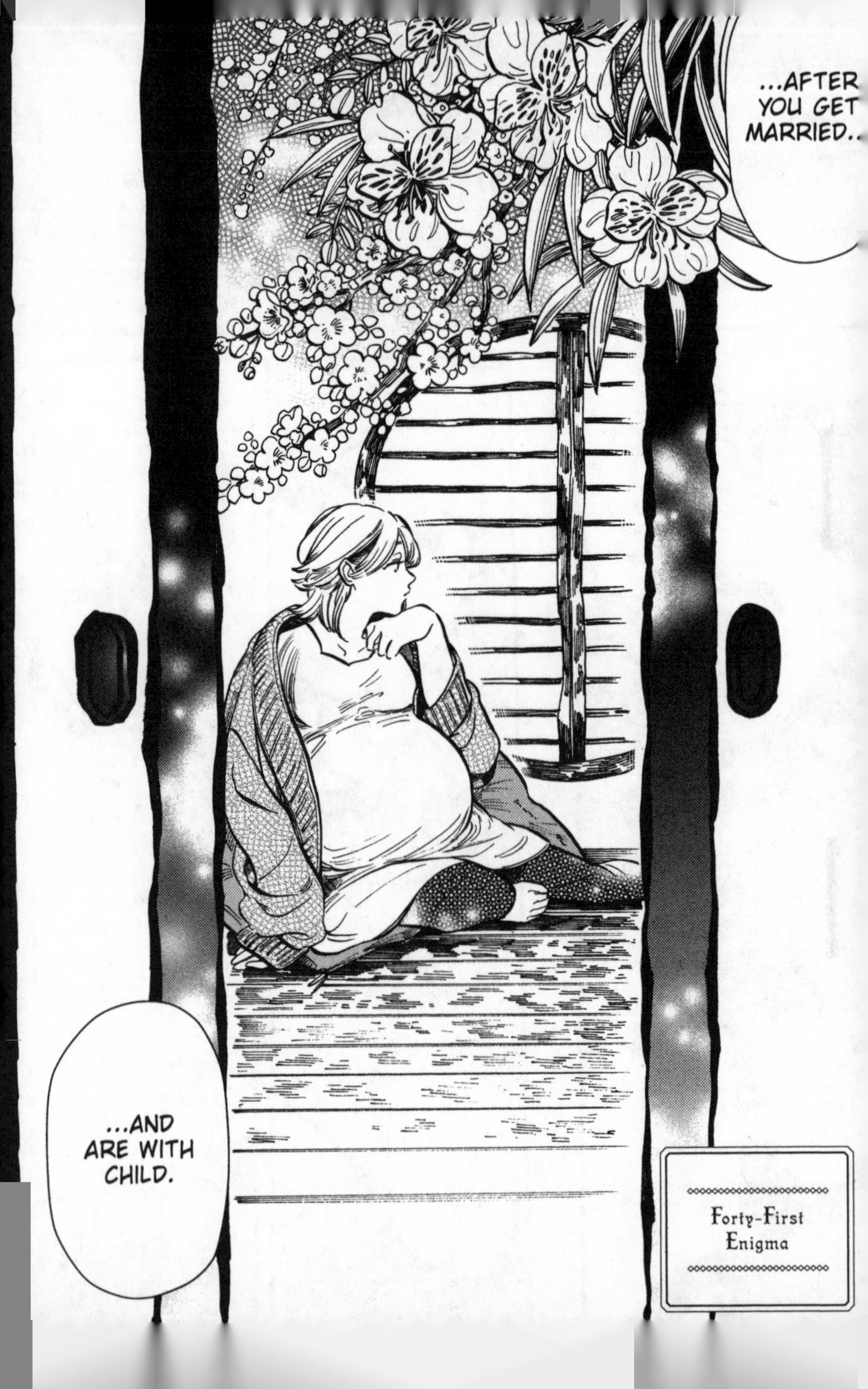
...AFTER YOU GET MARRIED...
...AND ARE WITH CHILD.
Forty-First Enigma

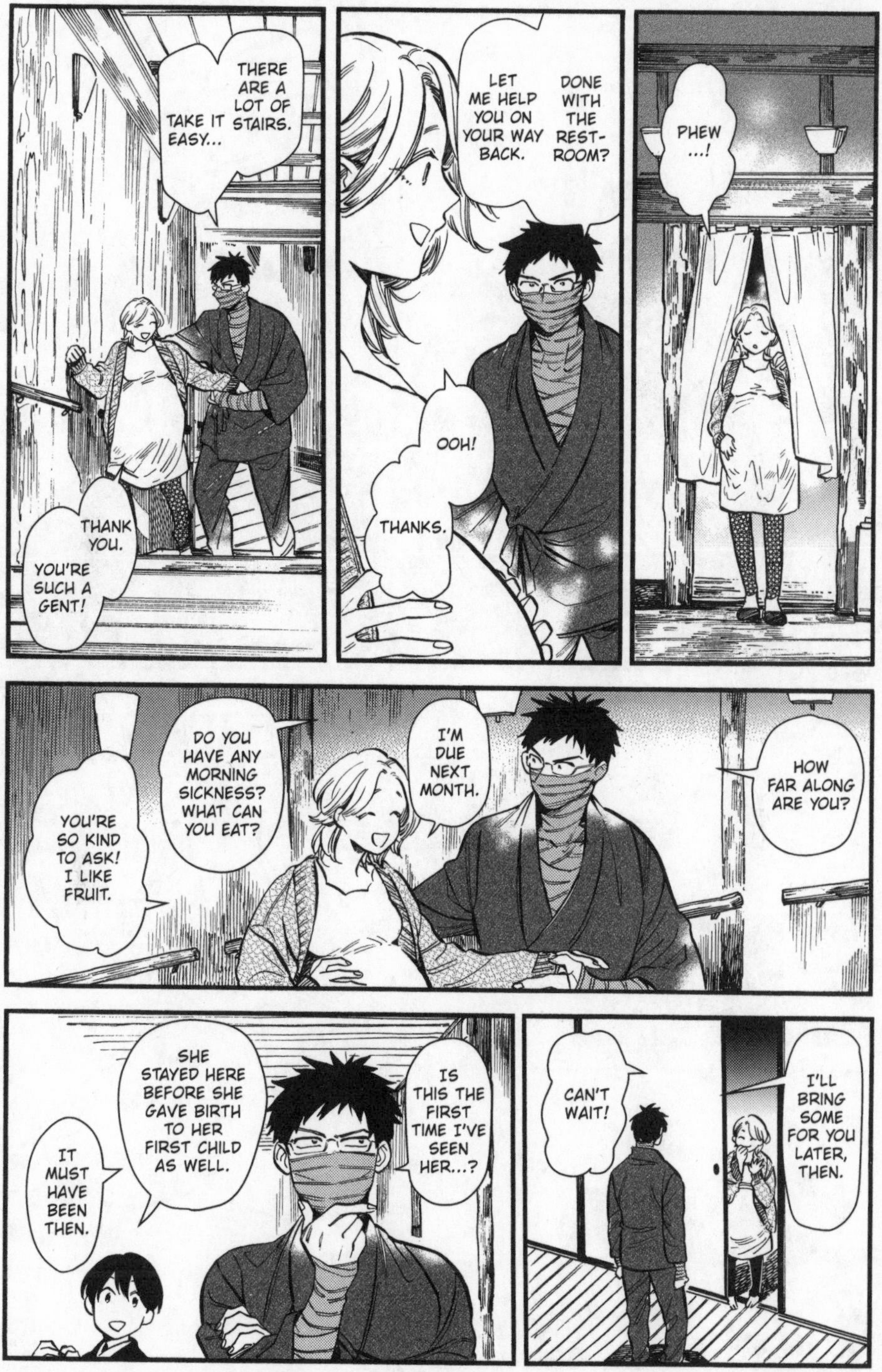
PHEW ...!
DONE WITH THE REST-ROOM?
LET ME HELP YOU ON YOUR WAY BACK.
OOH! THANKS.
THERE ARE A LOT OF STAIRS.
TAKE IT EASY...
THANK YOU. YOU'RE SUCH A GENT!
HOW FAR ALONG ARE YOU?
I'M DUE NEXT MONTH.
DO YOU HAVE ANY MORNING SICKNESS? WHAT CAN YOU EAT?
YOU'RE SO KIND TO ASK! I LIKE FRUIT.
I'LL BRING SOME FOR YOU LATER, THEN.
CAN'T WAIT!
IS THIS THE FIRST TIME I'VE SEEN HER...?
SHE STAYED HERE BEFORE SHE GAVE BIRTH TO HER FIRST CHILD AS WELL.
IT MUST HAVE BEEN THEN.

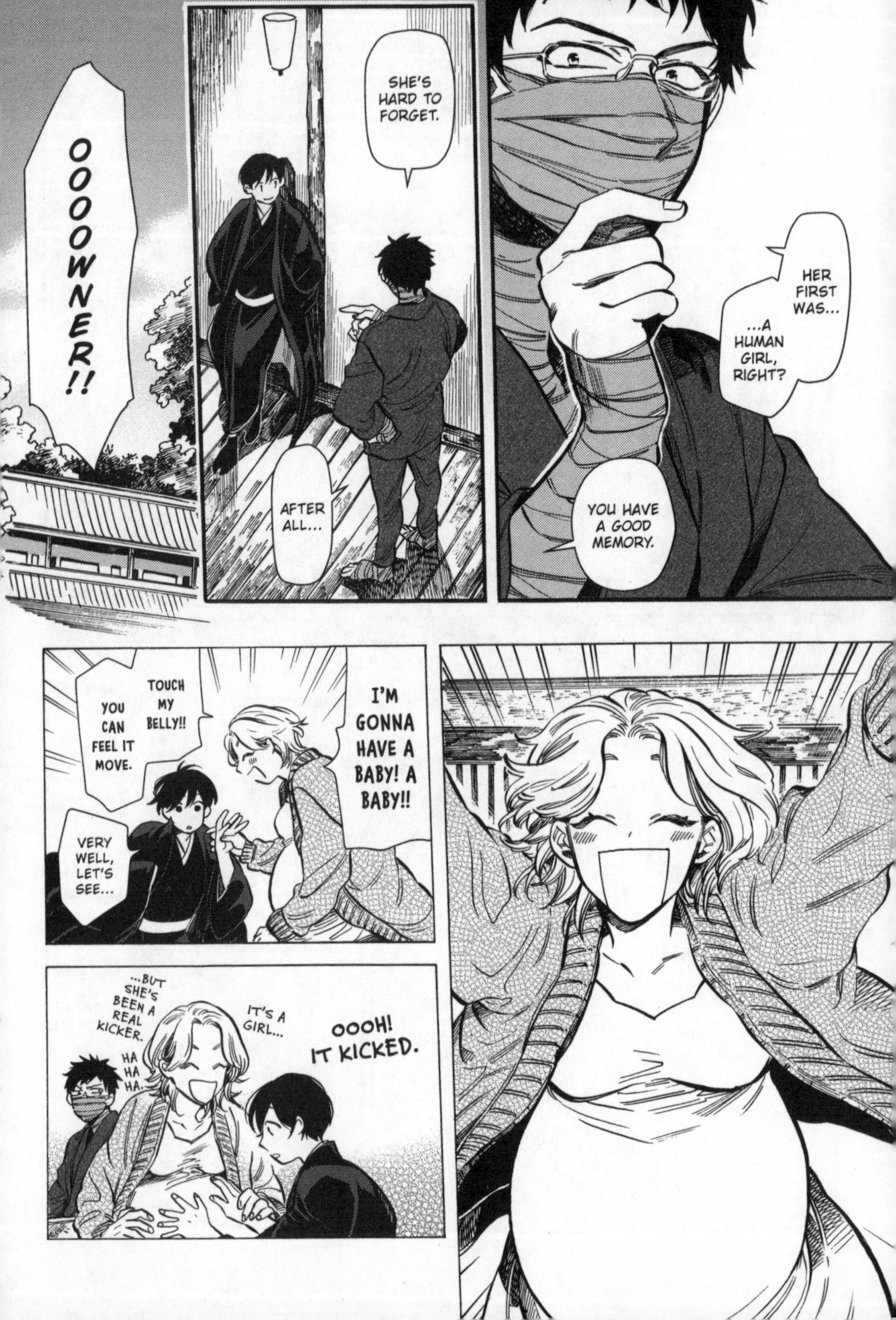
HER FIRST WAS...
...A HUMAN GIRL, RIGHT?
YOU HAVE A GOOD MEMORY.
SHE'S HARD TO FORGET.
AFTER ALL...
OOOOOWNER!!
I'M GONNA HAVE A BABY! A BABY!!
TOUCH MY BELLY!!
YOU CAN FEEL IT MOVE.
VERY WELL, LET'S SEE...
OOOH! IT KICKED.
IT'S A GIRL...
...BUT SHE'S BEEN A REAL KICKER.
HA HA HA.

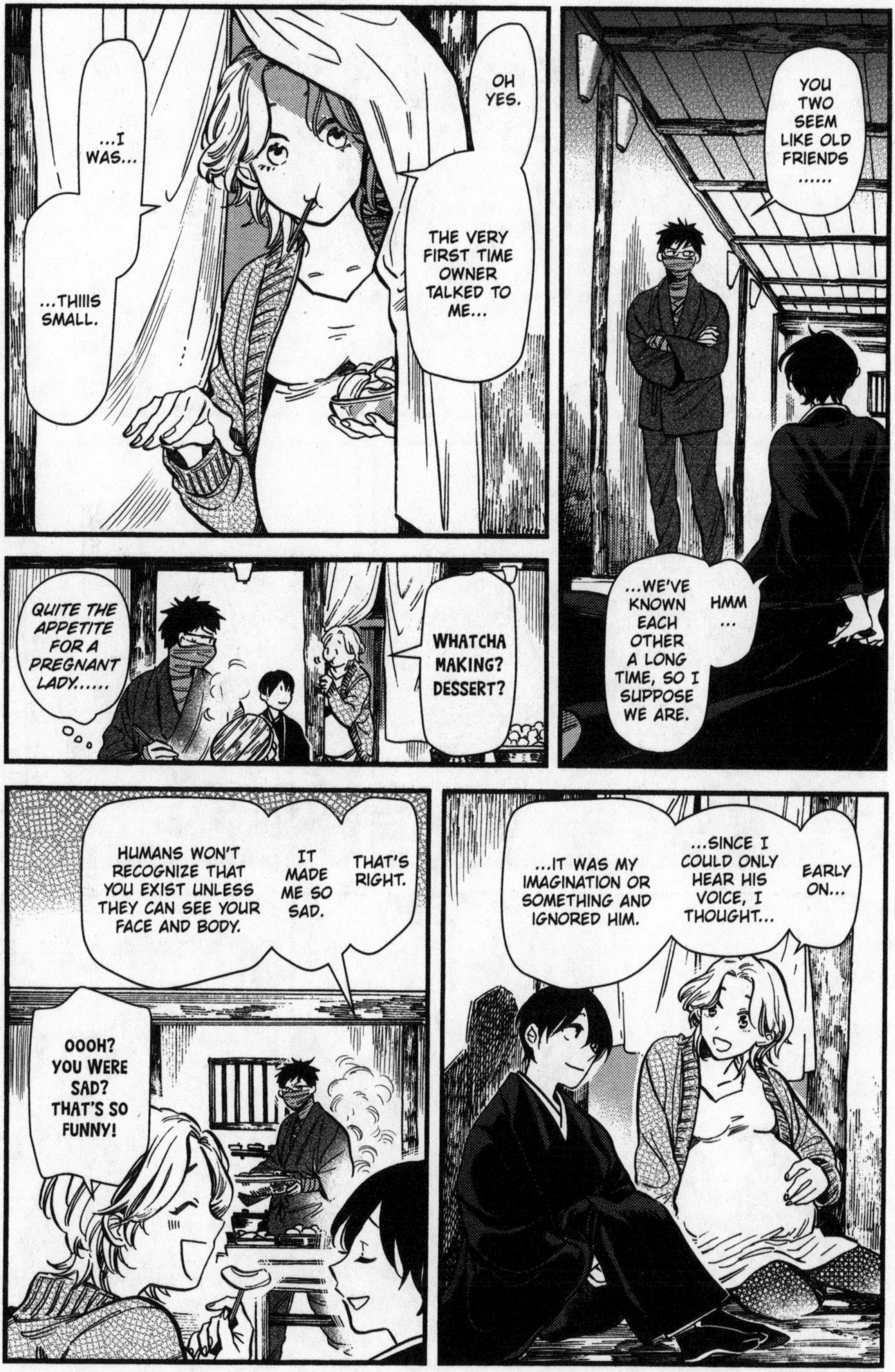
YOU TWO SEEM LIKE OLD FRIENDS ......
HMM ...
...WE'VE KNOWN EACH OTHER A LONG TIME, SO I SUPPOSE WE ARE.
OH YES.
THE VERY FIRST TIME OWNER TALKED TO ME...
...I WAS...
...THIIIS SMALL.
WHATCHA MAKING? DESSERT?
QUITE THE APPETITE FOR A PREGNANT LADY......
EARLY ON...
...SINCE I COULD ONLY HEAR HIS VOICE, I THOUGHT...
...IT WAS MY IMAGINATION OR SOMETHING AND IGNORED HIM.
THAT'S RIGHT.
IT MADE ME SO SAD.
HUMANS WON'T RECOGNIZE THAT YOU EXIST UNLESS THEY CAN SEE YOUR FACE AND BODY.
OOOH? YOU WERE SAD? THAT'S SO FUNNY!

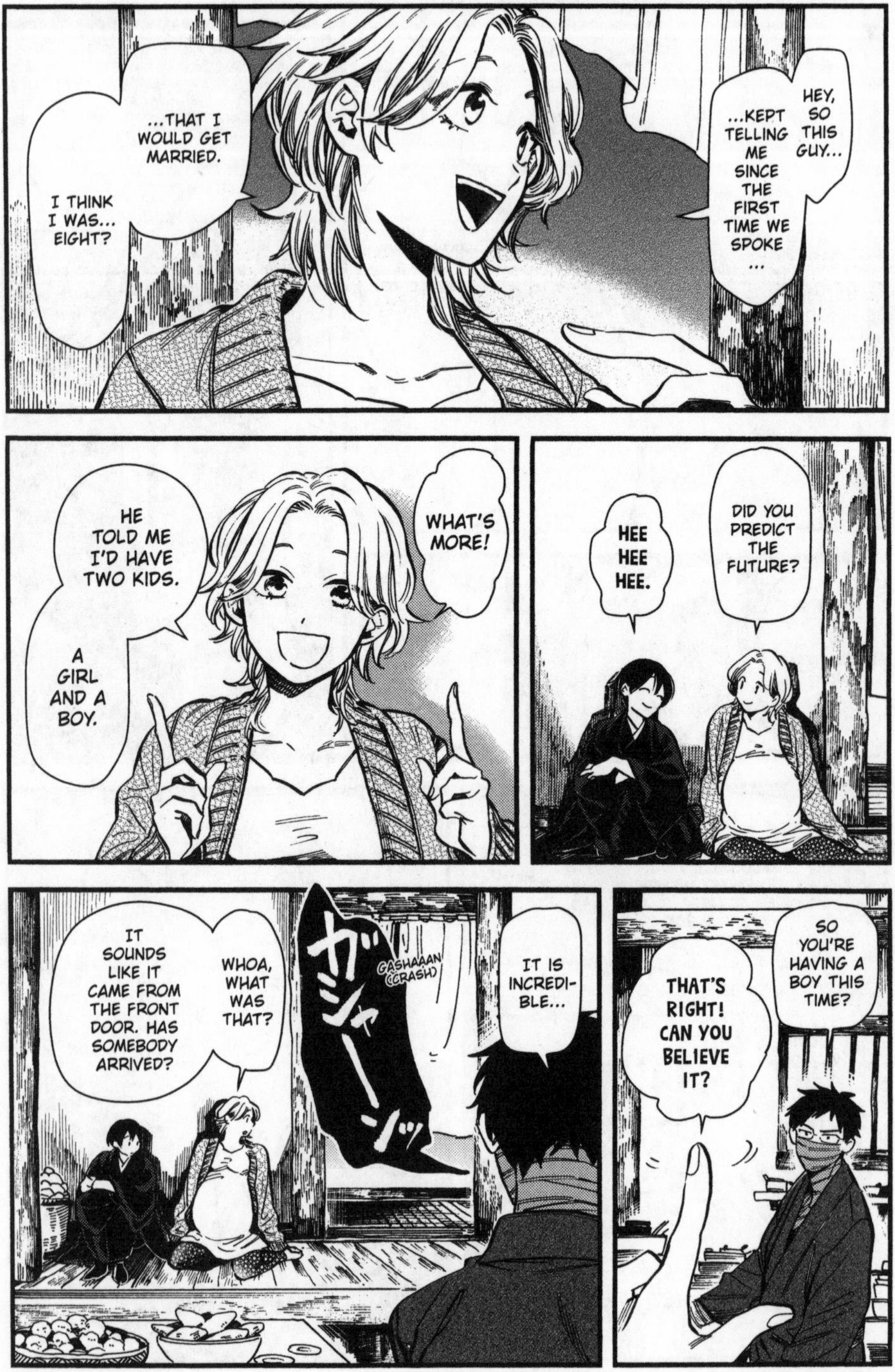
HEY, SO THIS GUY...
...KEPT TELLING ME SINCE THE FIRST TIME WE SPOKE...
...THAT I WOULD GET MARRIED.
I THINK I WAS... EIGHT?
DID YOU PREDICT THE FUTURE?
HEE HEE HEE.
WHAT'S MORE!
HE TOLD ME I'D HAVE TWO KIDS.
A GIRL AND A BOY.
SO YOU'RE HAVING A BOY THIS TIME?
THAT'S RIGHT! CAN YOU BELIEVE IT?
IT IS INCREDIBLE...
GASHAAAN (CRASH)
WHOA, WHAT WAS THAT?
IT SOUNDS LIKE IT CAME FROM THE FRONT DOOR. HAS SOMEBODY ARRIVED?

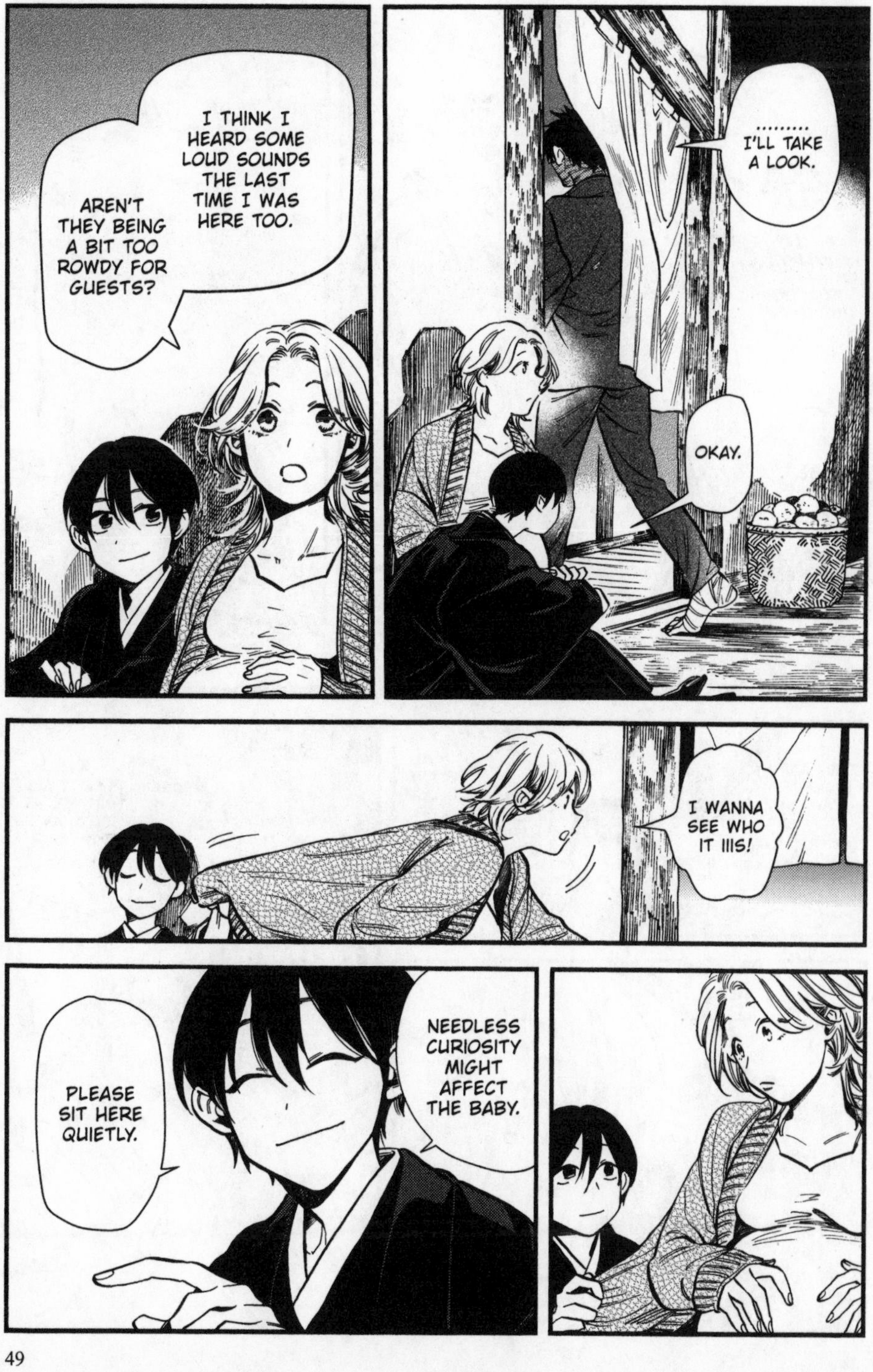
....
I'LL TAKE A LOOK.
OKAY.
I THINK I HEARD SOME LOUD SOUNDS THE LAST TIME I WAS HERE TOO.
AREN'T THEY BEING A BIT TOO ROWDY FOR GUESTS?
I WANNA SEE WHO IT IIIS!
NEEDLESS CURIOSITY MIGHT AFFECT THE BABY.
PLEASE SIT HERE QUIETLY.

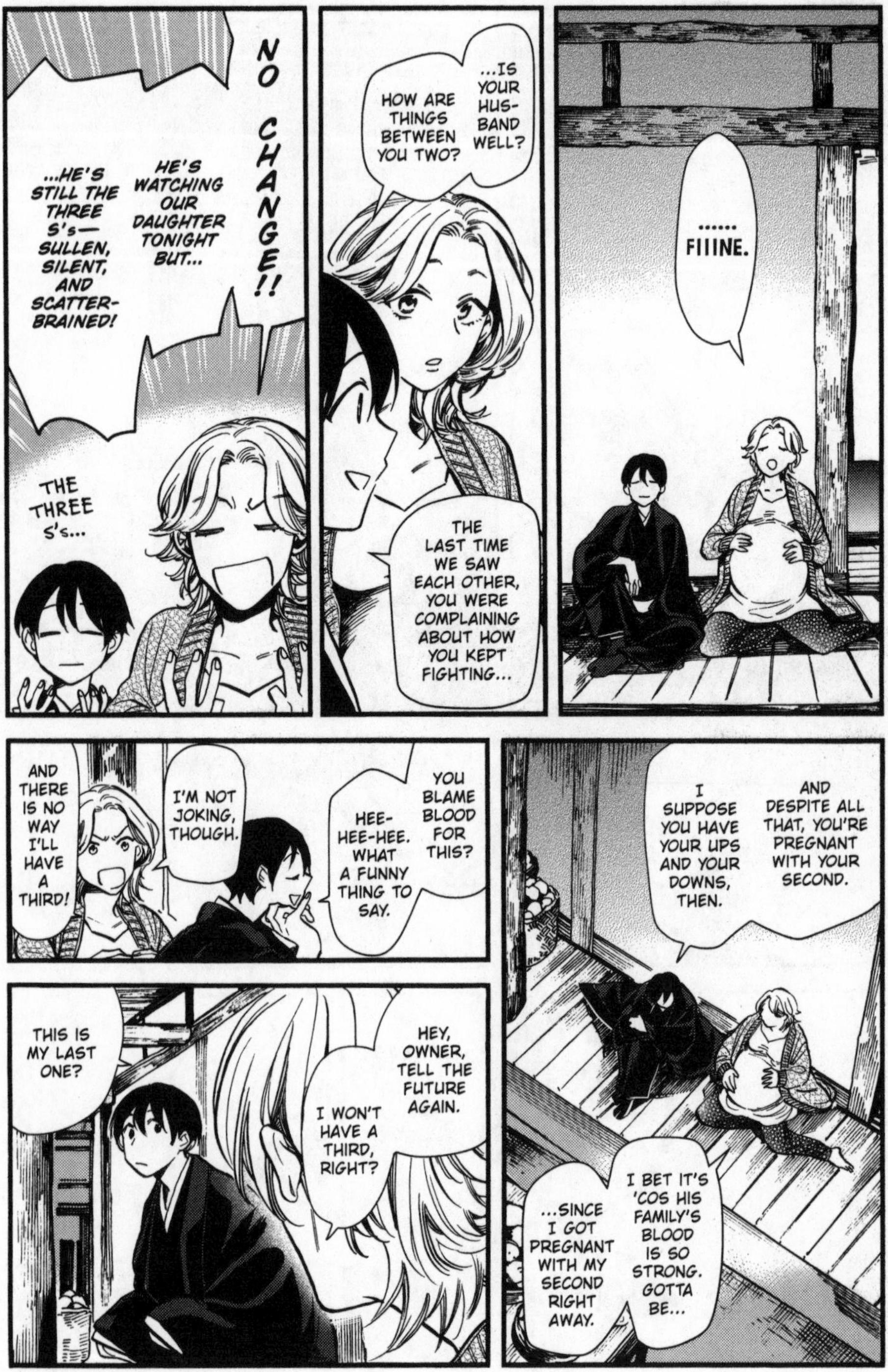
......FIIINE.
...IS YOUR HUSBAND WELL?
HOW ARE THINGS BETWEEN YOU TWO?
THE LAST TIME WE SAW EACH OTHER, YOU WERE COMPLAINING ABOUT HOW YOU KEPT FIGHTING...
NO CHANGE!!
HE'S WATCHING OUR DAUGHTER TONIGHT BUT...
...HE'S STILL THE THREE S's— SULLEN, SILENT, AND SCATTER-BRAINED!
THE THREE S's...
AND DESPITE ALL THAT, YOU'RE PREGNANT WITH YOUR SECOND.
I SUPPOSE YOU HAVE YOUR UPS AND YOUR DOWNS, THEN.
I BET IT'S 'COS HIS FAMILY'S BLOOD IS SO STRONG. GOTTA BE...
...SINCE I GOT PREGNANT WITH MY SECOND RIGHT AWAY.
YOU BLAME BLOOD FOR THIS?
HEE-HEE-HEE. WHAT A FUNNY THING TO SAY.
I'M NOT JOKING, THOUGH.
AND THERE IS NO WAY I'LL HAVE A THIRD!
HEY, OWNER, TELL THE FUTURE AGAIN.
I WON'T HAVE A THIRD, RIGHT?
THIS IS MY LAST ONE?

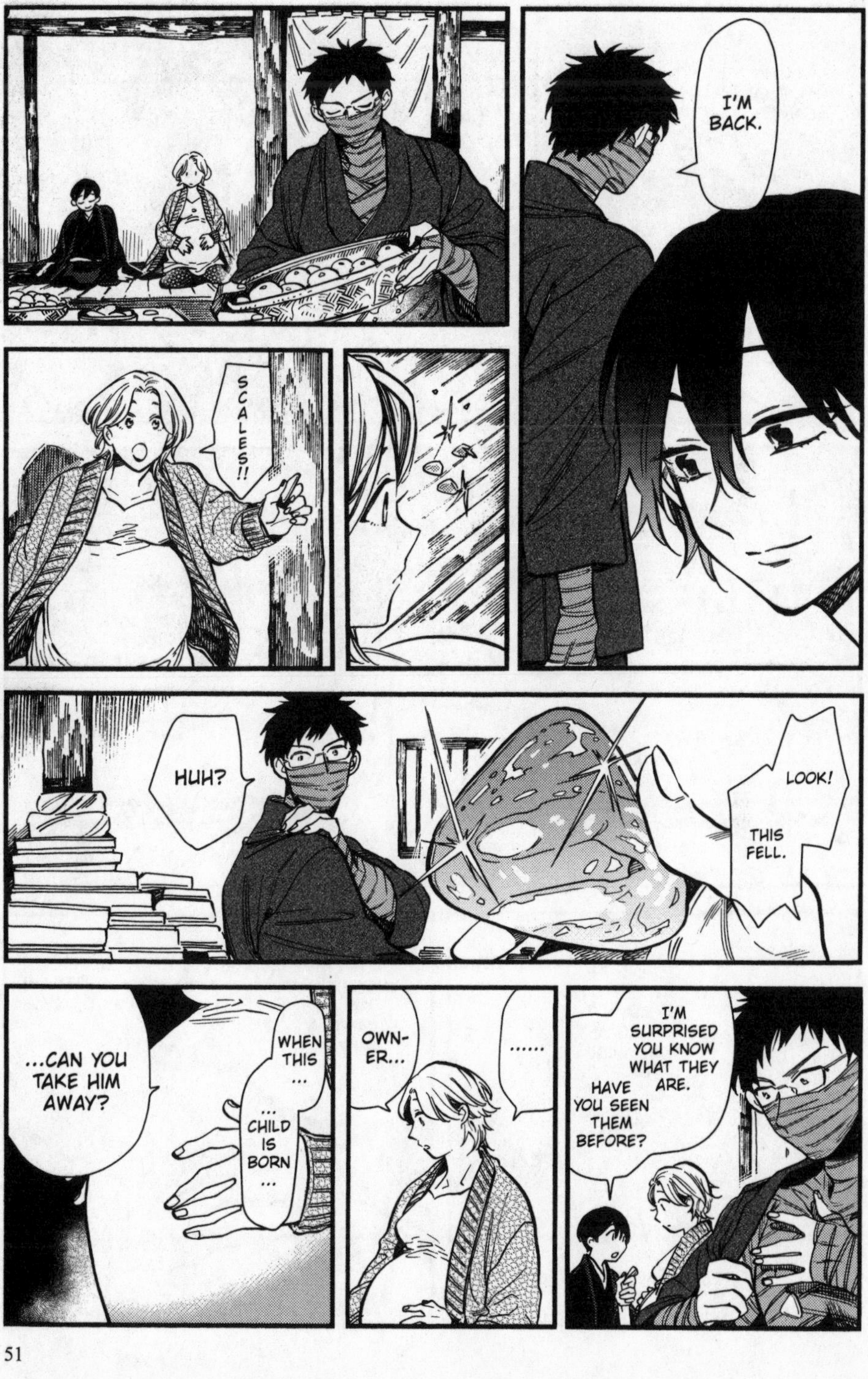
I'M BACK.
SCALES!!
LOOK! THIS FELL.
HUH?
I'M SURPRISED YOU KNOW WHAT THEY ARE.
HAVE YOU SEEN THEM BEFORE?
......
OWN-ER...
WHEN THIS ... ... CHILD IS BORN ...
...CAN YOU TAKE HIM AWAY?

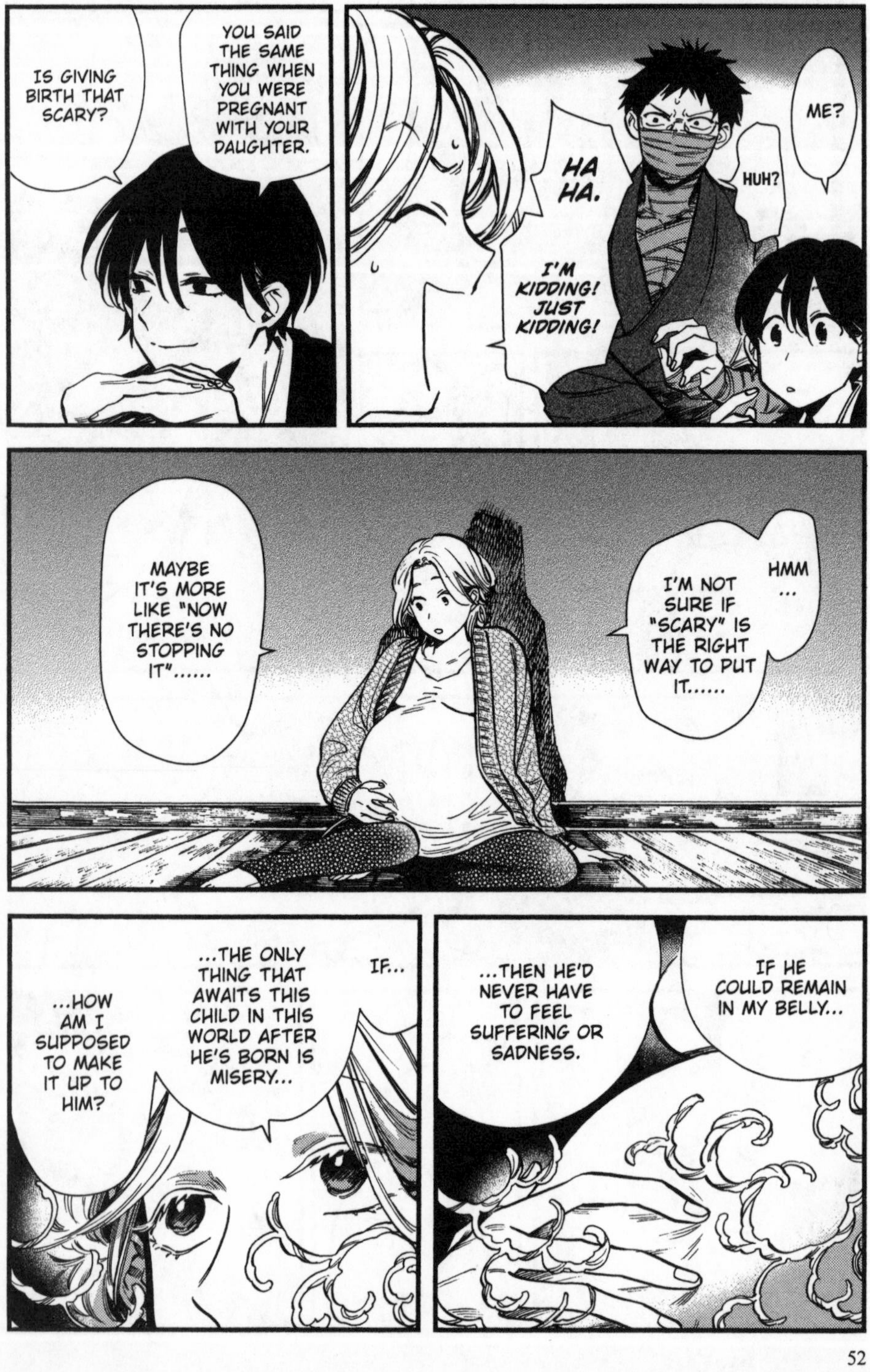
ME?
HUH?
HA HA.
I'M KIDDING! JUST KIDDING!
YOU SAID THE SAME THING WHEN YOU WERE PREGNANT WITH YOUR DAUGHTER.
IS GIVING BIRTH THAT SCARY?
HMM ...
I'M NOT SURE IF "SCARY" IS THE RIGHT WAY TO PUT IT......
MAYBE IT'S MORE LIKE "NOW THERE'S NO STOPPING IT"......
IF HE COULD REMAIN IN MY BELLY...
...THEN HE'D NEVER HAVE TO FEEL SUFFERING OR SADNESS.
IF...
...THE ONLY THING THAT AWAITS THIS CHILD IN THIS WORLD AFTER HE'S BORN IS MISERY...
...HOW AM I SUPPOSED TO MAKE IT UP TO HIM?

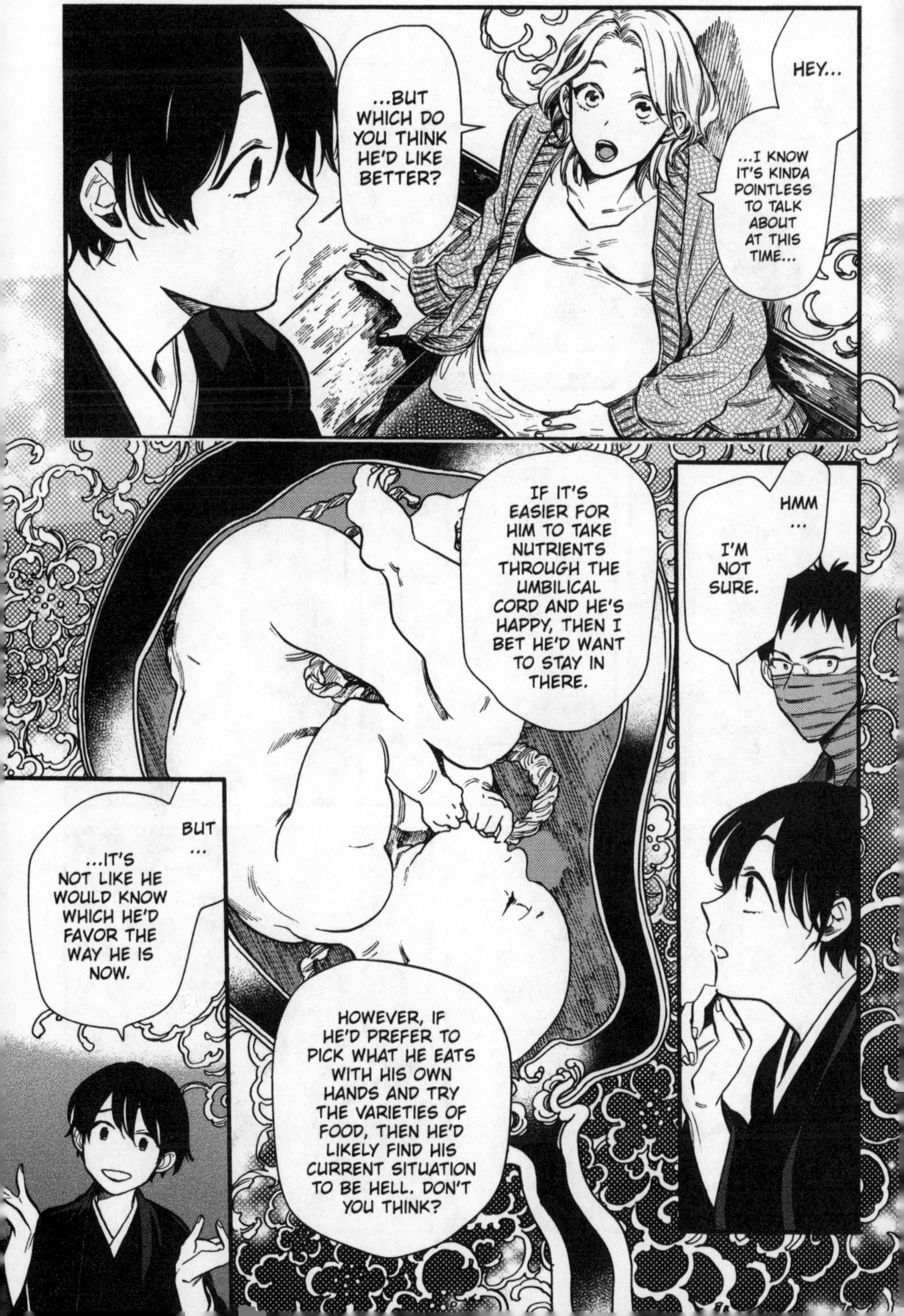
HEY...
...I KNOW IT'S KINDA POINTLESS TO TALK ABOUT AT THIS TIME...
...BUT WHICH DO YOU THINK HE'D LIKE BETTER?
HMM...
I'M NOT SURE.
IF IT'S EASIER FOR HIM TO TAKE NUTRIENTS THROUGH THE UMBILICAL CORD AND HE'S HAPPY, THEN I BET HE'D WANT TO STAY IN THERE.
HOWEVER, IF HE'D PREFER TO PICK WHAT HE EATS WITH HIS OWN HANDS AND TRY THE VARIETIES OF FOOD, THEN HE'D LIKELY FIND HIS CURRENT SITUATION TO BE HELL. DON'T YOU THINK?
BUT...
...IT'S NOT LIKE HE WOULD KNOW WHICH HE'D FAVOR THE WAY HE IS NOW.

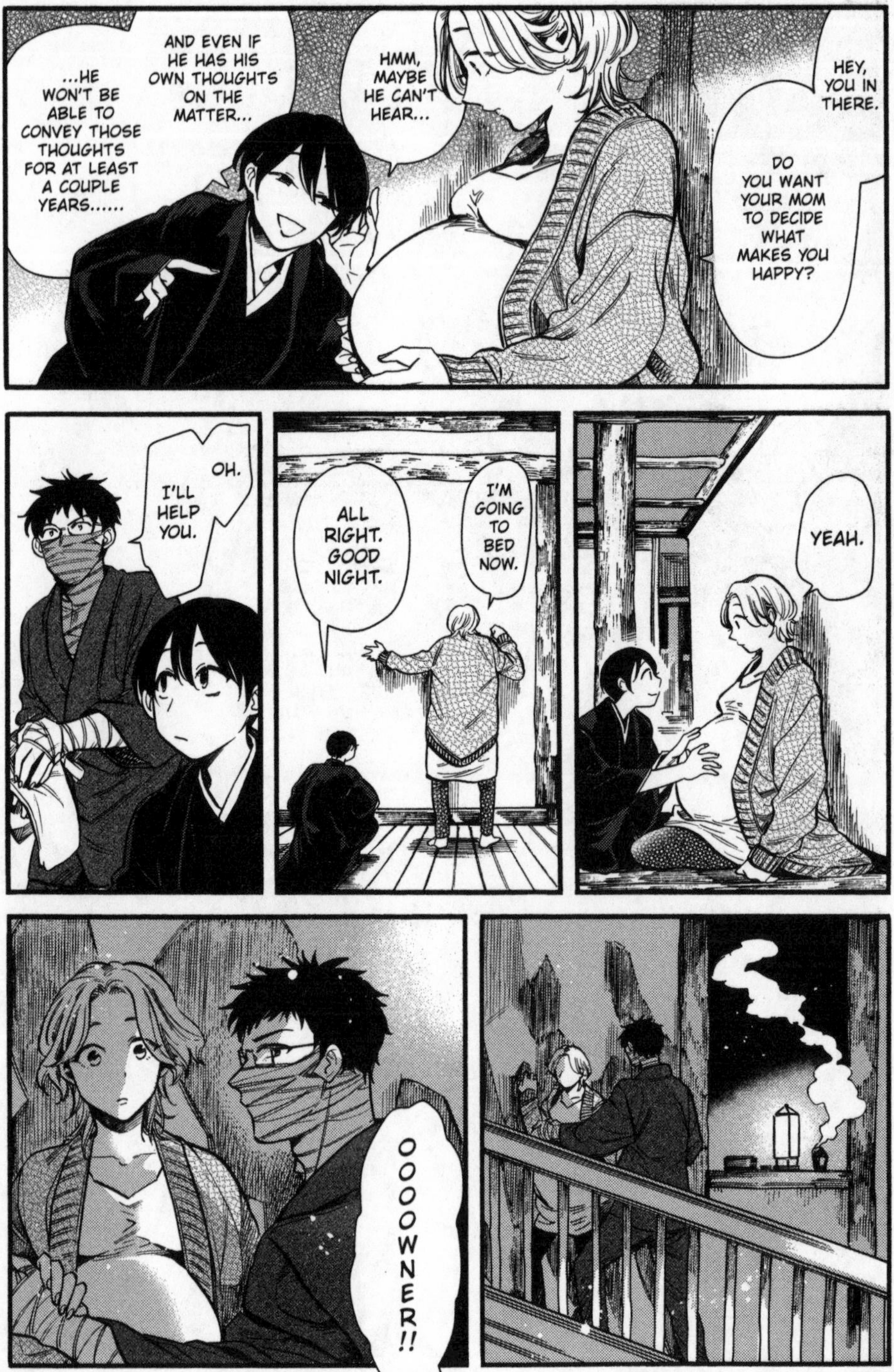
HEY, YOU IN THERE.
DO YOU WANT YOUR MOM TO DECIDE WHAT MAKES YOU HAPPY?
HMM, MAYBE HE CAN'T HEAR...
AND EVEN IF HE HAS HIS OWN THOUGHTS ON THE MATTER...
...HE WON'T BE ABLE TO CONVEY THOSE THOUGHTS FOR AT LEAST A COUPLE YEARS......
YEAH.
I'M GOING TO BED NOW.
ALL RIGHT. GOOD NIGHT.
OH. I'LL HELP YOU.
OOOOWNER!!

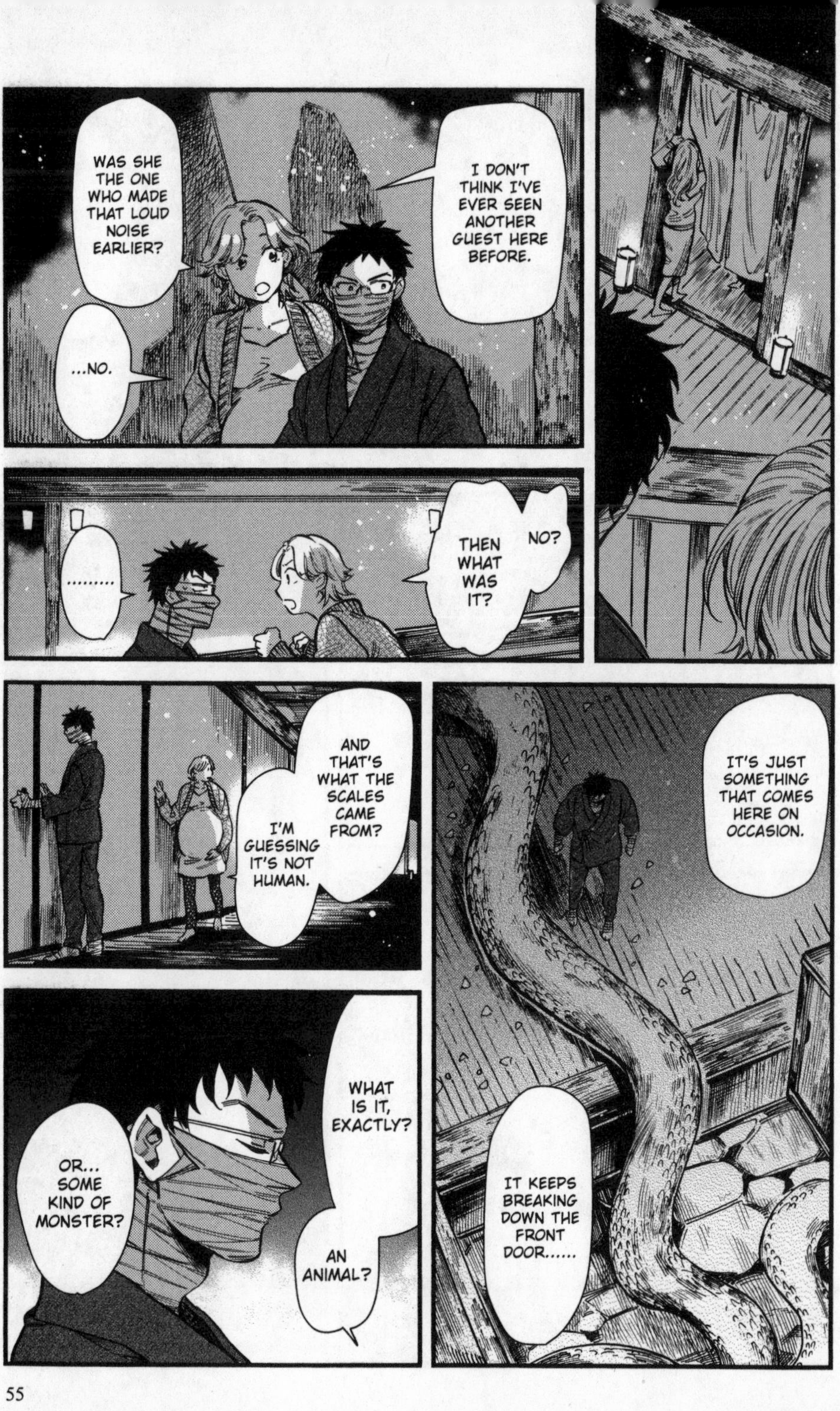
I DON'T THINK I'VE EVER SEEN ANOTHER GUEST HERE BEFORE.
WAS SHE THE ONE WHO MADE THAT LOUD NOISE EARLIER?
...NO.
NO?
THEN WHAT WAS IT?
....
IT'S JUST SOMETHING THAT COMES HERE ON OCCASION.
IT KEEPS BREAKING DOWN THE FRONT DOOR......
AND THAT'S WHAT THE SCALES CAME FROM?
I'M GUESSING IT'S NOT HUMAN.
WHAT IS IT, EXACTLY?
AN ANIMAL?
OR... SOME KIND OF MONSTER?

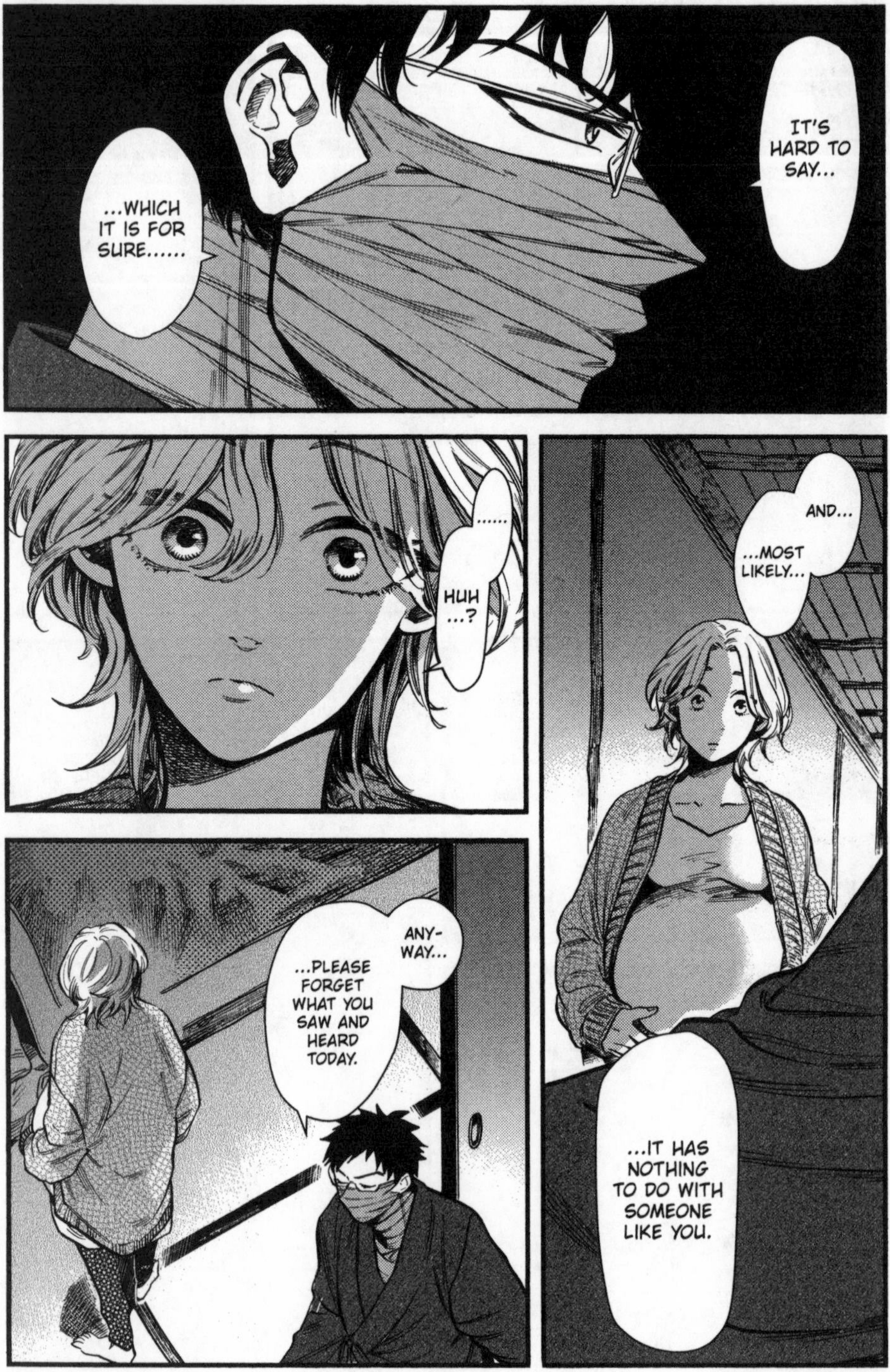
IT'S HARD TO SAY...
...WHICH IT IS FOR SURE......
AND...
...MOST LIKELY...
...IT HAS NOTHING TO DO WITH SOMEONE LIKE YOU.
......
HUH ...?
ANY-WAY...
...PLEASE FORGET WHAT YOU SAW AND HEARD TODAY.

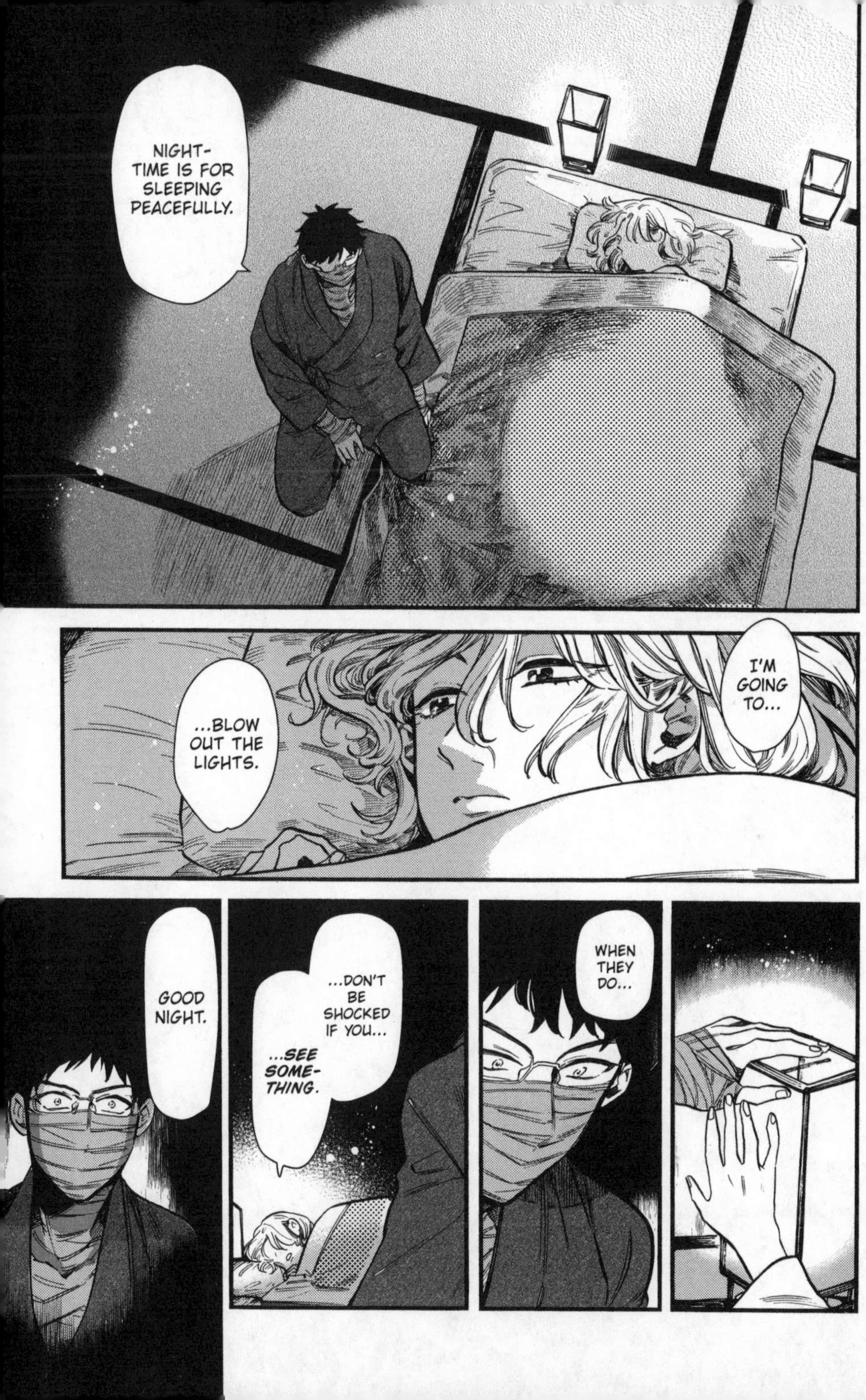
NIGHT-TIME IS FOR SLEEPING PEACEFULLY.
I'M GOING TO...
...BLOW OUT THE LIGHTS.
WHEN THEY DO...
...DON'T BE SHOCKED IF YOU...
...SEE SOMETHING.
GOOD NIGHT.

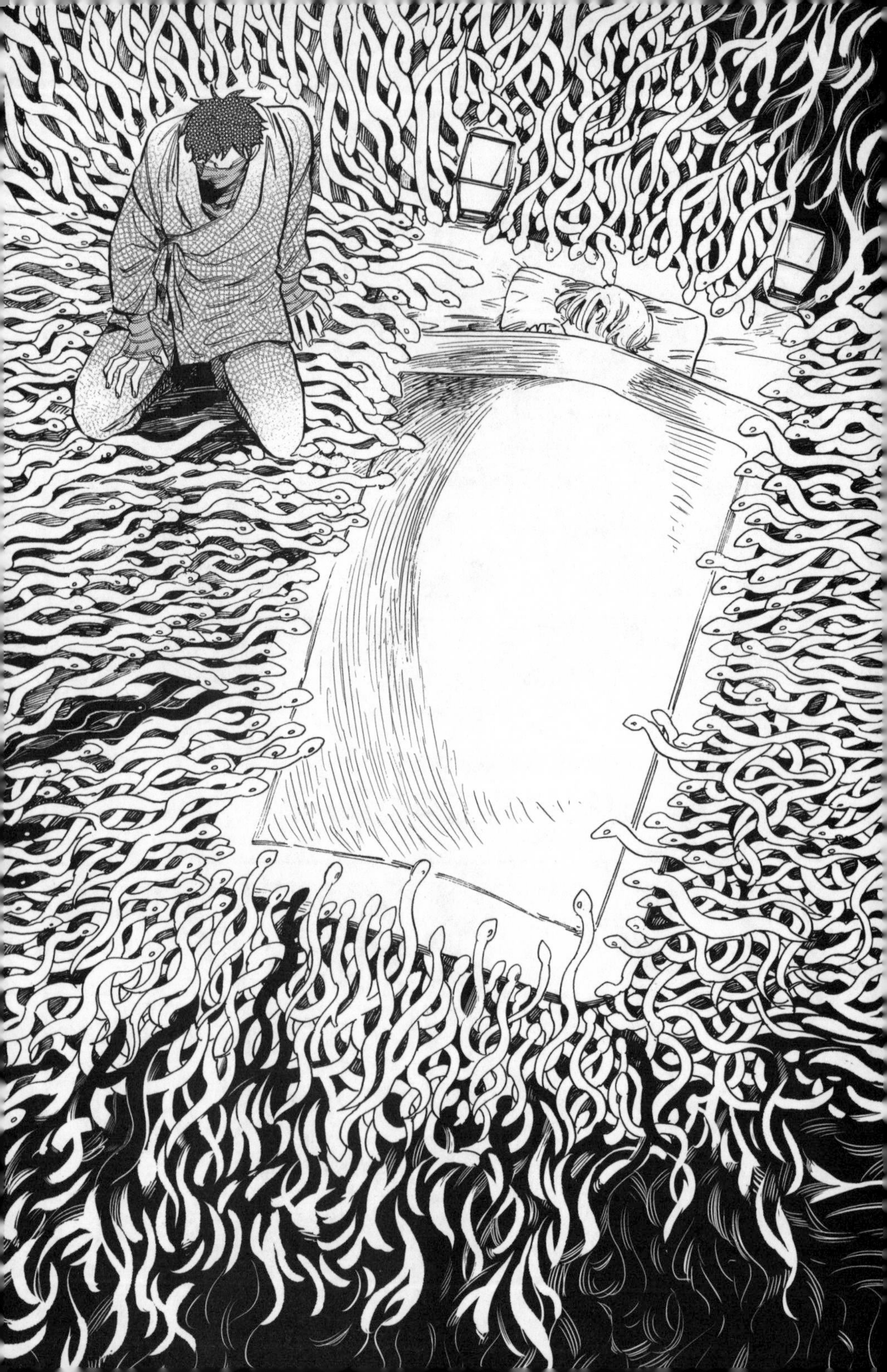

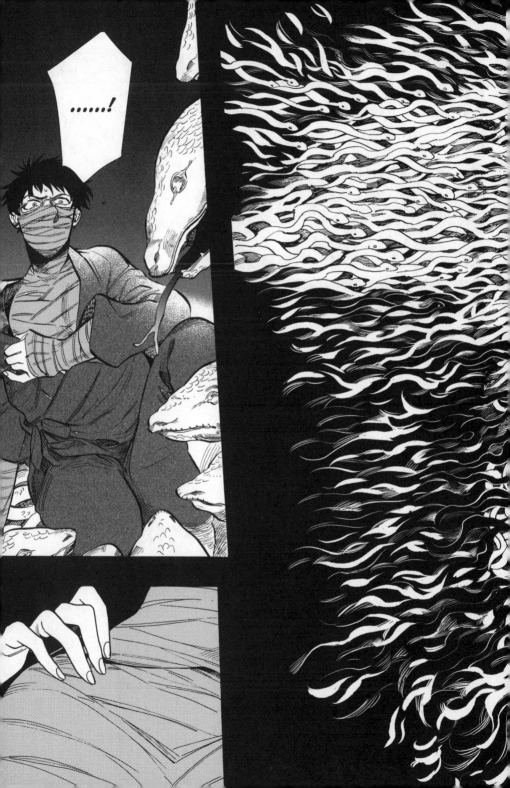

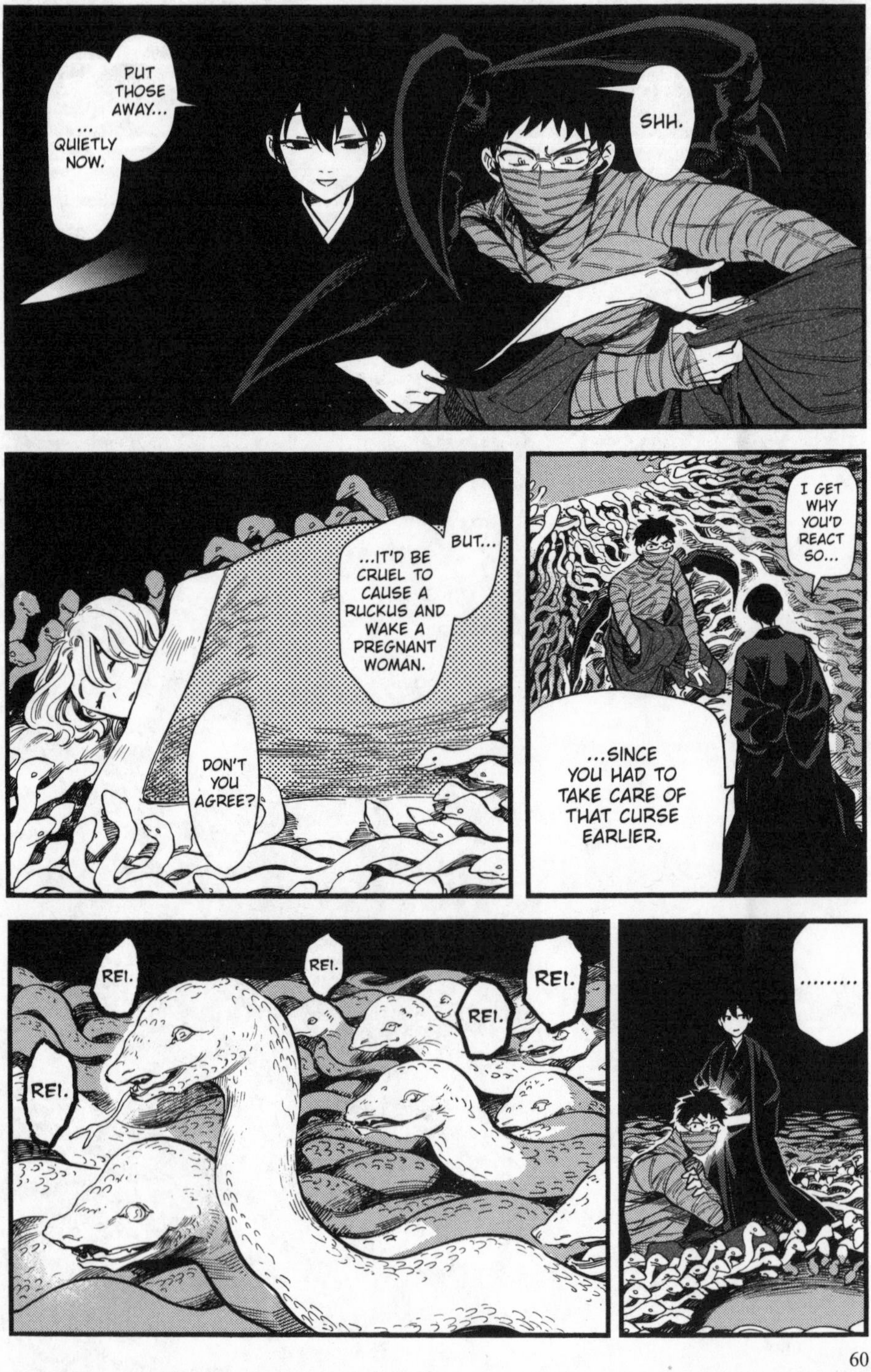
SHH.
PUT THOSE AWAY... ...QUIETLY NOW.
I GET WHY YOU'D REACT SO...
...SINCE YOU HAD TO TAKE CARE OF THAT CURSE EARLIER.
BUT...
...IT'D BE CRUEL TO CAUSE A RUCKUS AND WAKE A PREGNANT WOMAN.
DON'T YOU AGREE?
....
REI.
REI.
REI.
REI.
REI.

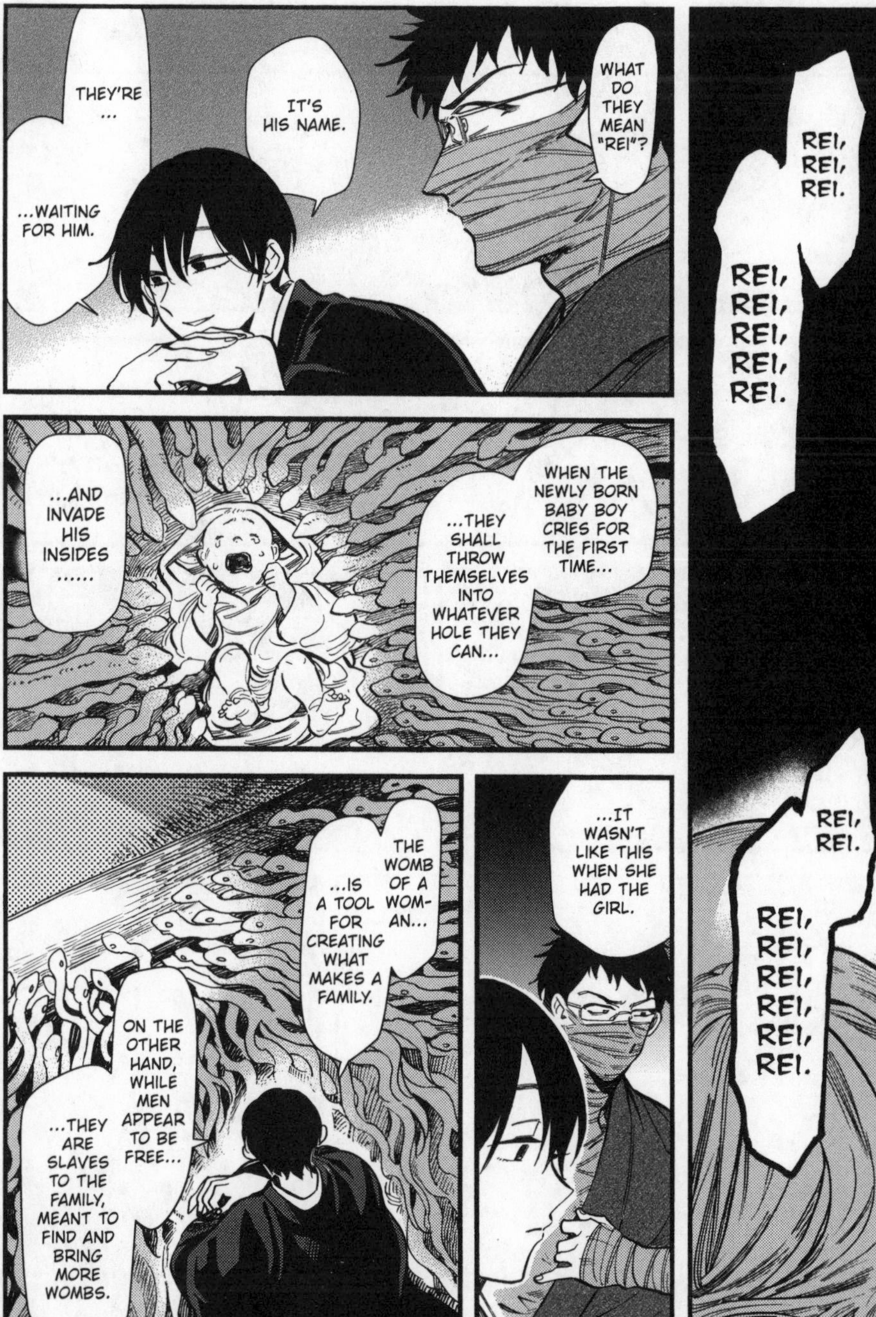
REI, REI, REI.
REI, REI, REI, REI, REI.
REI, REI.
REI, REI, REI, REI, REI, REI.
WHAT DO THEY MEAN "REI"?
IT'S HIS NAME.
THEY'RE ...
...WAITING FOR HIM.
WHEN THE NEWLY BORN BABY BOY CRIES FOR THE FIRST TIME...
...THEY SHALL THROW THEMSELVES INTO WHATEVER HOLE THEY CAN...
...AND INVADE HIS INSIDES ......
...IT WASN'T LIKE THIS WHEN SHE HAD THE GIRL.
THE WOMB OF A WOMAN...
...IS A TOOL FOR CREATING WHAT MAKES A FAMILY.
ON THE OTHER HAND, WHILE MEN APPEAR TO BE FREE...
...THEY ARE SLAVES TO THE FAMILY, MEANT TO FIND AND BRING MORE WOMBS.

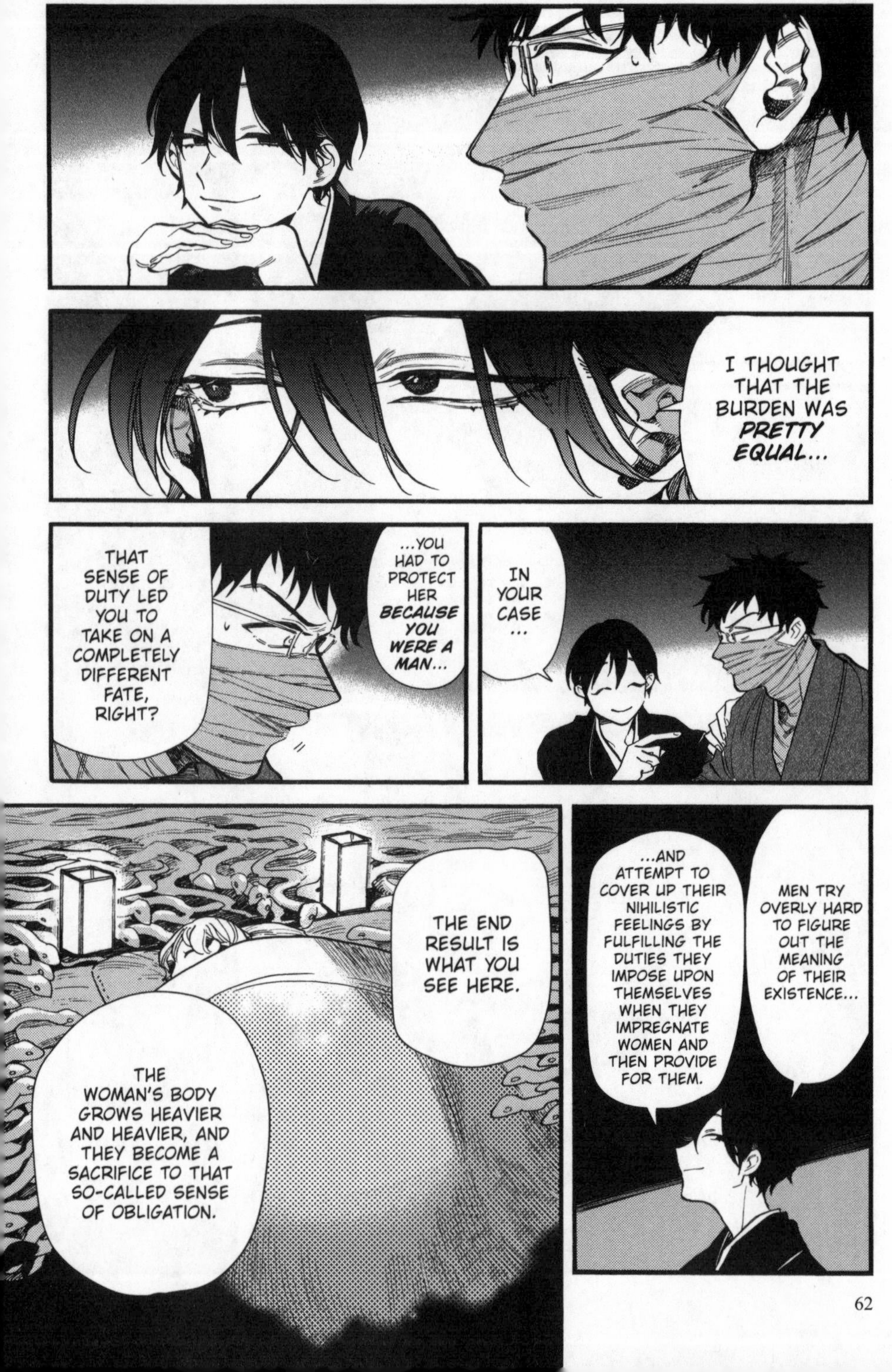
I THOUGHT THAT THE BURDEN WAS PRETTY EQUAL...
IN YOUR CASE ...
...YOU HAD TO PROTECT HER BECAUSE YOU WERE A MAN...
THAT SENSE OF DUTY LED YOU TO TAKE ON A COMPLETELY DIFFERENT FATE, RIGHT?
MEN TRY OVERLY HARD TO FIGURE OUT THE MEANING OF THEIR EXISTENCE...
...AND ATTEMPT TO COVER UP THEIR NIHILISTIC FEELINGS BY FULFILLING THE DUTIES THEY IMPOSE UPON THEMSELVES WHEN THEY IMPREGNATE WOMEN AND THEN PROVIDE FOR THEM.
THE END RESULT IS WHAT YOU SEE HERE.
THE WOMAN'S BODY GROWS HEAVIER AND HEAVIER, AND THEY BECOME A SACRIFICE TO THAT SO-CALLED SENSE OF OBLIGATION.

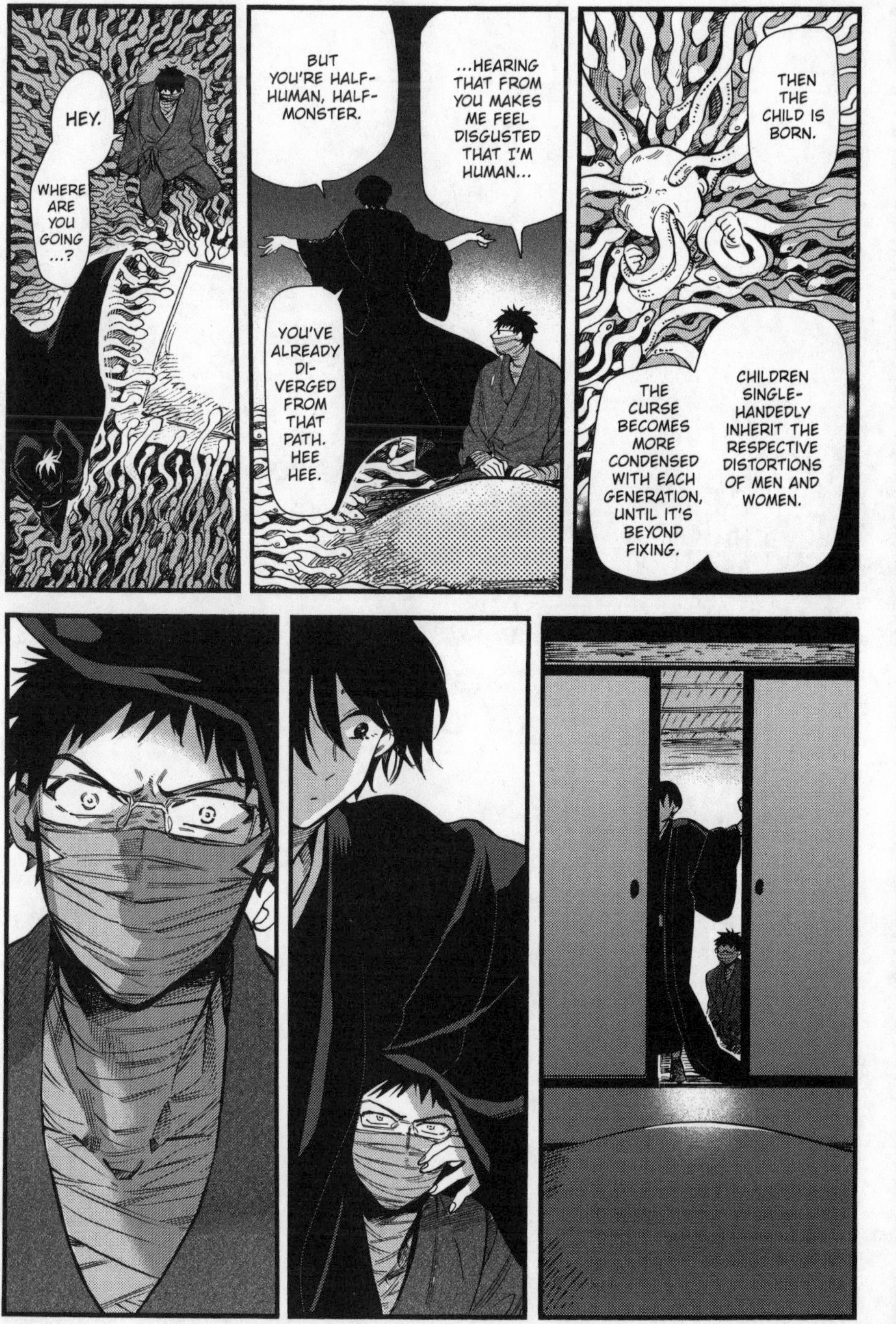
THEN THE CHILD IS BORN.
CHILDREN SINGLE-HANDEDLY INHERIT THE RESPECTIVE DISTORTIONS OF MEN AND WOMEN.
THE CURSE BECOMES MORE CONDENSED WITH EACH GENERATION, UNTIL IT'S BEYOND FIXING.
...HEARING THAT FROM YOU MAKES ME FEEL DISGUSTED THAT I'M HUMAN...
BUT YOU'RE HALF-HUMAN, HALF-MONSTER.
YOU'VE ALREADY DIVERGED FROM THAT PATH. HEE HEE.
HEY.
WHERE ARE YOU GOING ...?

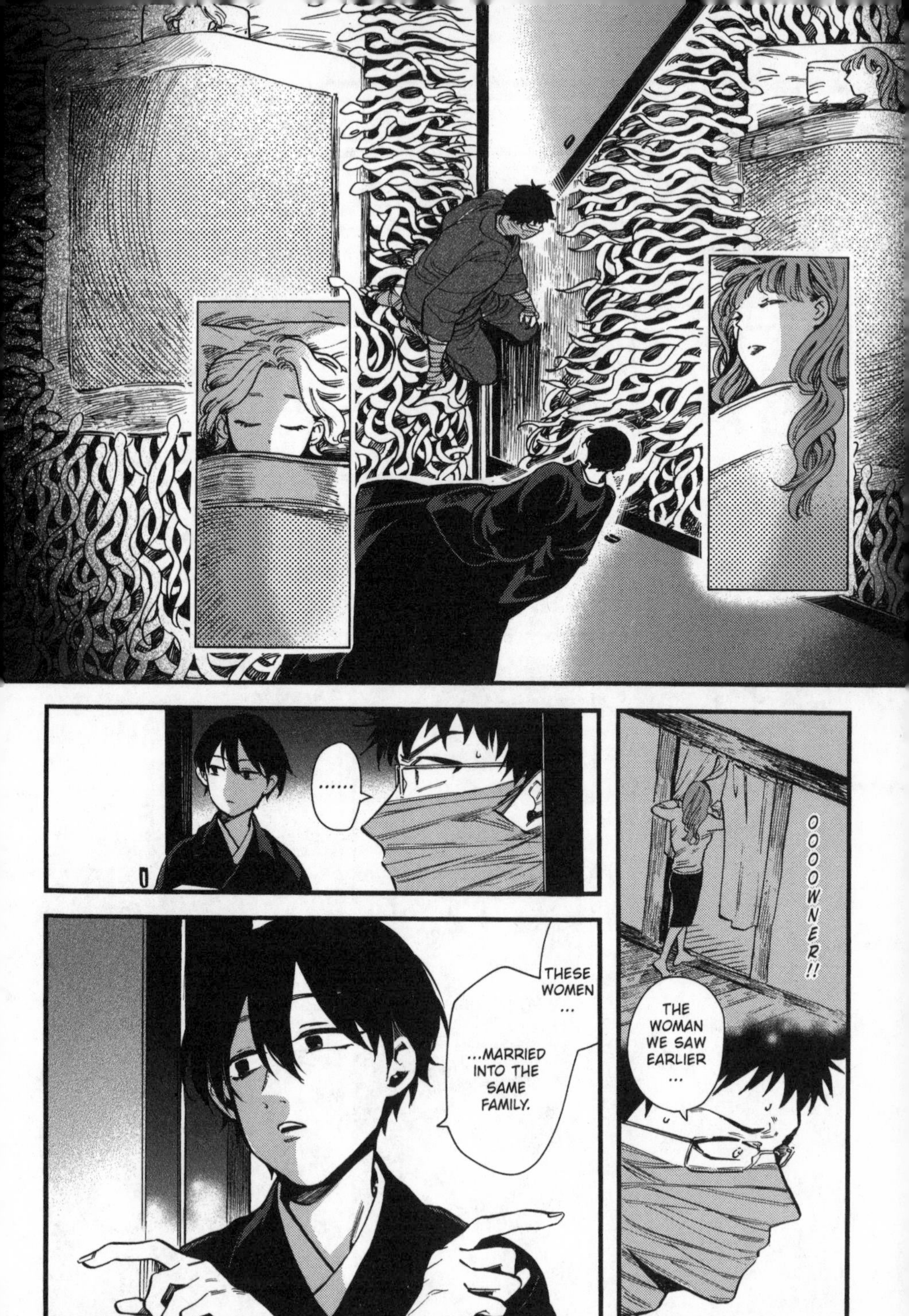
OOOOWNER!!
THE WOMAN WE SAW EARLIER ...
......
THESE WOMEN ...
...MARRIED INTO THE SAME FAMILY.

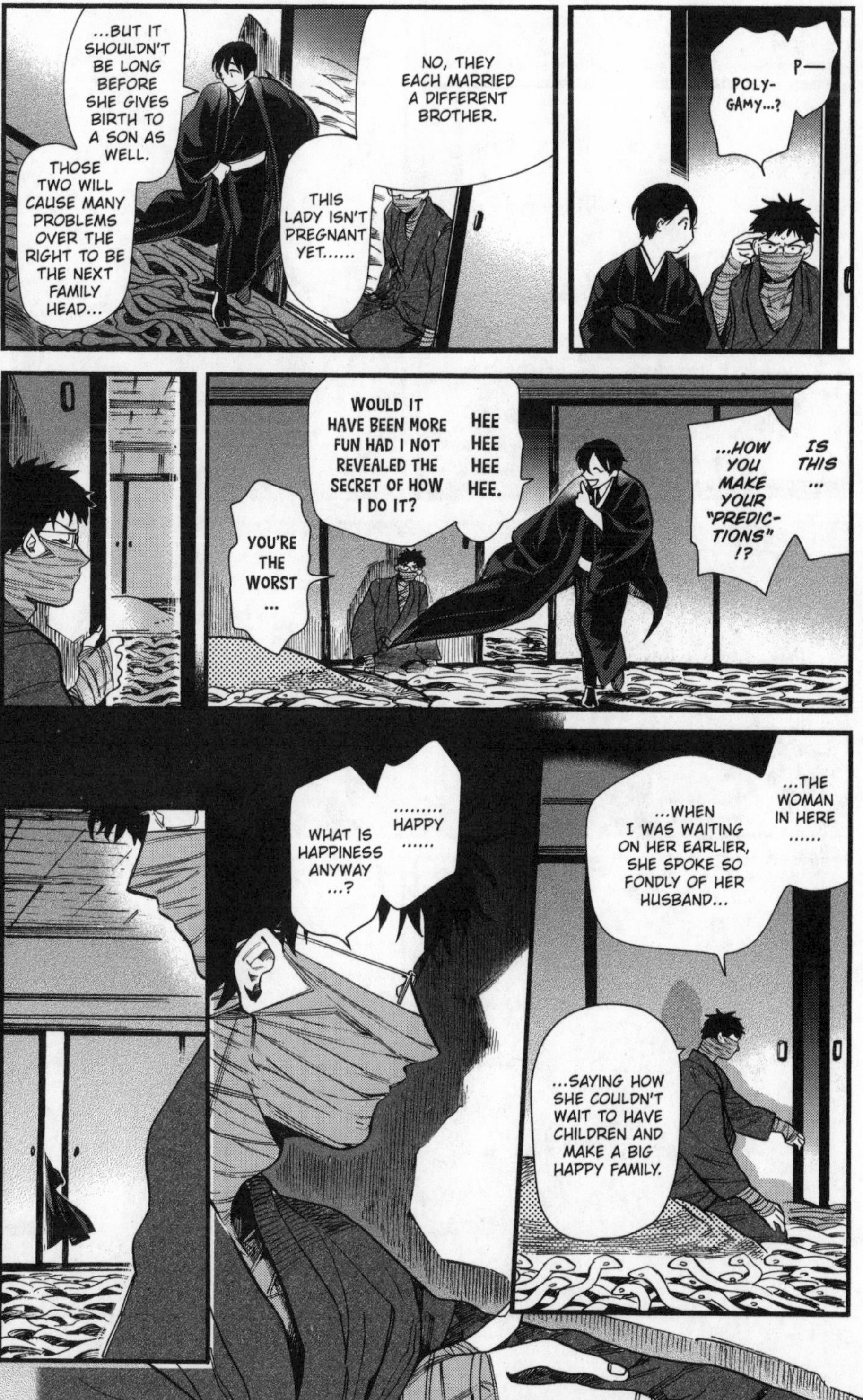
P— POLY-GAMY...?
NO, THEY EACH MARRIED A DIFFERENT BROTHER.
THIS LADY ISN'T PREGNANT YET......
...BUT IT SHOULDN'T BE LONG BEFORE SHE GIVES BIRTH TO A SON AS WELL.
THOSE TWO WILL CAUSE MANY PROBLEMS OVER THE RIGHT TO BE THE NEXT FAMILY HEAD...
IS THIS ...
...HOW YOU MAKE YOUR "PREDICTIONS" !?
HEE HEE HEE HEE.
WOULD IT HAVE BEEN MORE FUN HAD I NOT REVEALED THE SECRET OF HOW I DO IT?
YOU'RE THE WORST ...
...THE WOMAN IN HERE ......
...WHEN I WAS WAITING ON HER EARLIER, SHE SPOKE SO FONDLY OF HER HUSBAND...
...SAYING HOW SHE COULDN'T WAIT TO HAVE CHILDREN AND MAKE A BIG HAPPY FAMILY.
.... HAPPY ......
WHAT IS HAPPINESS ANYWAY ...?

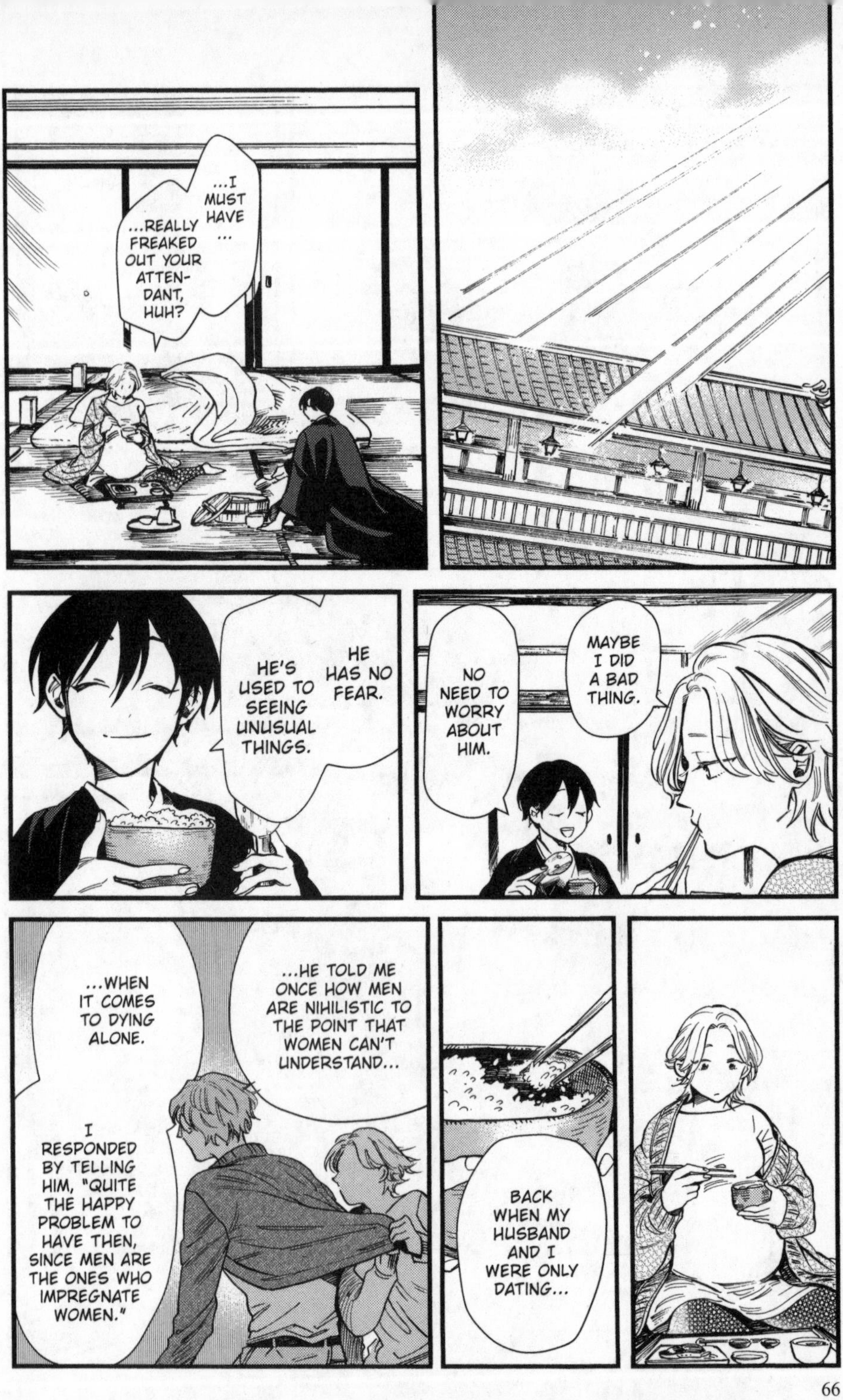
...I MUST HAVE...
...REALLY FREAKED OUT YOUR ATTENDANT, HUH?
MAYBE I DID A BAD THING.
NO NEED TO WORRY ABOUT HIM.
HE HAS NO FEAR.
HE'S USED TO SEEING UNUSUAL THINGS.
BACK WHEN MY HUSBAND AND I WERE ONLY DATING...
...HE TOLD ME ONCE HOW MEN ARE NIHILISTIC TO THE POINT THAT WOMEN CAN'T UNDERSTAND...
...WHEN IT COMES TO DYING ALONE.
I RESPONDED BY TELLING HIM, "QUITE THE HAPPY PROBLEM TO HAVE THEN, SINCE MEN ARE THE ONES WHO IMPREGNATE WOMEN."

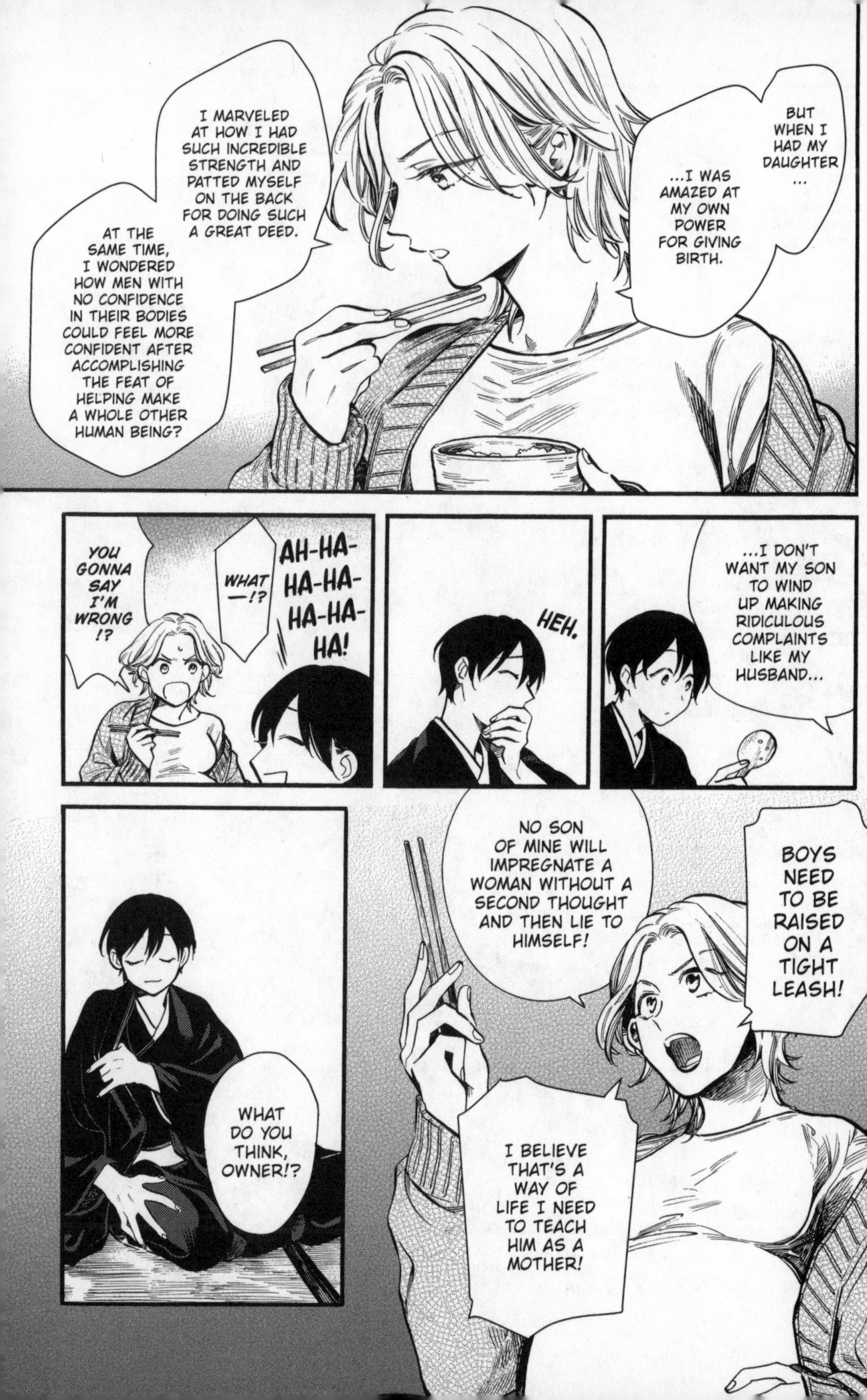
BUT WHEN I HAD MY DAUGHTER...
...I WAS AMAZED AT MY OWN POWER FOR GIVING BIRTH.
I MARVELED AT HOW I HAD SUCH INCREDIBLE STRENGTH AND PATTED MYSELF ON THE BACK FOR DOING SUCH A GREAT DEED.
AT THE SAME TIME, I WONDERED HOW MEN WITH NO CONFIDENCE IN THEIR BODIES COULD FEEL MORE CONFIDENT AFTER ACCOMPLISHING THE FEAT OF HELPING MAKE A WHOLE OTHER HUMAN BEING?
...I DON'T WANT MY SON TO WIND UP MAKING RIDICULOUS COMPLAINTS LIKE MY HUSBAND...
HEH.
AH-HA-HA-HA-HA-HA-HA!
WHAT—!?
YOU GONNA SAY I'M WRONG!?
BOYS NEED TO BE RAISED ON A TIGHT LEASH!
NO SON OF MINE WILL IMPREGNATE A WOMAN WITHOUT A SECOND THOUGHT AND THEN LIE TO HIMSELF!
I BELIEVE THAT'S A WAY OF LIFE I NEED TO TEACH HIM AS A MOTHER!
WHAT DO YOU THINK, OWNER!?

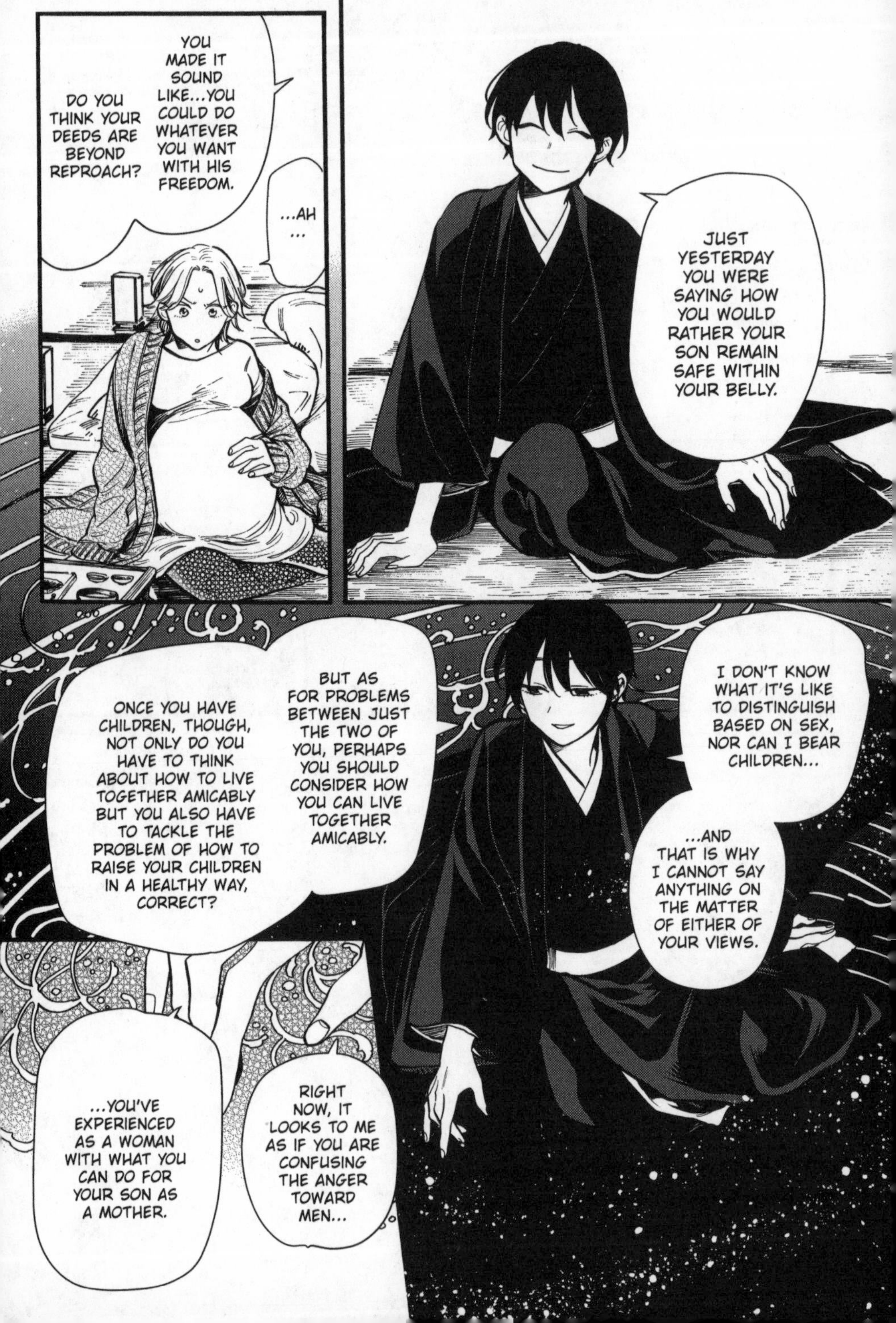
JUST YESTERDAY YOU WERE SAYING HOW YOU WOULD RATHER YOUR SON REMAIN SAFE WITHIN YOUR BELLY.
YOU MADE IT SOUND LIKE...YOU COULD DO WHATEVER YOU WANT WITH HIS FREEDOM.
DO YOU THINK YOUR DEEDS ARE BEYOND REPROACH?
...AH ...
I DON'T KNOW WHAT IT'S LIKE TO DISTINGUISH BASED ON SEX, NOR CAN I BEAR CHILDREN...
...AND THAT IS WHY I CANNOT SAY ANYTHING ON THE MATTER OF EITHER OF YOUR VIEWS.
BUT AS FOR PROBLEMS BETWEEN JUST THE TWO OF YOU, PERHAPS YOU SHOULD CONSIDER HOW YOU CAN LIVE TOGETHER AMICABLY.
ONCE YOU HAVE CHILDREN, THOUGH, NOT ONLY DO YOU HAVE TO THINK ABOUT HOW TO LIVE TOGETHER AMICABLY BUT YOU ALSO HAVE TO TACKLE THE PROBLEM OF HOW TO RAISE YOUR CHILDREN IN A HEALTHY WAY, CORRECT?
RIGHT NOW, IT LOOKS TO ME AS IF YOU ARE CONFUSING THE ANGER TOWARD MEN...
...YOU'VE EXPERIENCED AS A WOMAN WITH WHAT YOU CAN DO FOR YOUR SON AS A MOTHER.

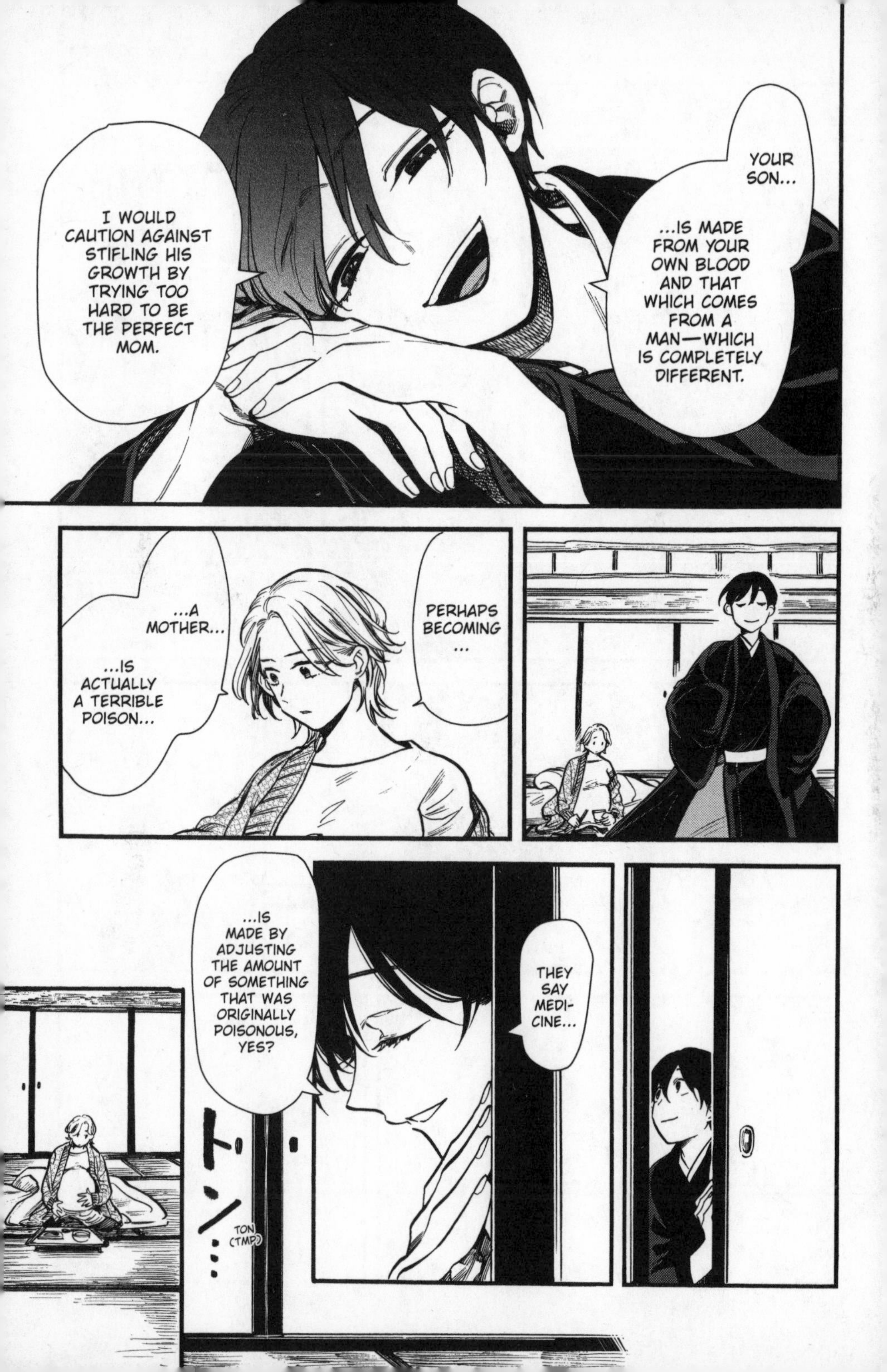
YOUR SON...
...IS MADE FROM YOUR OWN BLOOD AND THAT WHICH COMES FROM A MAN—WHICH IS COMPLETELY DIFFERENT.
I WOULD CAUTION AGAINST STIFLING HIS GROWTH BY TRYING TOO HARD TO BE THE PERFECT MOM.
PERHAPS BECOMING ...
...A MOTHER...
...IS ACTUALLY A TERRIBLE POISON...
THEY SAY MEDI-CINE...
...IS MADE BY ADJUSTING THE AMOUNT OF SOMETHING THAT WAS ORIGINALLY POISONOUS, YES?
TON (TMP)

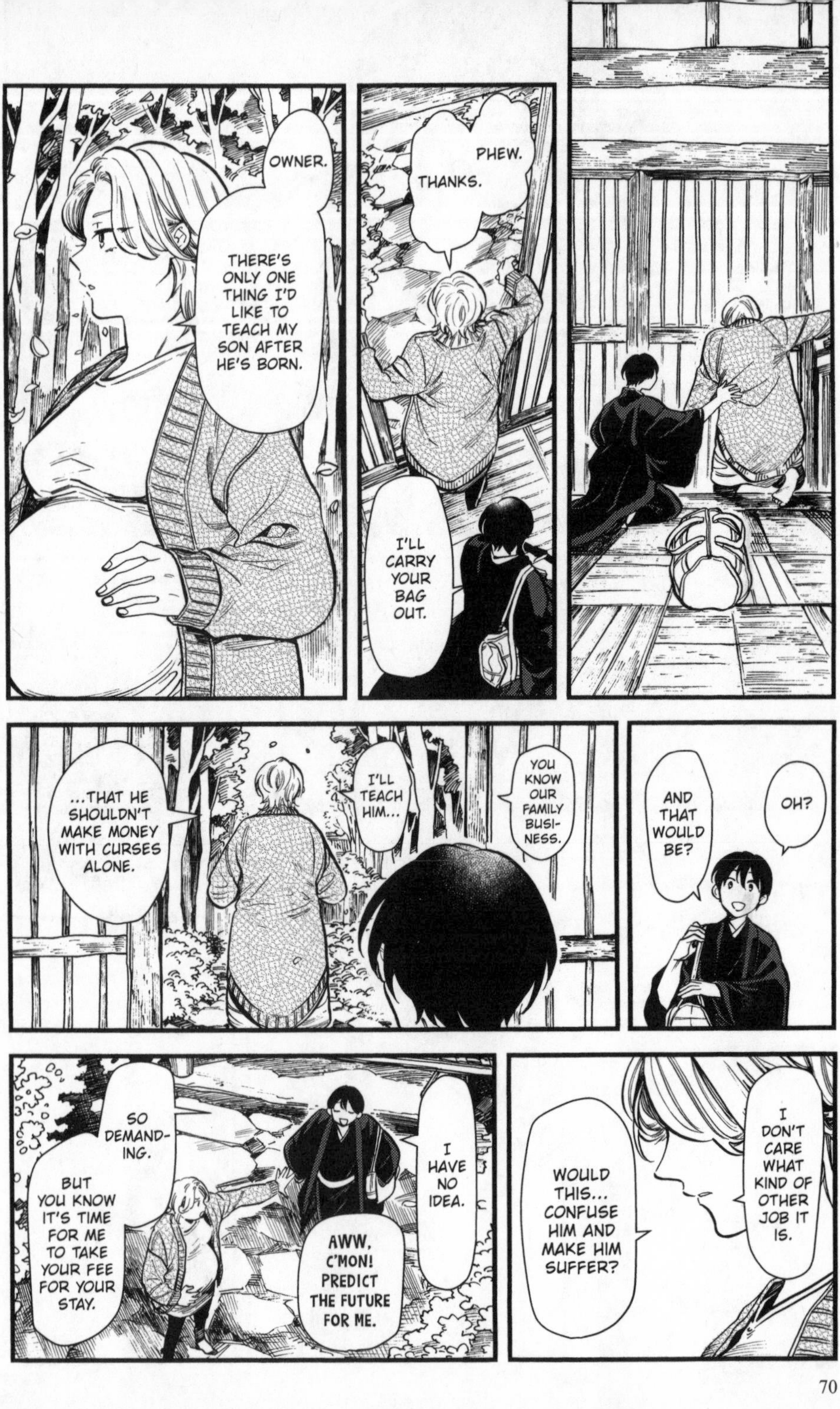
PHEW. THANKS.
I'LL CARRY YOUR BAG OUT.
OWNER.
THERE'S ONLY ONE THING I'D LIKE TO TEACH MY SON AFTER HE'S BORN.
OH?
AND THAT WOULD BE?
YOU KNOW OUR FAMILY BUSI-NESS.
I'LL TEACH HIM...
...THAT HE SHOULDN'T MAKE MONEY WITH CURSES ALONE.
I DON'T CARE WHAT KIND OF OTHER JOB IT IS.
WOULD THIS... CONFUSE HIM AND MAKE HIM SUFFER?
I HAVE NO IDEA.
AWW, C'MON! PREDICT THE FUTURE FOR ME.
SO DEMAND-ING.
BUT YOU KNOW IT'S TIME FOR ME TO TAKE YOUR FEE FOR YOUR STAY.

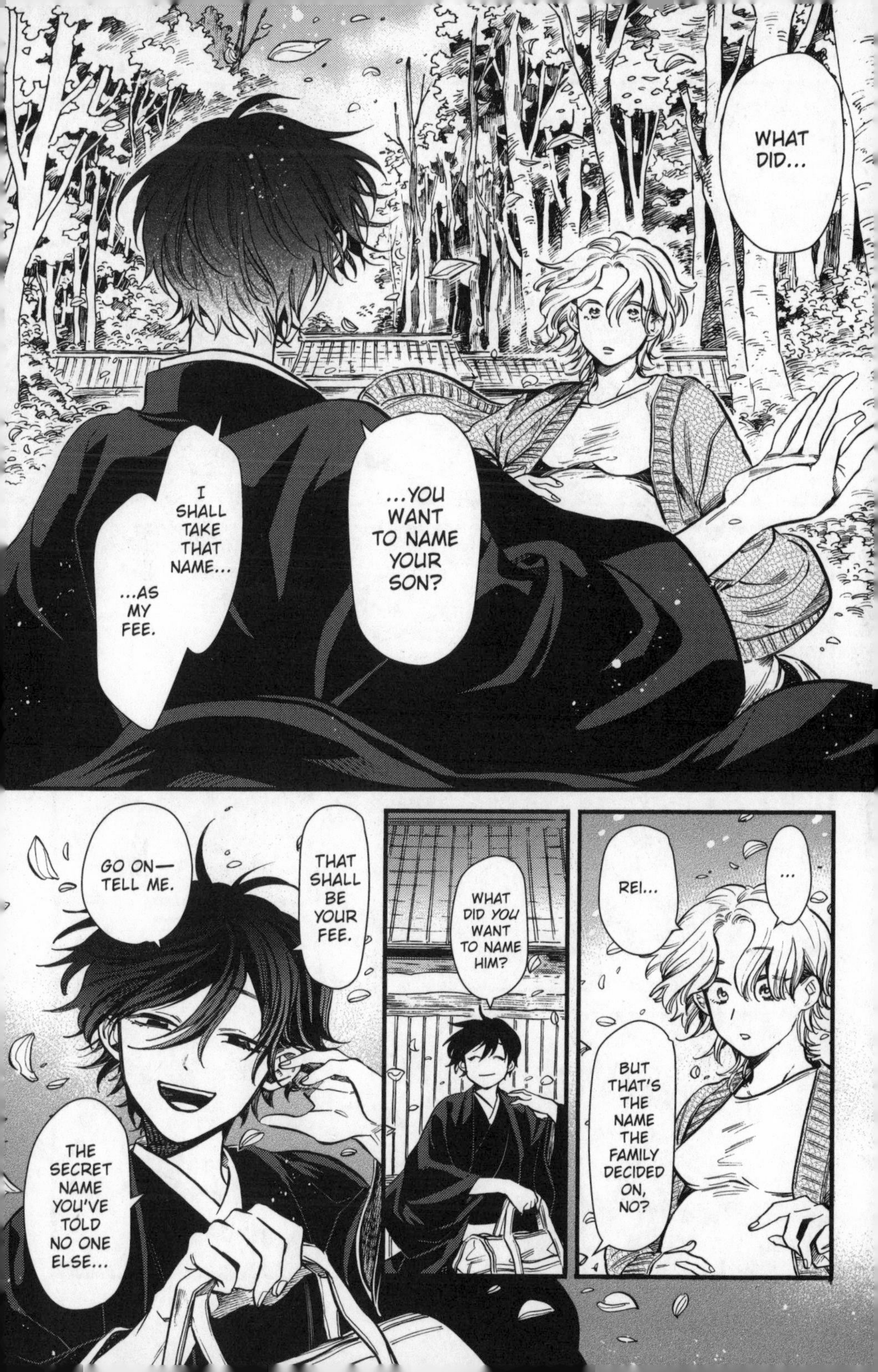
WHAT DID...
...YOU WANT TO NAME YOUR SON?
I SHALL TAKE THAT NAME...
...AS MY FEE.
...
REI...
BUT THAT'S THE NAME THE FAMILY DECIDED ON, NO?
WHAT DID *YOU* WANT TO NAME HIM?
THAT SHALL BE YOUR FEE.
GO ON—TELL ME.
THE SECRET NAME YOU'VE TOLD NO ONE ELSE...

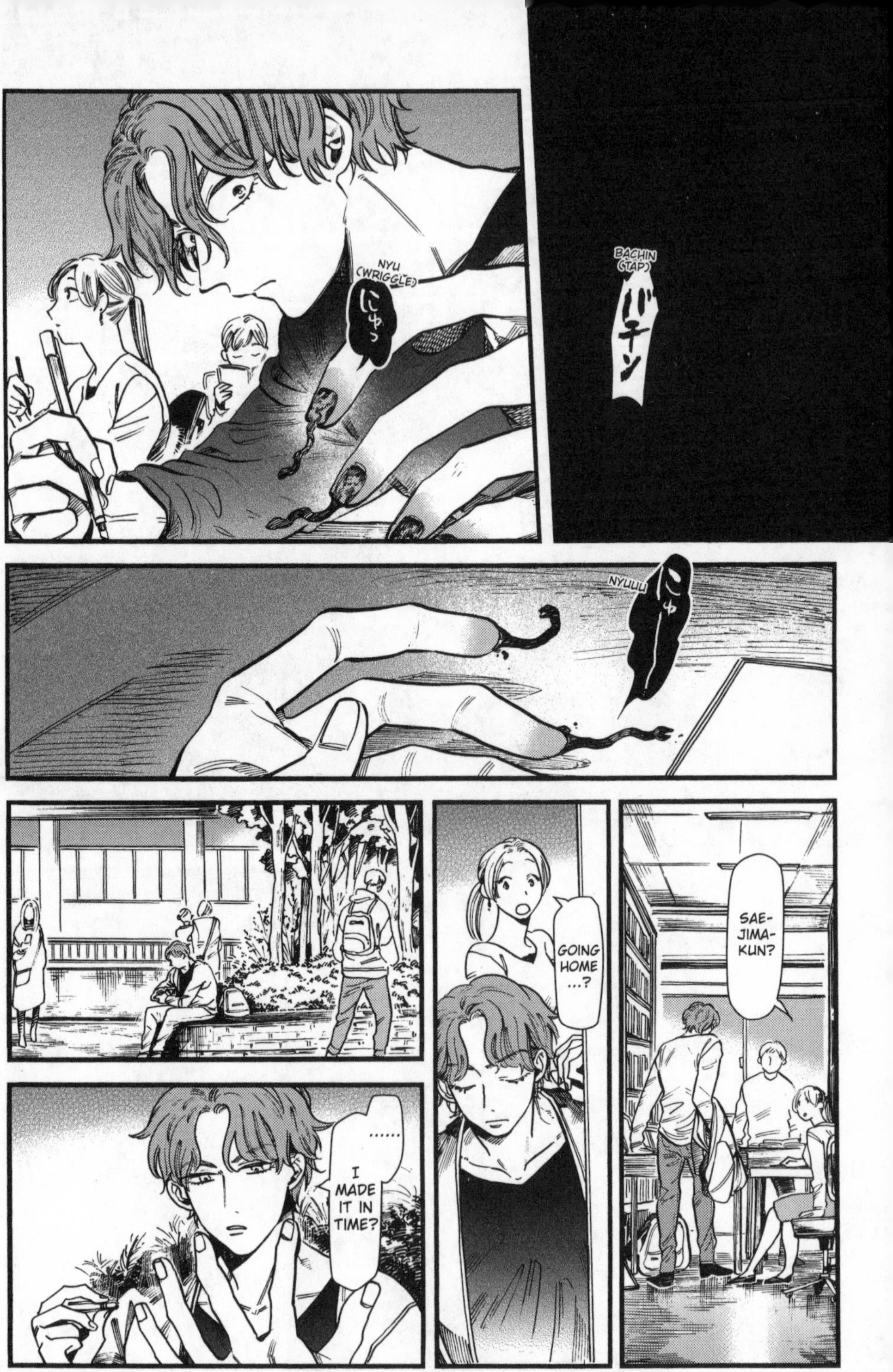
BACHIN (TAP)
バチン
NYU (WRIGGLE)
にゅっ
NYUUU
にゅ
SAE-JIMA-KUN?
GOING HOME ...?
......
I MADE IT IN TIME?

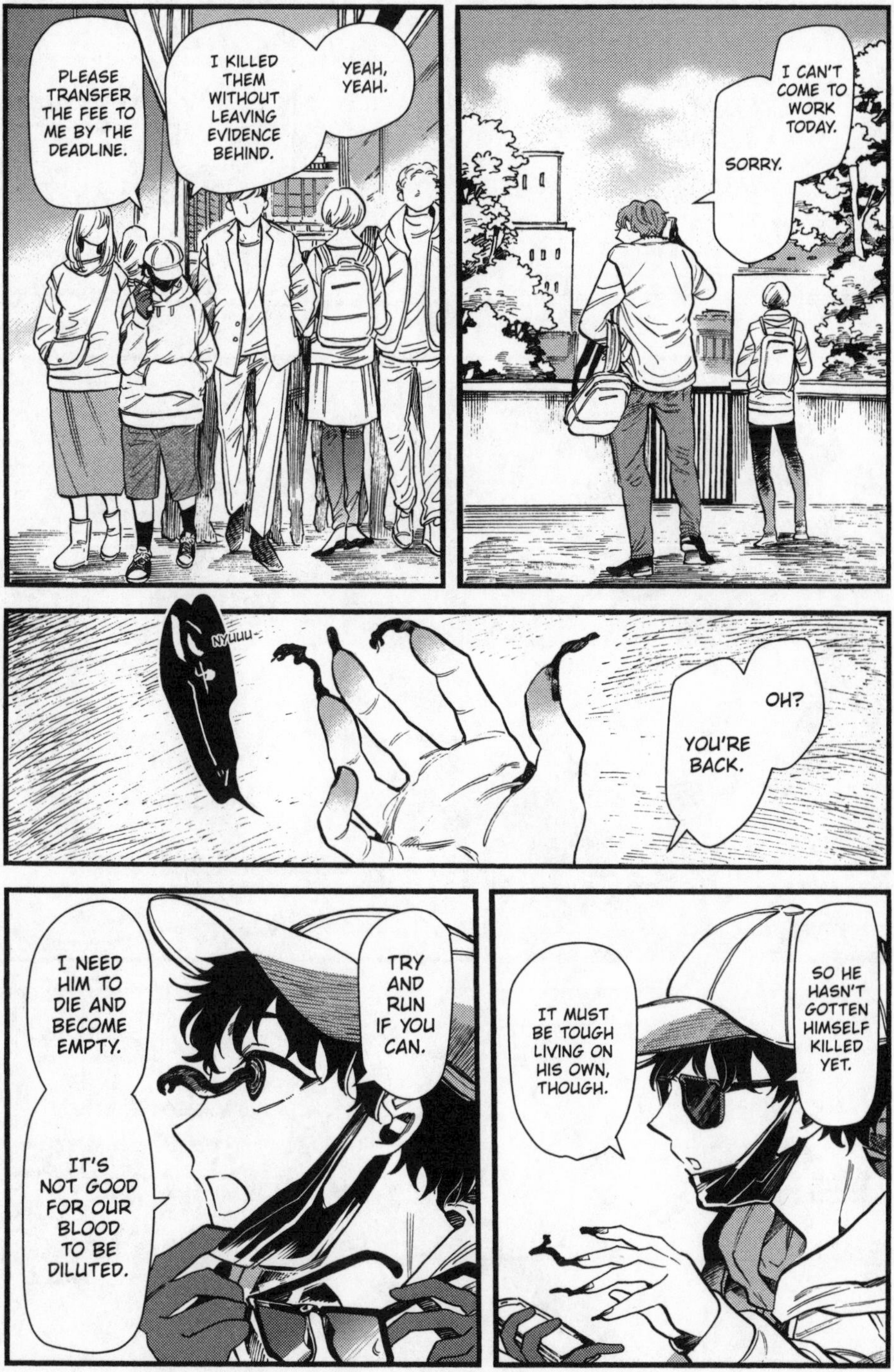
I CAN'T COME TO WORK TODAY.
SORRY.
YEAH, YEAH.
I KILLED THEM WITHOUT LEAVING EVIDENCE BEHIND.
PLEASE TRANSFER THE FEE TO ME BY THE DEADLINE.
OH?
YOU'RE BACK.
NYUUU-
SO HE HASN'T GOTTEN HIMSELF KILLED YET.
IT MUST BE TOUGH LIVING ON HIS OWN, THOUGH.
TRY AND RUN IF YOU CAN.
I NEED HIM TO DIE AND BECOME EMPTY.
IT'S NOT GOOD FOR OUR BLOOD TO BE DILUTED.

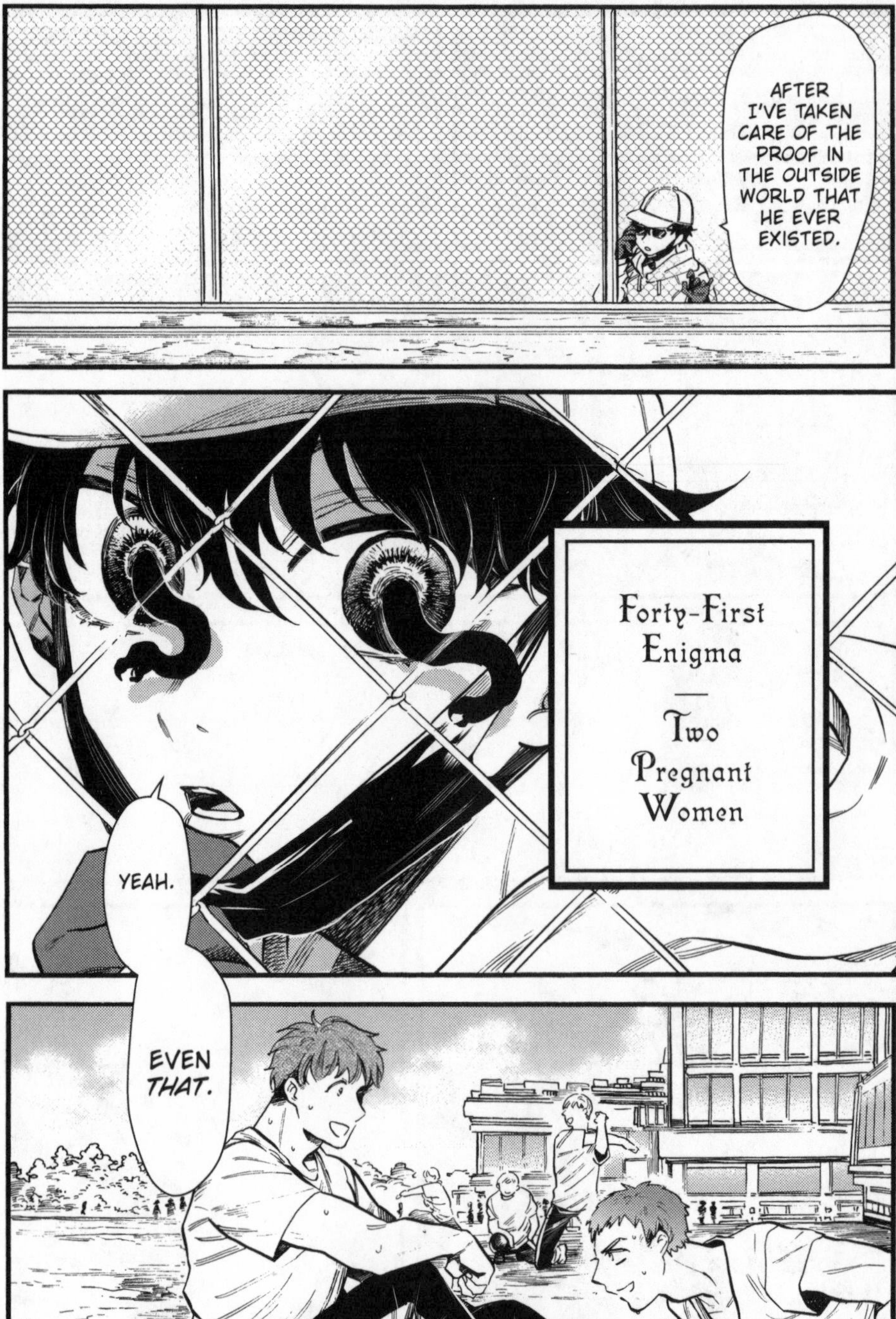
AFTER I'VE TAKEN CARE OF THE PROOF IN THE OUTSIDE WORLD THAT HE EVER EXISTED.
Forty-First Enigma — Two Pregnant Women
YEAH.
EVEN THAT.

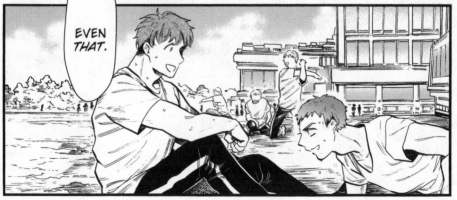

Phantom Tales of the Night

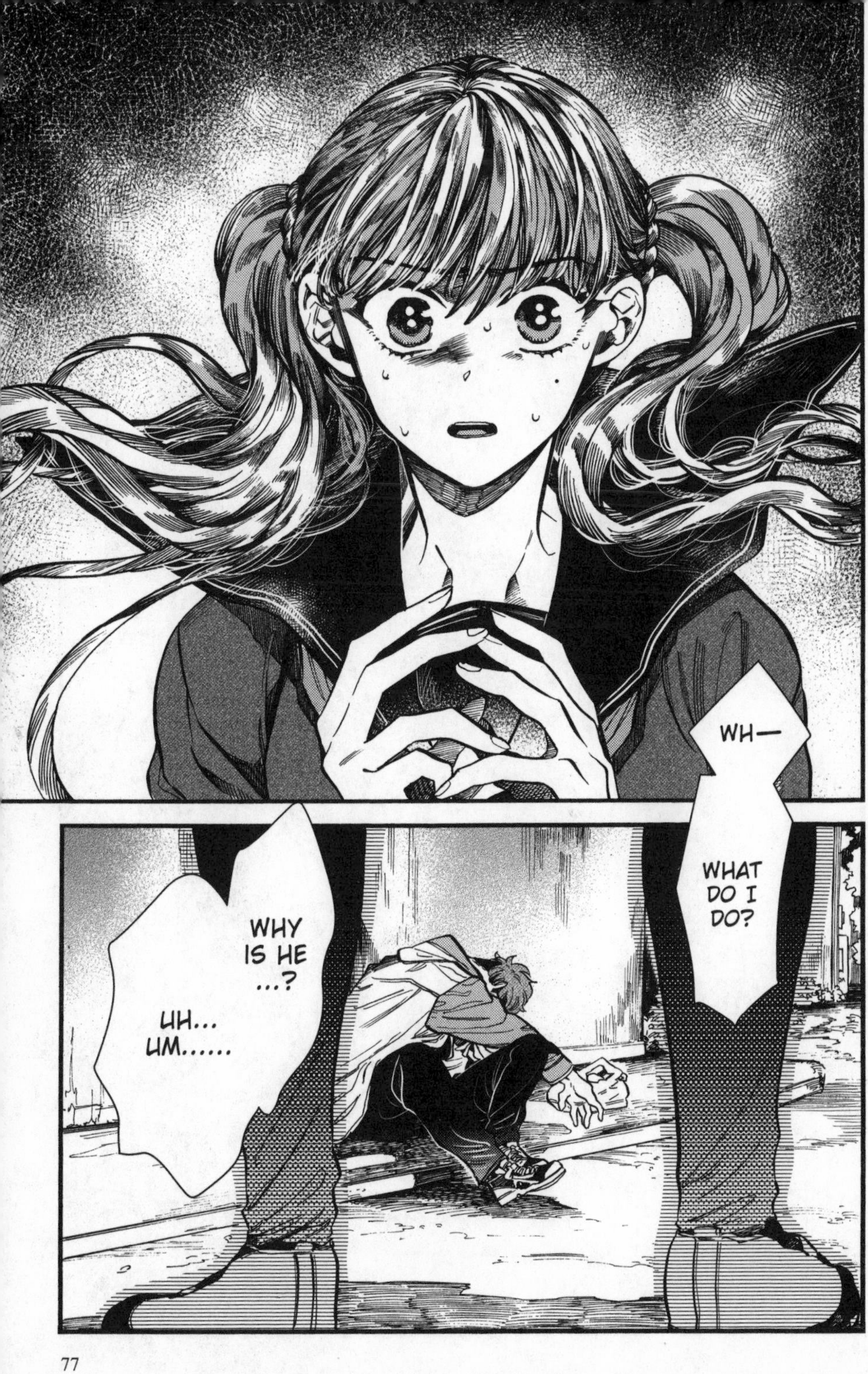
WH—
WHAT DO I DO?
WHY IS HE ...?
UH... UM......

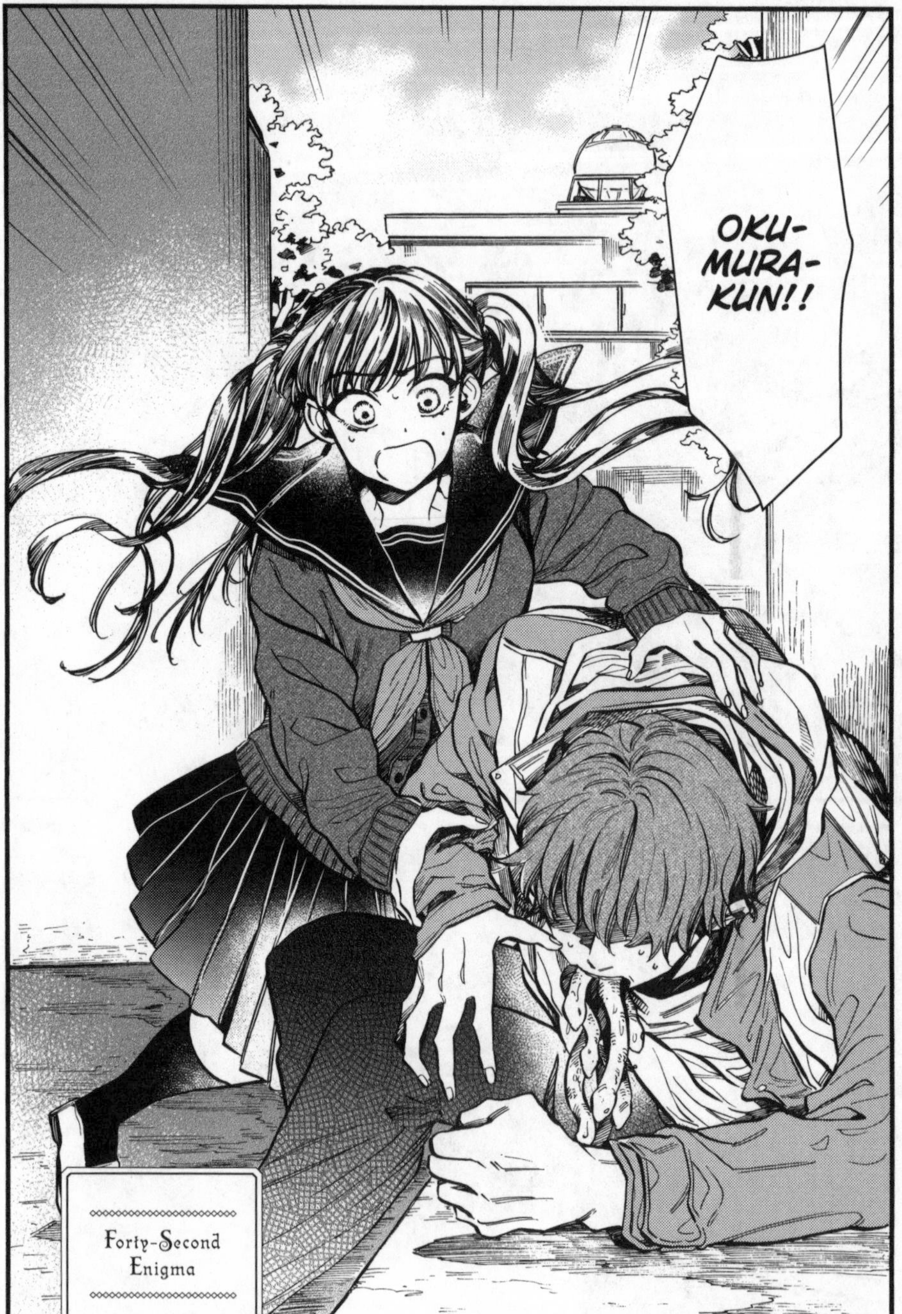
OKU-MURA-KUN!!
Forty-Second Enigma

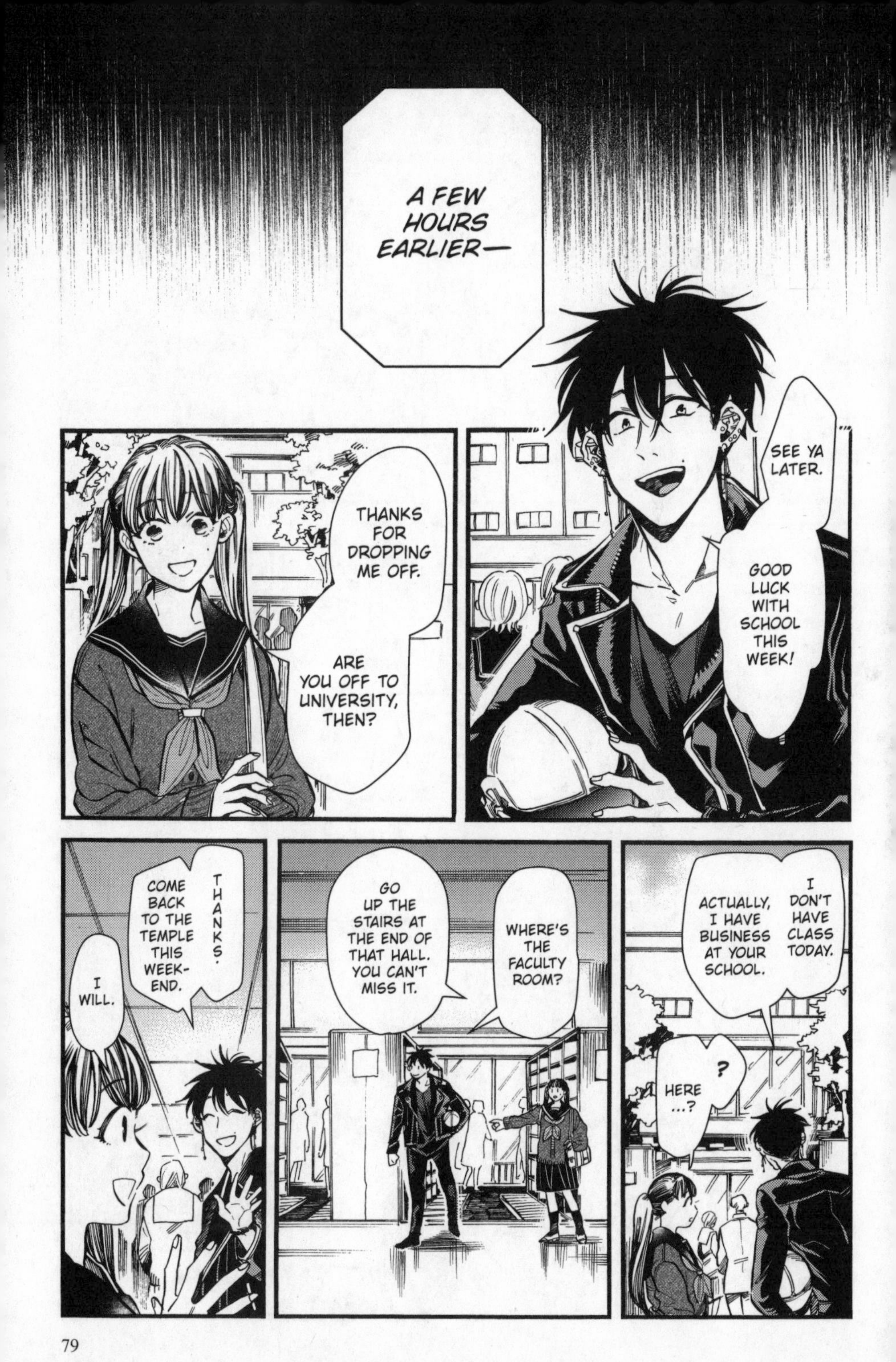
A FEW HOURS EARLIER—
SEE YA LATER.
GOOD LUCK WITH SCHOOL THIS WEEK!
THANKS FOR DROPPING ME OFF.
ARE YOU OFF TO UNIVERSITY, THEN?
I DON'T HAVE CLASS TODAY.
ACTUALLY, I HAVE BUSINESS AT YOUR SCHOOL.
?
HERE ...?
WHERE'S THE FACULTY ROOM?
GO UP THE STAIRS AT THE END OF THAT HALL. YOU CAN'T MISS IT.
THANKS.
COME BACK TO THE TEMPLE THIS WEEK-END.
I WILL.

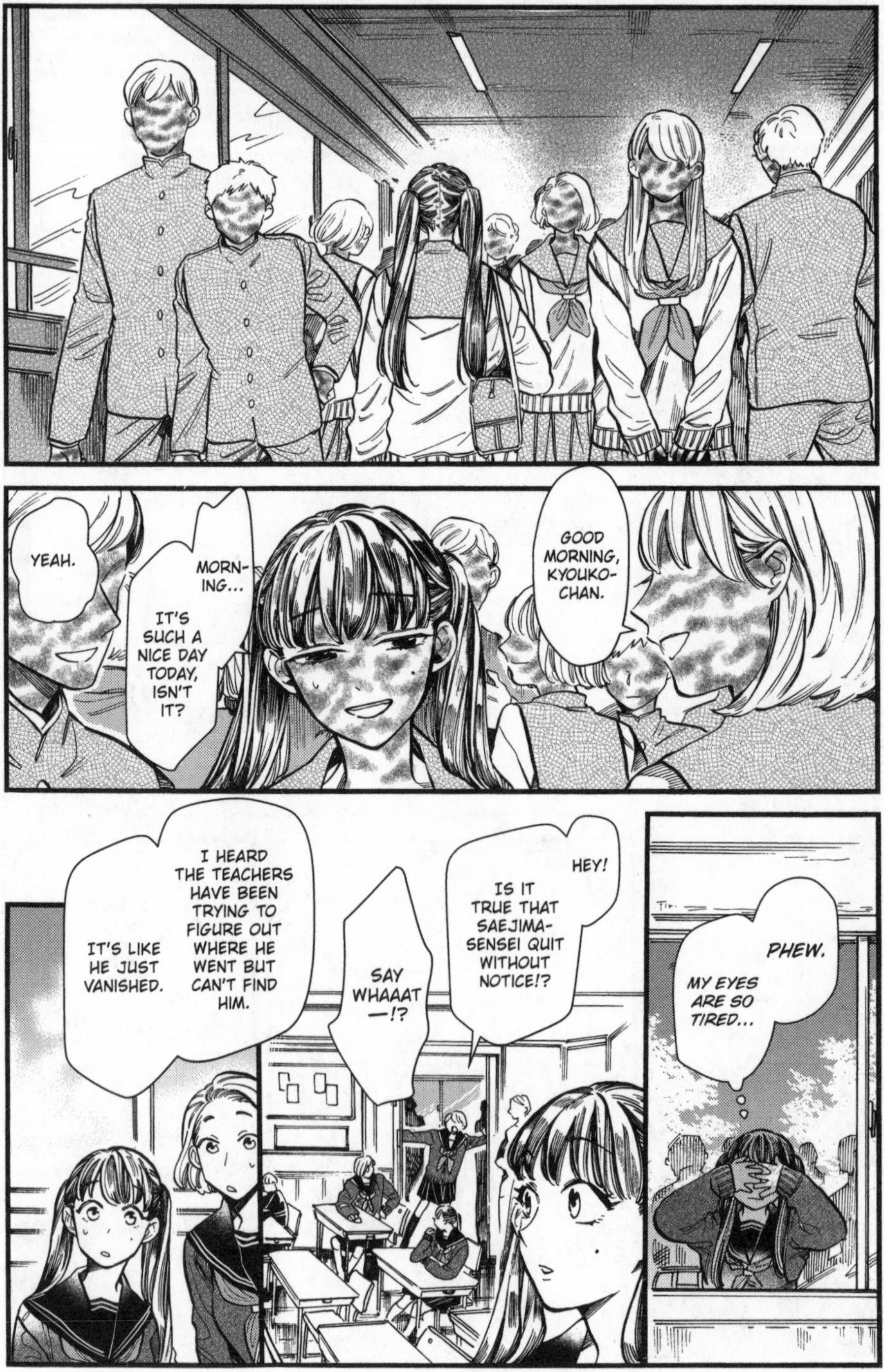
GOOD MORNING, KYOUKO-CHAN.
MORNING... IT'S SUCH A NICE DAY TODAY, ISN'T IT?
YEAH.
PHEW.
MY EYES ARE SO TIRED...
HEY!
IS IT TRUE THAT SAEJIMA-SENSEI QUIT WITHOUT NOTICE!?
SAY WHAAAT—!?
I HEARD THE TEACHERS HAVE BEEN TRYING TO FIGURE OUT WHERE HE WENT BUT CAN'T FIND HIM.
IT'S LIKE HE JUST VANISHED.

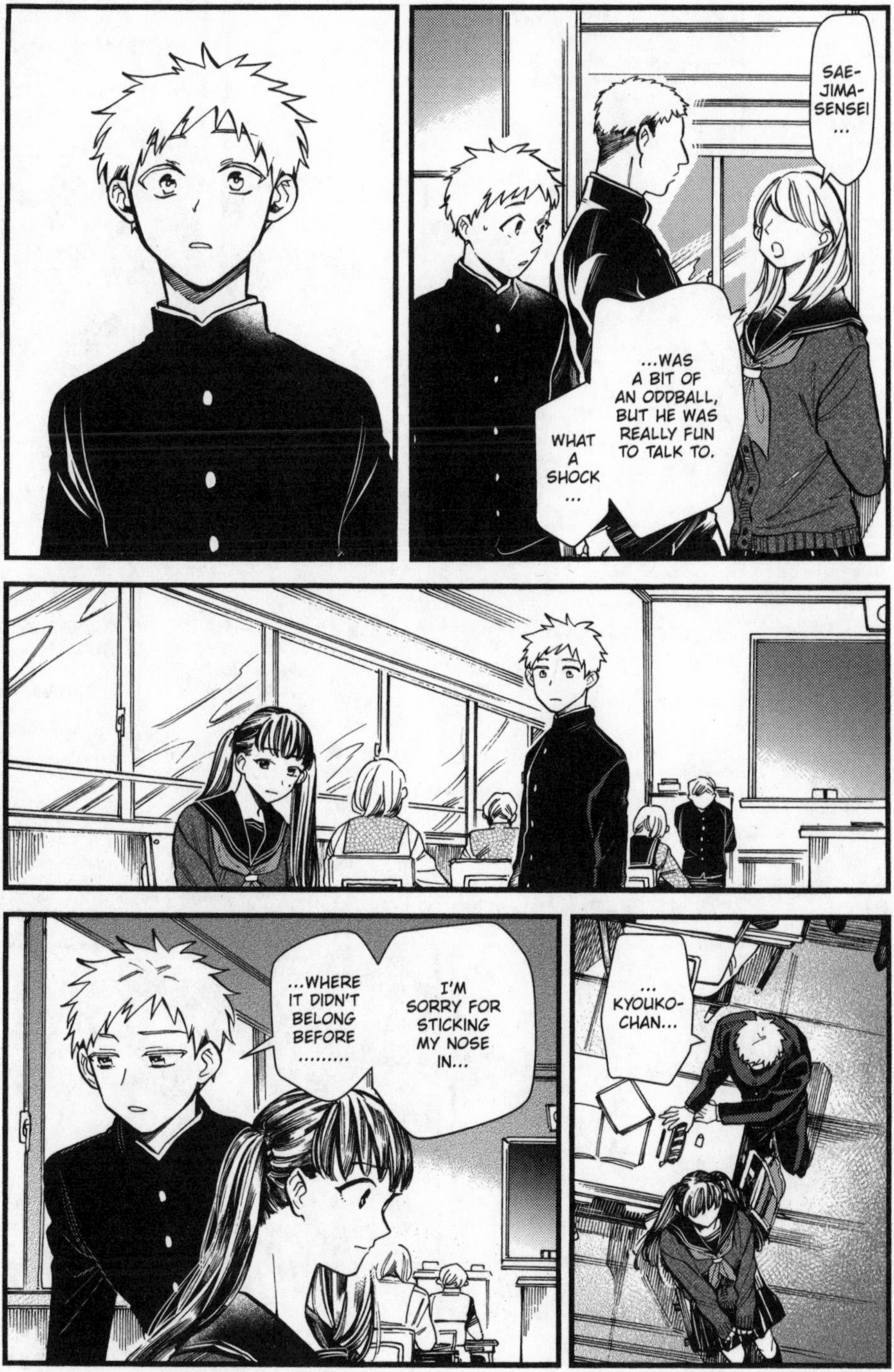
SAE-JIMA-SENSEI...
...WAS A BIT OF AN ODDBALL, BUT HE WAS REALLY FUN TO TALK TO.
WHAT A SHOCK...
...KYOUKO-CHAN...
I'M SORRY FOR STICKING MY NOSE IN...
...WHERE IT DIDN'T BELONG BEFORE ....

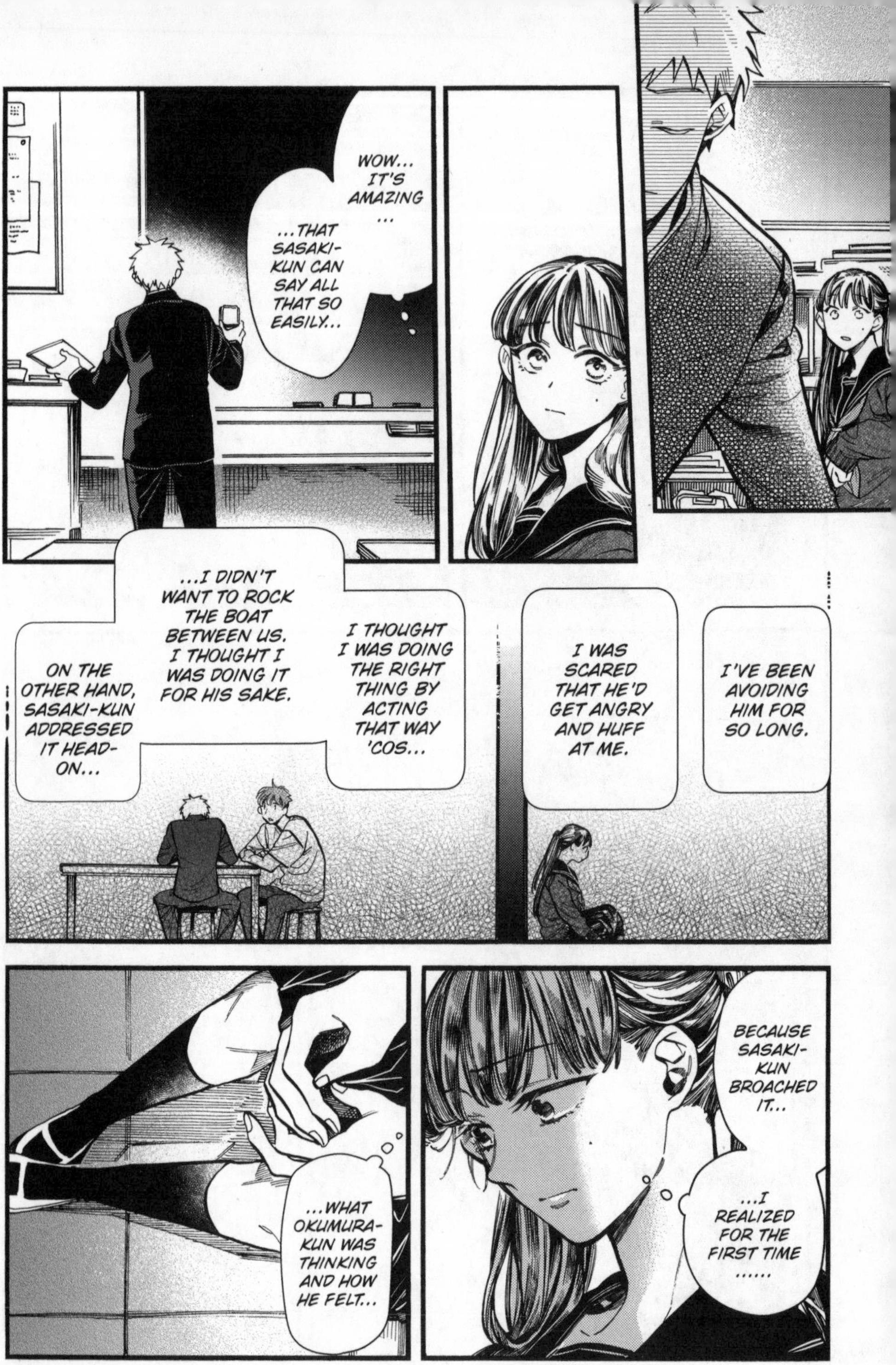

WOW... IT'S AMAZING ...
...THAT SASAKI-KUN CAN SAY ALL THAT SO EASILY...
I'VE BEEN AVOIDING HIM FOR SO LONG.
I WAS SCARED THAT HE'D GET ANGRY AND HUFF AT ME.
I THOUGHT I WAS DOING THE RIGHT THING BY ACTING THAT WAY 'COS...
...I DIDN'T WANT TO ROCK THE BOAT BETWEEN US. I THOUGHT I WAS DOING IT FOR HIS SAKE.
ON THE OTHER HAND, SASAKI-KUN ADDRESSED IT HEAD-ON...
BECAUSE SASAKI-KUN BROACHED IT...
...I REALIZED FOR THE FIRST TIME ......
...WHAT OKUMURA-KUN WAS THINKING AND HOW HE FELT...

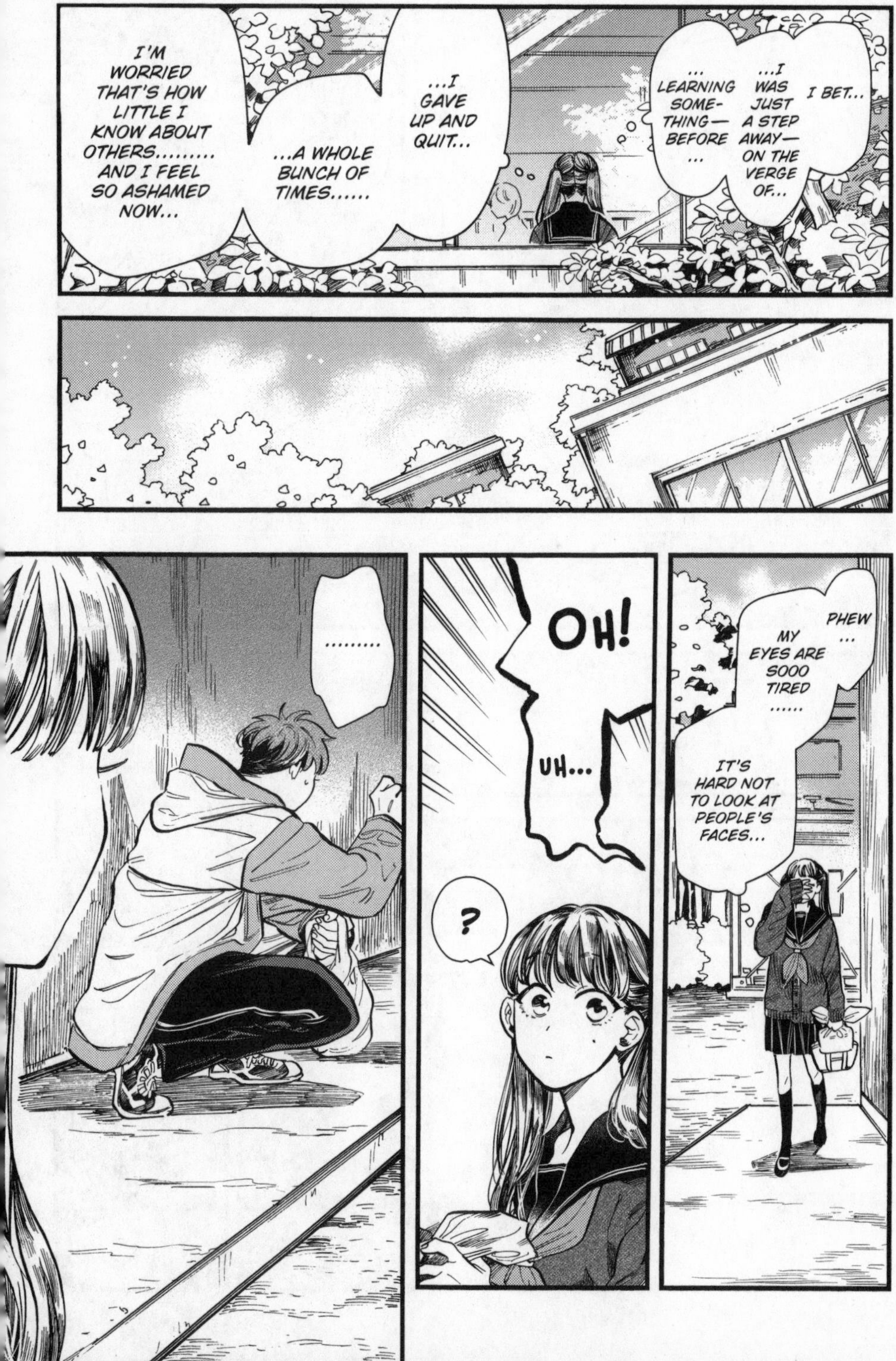
I BET...
...I WAS JUST A STEP AWAY— ON THE VERGE OF...
... LEARNING SOME-THING— BEFORE ...
...I GAVE UP AND QUIT...
...A WHOLE BUNCH OF TIMES......
I'M WORRIED THAT'S HOW LITTLE I KNOW ABOUT OTHERS......... AND I FEEL SO ASHAMED NOW...
PHEW ...
MY EYES ARE SOOO TIRED ......
IT'S HARD NOT TO LOOK AT PEOPLE'S FACES...
OH!
UH...
?
....

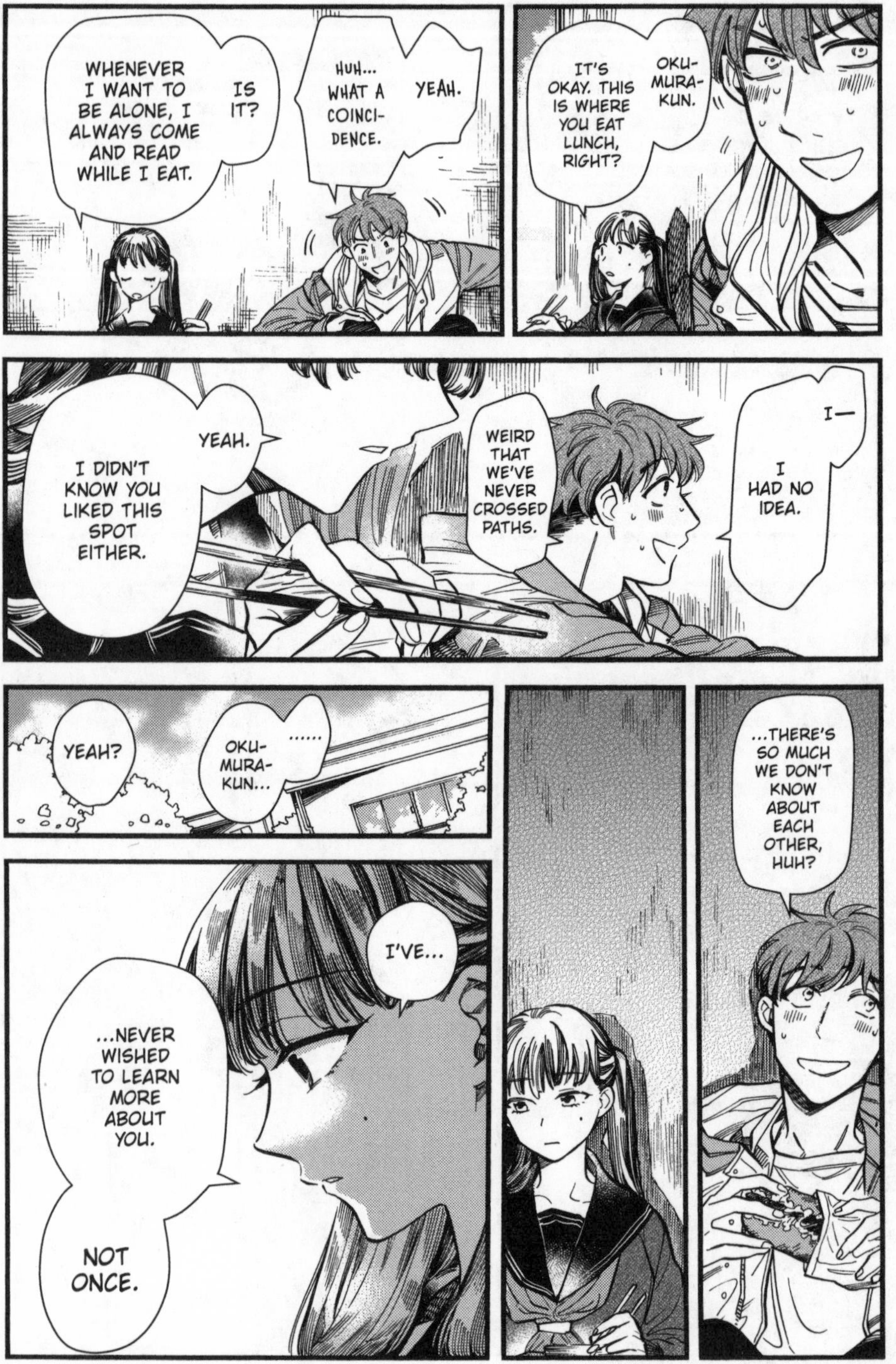
OKU-MURA-KUN.
IT'S OKAY. THIS IS WHERE YOU EAT LUNCH, RIGHT?
YEAH.
HUH... WHAT A COINCIDENCE.
IS IT?
WHENEVER I WANT TO BE ALONE, I ALWAYS COME AND READ WHILE I EAT.
I—
I HAD NO IDEA.
WEIRD THAT WE'VE NEVER CROSSED PATHS.
YEAH.
I DIDN'T KNOW YOU LIKED THIS SPOT EITHER.
...THERE'S SO MUCH WE DON'T KNOW ABOUT EACH OTHER, HUH?
......
OKU-MURA-KUN...
YEAH?
I'VE...
...NEVER WISHED TO LEARN MORE ABOUT YOU.
NOT ONCE.

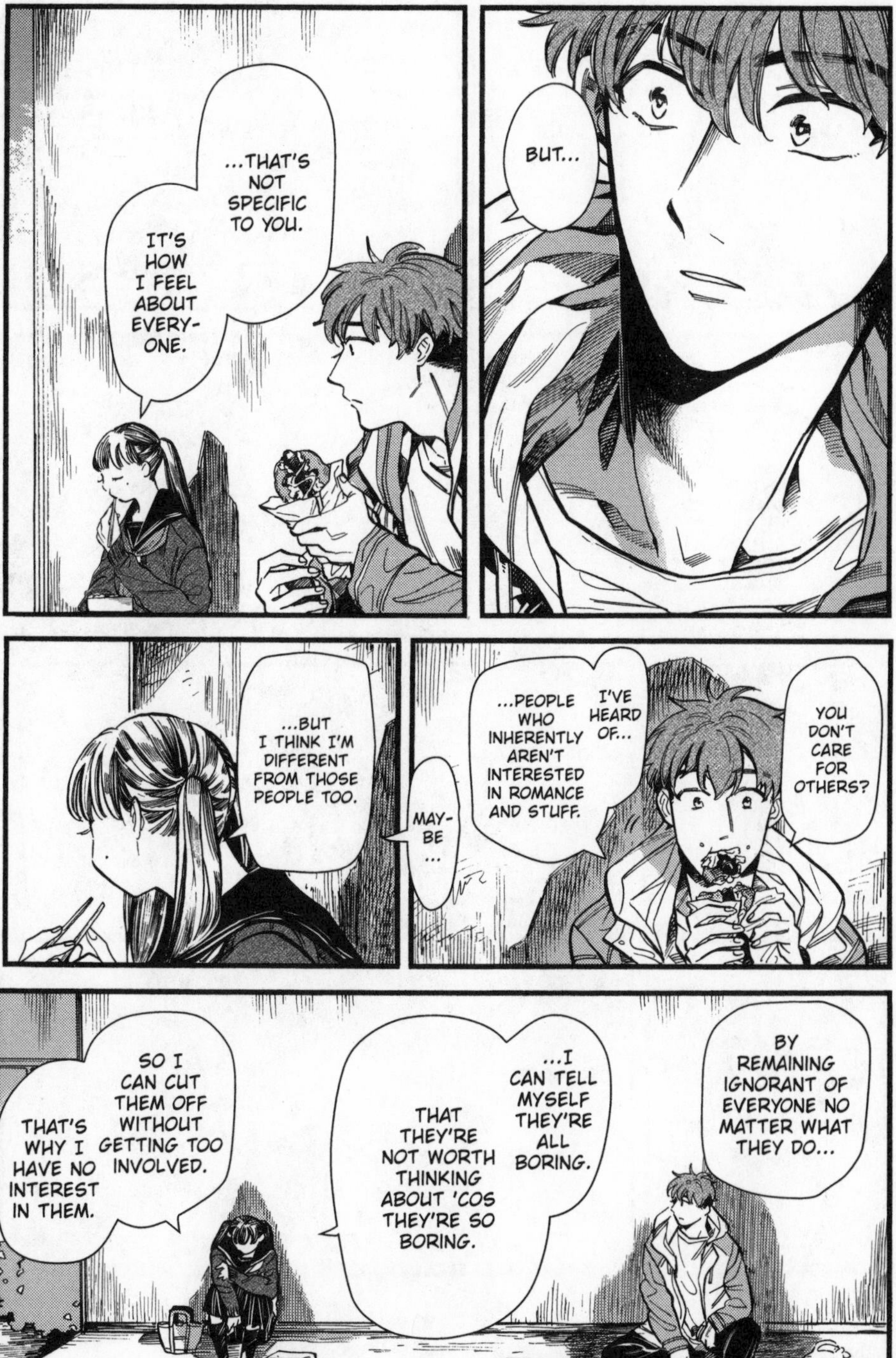
BUT...
...THAT'S NOT SPECIFIC TO YOU.
IT'S HOW I FEEL ABOUT EVERYONE.
YOU DON'T CARE FOR OTHERS?
I'VE HEARD OF...
...PEOPLE WHO INHERENTLY AREN'T INTERESTED IN ROMANCE AND STUFF.
MAYBE...
...BUT I THINK I'M DIFFERENT FROM THOSE PEOPLE TOO.
BY REMAINING IGNORANT OF EVERYONE NO MATTER WHAT THEY DO...
...I CAN TELL MYSELF THEY'RE ALL BORING.
THAT THEY'RE NOT WORTH THINKING ABOUT 'COS THEY'RE SO BORING.
SO I CAN CUT THEM OFF WITHOUT GETTING TOO INVOLVED.
THAT'S WHY I HAVE NO INTEREST IN THEM.

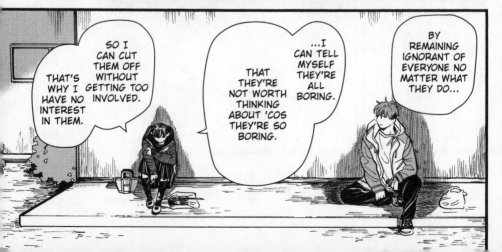

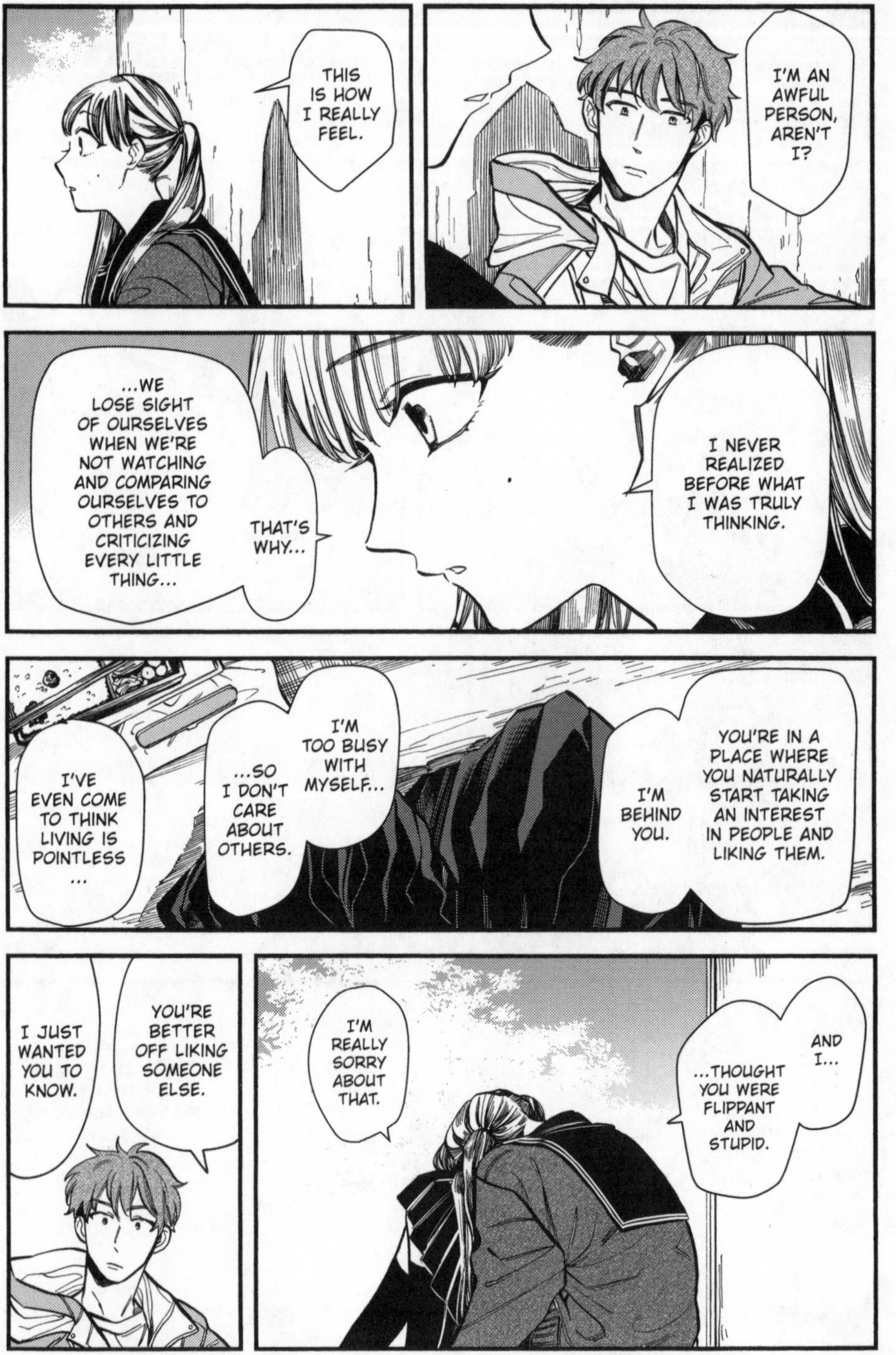
I'M AN AWFUL PERSON, AREN'T I?
THIS IS HOW I REALLY FEEL.
I NEVER REALIZED BEFORE WHAT I WAS TRULY THINKING.
THAT'S WHY...
...WE LOSE SIGHT OF OURSELVES WHEN WE'RE NOT WATCHING AND COMPARING OURSELVES TO OTHERS AND CRITICIZING EVERY LITTLE THING...
YOU'RE IN A PLACE WHERE YOU NATURALLY START TAKING AN INTEREST IN PEOPLE AND LIKING THEM.
I'M BEHIND YOU.
I'M TOO BUSY WITH MYSELF...
...SO I DON'T CARE ABOUT OTHERS.
I'VE EVEN COME TO THINK LIVING IS POINTLESS ...
AND I...
...THOUGHT YOU WERE FLIPPANT AND STUPID.
I'M REALLY SORRY ABOUT THAT.
YOU'RE BETTER OFF LIKING SOMEONE ELSE.
I JUST WANTED YOU TO KNOW.

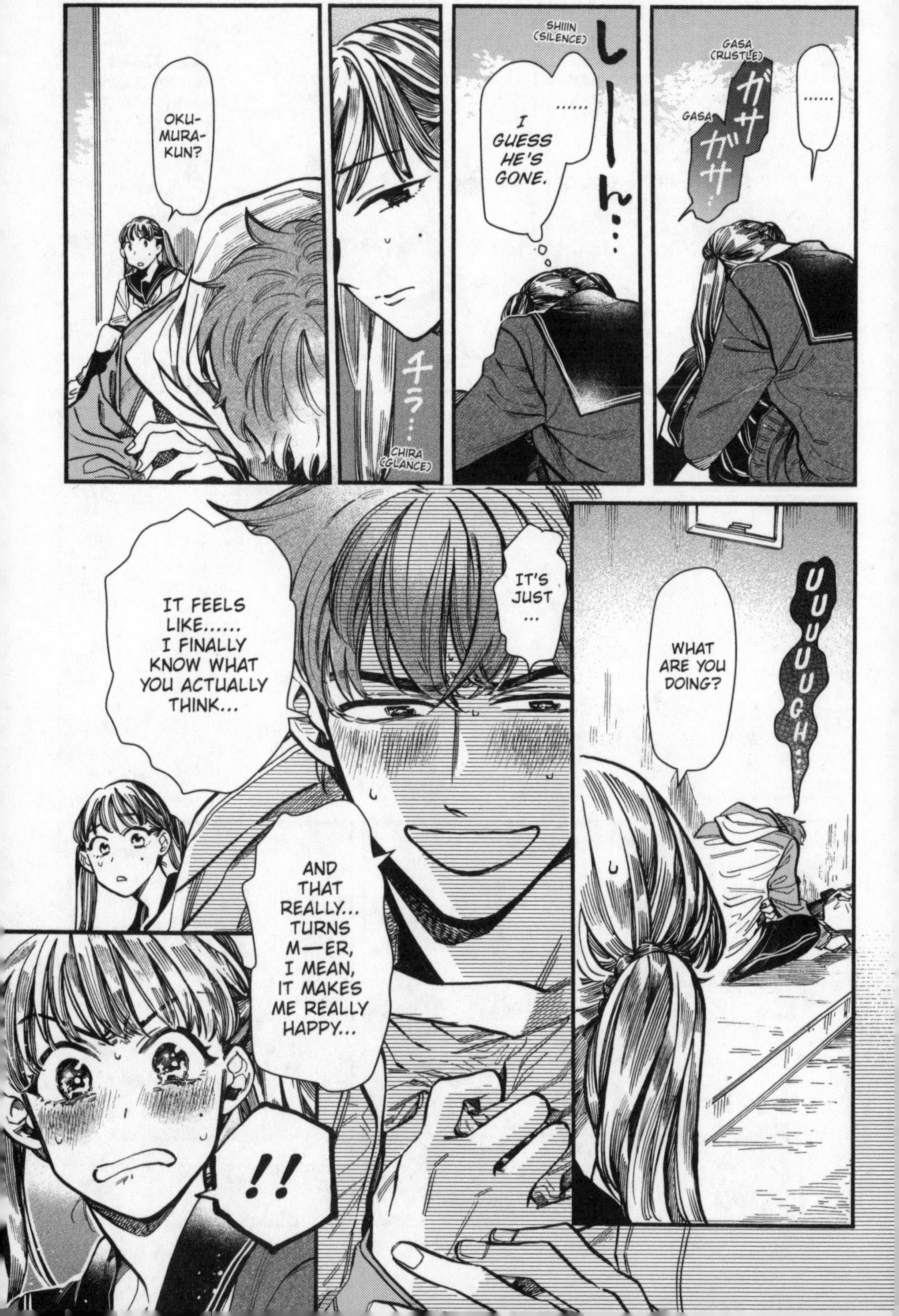
......
GASA (RUSTLE)
ガサ
GASA
ガサ
SHIIIN (SILENCE)
しーん...
...... I GUESS HE'S GONE.
チラ...
CHIRA (GLANCE)
OKU-MURA-KUN?
UUUUUGH...
WHAT ARE YOU DOING?
IT'S JUST ...
IT FEELS LIKE...... I FINALLY KNOW WHAT YOU ACTUALLY THINK...
AND THAT REALLY... TURNS M—ER, I MEAN, IT MAKES ME REALLY HAPPY...
!!

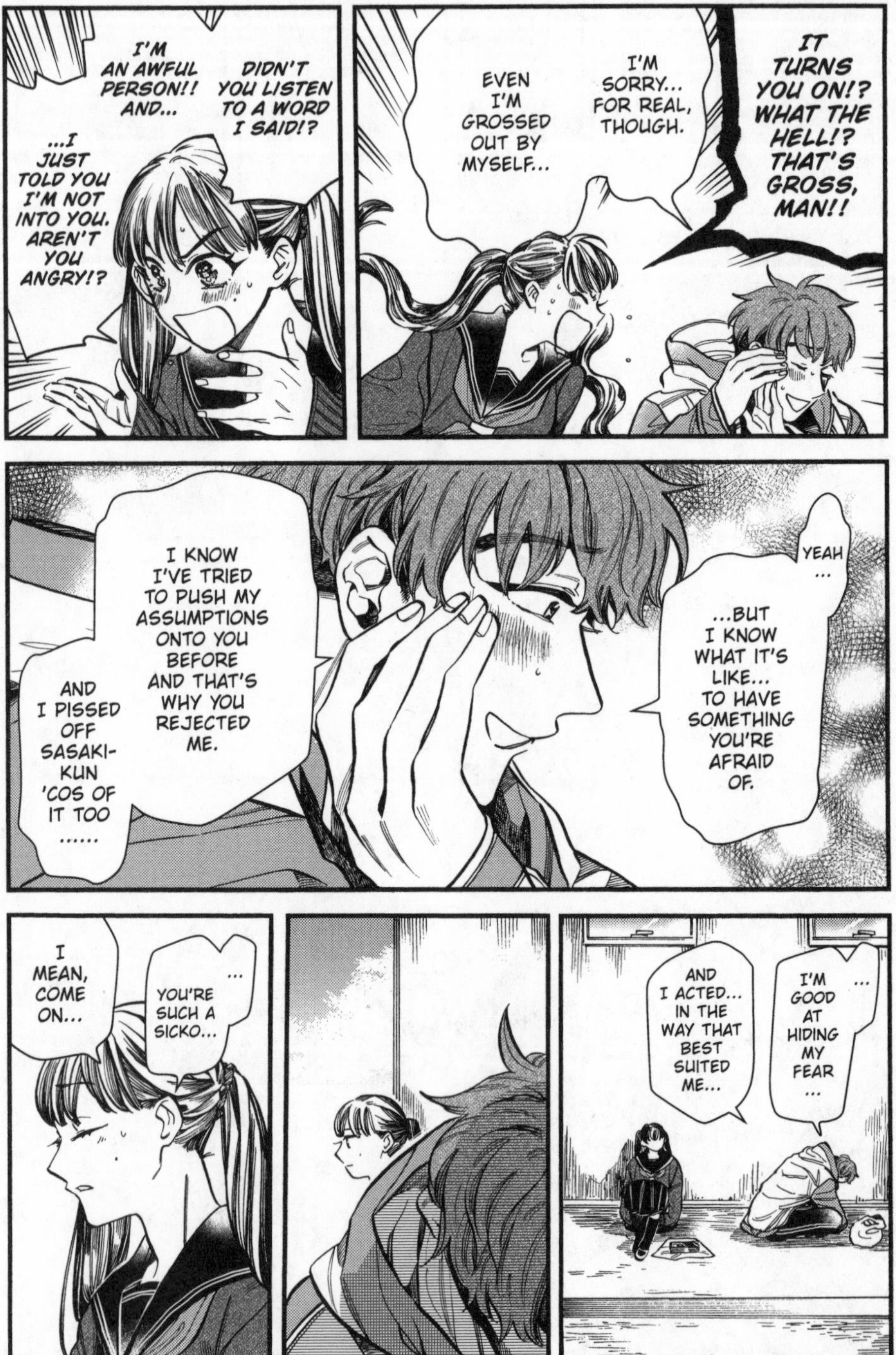
IT TURNS YOU ON!? WHAT THE HELL!? THAT'S GROSS, MAN!!
I'M SORRY... FOR REAL, THOUGH.
EVEN I'M GROSSED OUT BY MYSELF...
DIDN'T YOU LISTEN TO A WORD I SAID!?
I'M AN AWFUL PERSON!! AND...
...I JUST TOLD YOU I'M NOT INTO YOU. AREN'T YOU ANGRY!?
YEAH ...
...BUT I KNOW WHAT IT'S LIKE... TO HAVE SOMETHING YOU'RE AFRAID OF.
I KNOW I'VE TRIED TO PUSH MY ASSUMPTIONS ONTO YOU BEFORE AND THAT'S WHY YOU REJECTED ME.
AND I PISSED OFF SASAKI-KUN 'COS OF IT TOO ......
... I'M GOOD AT HIDING MY FEAR ...
AND I ACTED... IN THE WAY THAT BEST SUITED ME...
... YOU'RE SUCH A SICKO...
I MEAN, COME ON...

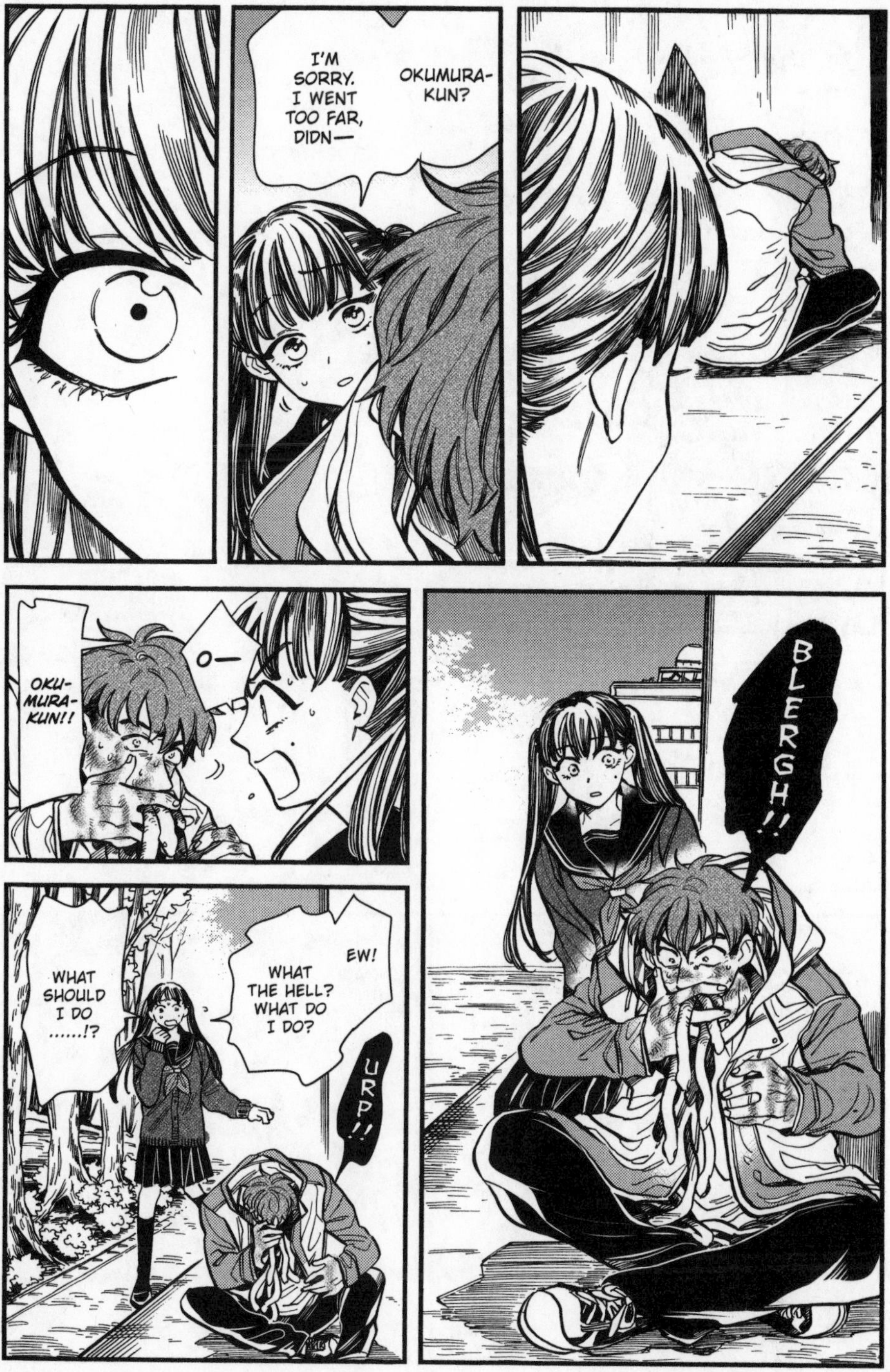
OKUMURA-KUN?
I'M SORRY. I WENT TOO FAR, DIDN—
BLERGH!!
O—
OKUMURA-KUN!!
EW!
WHAT THE HELL? WHAT DO I DO?
URP!!
WHAT SHOULD I DO ......!?

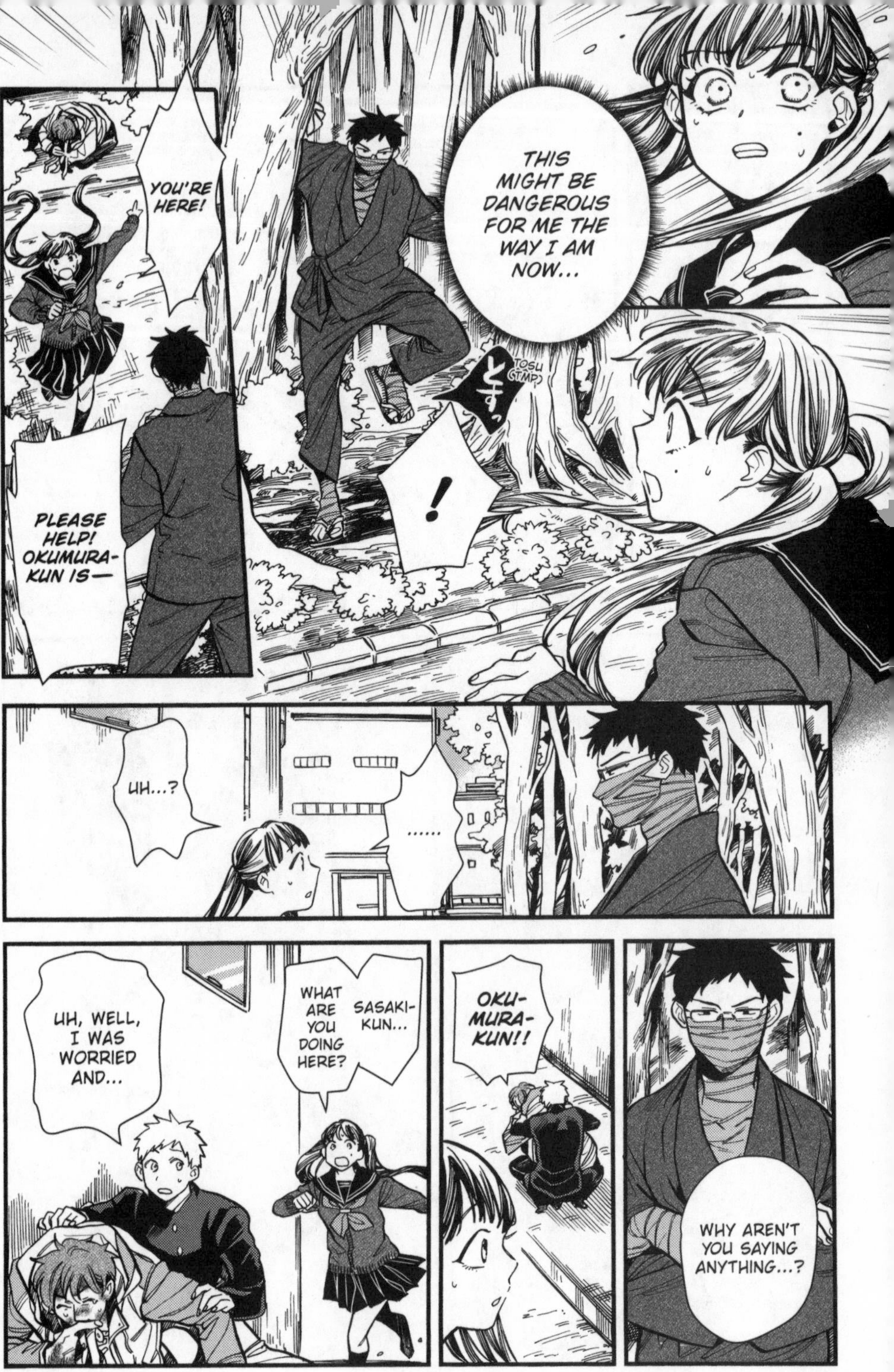
THIS MIGHT BE DANGEROUS FOR ME THE WAY I AM NOW...
とすっ
TOSU (TMP)
!
YOU'RE HERE!
PLEASE HELP! OKUMURA-KUN IS—
......
UH...?
WHY AREN'T YOU SAYING ANYTHING...?
OKUMURA-KUN!!
SASAKI-KUN...
WHAT ARE YOU DOING HERE?
UH, WELL, I WAS WORRIED AND...

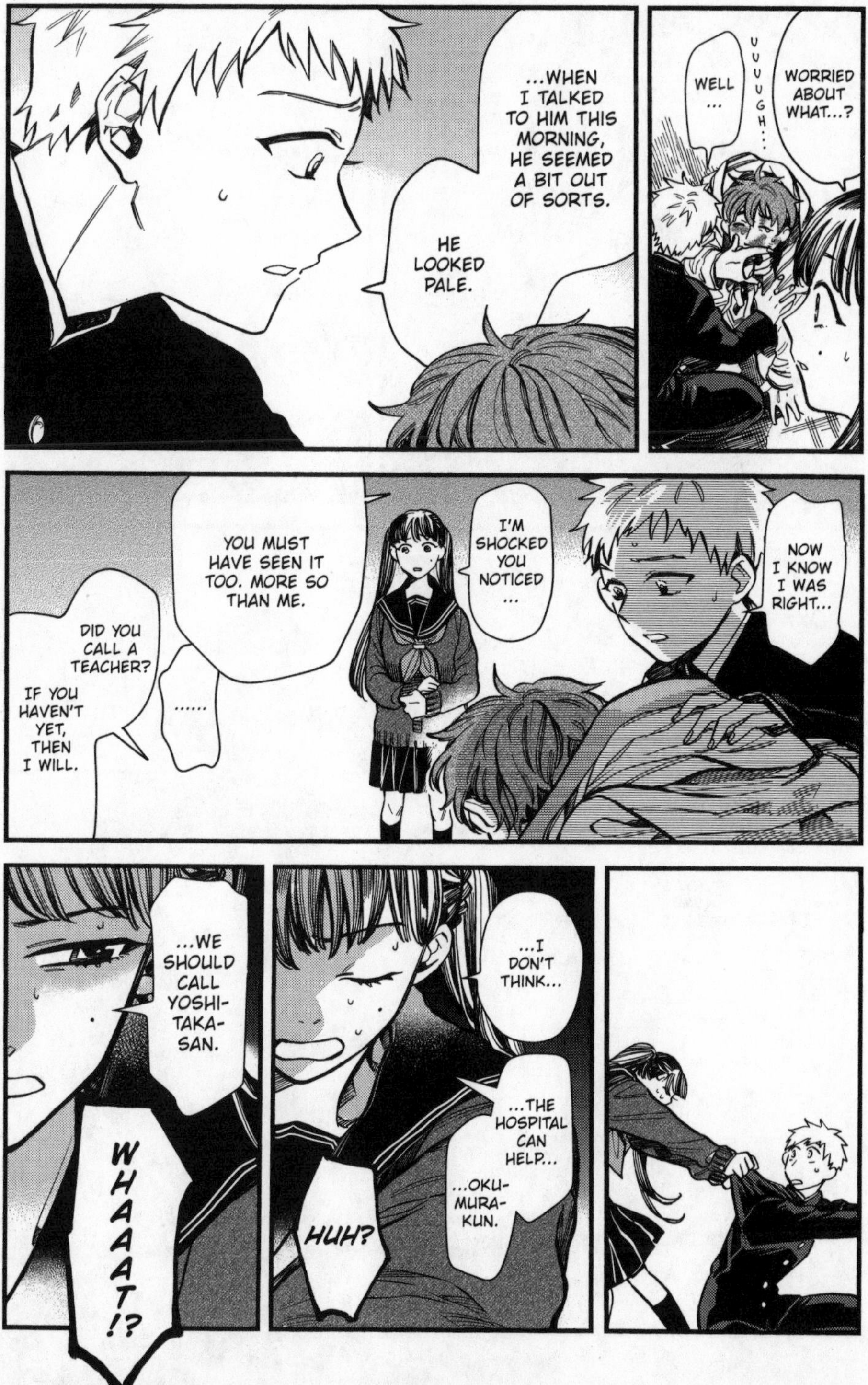
WORRIED ABOUT WHAT...?
UUUUGH...
WELL...
...WHEN I TALKED TO HIM THIS MORNING, HE SEEMED A BIT OUT OF SORTS.
HE LOOKED PALE.
NOW I KNOW I WAS RIGHT...
I'M SHOCKED YOU NOTICED...
YOU MUST HAVE SEEN IT TOO. MORE SO THAN ME.
......
DID YOU CALL A TEACHER?
IF YOU HAVEN'T YET, THEN I WILL.
...I DON'T THINK...
...THE HOSPITAL CAN HELP...
...OKU-MURA-KUN.
HUH?
...WE SHOULD CALL YOSHI-TAKA-SAN.
WHAAAT!?

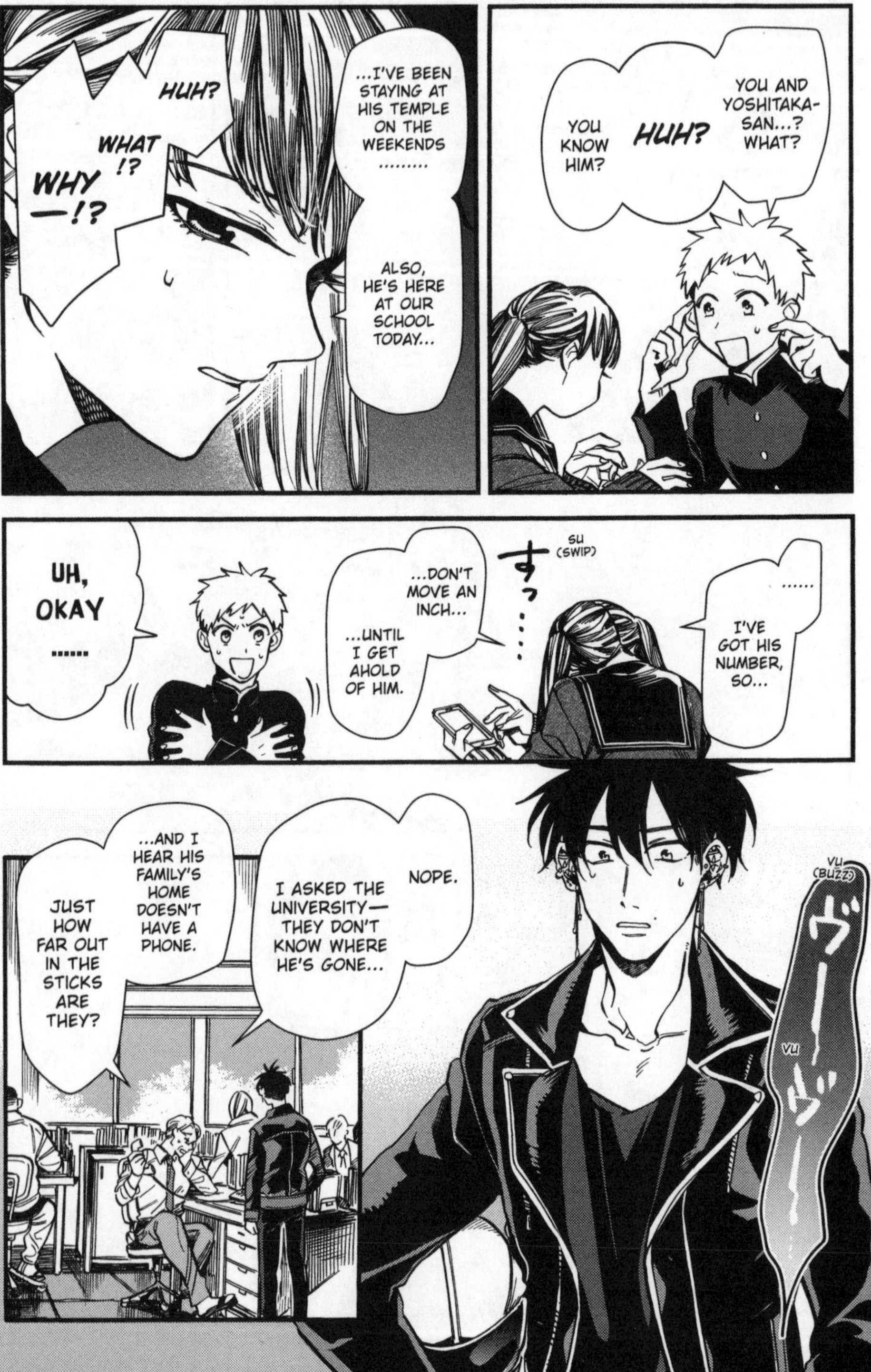
YOU AND YOSHITAKA-SAN...? WHAT?
HUH?
YOU KNOW HIM?
...I'VE BEEN STAYING AT HIS TEMPLE ON THE WEEKENDS ....
HUH? WHAT!? WHY—!?
ALSO, HE'S HERE AT OUR SCHOOL TODAY...
...... I'VE GOT HIS NUMBER, SO...
すっ…
SU (SWIP)
...DON'T MOVE AN INCH...
...UNTIL I GET AHOLD OF HIM.
UH, OKAY ......
ヴーッ
VU (BUZZ)
VU
NOPE.
I ASKED THE UNIVERSITY—THEY DON'T KNOW WHERE HE'S GONE...
...AND I HEAR HIS FAMILY'S HOME DOESN'T HAVE A PHONE.
JUST HOW FAR OUT IN THE STICKS ARE THEY?

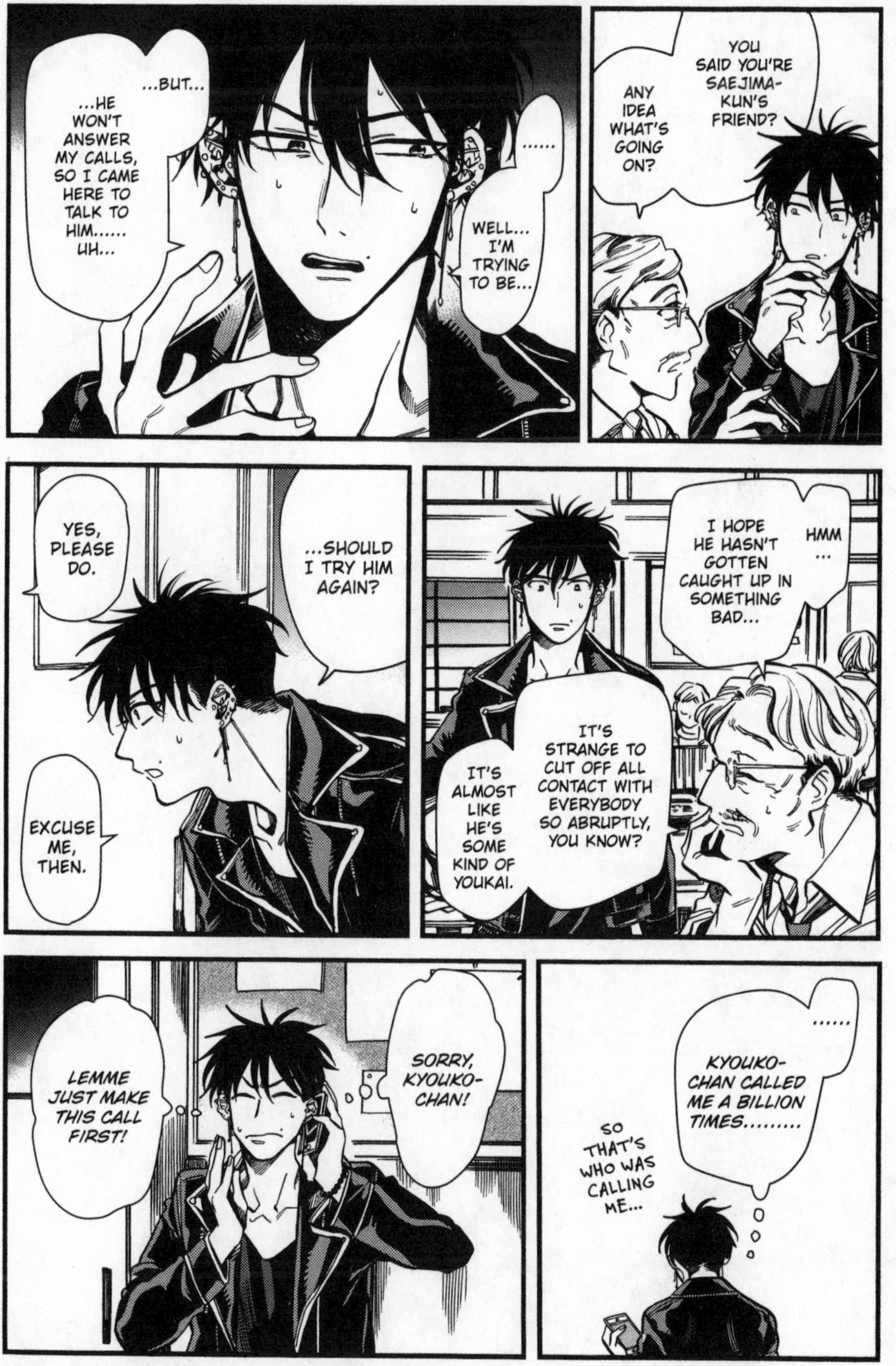
YOU SAID YOU'RE SAEJIMA-KUN'S FRIEND?
ANY IDEA WHAT'S GOING ON?
......
WELL... I'M TRYING TO BE...
...BUT...
...HE WON'T ANSWER MY CALLS, SO I CAME HERE TO TALK TO HIM...... UH...
HMM...
I HOPE HE HASN'T GOTTEN CAUGHT UP IN SOMETHING BAD...
IT'S STRANGE TO CUT OFF ALL CONTACT WITH EVERYBODY SO ABRUPTLY, YOU KNOW?
IT'S ALMOST LIKE HE'S SOME KIND OF YOUKAI.
...SHOULD I TRY HIM AGAIN?
YES, PLEASE DO.
EXCUSE ME, THEN.
......
KYOUKO-CHAN CALLED ME A BILLION TIMES.........
SO THAT'S WHO WAS CALLING ME...
SORRY, KYOUKO-CHAN!
LEMME JUST MAKE THIS CALL FIRST!

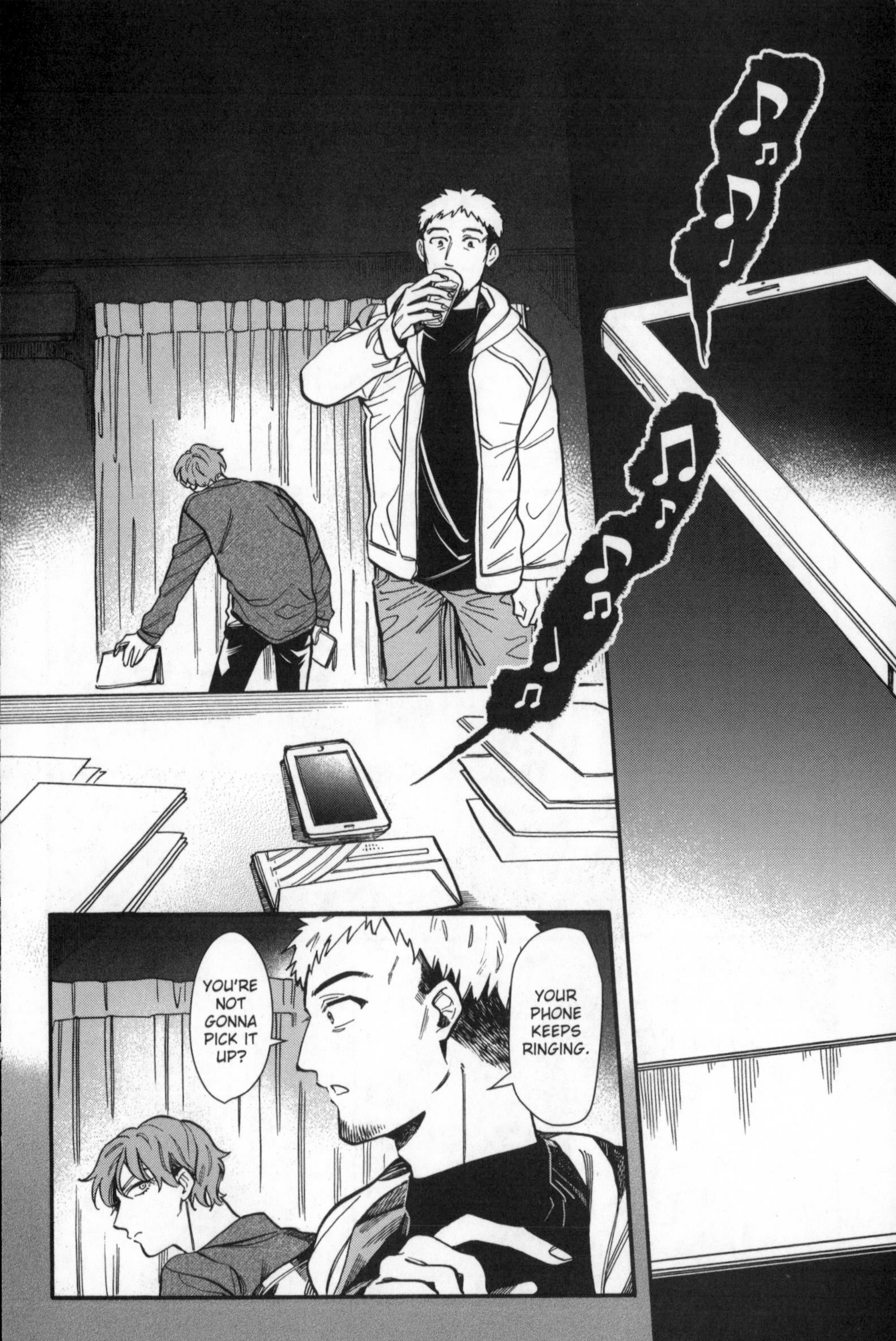
YOUR PHONE KEEPS RINGING.
YOU'RE NOT GONNA PICK IT UP?

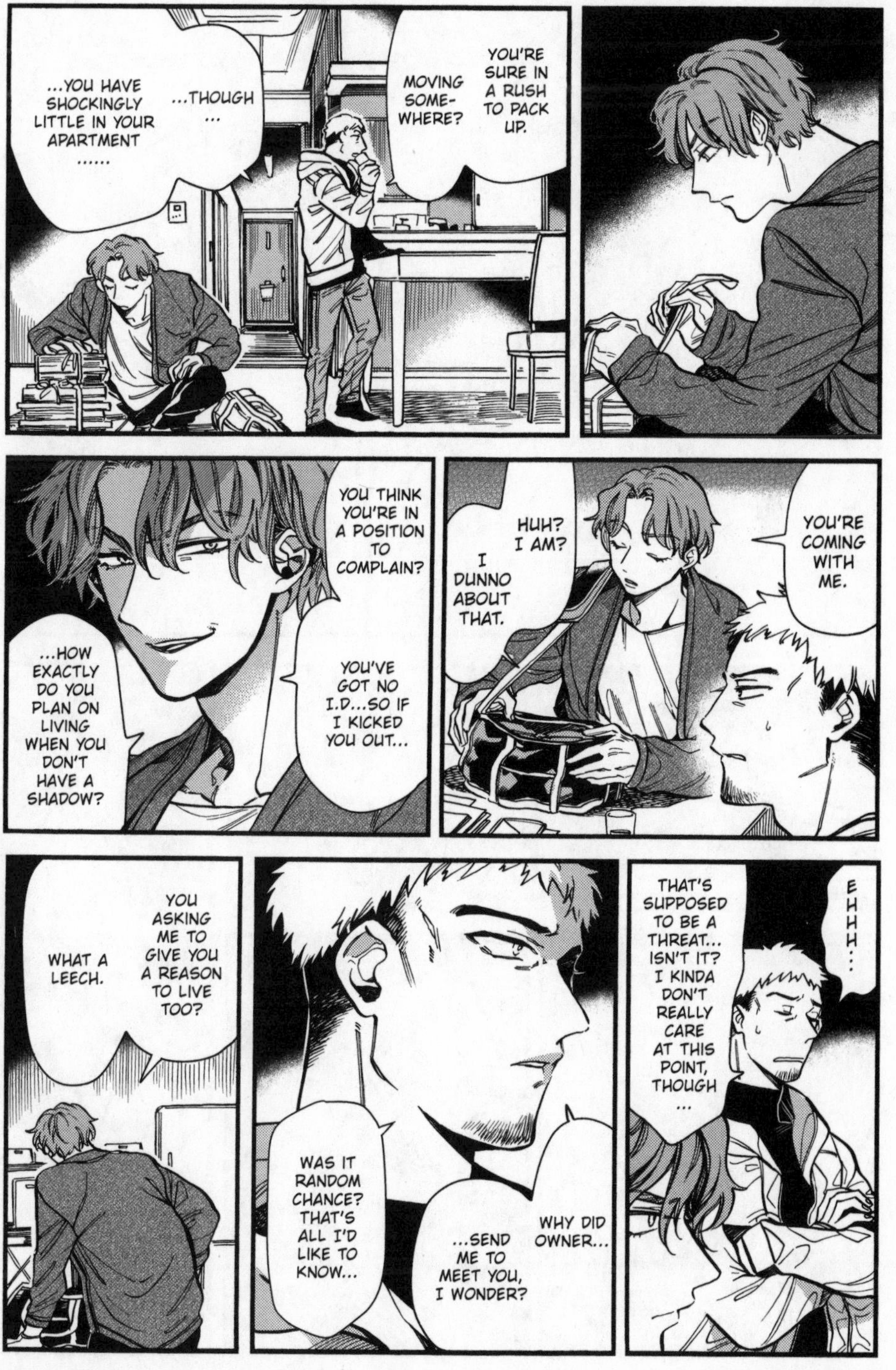
YOU'RE SURE IN A RUSH TO PACK UP.
MOVING SOME-WHERE?
...THOUGH...
...YOU HAVE SHOCKINGLY LITTLE IN YOUR APARTMENT ......
YOU'RE COMING WITH ME.
HUH? I AM?
I DUNNO ABOUT THAT.
YOU THINK YOU'RE IN A POSITION TO COMPLAIN?
YOU'VE GOT NO I.D...SO IF I KICKED YOU OUT...
...HOW EXACTLY DO YOU PLAN ON LIVING WHEN YOU DON'T HAVE A SHADOW?
EHHH...
THAT'S SUPPOSED TO BE A THREAT... ISN'T IT? I KINDA DON'T REALLY CARE AT THIS POINT, THOUGH...
WHY DID OWNER...
...SEND ME TO MEET YOU, I WONDER?
WAS IT RANDOM CHANCE? THAT'S ALL I'D LIKE TO KNOW...
YOU ASKING ME TO GIVE YOU A REASON TO LIVE TOO?
WHAT A LEECH.

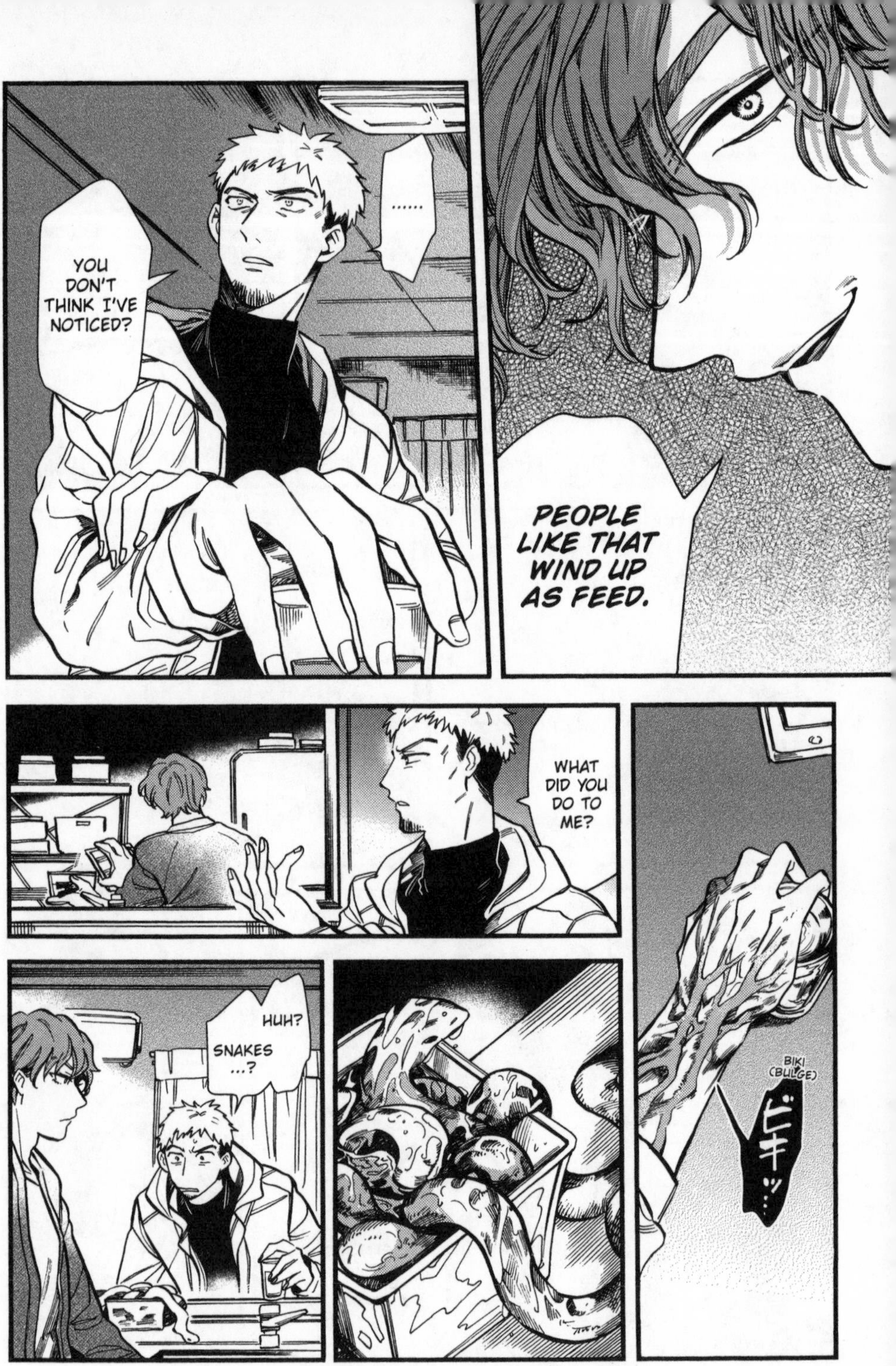
PEOPLE LIKE THAT WIND UP AS FEED.
......
YOU DON'T THINK I'VE NOTICED?
BIKI (BULGE)
ビキッ…
WHAT DID YOU DO TO ME?
HUH?
SNAKES ...?

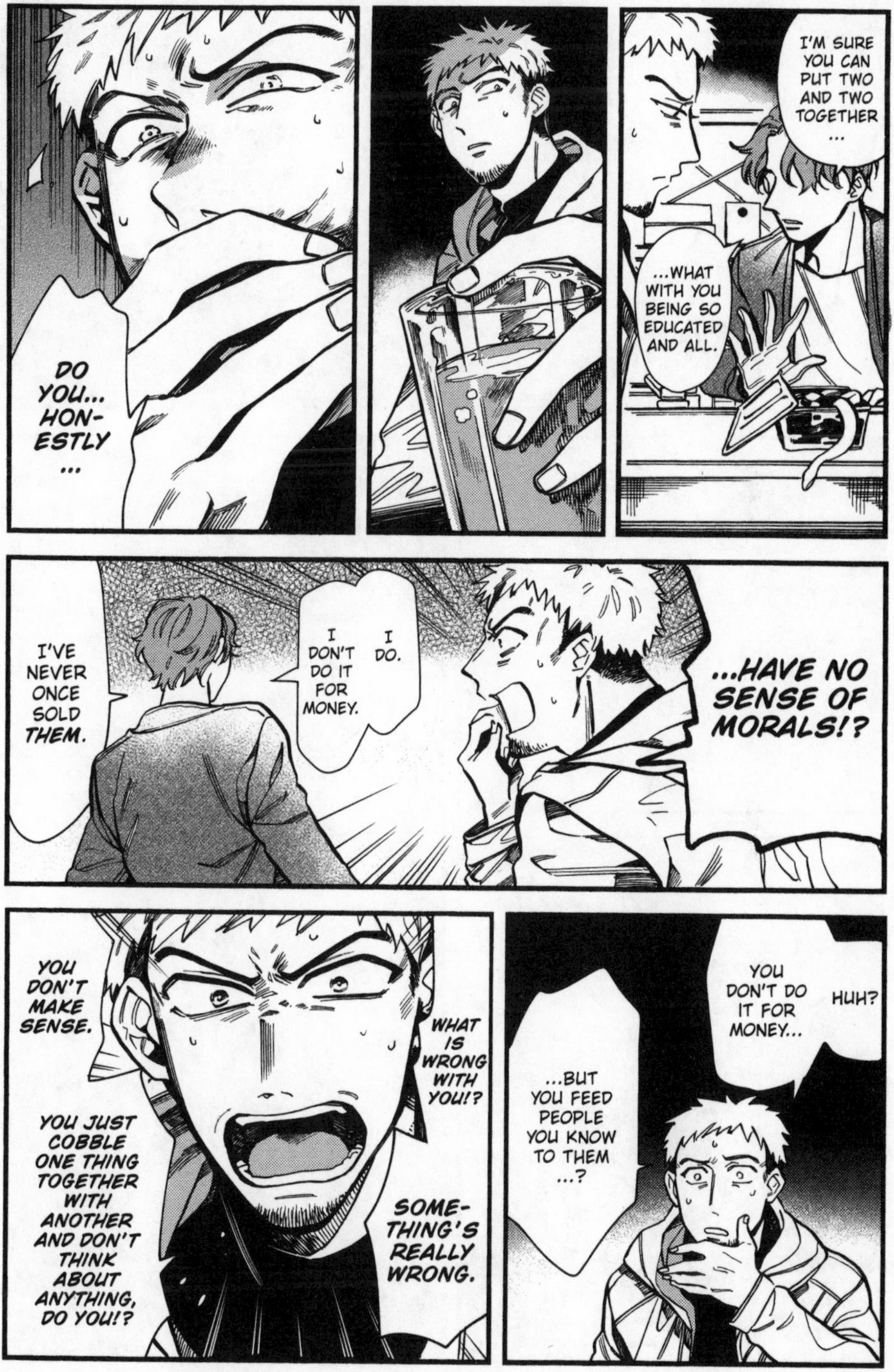
I'M SURE YOU CAN PUT TWO AND TWO TOGETHER ...
...WHAT WITH YOU BEING SO EDUCATED AND ALL.
DO YOU... HONESTLY ...
...HAVE NO SENSE OF MORALS!?
I DO.
I DON'T DO IT FOR MONEY.
I'VE NEVER ONCE SOLD THEM.
HUH?
YOU DON'T DO IT FOR MONEY...
...BUT YOU FEED PEOPLE YOU KNOW TO THEM ...?
WHAT IS WRONG WITH YOU!?
YOU DON'T MAKE SENSE.
SOMETHING'S REALLY WRONG.
YOU JUST COBBLE ONE THING TOGETHER WITH ANOTHER AND DON'T THINK ABOUT ANYTHING, DO YOU!?

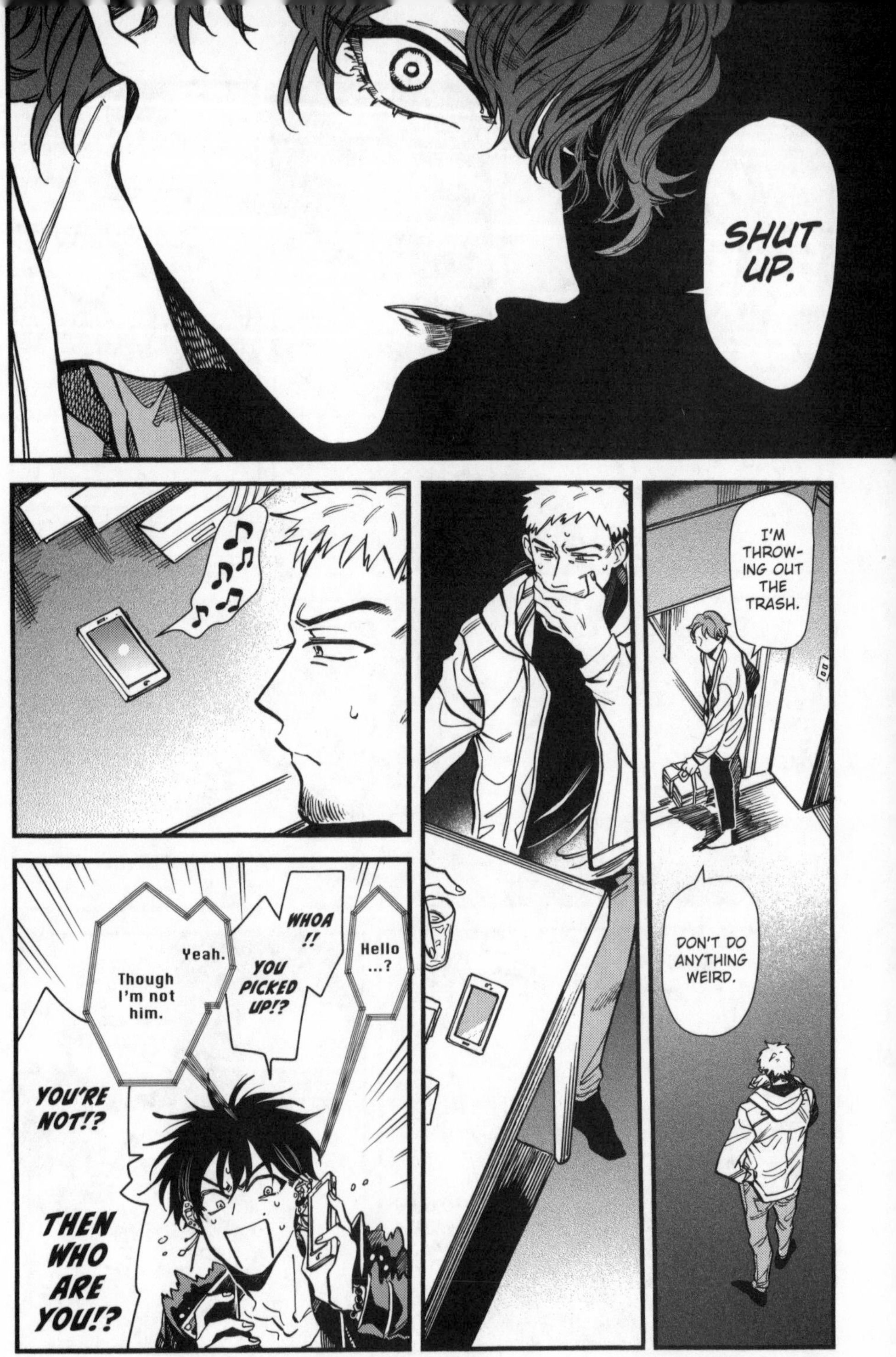
SHUT UP.
I'M THROWING OUT THE TRASH.
DON'T DO ANYTHING WEIRD.
Hello ...?
WHOA!! YOU PICKED UP!?
Yeah.
Though I'm not him.
YOU'RE NOT!?
THEN WHO ARE YOU!?

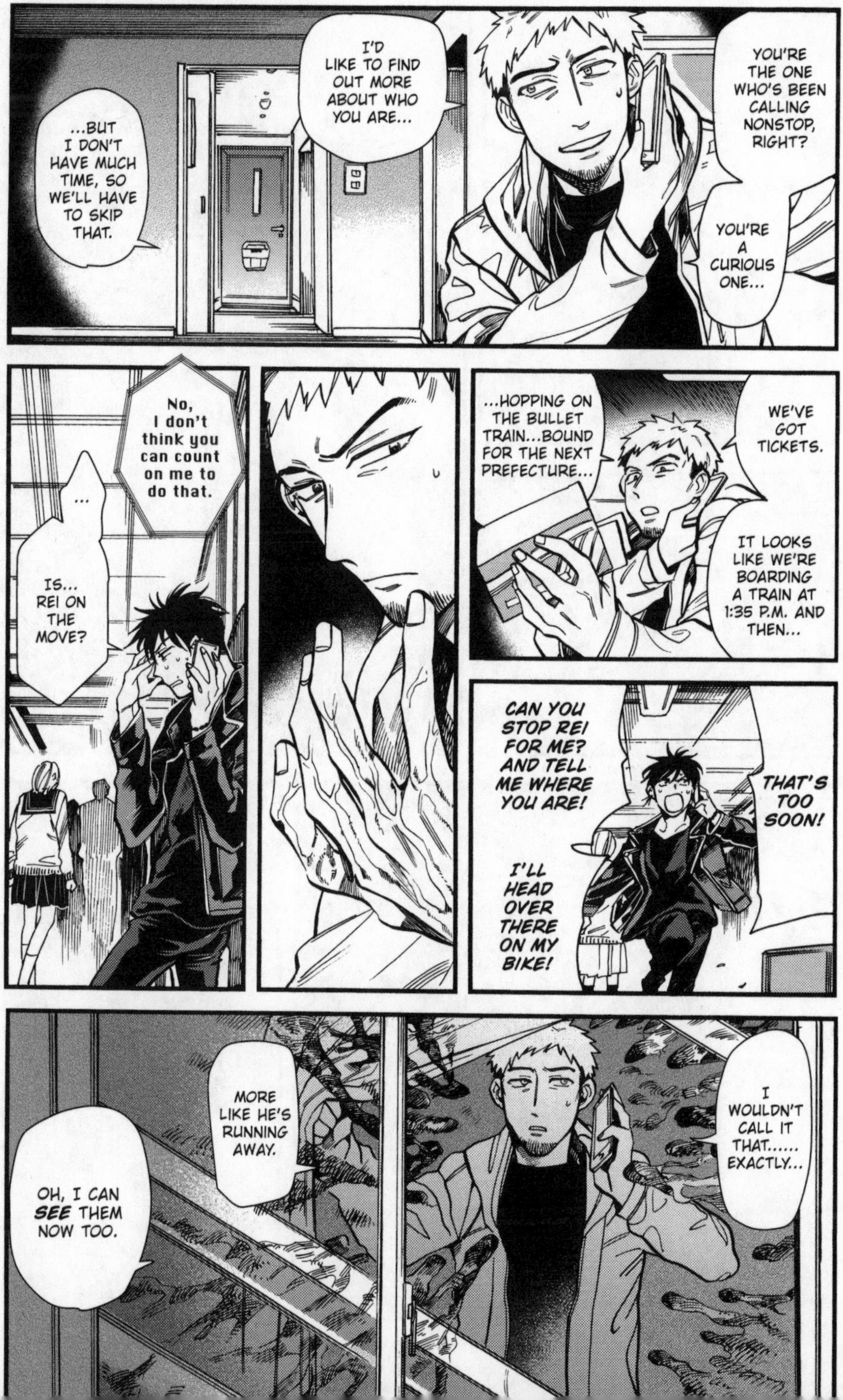
YOU'RE THE ONE WHO'S BEEN CALLING NONSTOP, RIGHT?
YOU'RE A CURIOUS ONE...
I'D LIKE TO FIND OUT MORE ABOUT WHO YOU ARE...
...BUT I DON'T HAVE MUCH TIME, SO WE'LL HAVE TO SKIP THAT.
WE'VE GOT TICKETS.
IT LOOKS LIKE WE'RE BOARDING A TRAIN AT 1:35 P.M. AND THEN...
...HOPPING ON THE BULLET TRAIN...BOUND FOR THE NEXT PREFECTURE...
THAT'S TOO SOON!
CAN YOU STOP REI FOR ME? AND TELL ME WHERE YOU ARE!
I'LL HEAD OVER THERE ON MY BIKE!
No, I don't think you can count on me to do that.
...
IS... REI ON THE MOVE?
I WOULDN'T CALL IT THAT...... EXACTLY...
MORE LIKE HE'S RUNNING AWAY.
OH, I CAN ***SEE*** THEM NOW TOO.

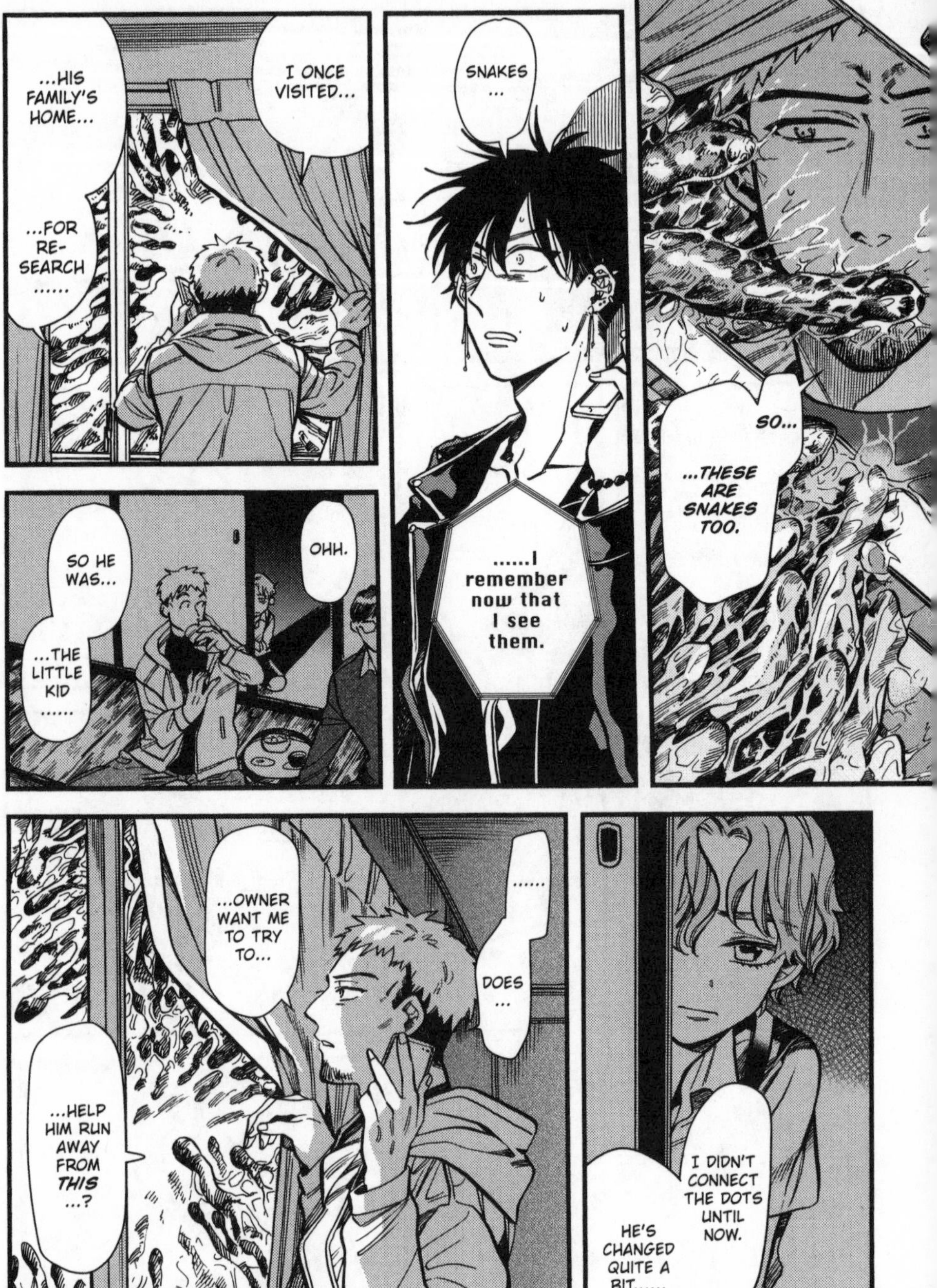
SO...
...THESE ARE SNAKES TOO.
SNAKES ...
......I remember now that I see them.
I ONCE VISITED...
...HIS FAMILY'S HOME...
...FOR RE-SEARCH ......
OHH.
SO HE WAS...
...THE LITTLE KID ......
I DIDN'T CONNECT THE DOTS UNTIL NOW.
HE'S CHANGED QUITE A BIT......
......
DOES ...
...OWNER WANT ME TO TRY TO...
...HELP HIM RUN AWAY FROM *THIS* ...?

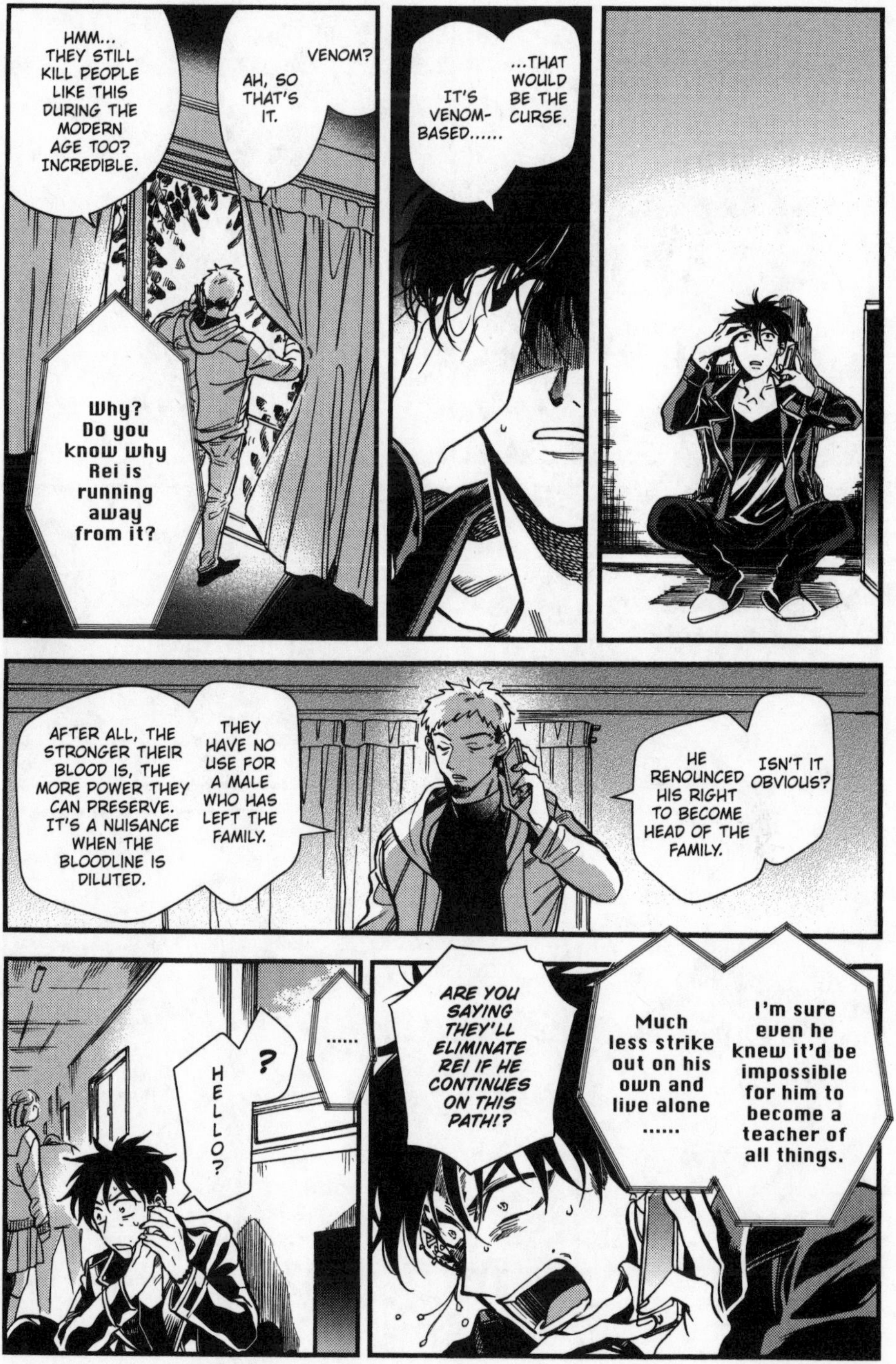
...THAT WOULD BE THE CURSE.
IT'S VENOM-BASED......
VENOM?
AH, SO THAT'S IT.
HMM... THEY STILL KILL PEOPLE LIKE THIS DURING THE MODERN AGE TOO? INCREDIBLE.
Why? Do you know why Rei is running away from it?
ISN'T IT OBVIOUS?
HE RENOUNCED HIS RIGHT TO BECOME HEAD OF THE FAMILY.
THEY HAVE NO USE FOR A MALE WHO HAS LEFT THE FAMILY.
AFTER ALL, THE STRONGER THEIR BLOOD IS, THE MORE POWER THEY CAN PRESERVE. IT'S A NUISANCE WHEN THE BLOODLINE IS DILUTED.
I'm sure even he knew it'd be impossible for him to become a teacher of all things.
Much less strike out on his own and live alone ......
ARE YOU SAYING THEY'LL ELIMINATE REI IF HE CONTINUES ON THIS PATH!?
......
?
HELLO?

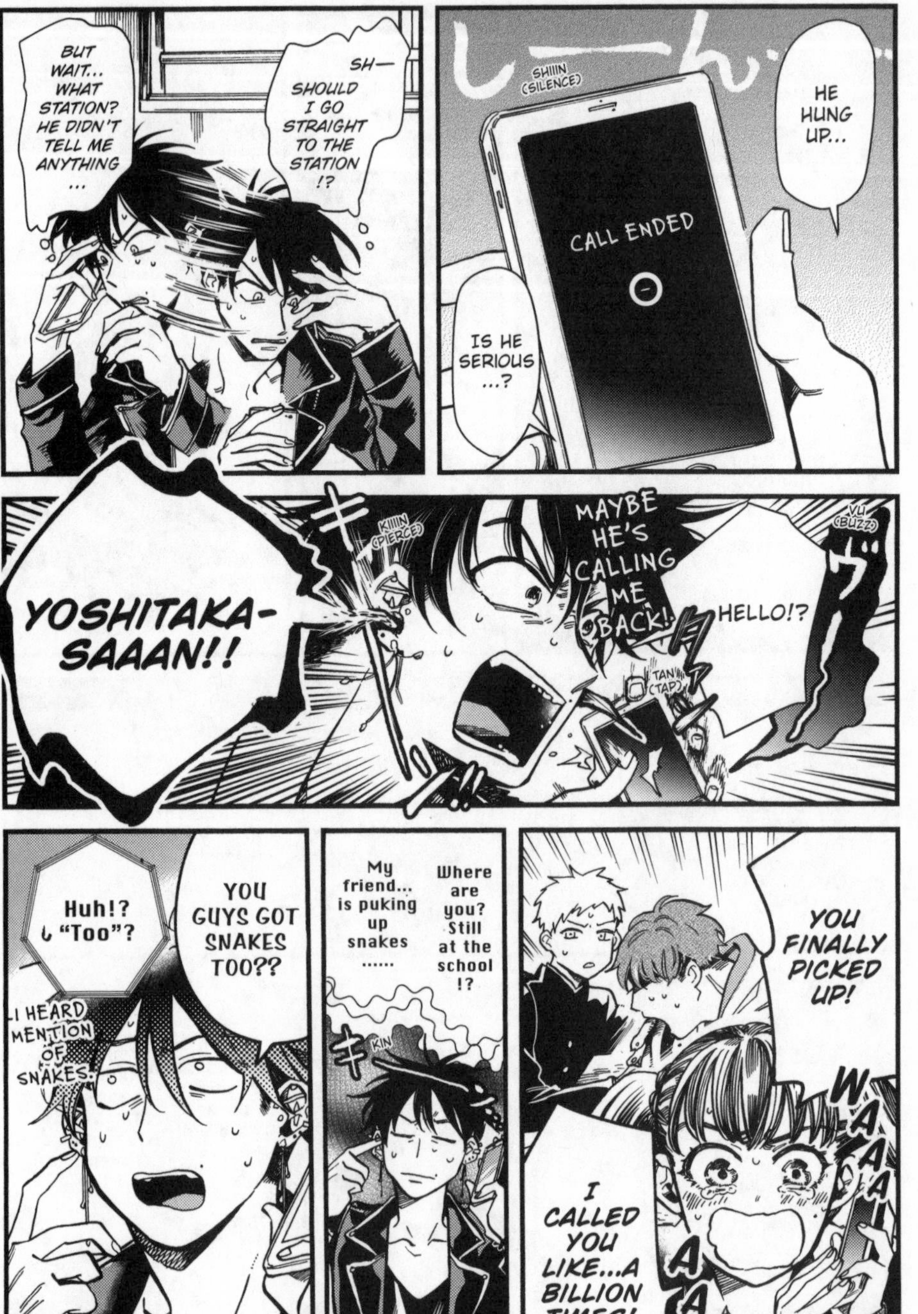
SHIIIN (SILENCE)
HE HUNG UP...
CALL ENDED
IS HE SERIOUS ...?
SH— SHOULD I GO STRAIGHT TO THE STATION !?
BUT WAIT... WHAT STATION? HE DIDN'T TELL ME ANYTHING ...
VU (BUZZ)
HELLO!?
MAYBE HE'S CALLING ME BACK!
TAN (TAP)
KIIIN (PIERCE)
YOSHITAKA-SAAAN!!
YOU FINALLY PICKED UP!
WAAAAAAAAH!
I CALLED YOU LIKE...A BILLION TIMES!
Where are you? Still at the school !?
My friend... is puking up snakes ......
KIN
YOU GUYS GOT SNAKES TOO??
Huh!? "Too"?
I HEARD MENTION OF SNAKES.

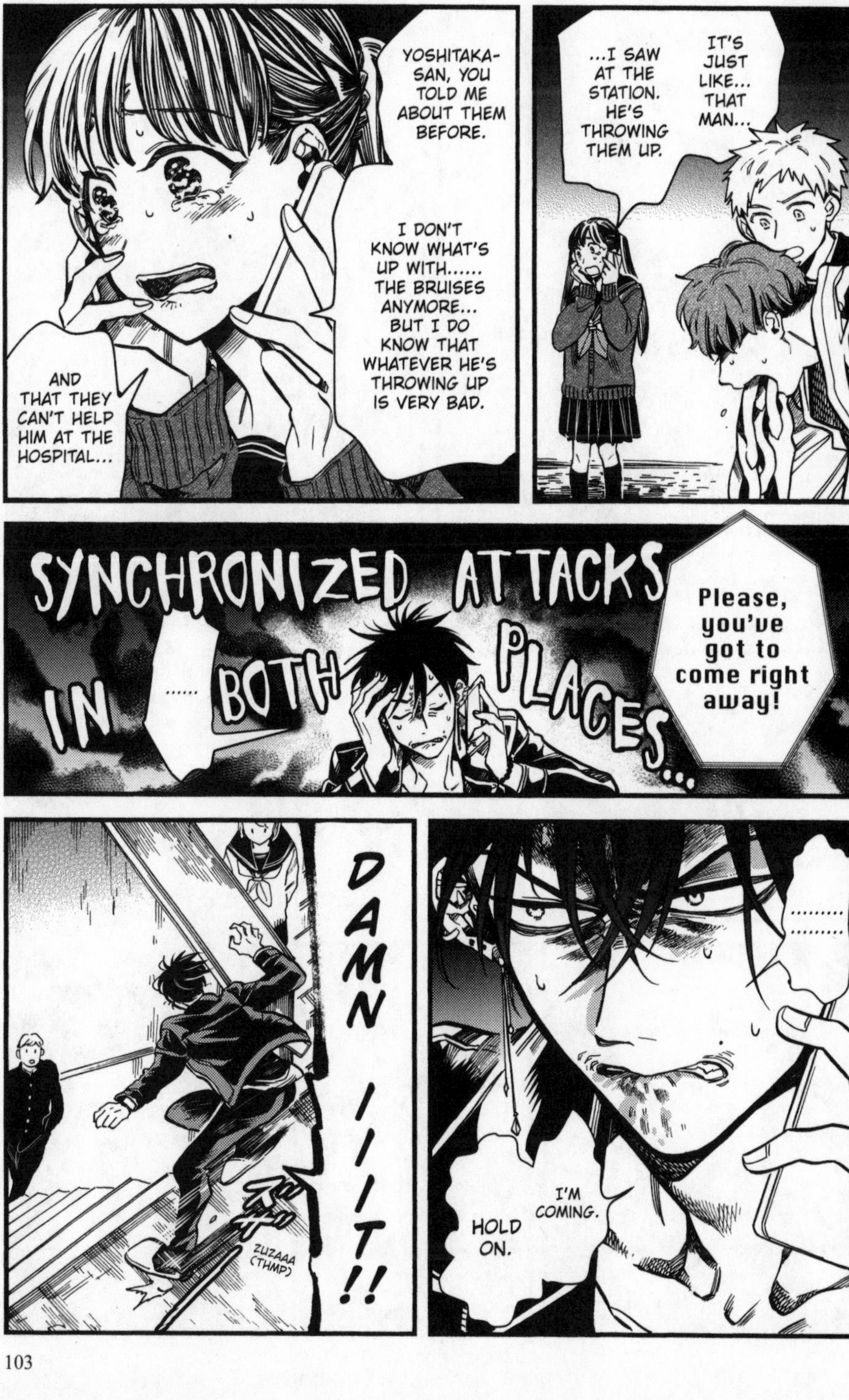
IT'S JUST LIKE... THAT MAN...
...I SAW AT THE STATION. HE'S THROWING THEM UP.
YOSHITAKA-SAN, YOU TOLD ME ABOUT THEM BEFORE.
I DON'T KNOW WHAT'S UP WITH...... THE BRUISES ANYMORE... BUT I DO KNOW THAT WHATEVER HE'S THROWING UP IS VERY BAD.
AND THAT THEY CAN'T HELP HIM AT THE HOSPITAL...
Please, you've got to come right away!
SYNCHRONIZED ATTACKS IN BOTH PLACES...
......
....
I'M COMING.
HOLD ON.
DAMN IIIIT!!
ZUZAAA (THMP)

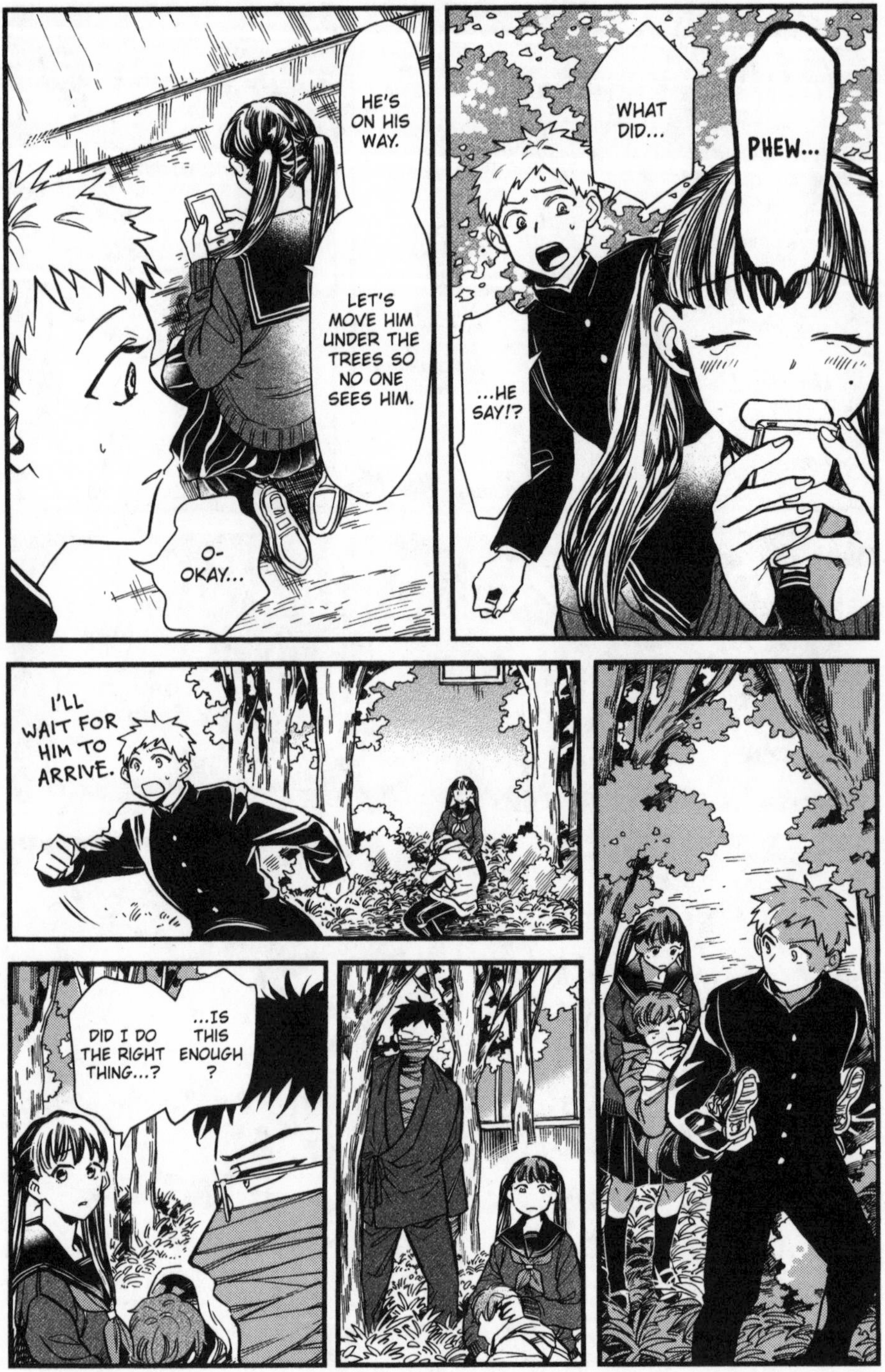
PHEW...
WHAT DID...
...HE SAY!?
HE'S ON HIS WAY.
LET'S MOVE HIM UNDER THE TREES SO NO ONE SEES HIM.
O-OKAY...
I'LL WAIT FOR HIM TO ARRIVE.
...IS THIS ENOUGH?
DID I DO THE RIGHT THING...?

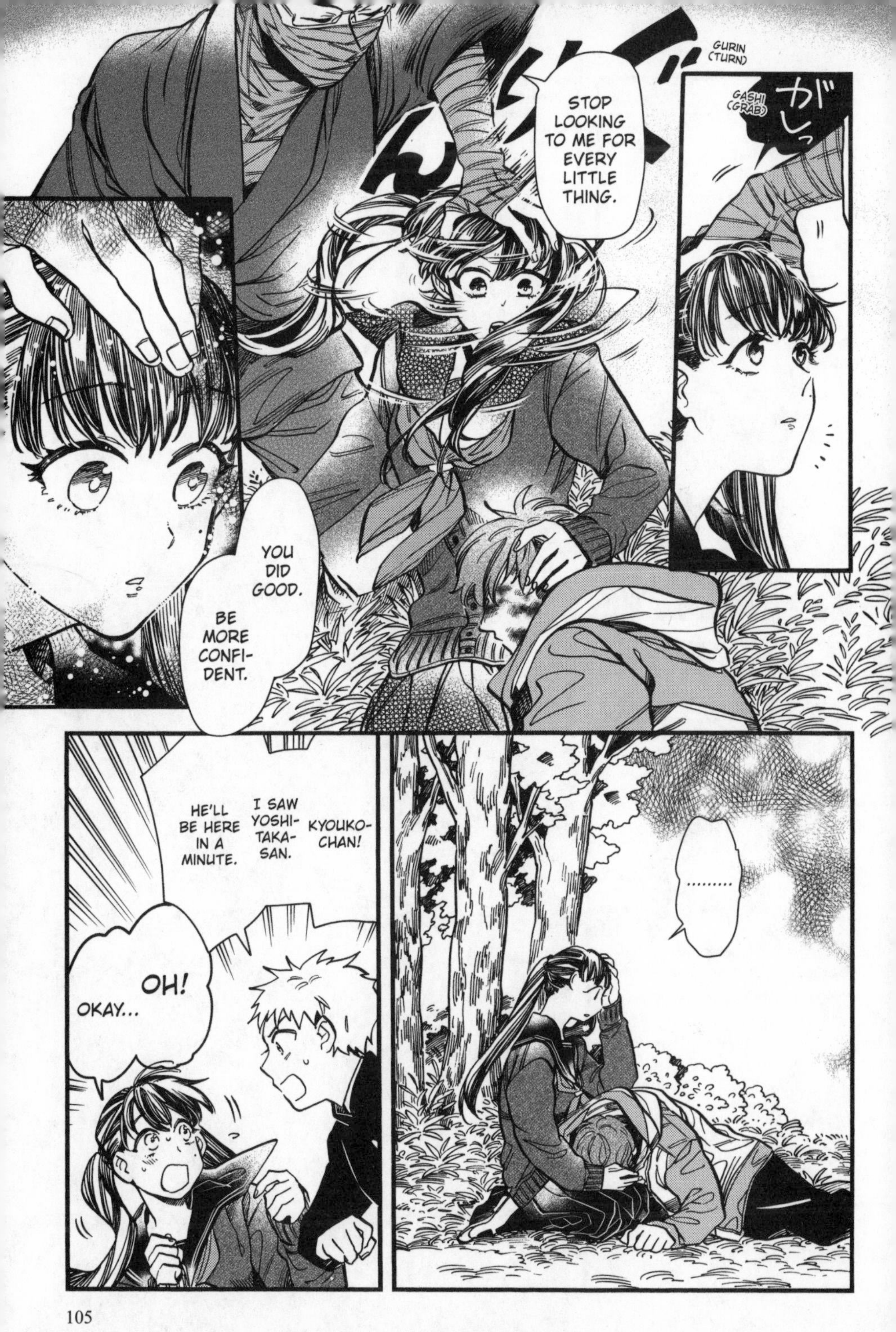
GASHI (GRAB)
がしっ
GURIN (TURN)
STOP LOOKING TO ME FOR EVERY LITTLE THING.
YOU DID GOOD.
BE MORE CONFIDENT.
....
KYOUKO-CHAN!
I SAW YOSHITAKA-SAN.
HE'LL BE HERE IN A MINUTE.
OH! OKAY...

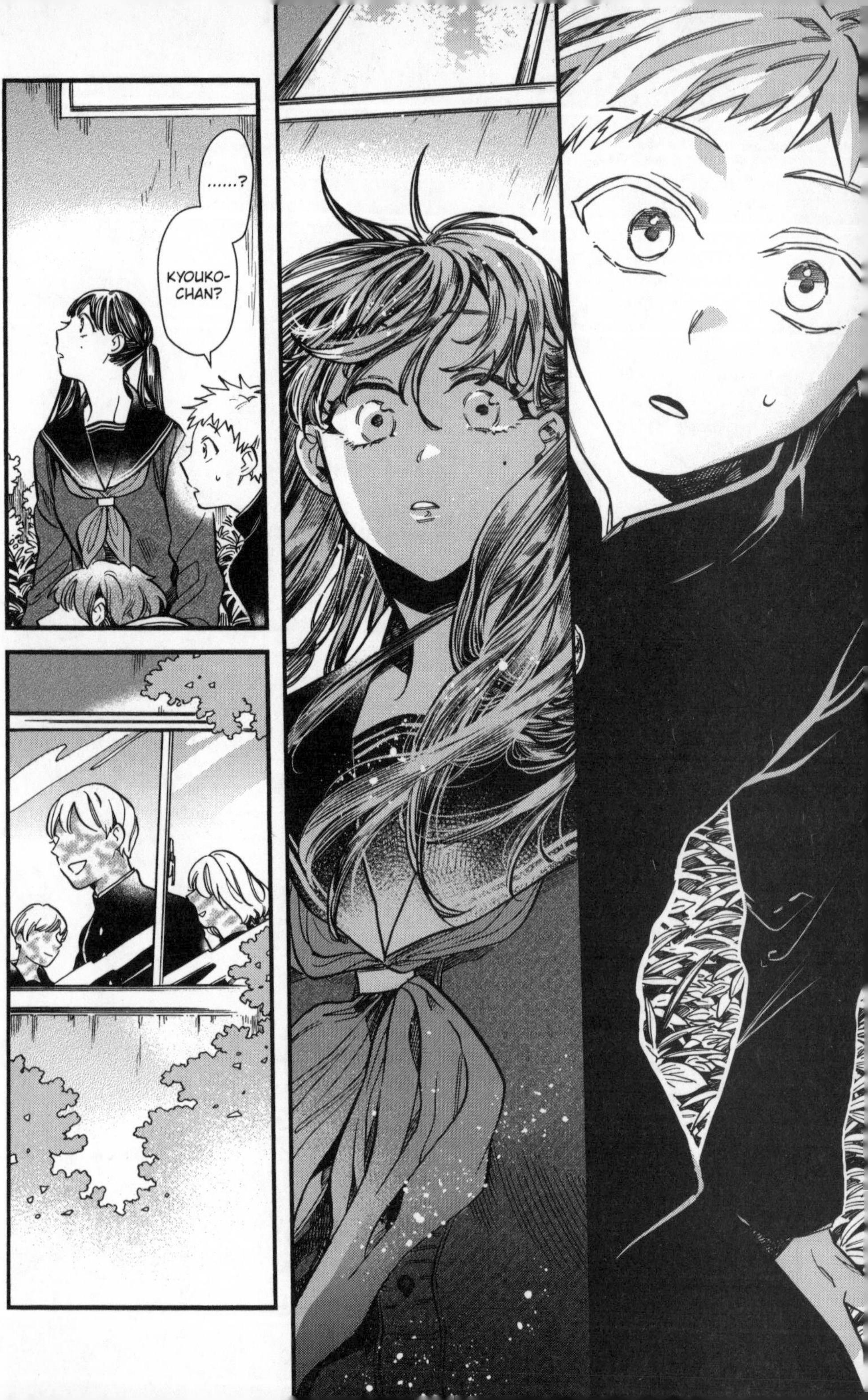

......?
KYOUKO-CHAN?

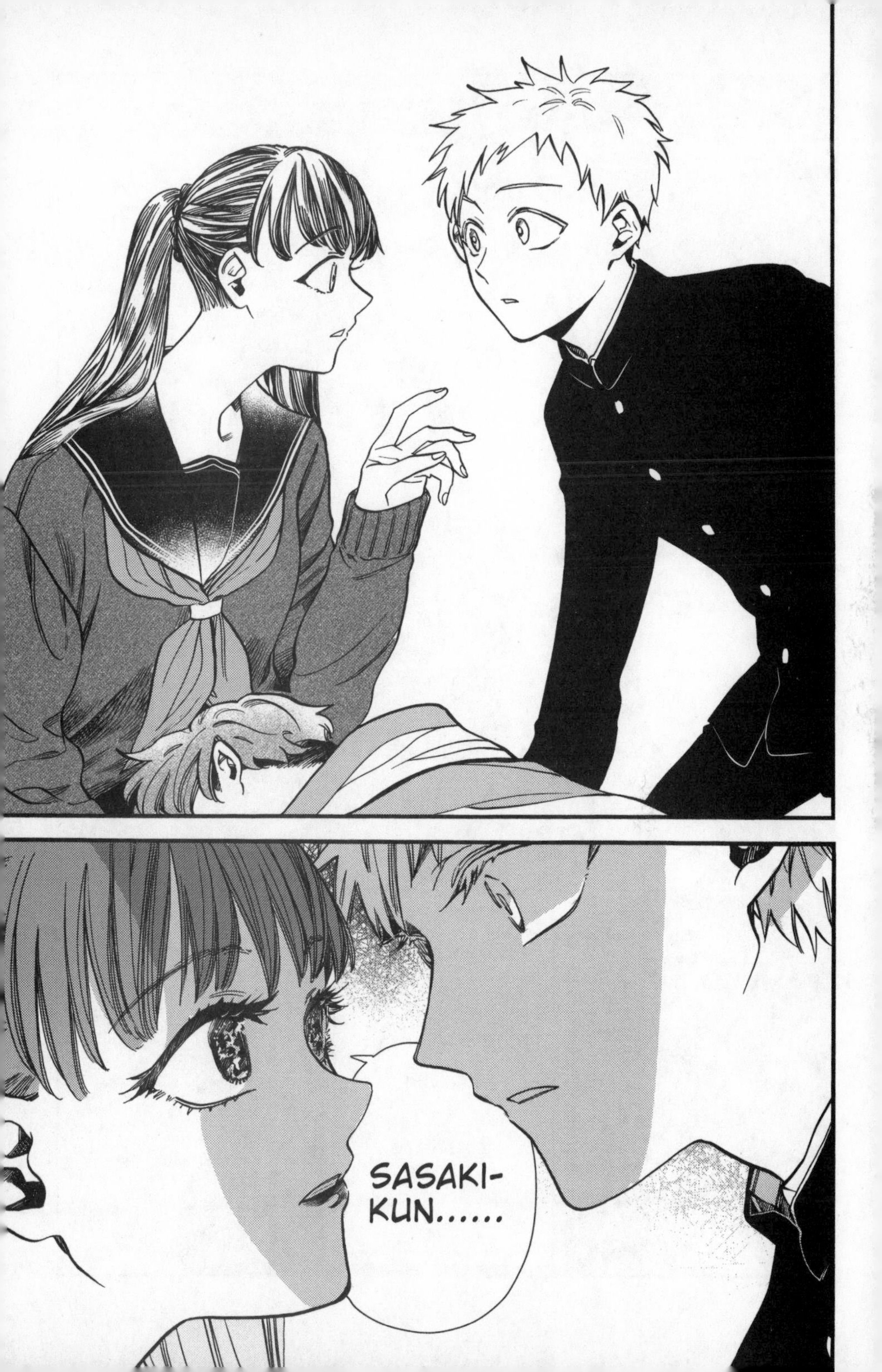
SASAKI-KUN......

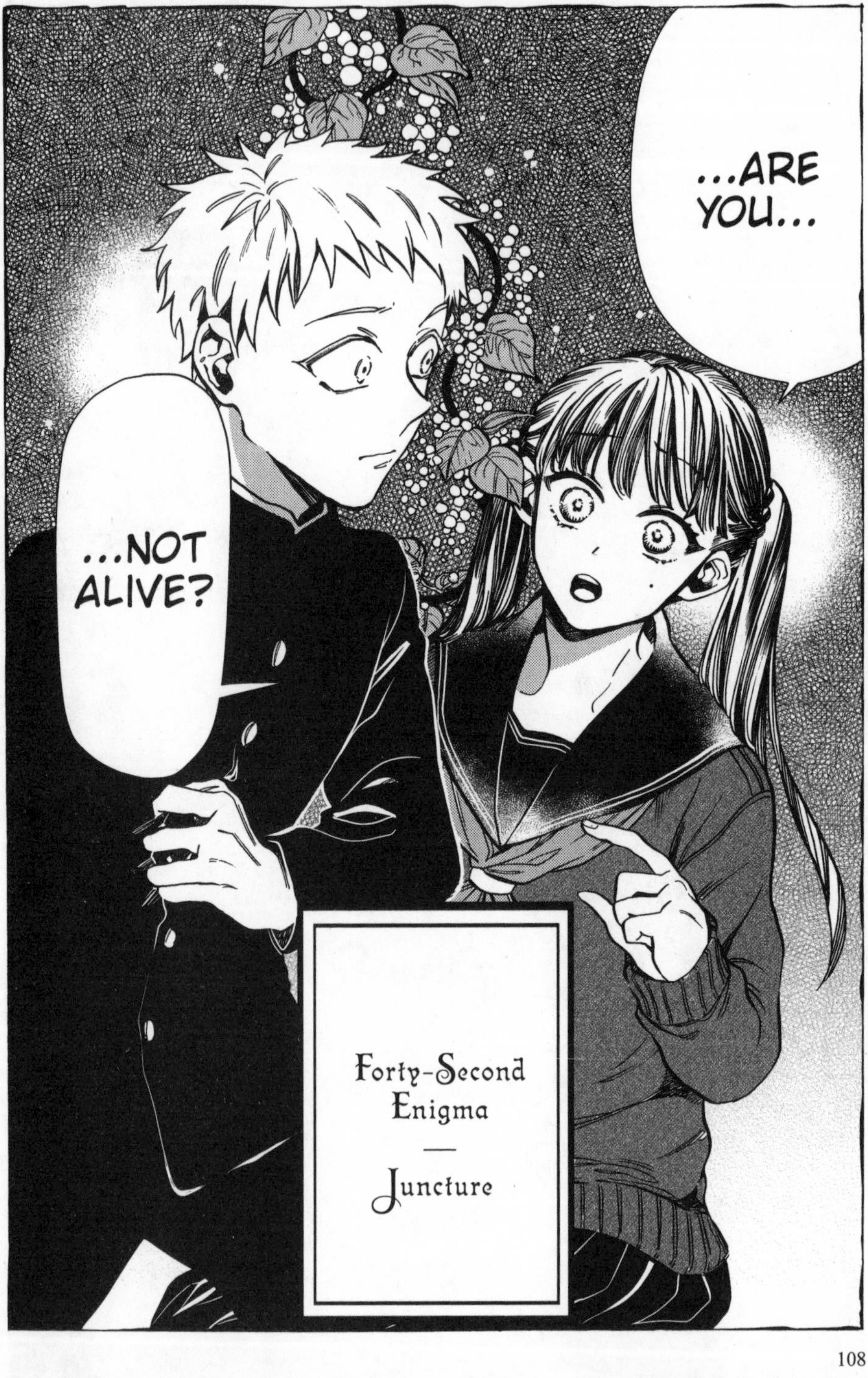
...ARE YOU...
...NOT ALIVE?
Forty-Second Enigma
—
Juncture

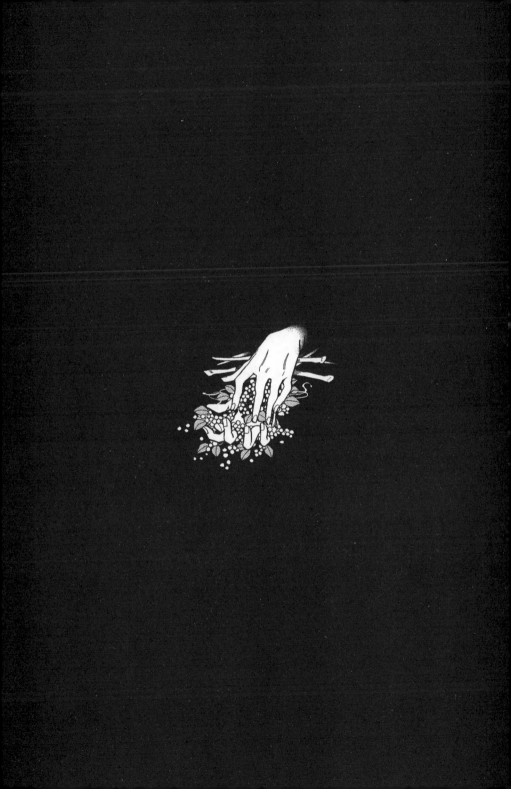

Phantom Tales of the Night

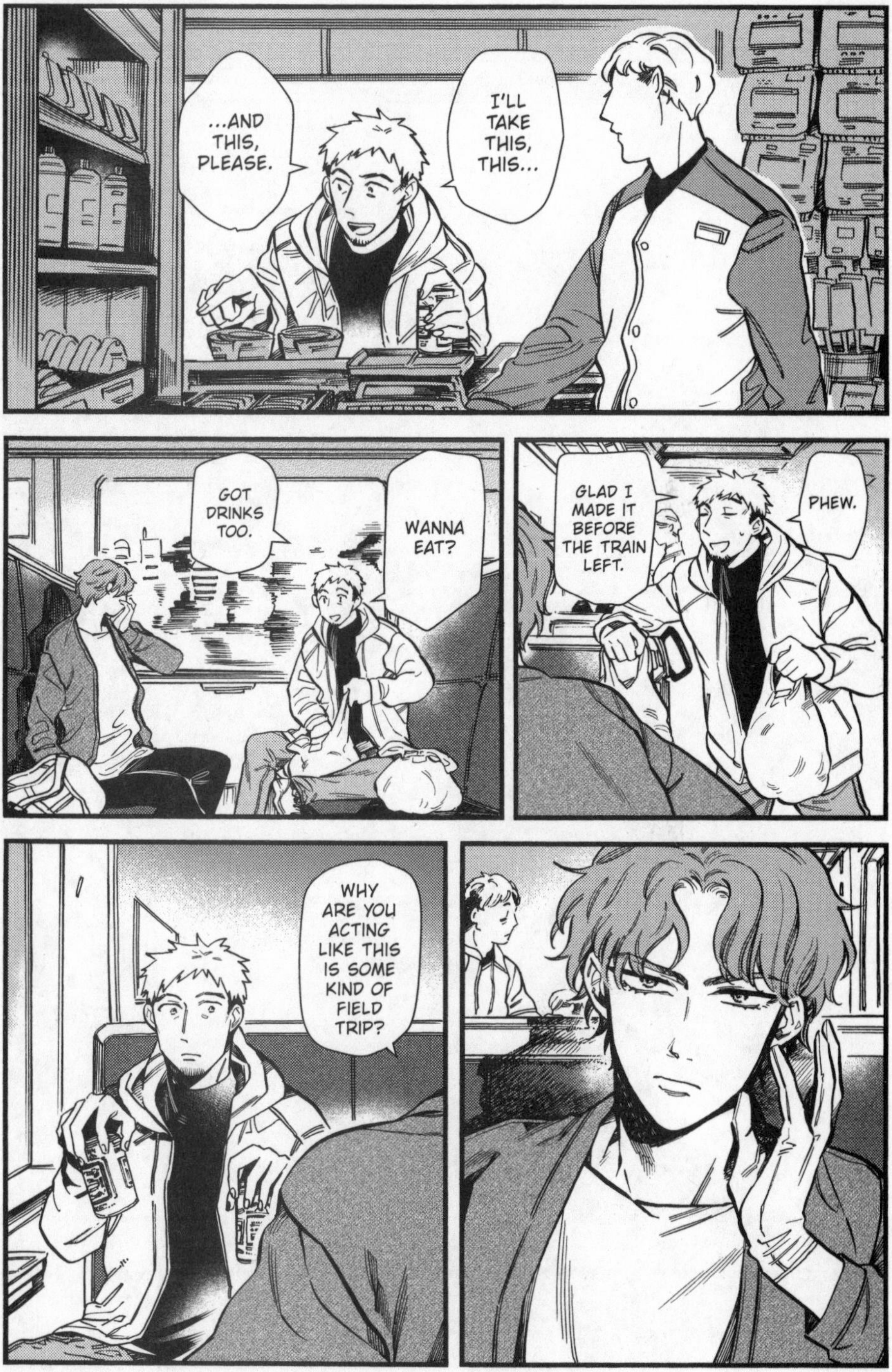
I'LL TAKE THIS, THIS...
...AND THIS, PLEASE.
PHEW.
GLAD I MADE IT BEFORE THE TRAIN LEFT.
WANNA EAT?
GOT DRINKS TOO.
WHY ARE YOU ACTING LIKE THIS IS SOME KIND OF FIELD TRIP?

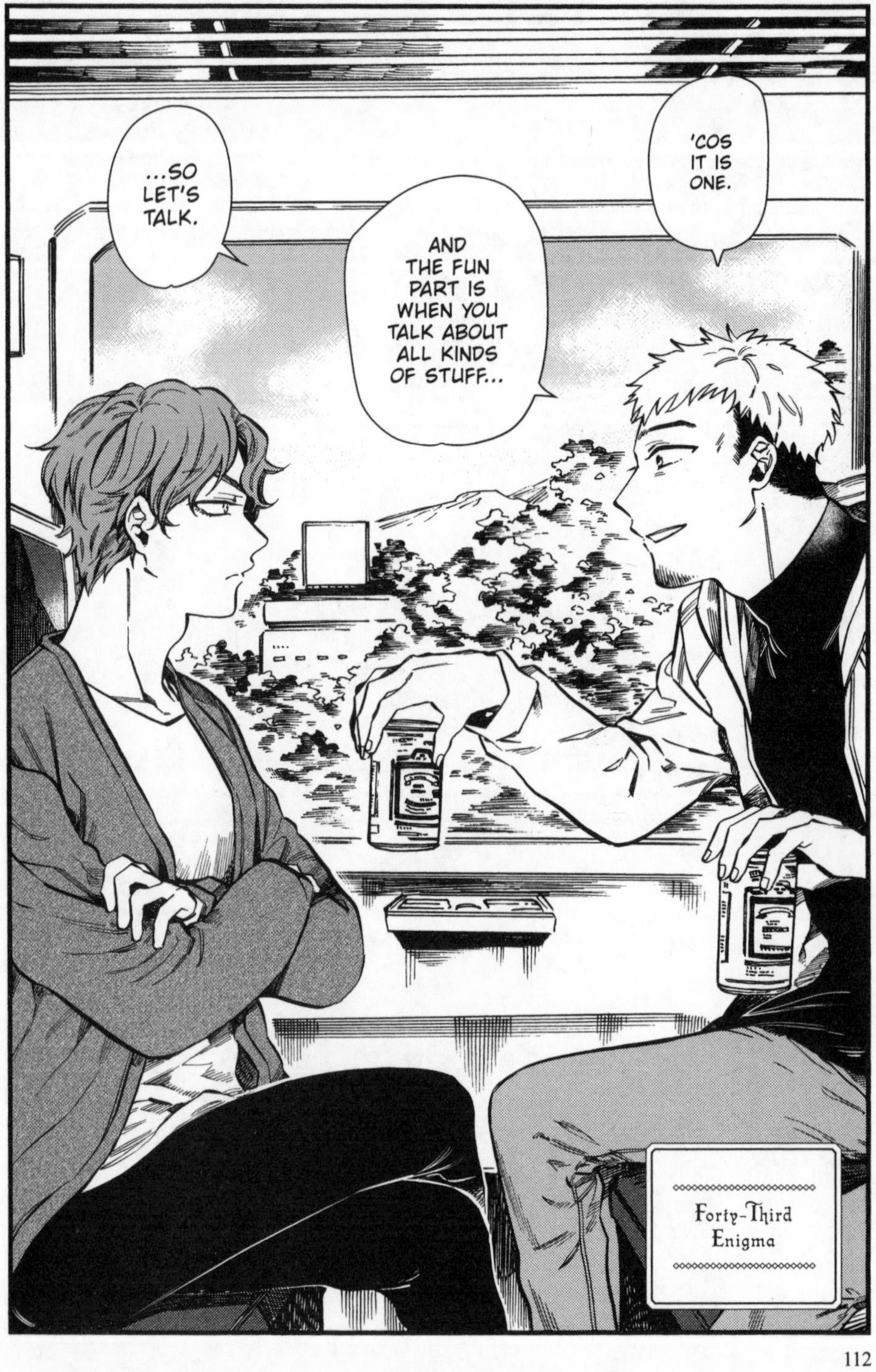
'COS IT IS ONE.
AND THE FUN PART IS WHEN YOU TALK ABOUT ALL KINDS OF STUFF...
...SO LET'S TALK.
Forty-Third Enigma

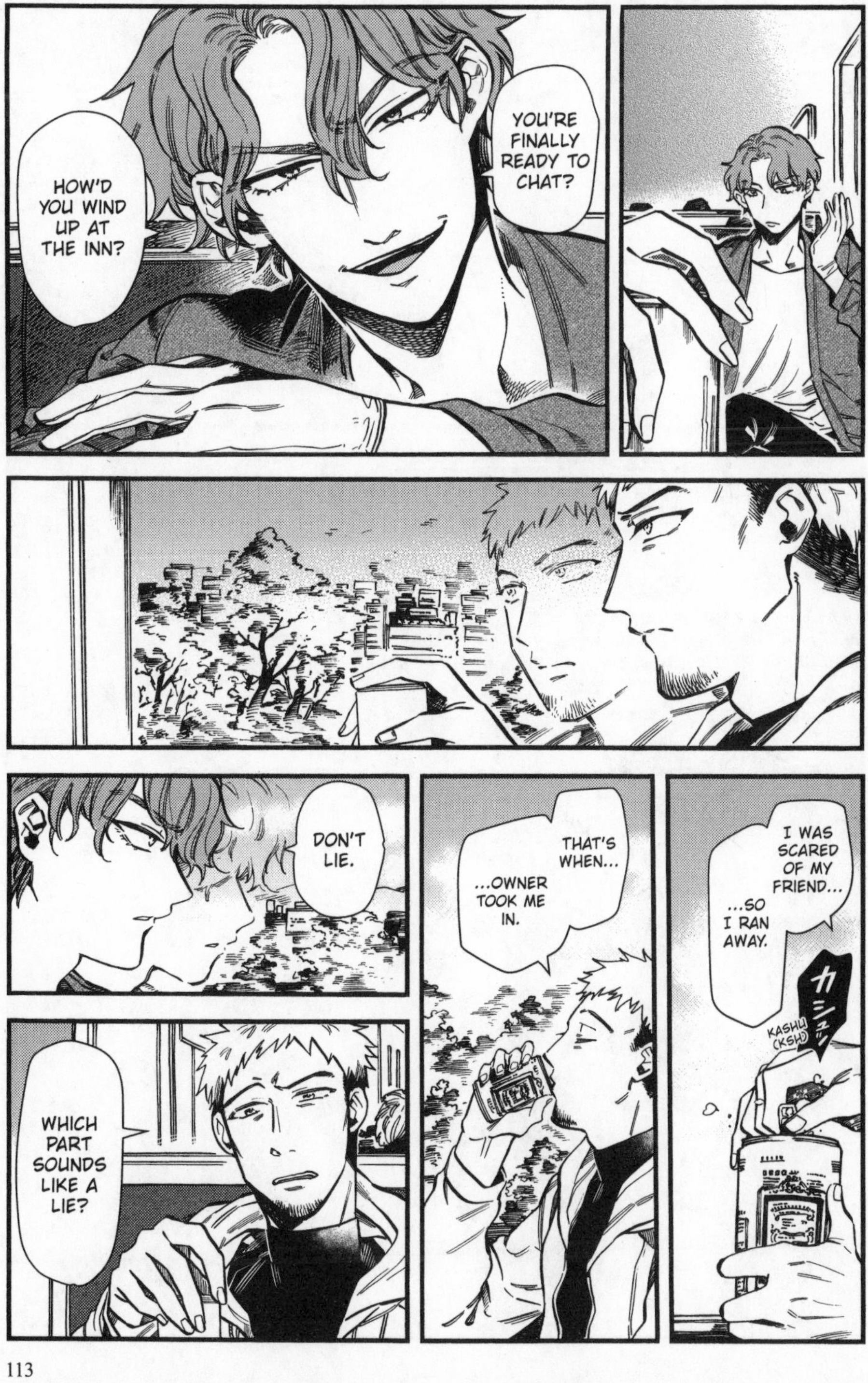
YOU'RE FINALLY READY TO CHAT?
HOW'D YOU WIND UP AT THE INN?
I WAS SCARED OF MY FRIEND...
...SO I RAN AWAY.
カシュ
KASHU (KSH)
THAT'S WHEN...
...OWNER TOOK ME IN.
DON'T LIE.
WHICH PART SOUNDS LIKE A LIE?

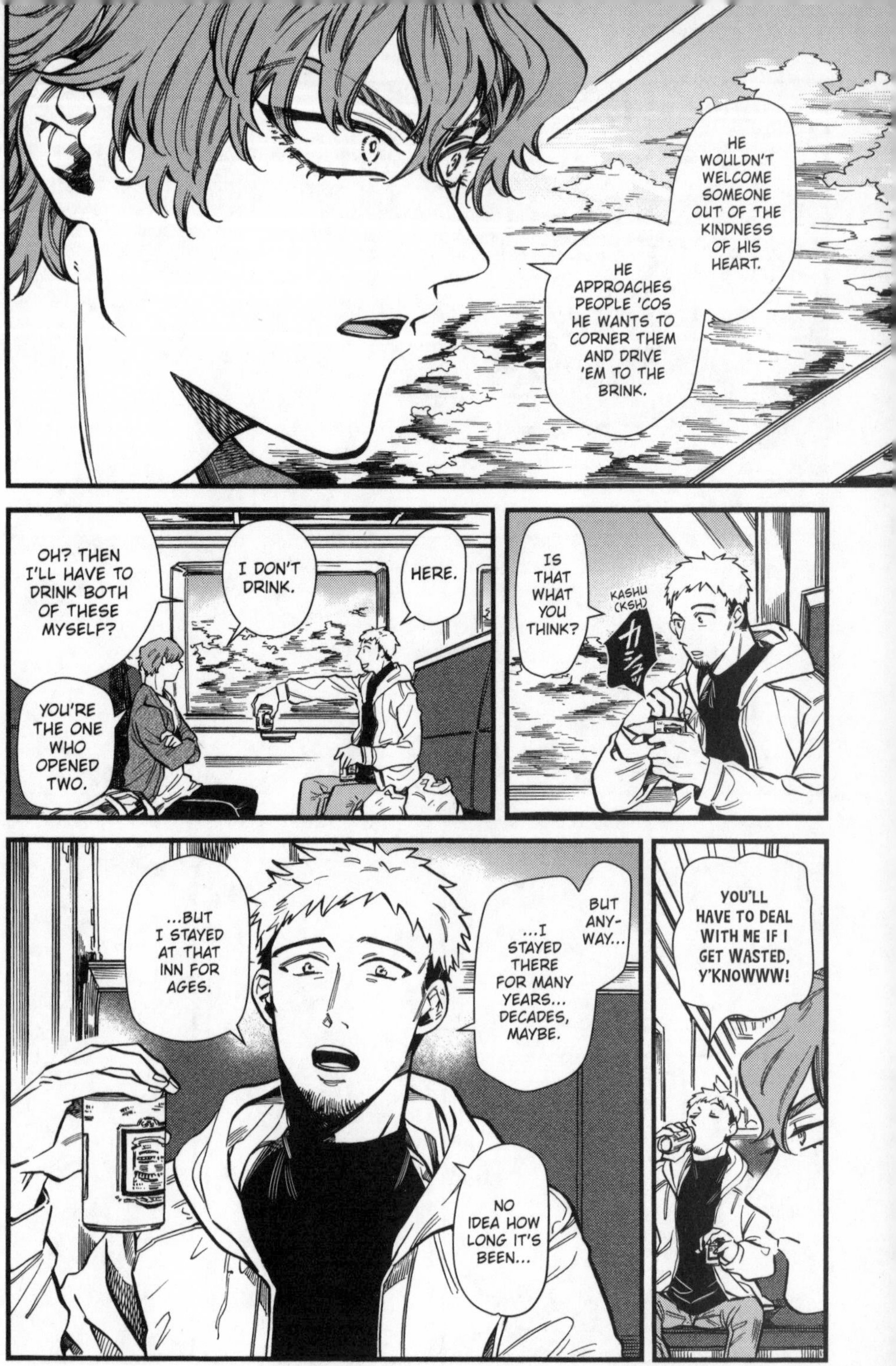
HE WOULDN'T WELCOME SOMEONE OUT OF THE KINDNESS OF HIS HEART.
HE APPROACHES PEOPLE 'COS HE WANTS TO CORNER THEM AND DRIVE 'EM TO THE BRINK.
IS THAT WHAT YOU THINK?
KASHU (KSH)
HERE.
I DON'T DRINK.
OH? THEN I'LL HAVE TO DRINK BOTH OF THESE MYSELF?
YOU'RE THE ONE WHO OPENED TWO.
YOU'LL HAVE TO DEAL WITH ME IF I GET WASTED, Y'KNOWWW!
BUT ANY-WAY...
...I STAYED THERE FOR MANY YEARS... DECADES, MAYBE.
...BUT I STAYED AT THAT INN FOR AGES.
NO IDEA HOW LONG IT'S BEEN...

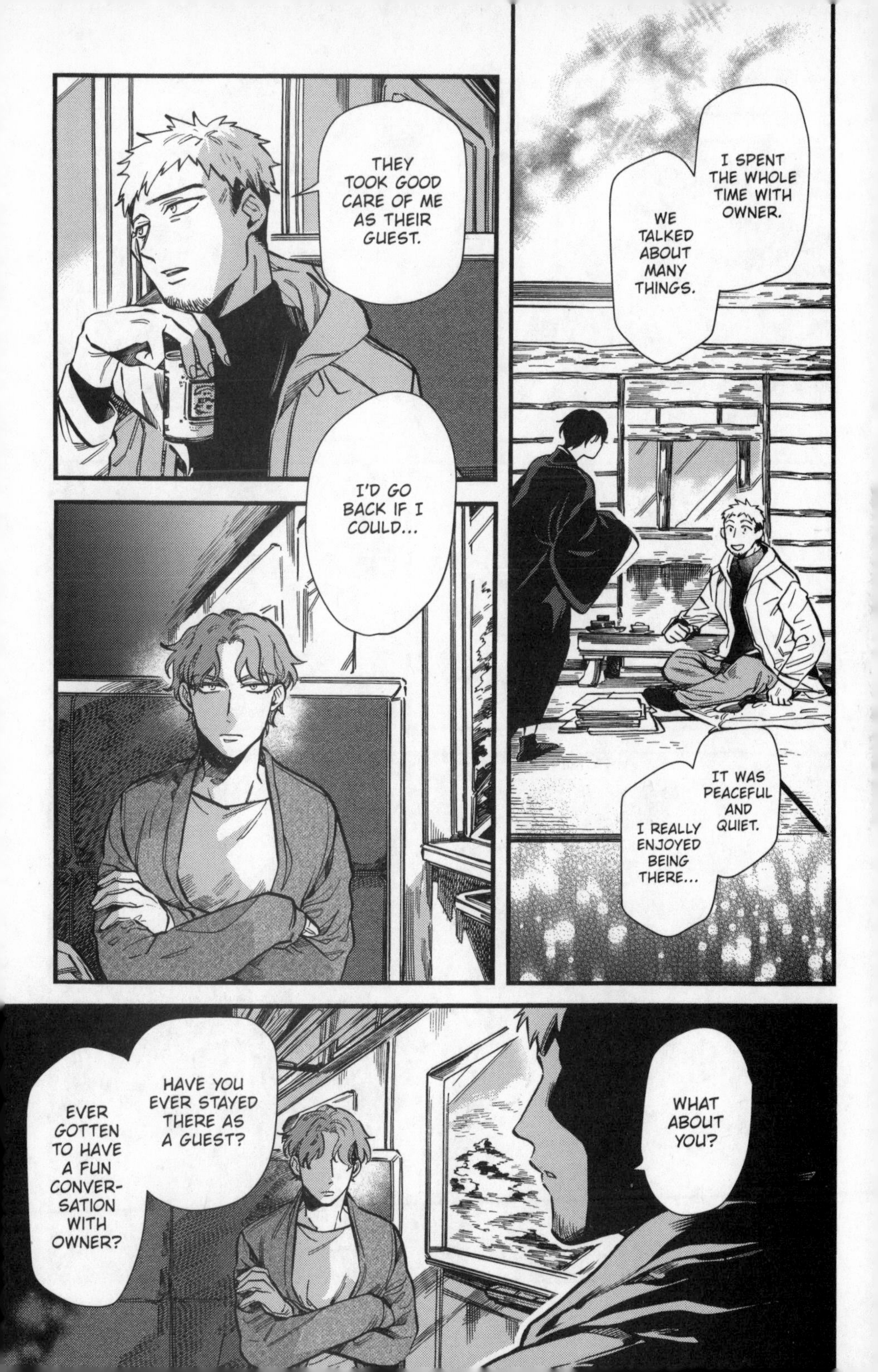
I SPENT THE WHOLE TIME WITH OWNER.
WE TALKED ABOUT MANY THINGS.
IT WAS PEACEFUL AND QUIET.
I REALLY ENJOYED BEING THERE...
THEY TOOK GOOD CARE OF ME AS THEIR GUEST.
I'D GO BACK IF I COULD...
WHAT ABOUT YOU?
HAVE YOU EVER STAYED THERE AS A GUEST?
EVER GOTTEN TO HAVE A FUN CONVER-SATION WITH OWNER?

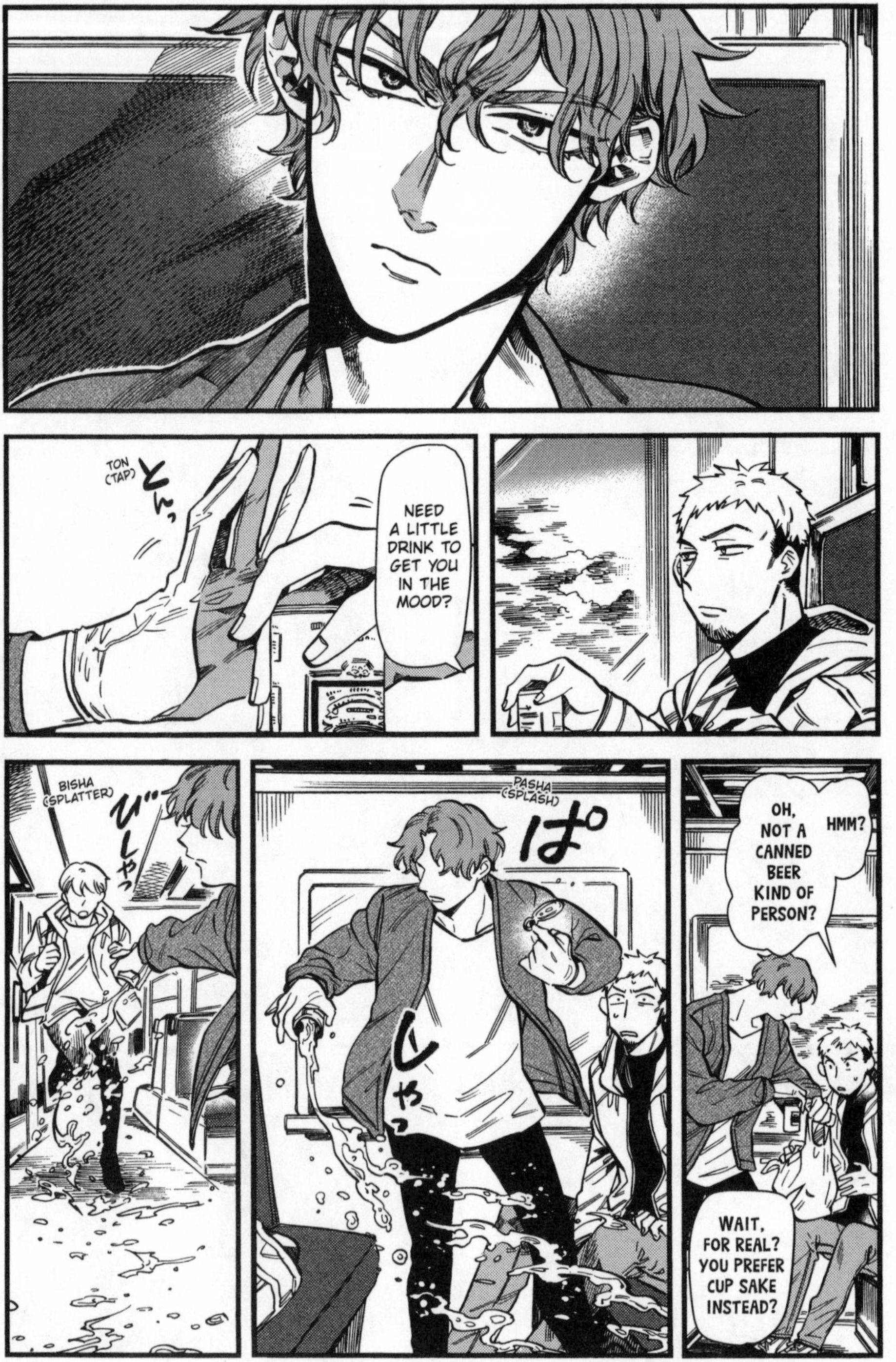

TON (TAP)
とんっ
NEED A LITTLE DRINK TO GET YOU IN THE MOOD?
HMM?
OH, NOT A CANNED BEER KIND OF PERSON?
WAIT, FOR REAL? YOU PREFER CUP SAKE INSTEAD?
PASHA (SPLASH)
ぱしゃっ
BISHA (SPLATTER)
びしゃっ

ゾ
ZO
(SLITHER)

ゾ
ZO

ゾ
ZO

ド
ZO

ゾ
ZO

ゾ
ZO

ゾ
ZO

AAH! IT BURNS!

IT BURNS!

HERE THEY COME.

SNAKES —!?

WHOA!?

PETO (PLIP)
ペと

PETO
ペと

PETO
ペと…

GOOOOOOO (RUMBLE)
ゴォォ
オ
オ

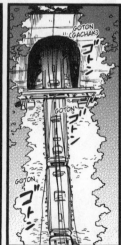

GOTON (GACHAK)
ゴトン

GOTON
ゴトン

GOTON
ゴトン

GOTON
ゴトン

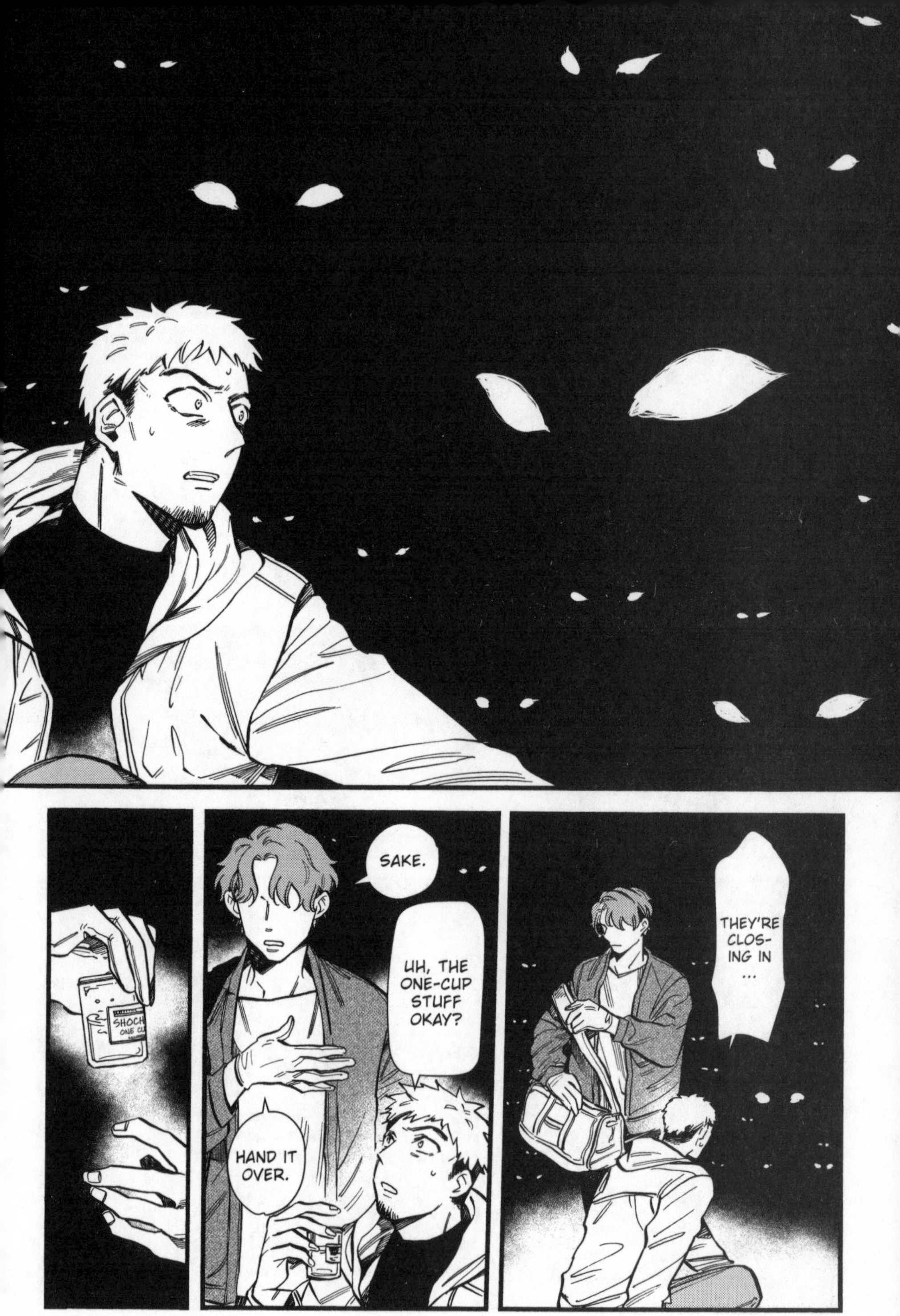
THEY'RE CLOS-ING IN ...
SAKE.
UH, THE ONE-CUP STUFF OKAY?
HAND IT OVER.

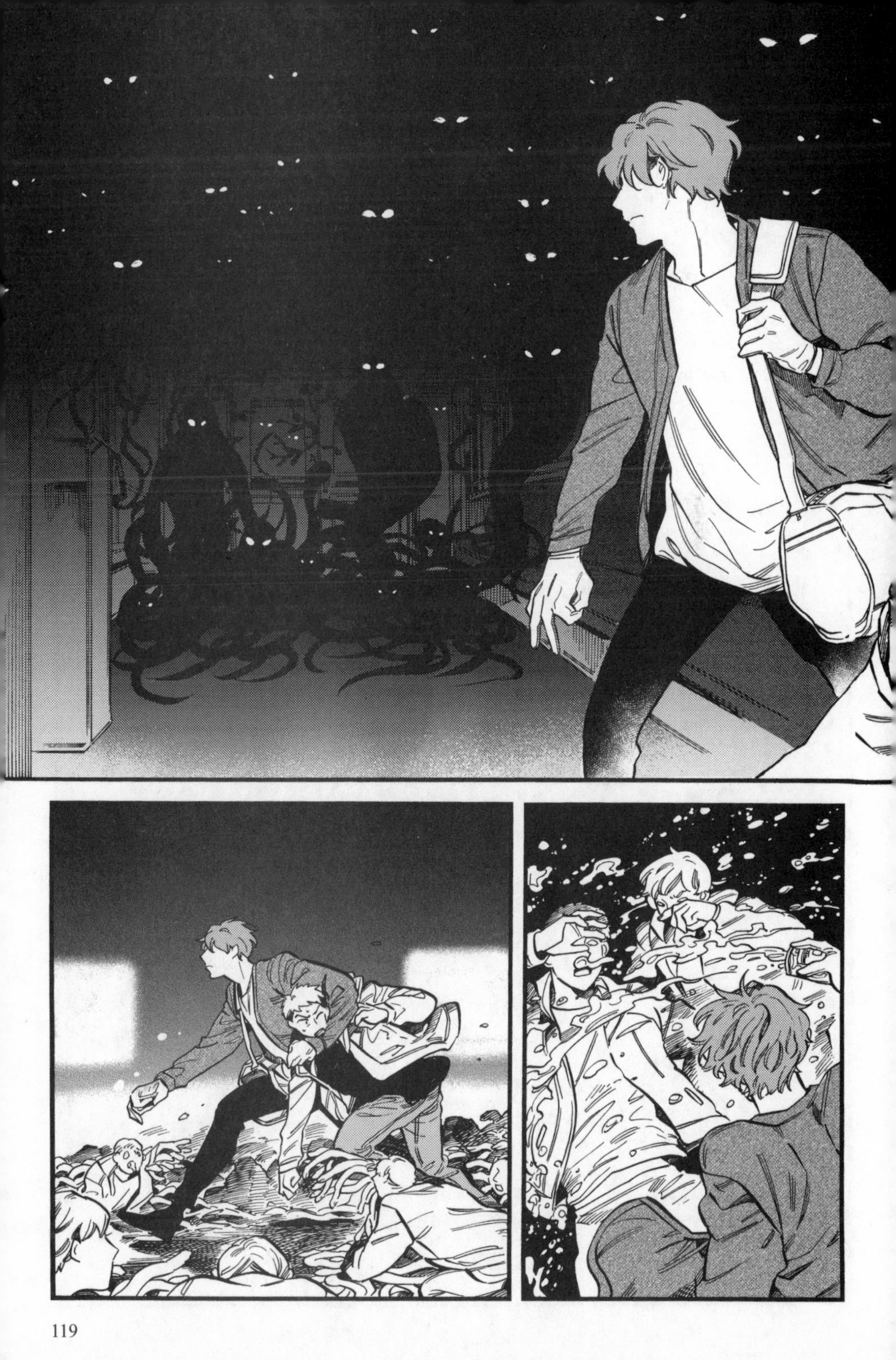

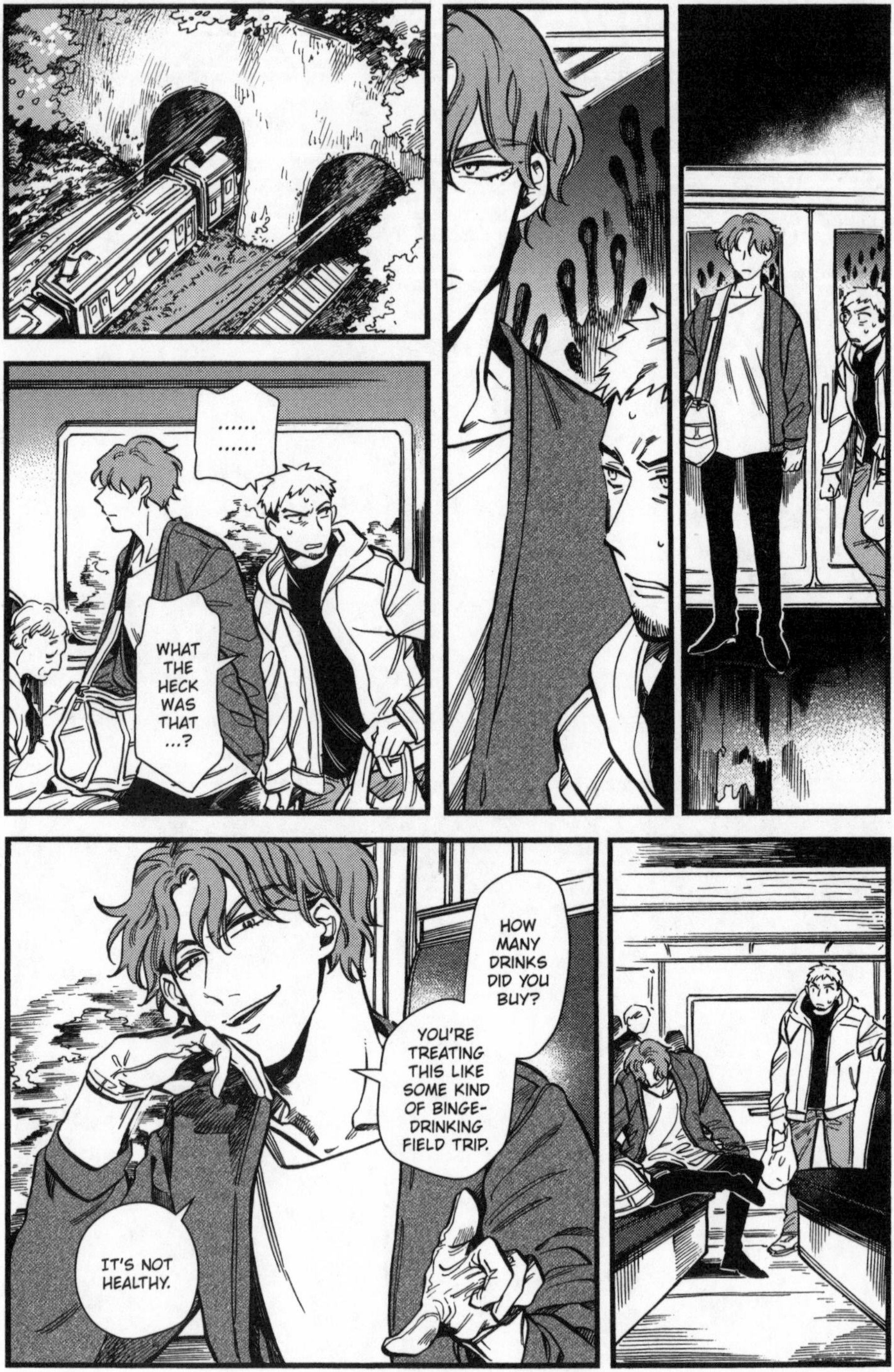
......
......
WHAT THE HECK WAS THAT ...?
HOW MANY DRINKS DID YOU BUY?
YOU'RE TREATING THIS LIKE SOME KIND OF BINGE-DRINKING FIELD TRIP.
IT'S NOT HEALTHY.

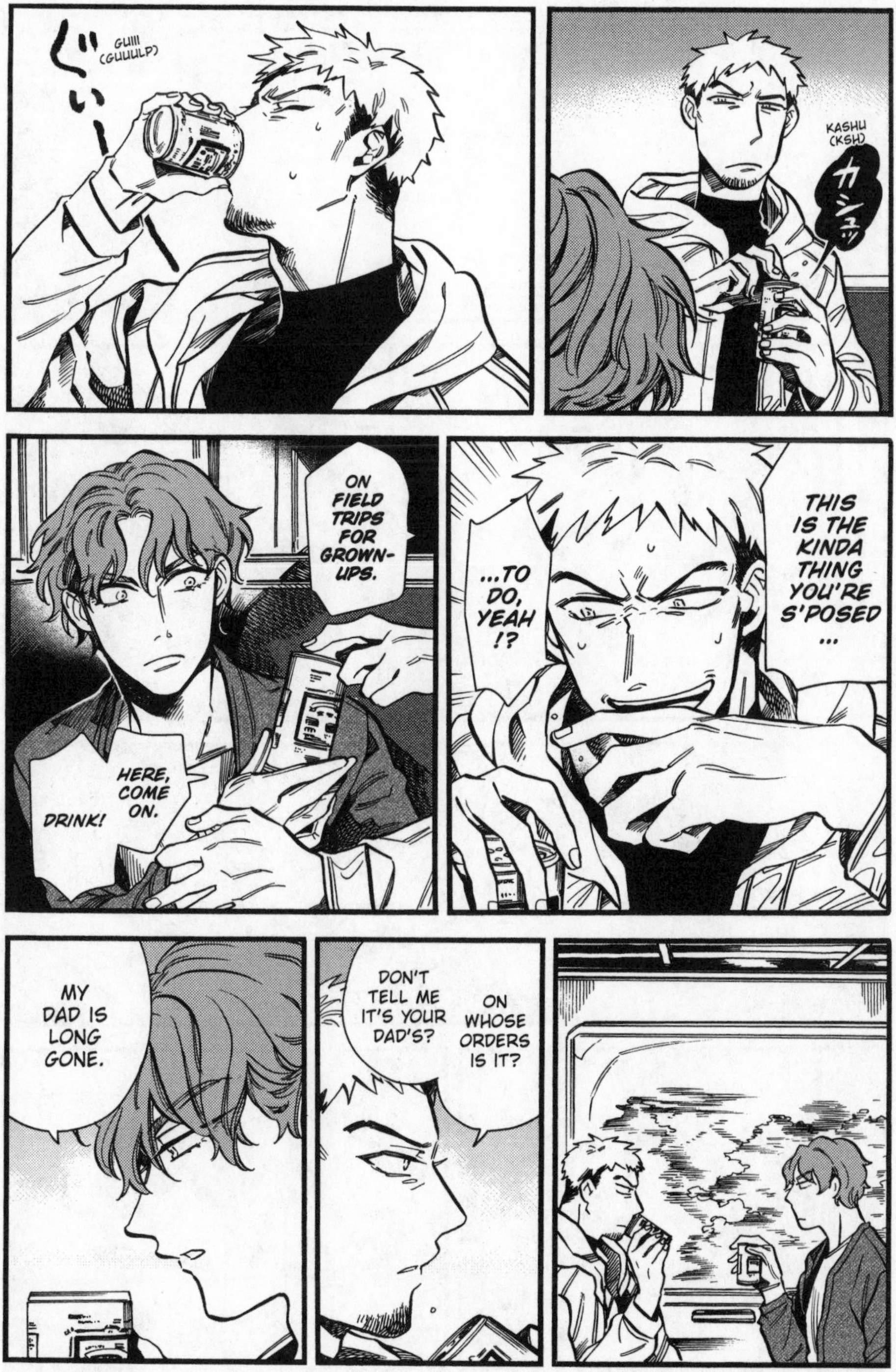
KASHU (KSH)
カシュッ
ぐいー
GUIII (GUUULP)
THIS IS THE KINDA THING YOU'RE S'POSED...
...TO DO, YEAH!?
ON FIELD TRIPS FOR GROWN-UPS.
HERE, COME ON.
DRINK!
ON WHOSE ORDERS IS IT?
DON'T TELL ME IT'S YOUR DAD'S?
MY DAD IS LONG GONE.

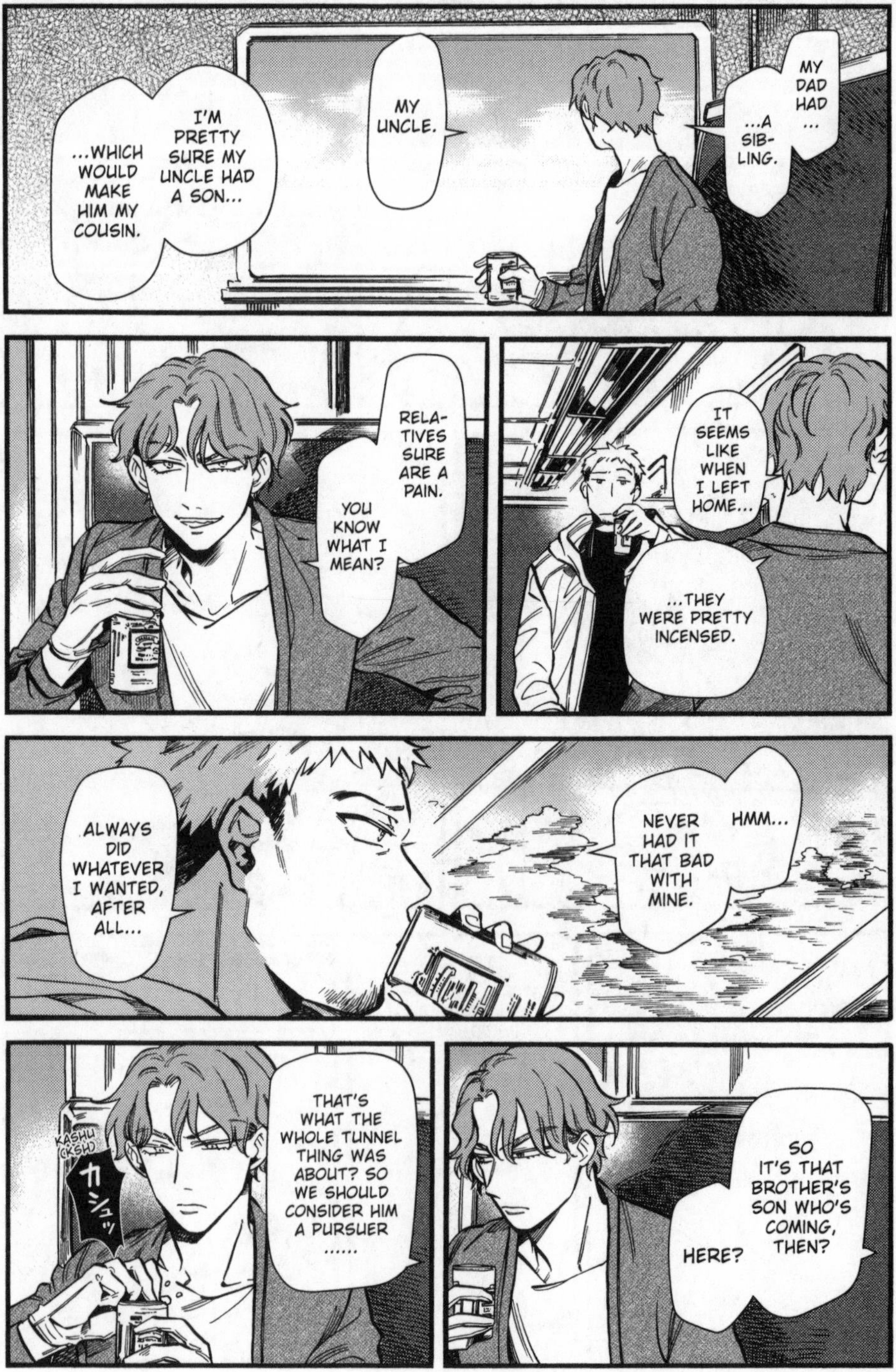
MY DAD HAD...
...A SIBLING.
MY UNCLE.
I'M PRETTY SURE MY UNCLE HAD A SON...
...WHICH WOULD MAKE HIM MY COUSIN.
IT SEEMS LIKE WHEN I LEFT HOME...
...THEY WERE PRETTY INCENSED.
RELATIVES SURE ARE A PAIN.
YOU KNOW WHAT I MEAN?
HMM...
NEVER HAD IT THAT BAD WITH MINE.
ALWAYS DID WHATEVER I WANTED, AFTER ALL...
SO IT'S THAT BROTHER'S SON WHO'S COMING, THEN?
HERE?
カシュッ
KASHU (KSH)
THAT'S WHAT THE WHOLE TUNNEL THING WAS ABOUT? SO WE SHOULD CONSIDER HIM A PURSUER ......

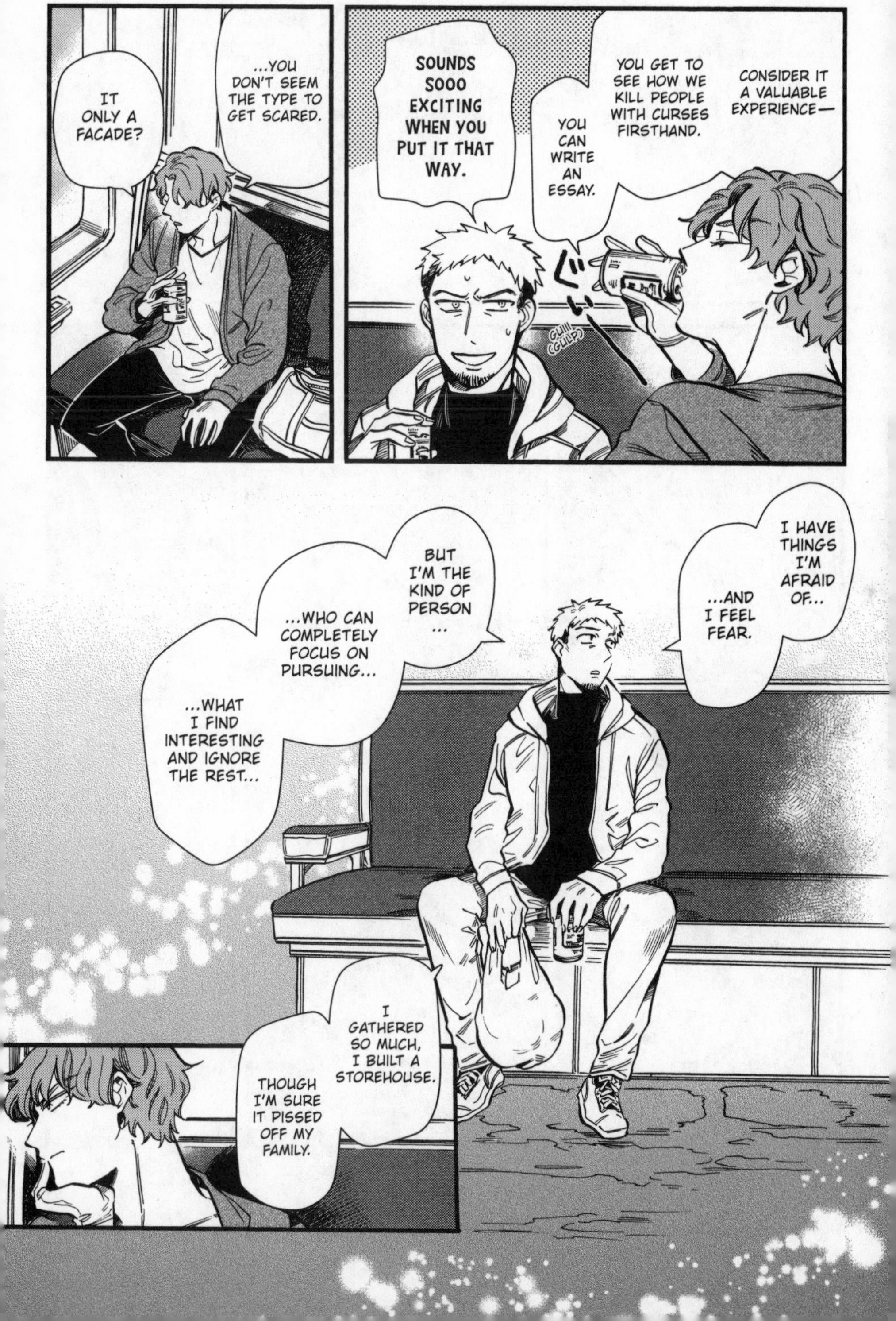
CONSIDER IT A VALUABLE EXPERIENCE—
YOU GET TO SEE HOW WE KILL PEOPLE WITH CURSES FIRSTHAND.
YOU CAN WRITE AN ESSAY.
ぐい
GUIII (GULP)
SOUNDS SOOO EXCITING WHEN YOU PUT IT THAT WAY.
...YOU DON'T SEEM THE TYPE TO GET SCARED.
IT ONLY A FACADE?
I HAVE THINGS I'M AFRAID OF...
...AND I FEEL FEAR.
BUT I'M THE KIND OF PERSON...
...WHO CAN COMPLETELY FOCUS ON PURSUING...
...WHAT I FIND INTERESTING AND IGNORE THE REST...
I GATHERED SO MUCH, I BUILT A STOREHOUSE.
THOUGH I'M SURE IT PISSED OFF MY FAMILY.

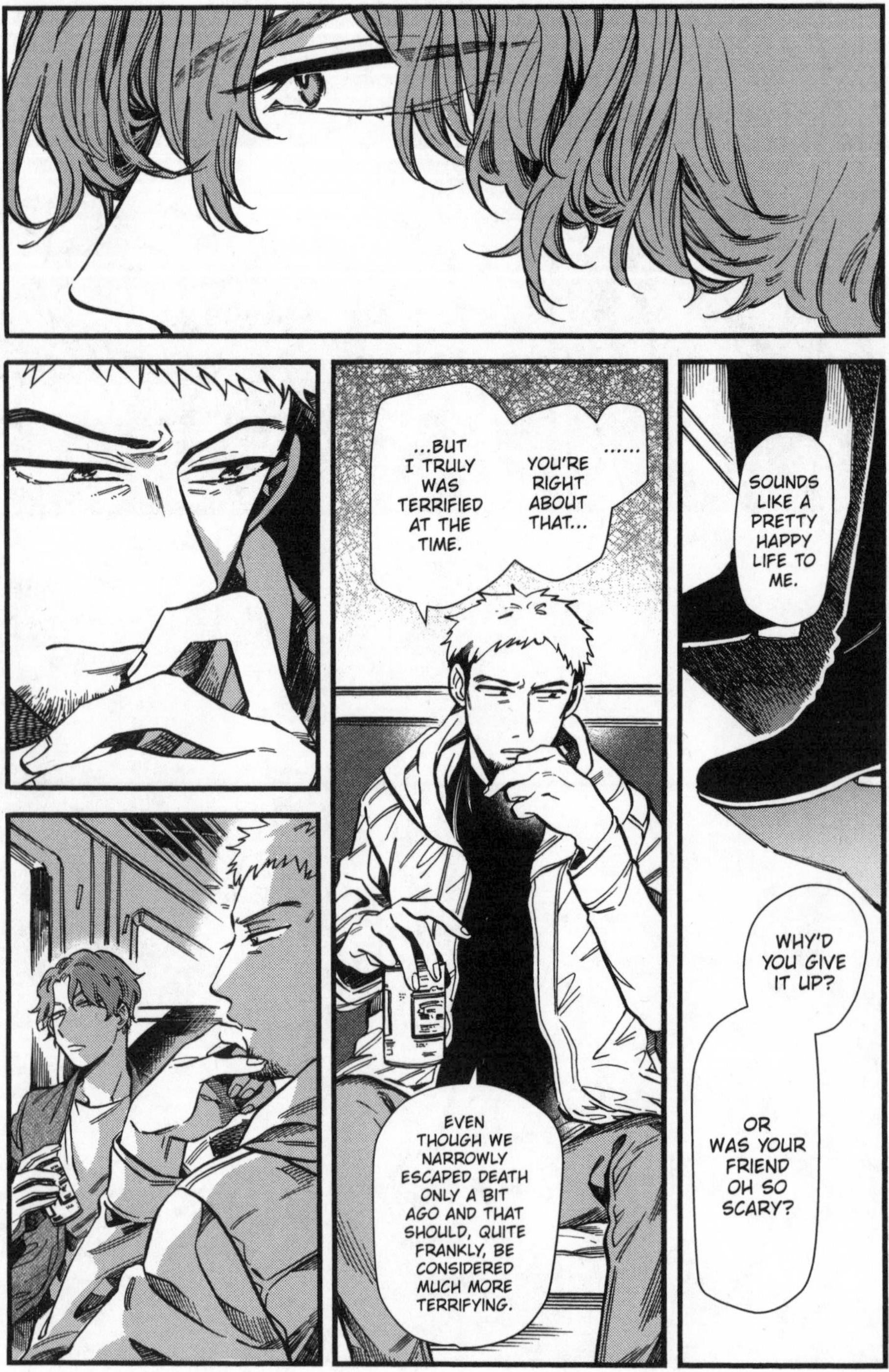
SOUNDS LIKE A PRETTY HAPPY LIFE TO ME.
WHY'D YOU GIVE IT UP?
OR WAS YOUR FRIEND OH SO SCARY?
......
YOU'RE RIGHT ABOUT THAT...
...BUT I TRULY WAS TERRIFIED AT THE TIME.
EVEN THOUGH WE NARROWLY ESCAPED DEATH ONLY A BIT AGO AND THAT SHOULD, QUITE FRANKLY, BE CONSIDERED MUCH MORE TERRIFYING.

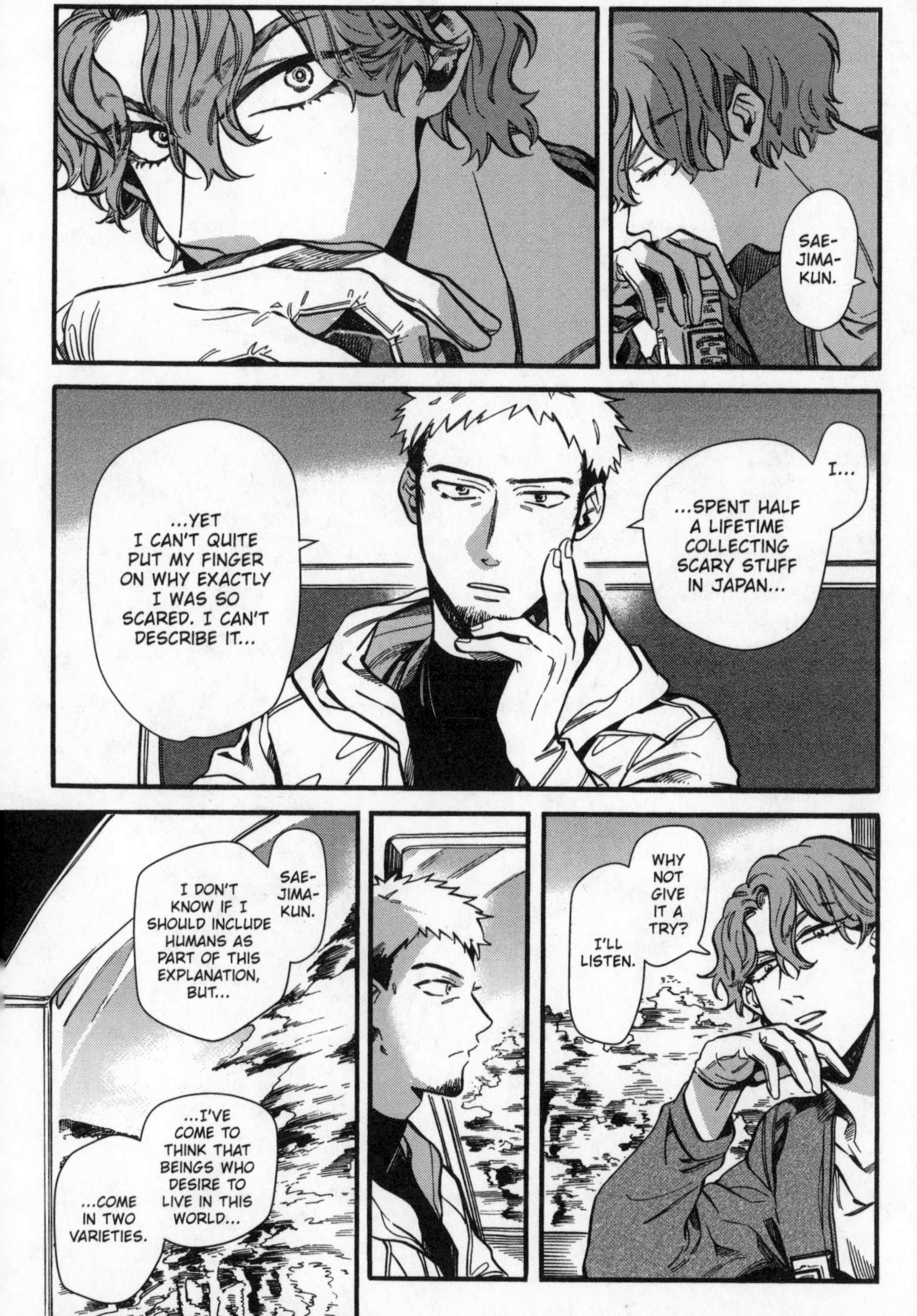
SAE-JIMA-KUN.
I...
...SPENT HALF A LIFETIME COLLECTING SCARY STUFF IN JAPAN...
...YET I CAN'T QUITE PUT MY FINGER ON WHY EXACTLY I WAS SO SCARED. I CAN'T DESCRIBE IT...
WHY NOT GIVE IT A TRY?
I'LL LISTEN.
SAE-JIMA-KUN.
I DON'T KNOW IF I SHOULD INCLUDE HUMANS AS PART OF THIS EXPLANATION, BUT...
...I'VE COME TO THINK THAT BEINGS WHO DESIRE TO LIVE IN THIS WORLD...
...COME IN TWO VARIETIES.

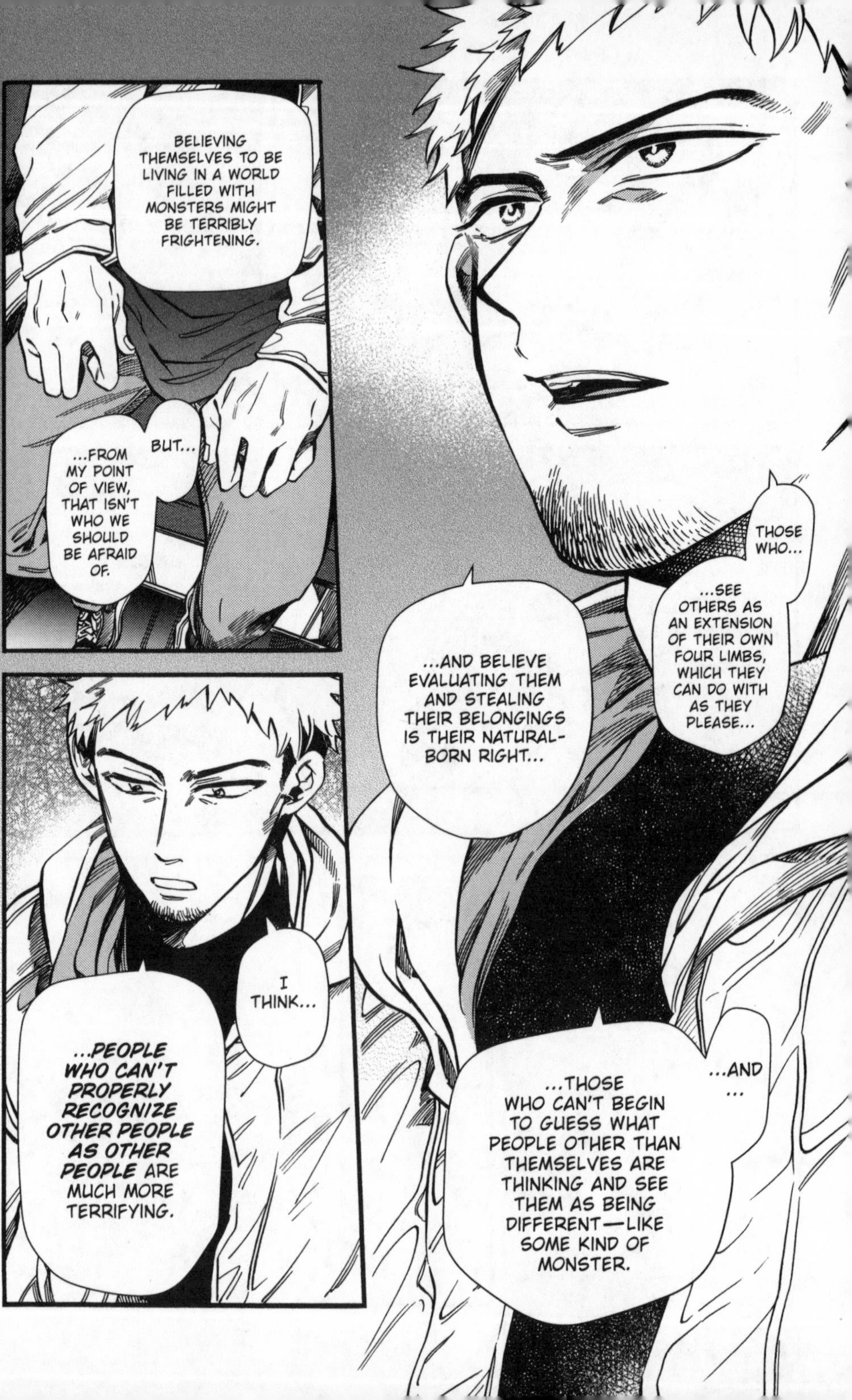

THOSE WHO...
...SEE OTHERS AS AN EXTENSION OF THEIR OWN FOUR LIMBS, WHICH THEY CAN DO WITH AS THEY PLEASE...
...AND BELIEVE EVALUATING THEM AND STEALING THEIR BELONGINGS IS THEIR NATURAL-BORN RIGHT...
...AND...
...THOSE WHO CAN'T BEGIN TO GUESS WHAT PEOPLE OTHER THAN THEMSELVES ARE THINKING AND SEE THEM AS BEING DIFFERENT—LIKE SOME KIND OF MONSTER.
BELIEVING THEMSELVES TO BE LIVING IN A WORLD FILLED WITH MONSTERS MIGHT BE TERRIBLY FRIGHTENING.
BUT...
...FROM MY POINT OF VIEW, THAT ISN'T WHO WE SHOULD BE AFRAID OF.
I THINK...
...PEOPLE WHO CAN'T PROPERLY RECOGNIZE OTHER PEOPLE AS OTHER PEOPLE ARE MUCH MORE TERRIFYING.

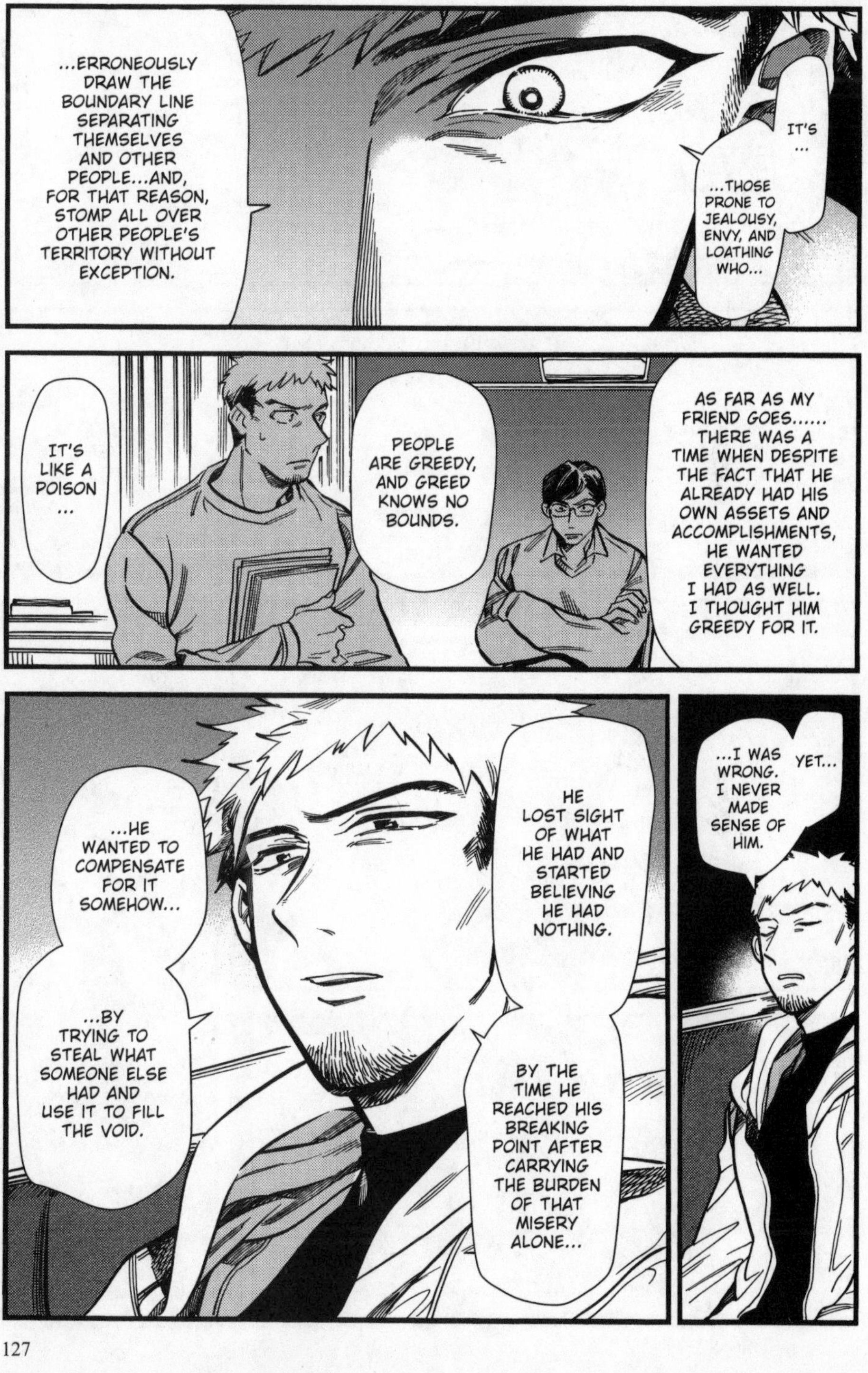
IT'S ...
...THOSE PRONE TO JEALOUSY, ENVY, AND LOATHING WHO...
...ERRONEOUSLY DRAW THE BOUNDARY LINE SEPARATING THEMSELVES AND OTHER PEOPLE...AND, FOR THAT REASON, STOMP ALL OVER OTHER PEOPLE'S TERRITORY WITHOUT EXCEPTION.
AS FAR AS MY FRIEND GOES...... THERE WAS A TIME WHEN DESPITE THE FACT THAT HE ALREADY HAD HIS OWN ASSETS AND ACCOMPLISHMENTS, HE WANTED EVERYTHING I HAD AS WELL. I THOUGHT HIM GREEDY FOR IT.
PEOPLE ARE GREEDY, AND GREED KNOWS NO BOUNDS.
IT'S LIKE A POISON ...
YET...
...I WAS WRONG. I NEVER MADE SENSE OF HIM.
HE LOST SIGHT OF WHAT HE HAD AND STARTED BELIEVING HE HAD NOTHING.
BY THE TIME HE REACHED HIS BREAKING POINT AFTER CARRYING THE BURDEN OF THAT MISERY ALONE...
...HE WANTED TO COMPENSATE FOR IT SOMEHOW...
...BY TRYING TO STEAL WHAT SOMEONE ELSE HAD AND USE IT TO FILL THE VOID.

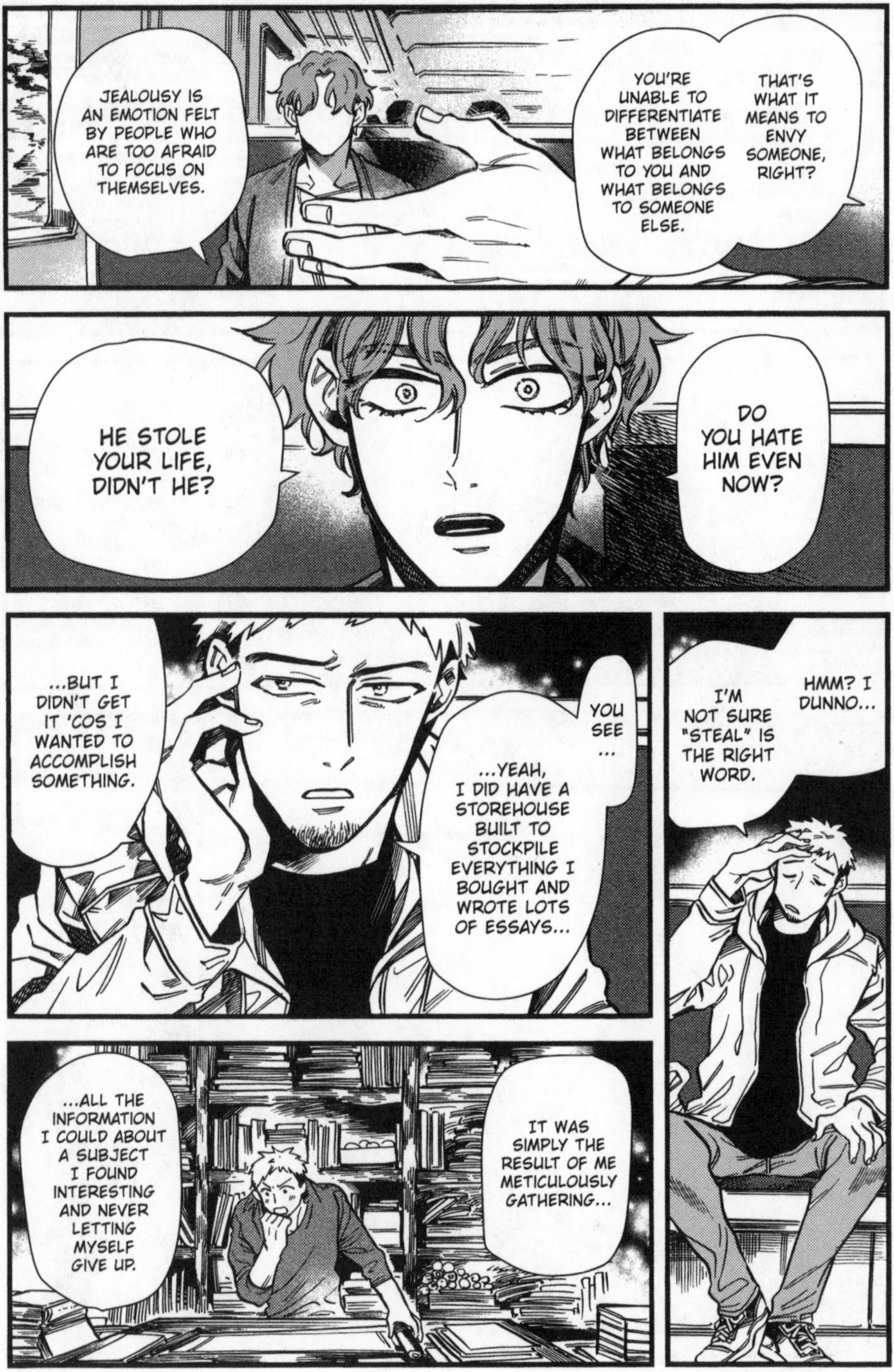
THAT'S WHAT IT MEANS TO ENVY SOMEONE, RIGHT?
YOU'RE UNABLE TO DIFFERENTIATE BETWEEN WHAT BELONGS TO YOU AND WHAT BELONGS TO SOMEONE ELSE.
JEALOUSY IS AN EMOTION FELT BY PEOPLE WHO ARE TOO AFRAID TO FOCUS ON THEMSELVES.
DO YOU HATE HIM EVEN NOW?
HE STOLE YOUR LIFE, DIDN'T HE?
HMM? I DUNNO...
I'M NOT SURE "STEAL" IS THE RIGHT WORD.
YOU SEE...
...YEAH, I DID HAVE A STOREHOUSE BUILT TO STOCKPILE EVERYTHING I BOUGHT AND WROTE LOTS OF ESSAYS...
...BUT I DIDN'T GET IT 'COS I WANTED TO ACCOMPLISH SOMETHING.
IT WAS SIMPLY THE RESULT OF ME METICULOUSLY GATHERING...
...ALL THE INFORMATION I COULD ABOUT A SUBJECT I FOUND INTERESTING AND NEVER LETTING MYSELF GIVE UP.

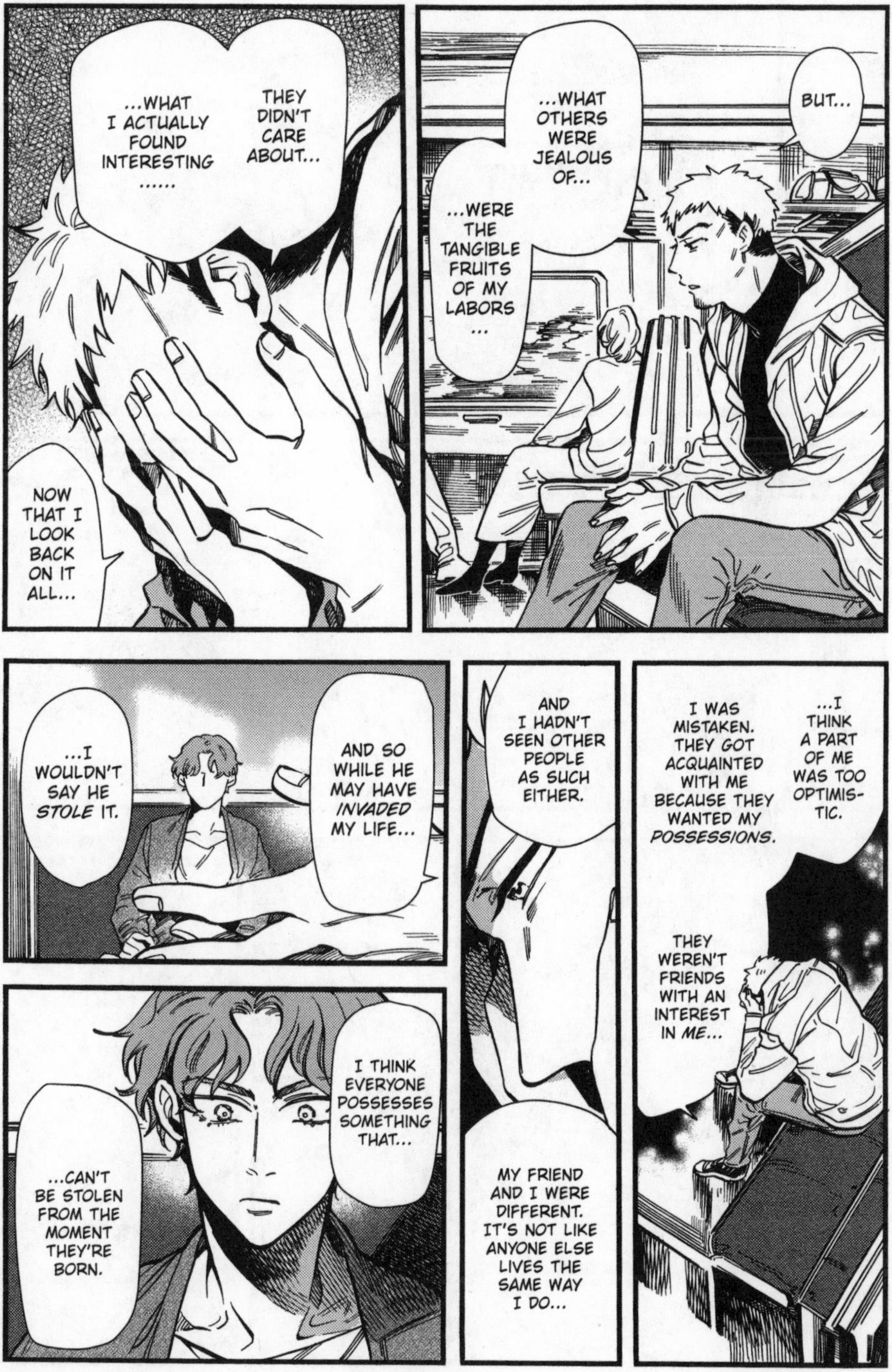
BUT...
...WHAT OTHERS WERE JEALOUS OF...
...WERE THE TANGIBLE FRUITS OF MY LABORS...
THEY DIDN'T CARE ABOUT...
...WHAT I ACTUALLY FOUND INTERESTING......
NOW THAT I LOOK BACK ON IT ALL...
...I THINK A PART OF ME WAS TOO OPTIMISTIC.
I WAS MISTAKEN. THEY GOT ACQUAINTED WITH ME BECAUSE THEY WANTED MY *POSSESSIONS*.
THEY WEREN'T FRIENDS WITH AN INTEREST IN *ME*...
AND I HADN'T SEEN OTHER PEOPLE AS SUCH EITHER.
MY FRIEND AND I WERE DIFFERENT. IT'S NOT LIKE ANYONE ELSE LIVES THE SAME WAY I DO...
AND SO WHILE HE MAY HAVE *INVADED* MY LIFE...
...I WOULDN'T SAY HE *STOLE* IT.
I THINK EVERYONE POSSESSES SOMETHING THAT...
...CAN'T BE STOLEN FROM THE MOMENT THEY'RE BORN.

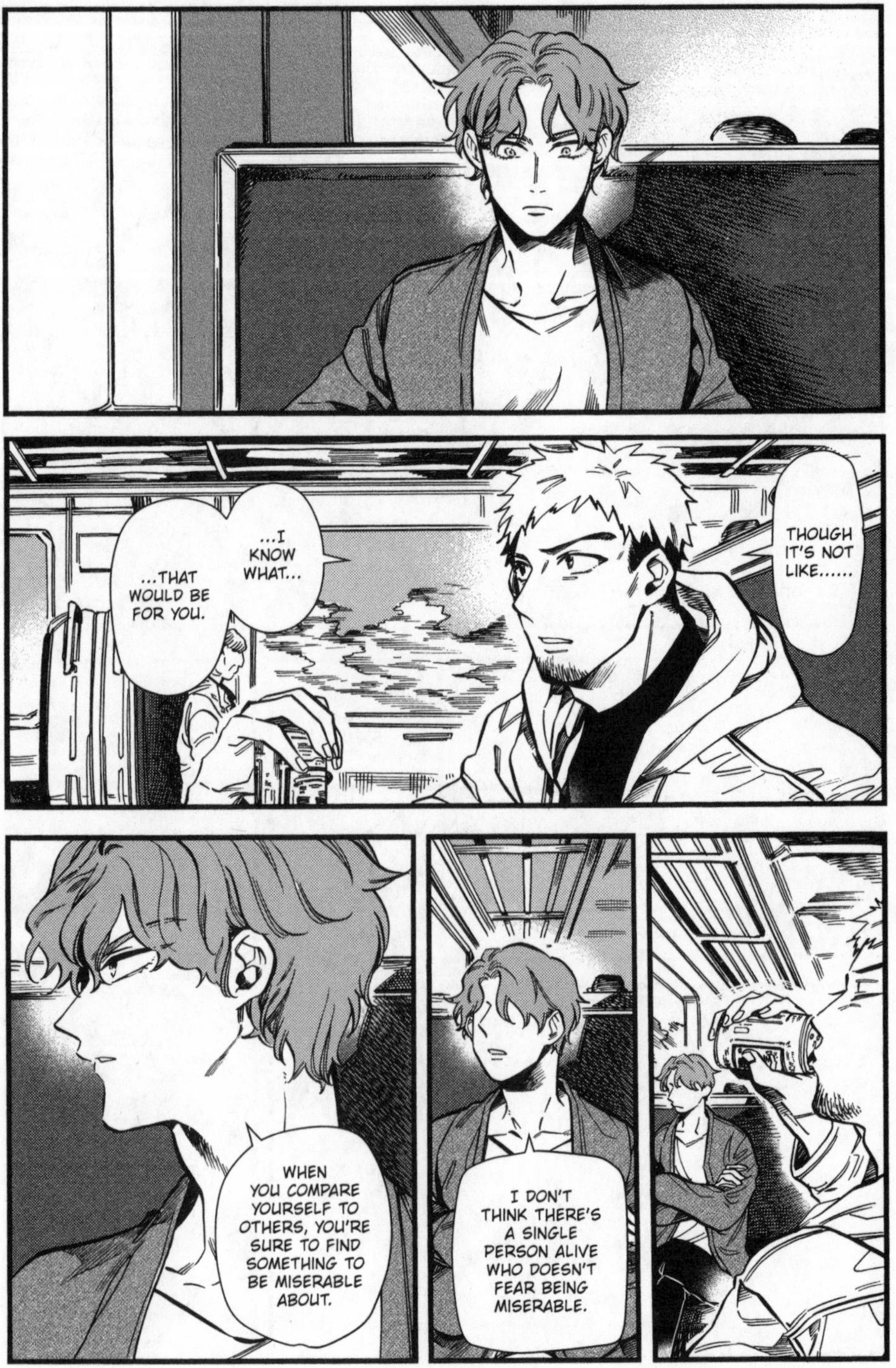
THOUGH IT'S NOT LIKE......
...I KNOW WHAT...
...THAT WOULD BE FOR YOU.
I DON'T THINK THERE'S A SINGLE PERSON ALIVE WHO DOESN'T FEAR BEING MISERABLE.
WHEN YOU COMPARE YOURSELF TO OTHERS, YOU'RE SURE TO FIND SOMETHING TO BE MISERABLE ABOUT.

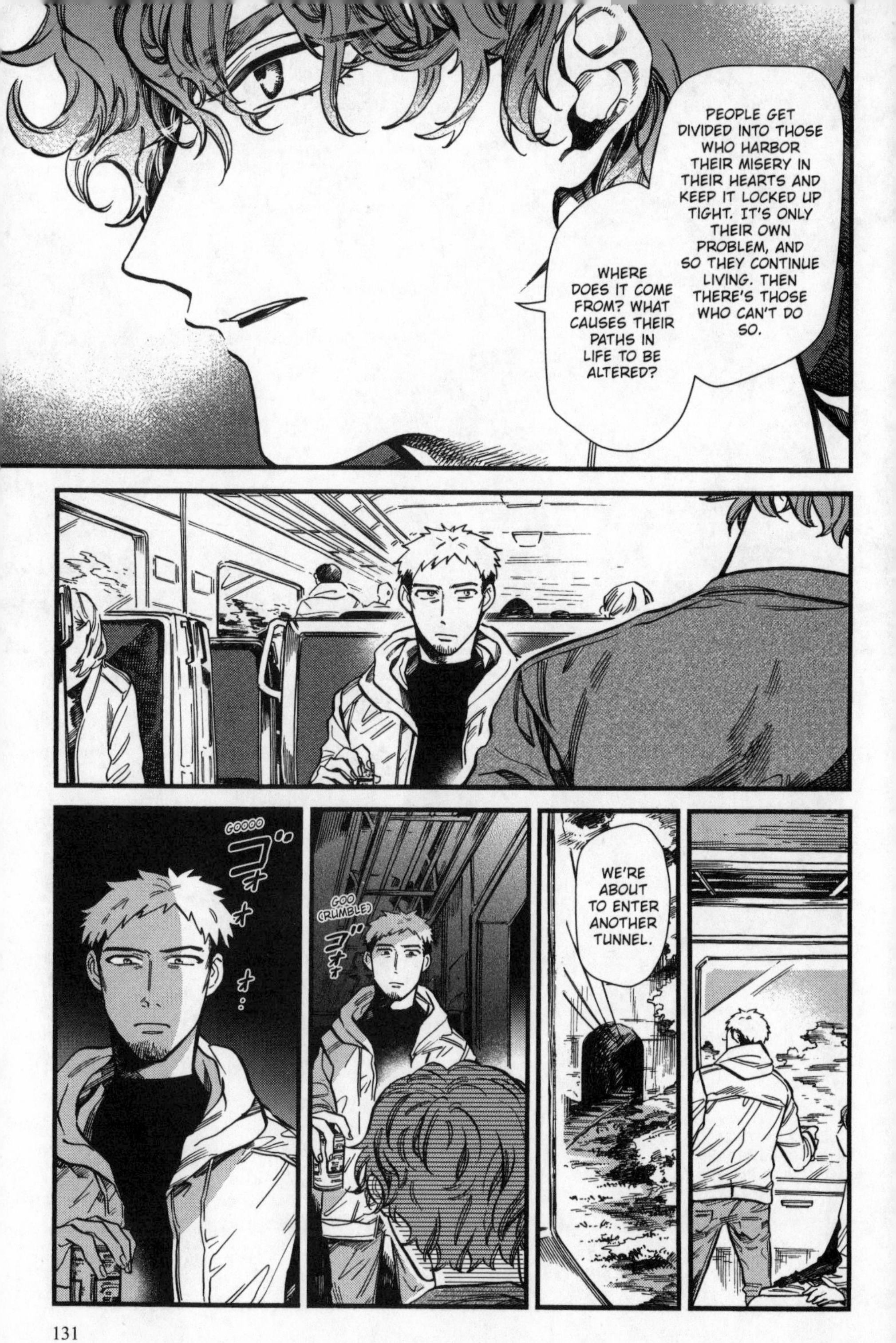
PEOPLE GET DIVIDED INTO THOSE WHO HARBOR THEIR MISERY IN THEIR HEARTS AND KEEP IT LOCKED UP TIGHT. IT'S ONLY THEIR OWN PROBLEM, AND SO THEY CONTINUE LIVING. THEN THERE'S THOSE WHO CAN'T DO SO.
WHERE DOES IT COME FROM? WHAT CAUSES THEIR PATHS IN LIFE TO BE ALTERED?
WE'RE ABOUT TO ENTER ANOTHER TUNNEL.
GOO (RUMBLE)
ゴォ
GOOOO
ゴォォォ…

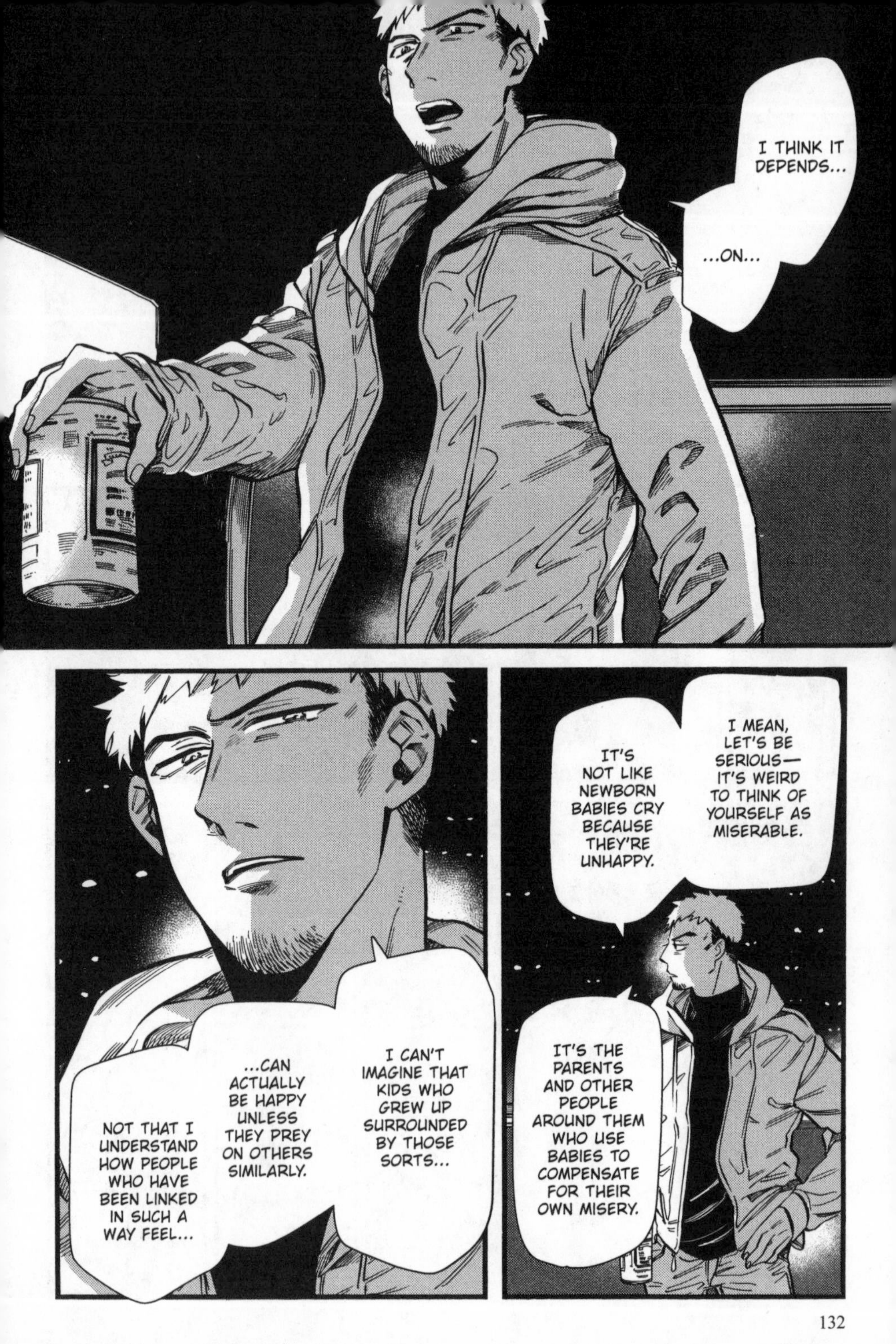
I THINK IT DEPENDS...
...ON...
I MEAN, LET'S BE SERIOUS— IT'S WEIRD TO THINK OF YOURSELF AS MISERABLE.
IT'S NOT LIKE NEWBORN BABIES CRY BECAUSE THEY'RE UNHAPPY.
IT'S THE PARENTS AND OTHER PEOPLE AROUND THEM WHO USE BABIES TO COMPENSATE FOR THEIR OWN MISERY.
I CAN'T IMAGINE THAT KIDS WHO GREW UP SURROUNDED BY THOSE SORTS...
...CAN ACTUALLY BE HAPPY UNLESS THEY PREY ON OTHERS SIMILARLY.
NOT THAT I UNDERSTAND HOW PEOPLE WHO HAVE BEEN LINKED IN SUCH A WAY FEEL...

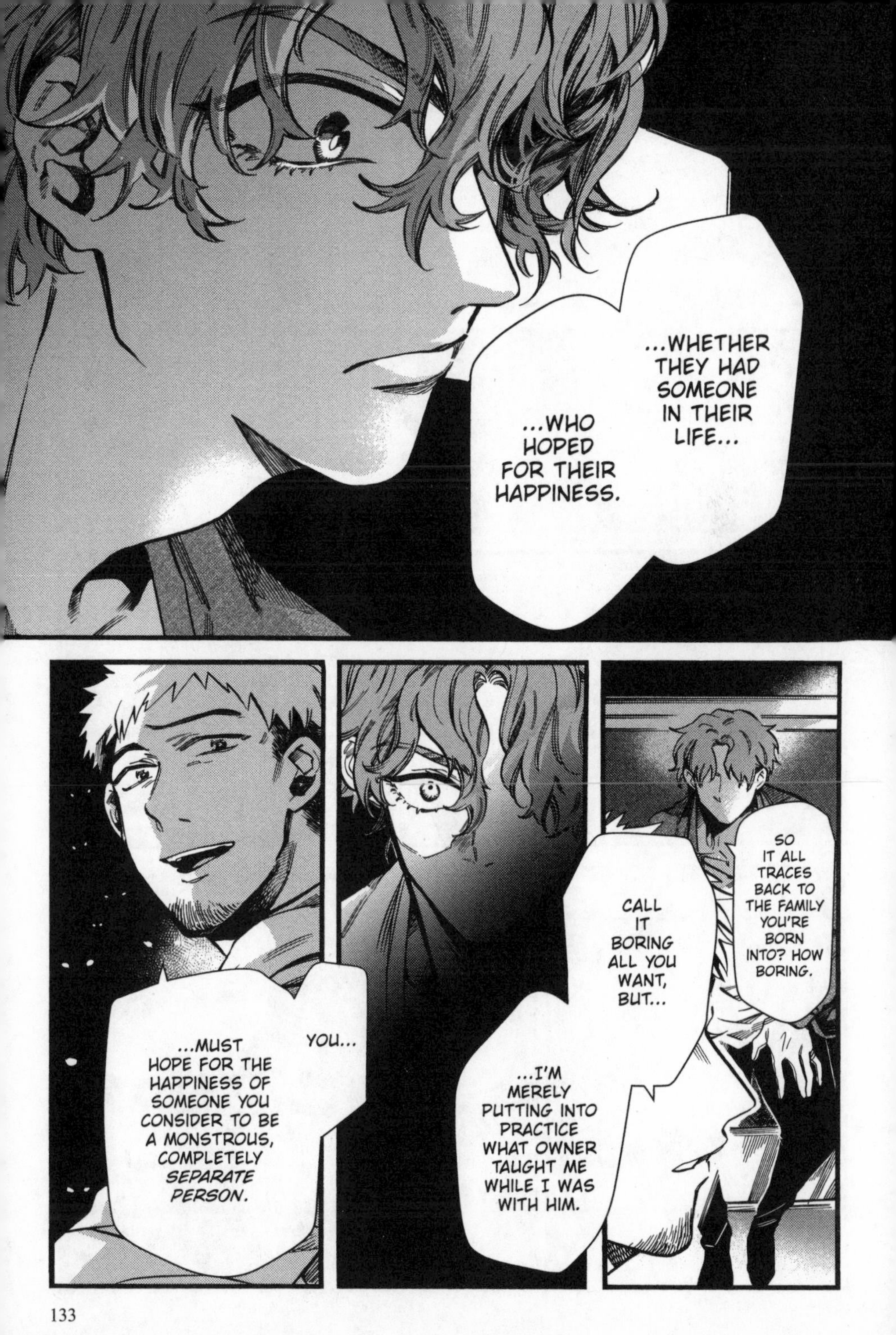
...WHETHER THEY HAD SOMEONE IN THEIR LIFE...
...WHO HOPED FOR THEIR HAPPINESS.
SO IT ALL TRACES BACK TO THE FAMILY YOU'RE BORN INTO? HOW BORING.
CALL IT BORING ALL YOU WANT, BUT...
...I'M MERELY PUTTING INTO PRACTICE WHAT OWNER TAUGHT ME WHILE I WAS WITH HIM.
YOU...
...MUST HOPE FOR THE HAPPINESS OF SOMEONE YOU CONSIDER TO BE A MONSTROUS, COMPLETELY *SEPARATE PERSON*.

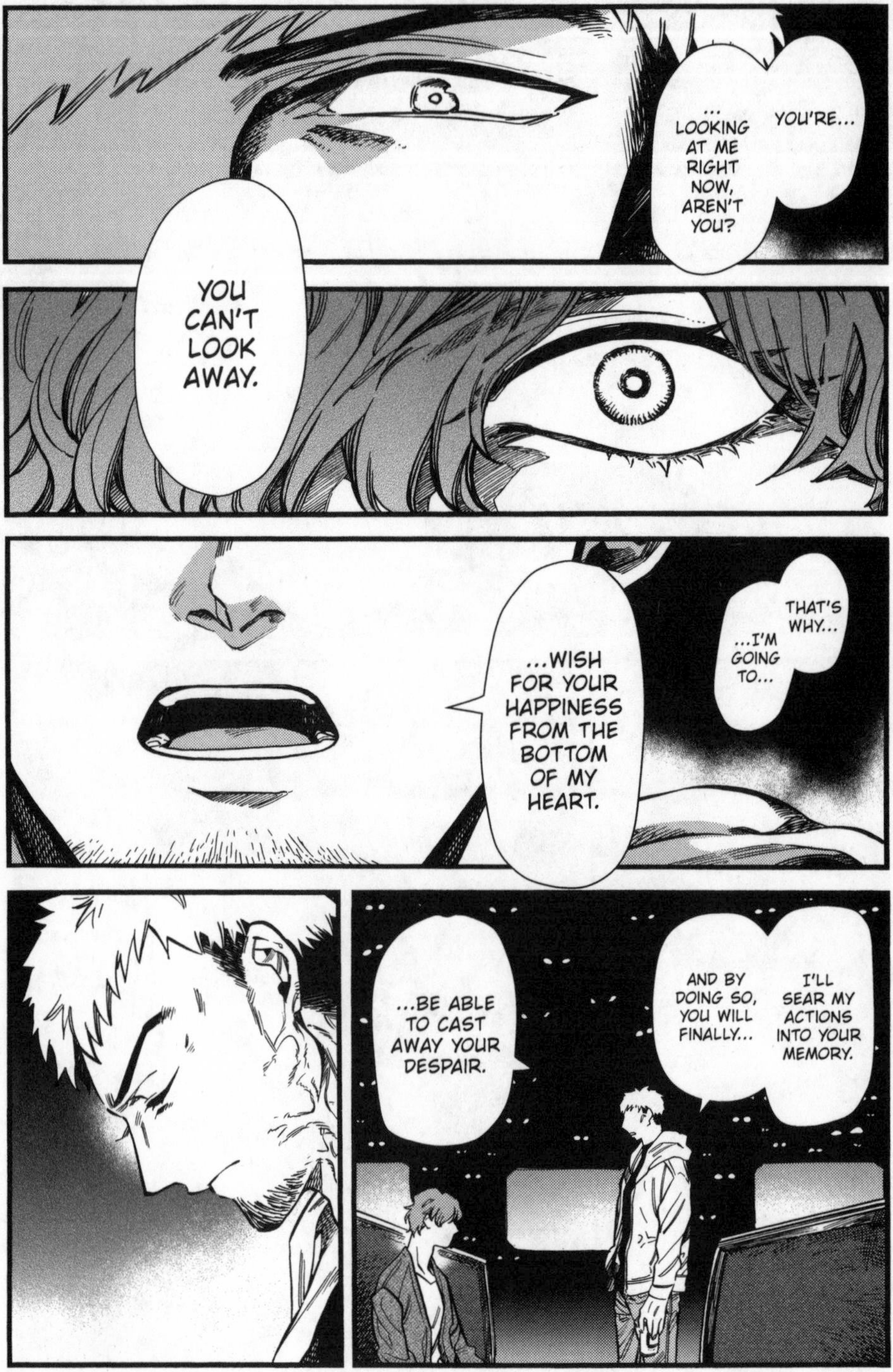
YOU'RE...
... LOOKING AT ME RIGHT NOW, AREN'T YOU?
YOU CAN'T LOOK AWAY.
THAT'S WHY...
...I'M GOING TO...
...WISH FOR YOUR HAPPINESS FROM THE BOTTOM OF MY HEART.
I'LL SEAR MY ACTIONS INTO YOUR MEMORY.
AND BY DOING SO, YOU WILL FINALLY...
...BE ABLE TO CAST AWAY YOUR DESPAIR.

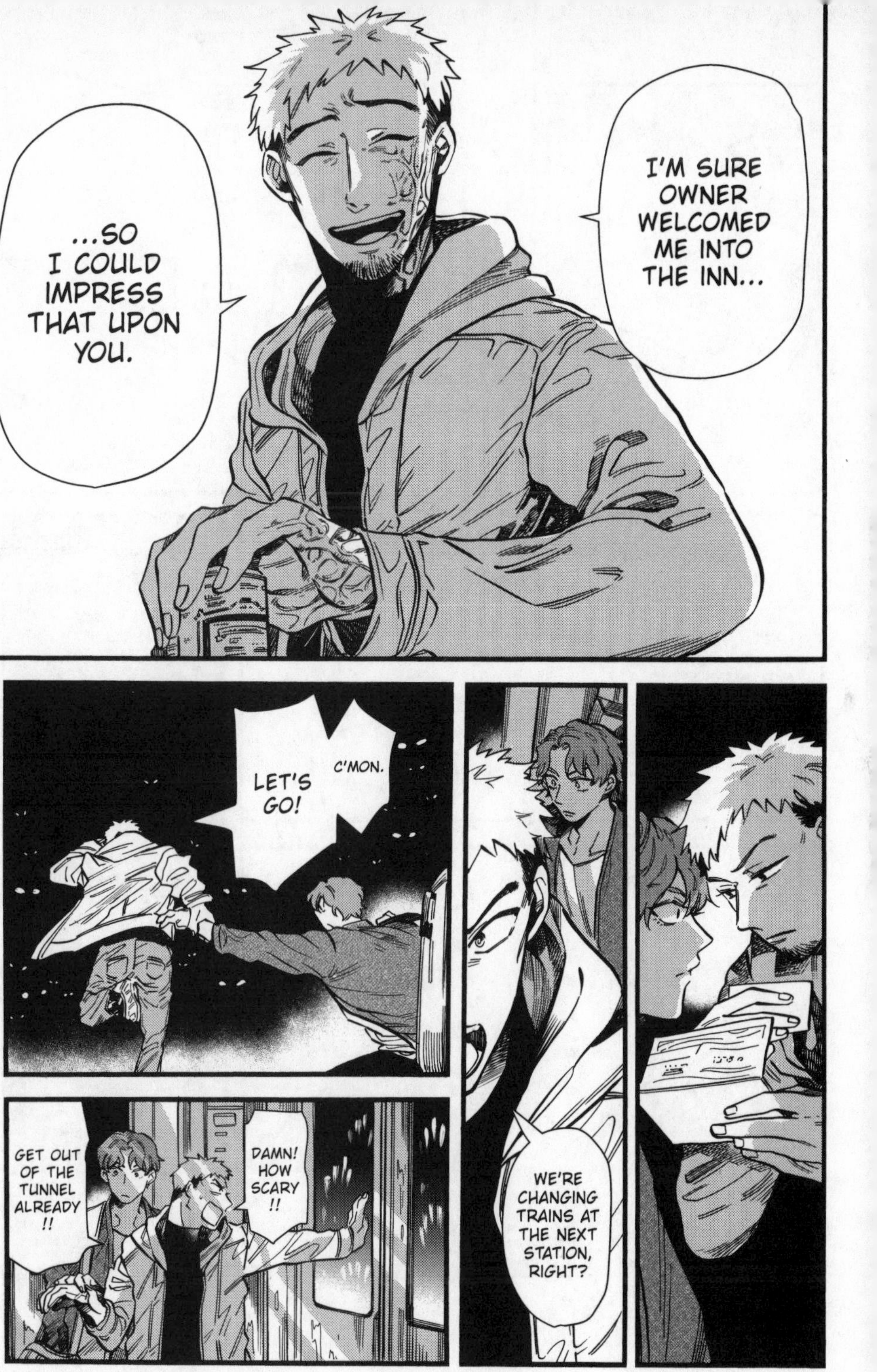
I'M SURE OWNER WELCOMED ME INTO THE INN...
...SO I COULD IMPRESS THAT UPON YOU.
WE'RE CHANGING TRAINS AT THE NEXT STATION, RIGHT?
C'MON.
LET'S GO!
DAMN! HOW SCARY!!
GET OUT OF THE TUNNEL ALREADY!!

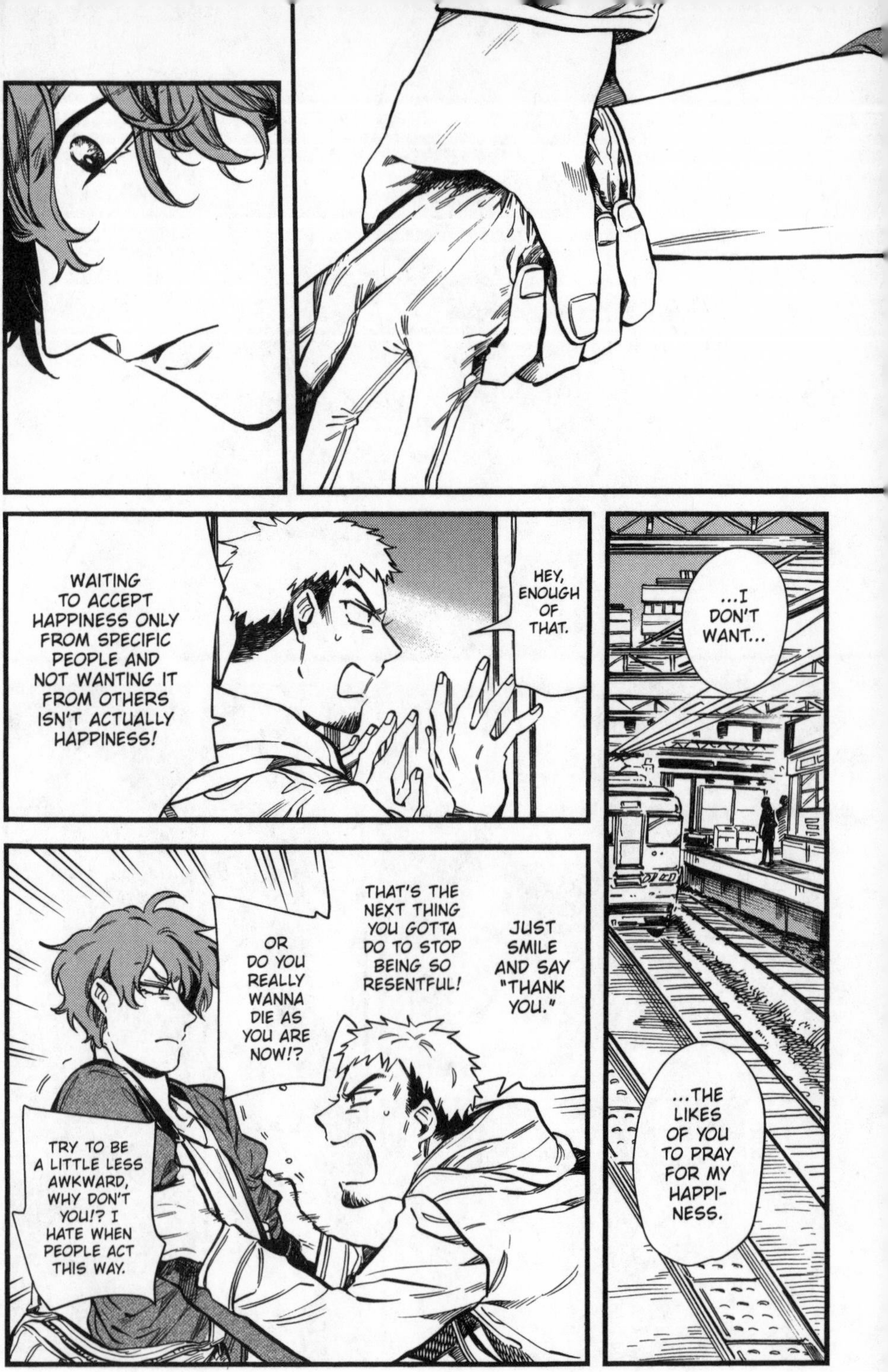
...I DON'T WANT...
...THE LIKES OF YOU TO PRAY FOR MY HAPPI-NESS.
HEY, ENOUGH OF THAT.
WAITING TO ACCEPT HAPPINESS ONLY FROM SPECIFIC PEOPLE AND NOT WANTING IT FROM OTHERS ISN'T ACTUALLY HAPPINESS!
JUST SMILE AND SAY "THANK YOU."
THAT'S THE NEXT THING YOU GOTTA DO TO STOP BEING SO RESENTFUL!
OR DO YOU REALLY WANNA DIE AS YOU ARE NOW!?
TRY TO BE A LITTLE LESS AWKWARD, WHY DON'T YOU!? I HATE WHEN PEOPLE ACT THIS WAY.

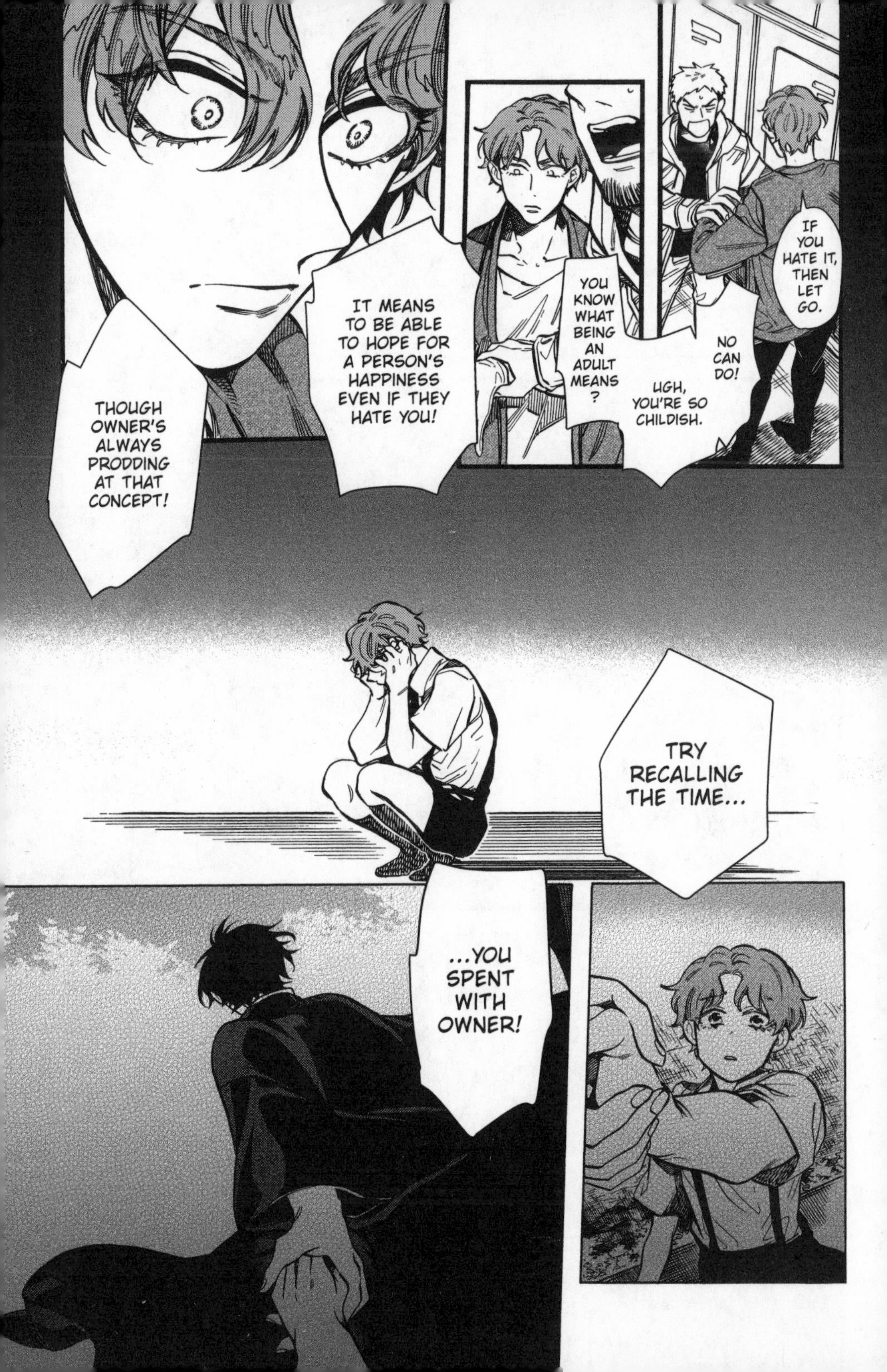
IF YOU HATE IT, THEN LET GO.
NO CAN DO!
UGH, YOU'RE SO CHILDISH.
YOU KNOW WHAT BEING AN ADULT MEANS?
IT MEANS TO BE ABLE TO HOPE FOR A PERSON'S HAPPINESS EVEN IF THEY HATE YOU!
THOUGH OWNER'S ALWAYS PRODDING AT THAT CONCEPT!
TRY RECALLING THE TIME...
...YOU SPENT WITH OWNER!

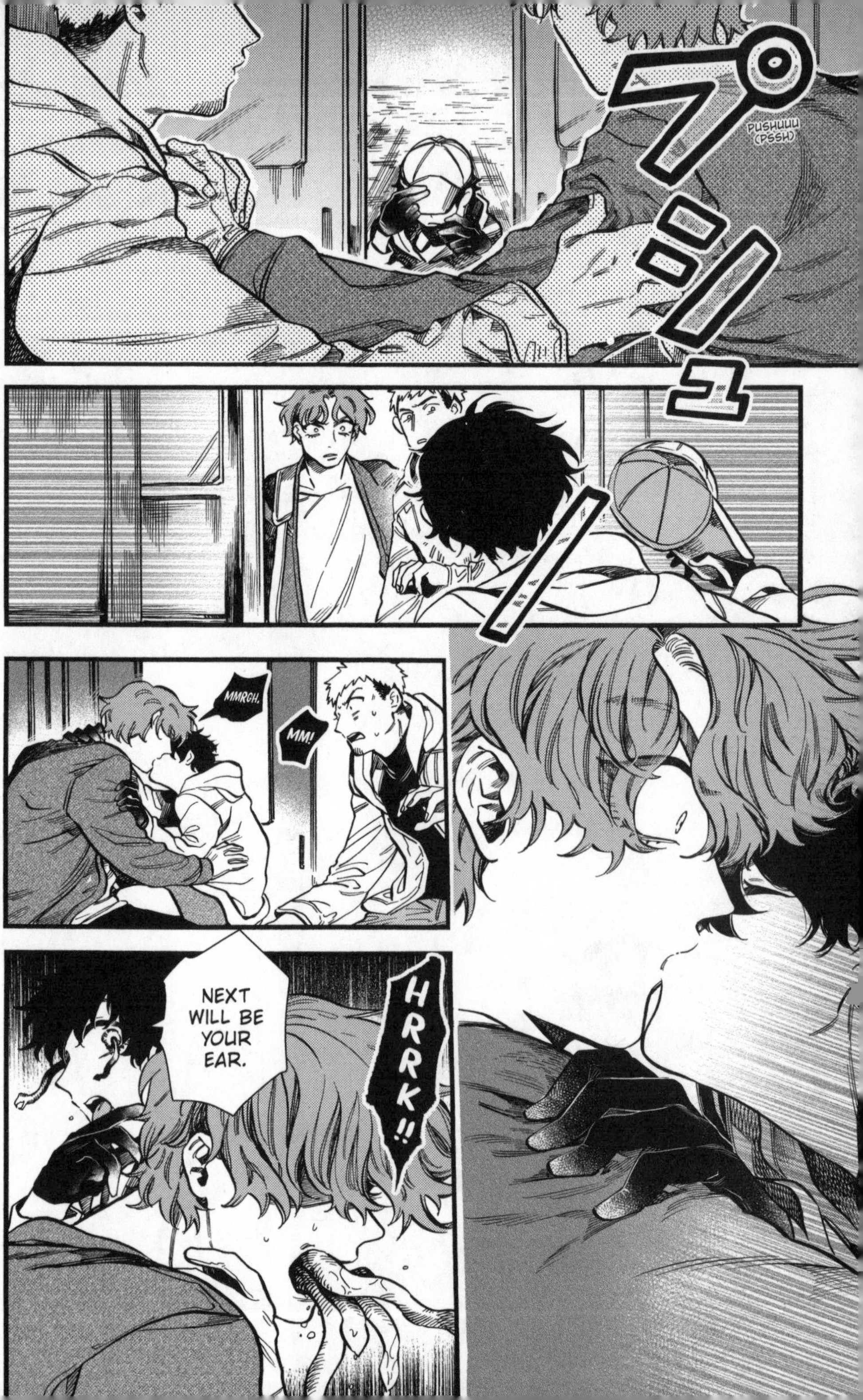
プシュ
PUSHUUU (PSSH)
MMRGH.
MM!
HRRK!!
NEXT WILL BE YOUR EAR.

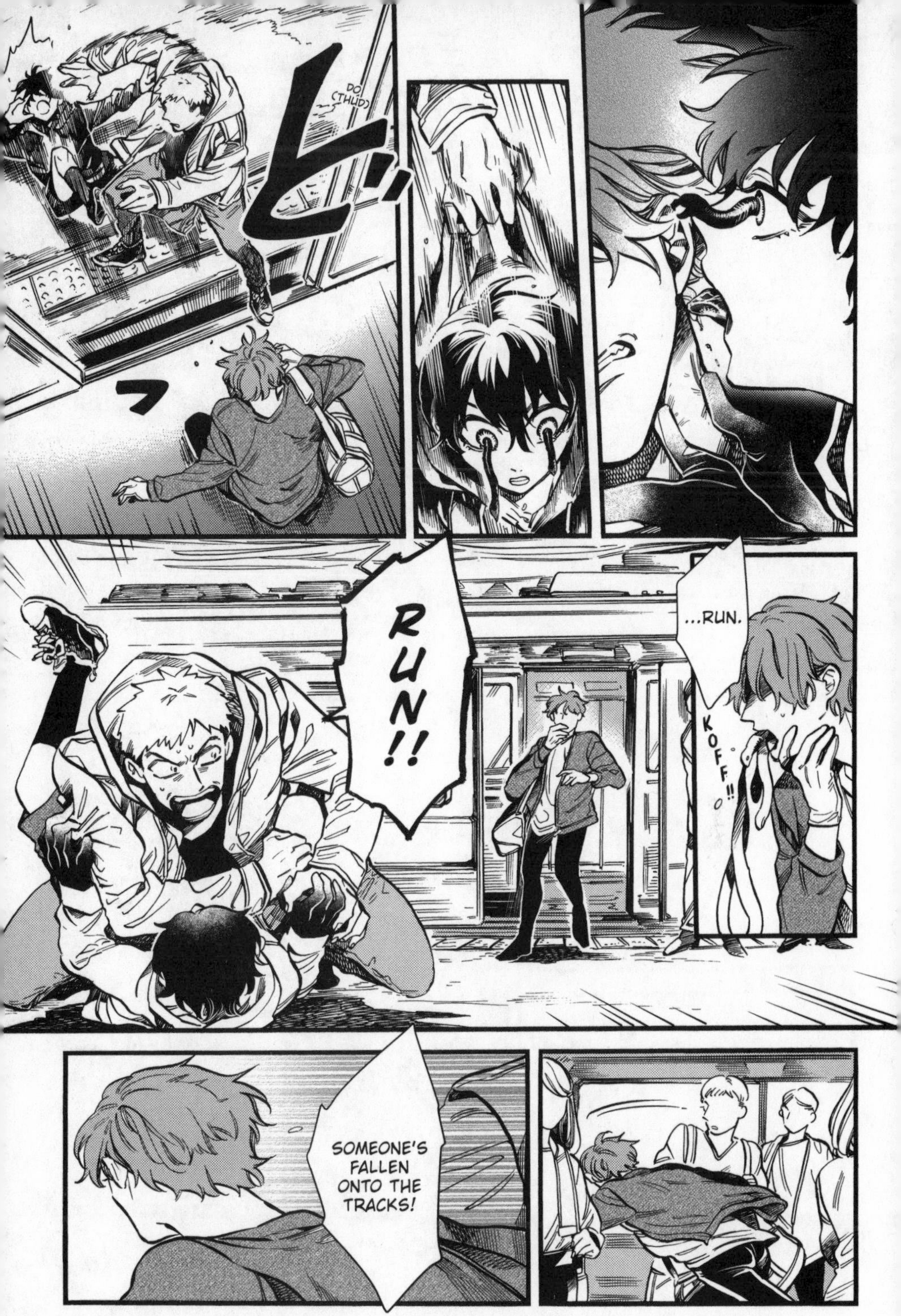
DO (THUD)
...RUN.
KOFF!!
RUN!!
SOMEONE'S FALLEN ONTO THE TRACKS!

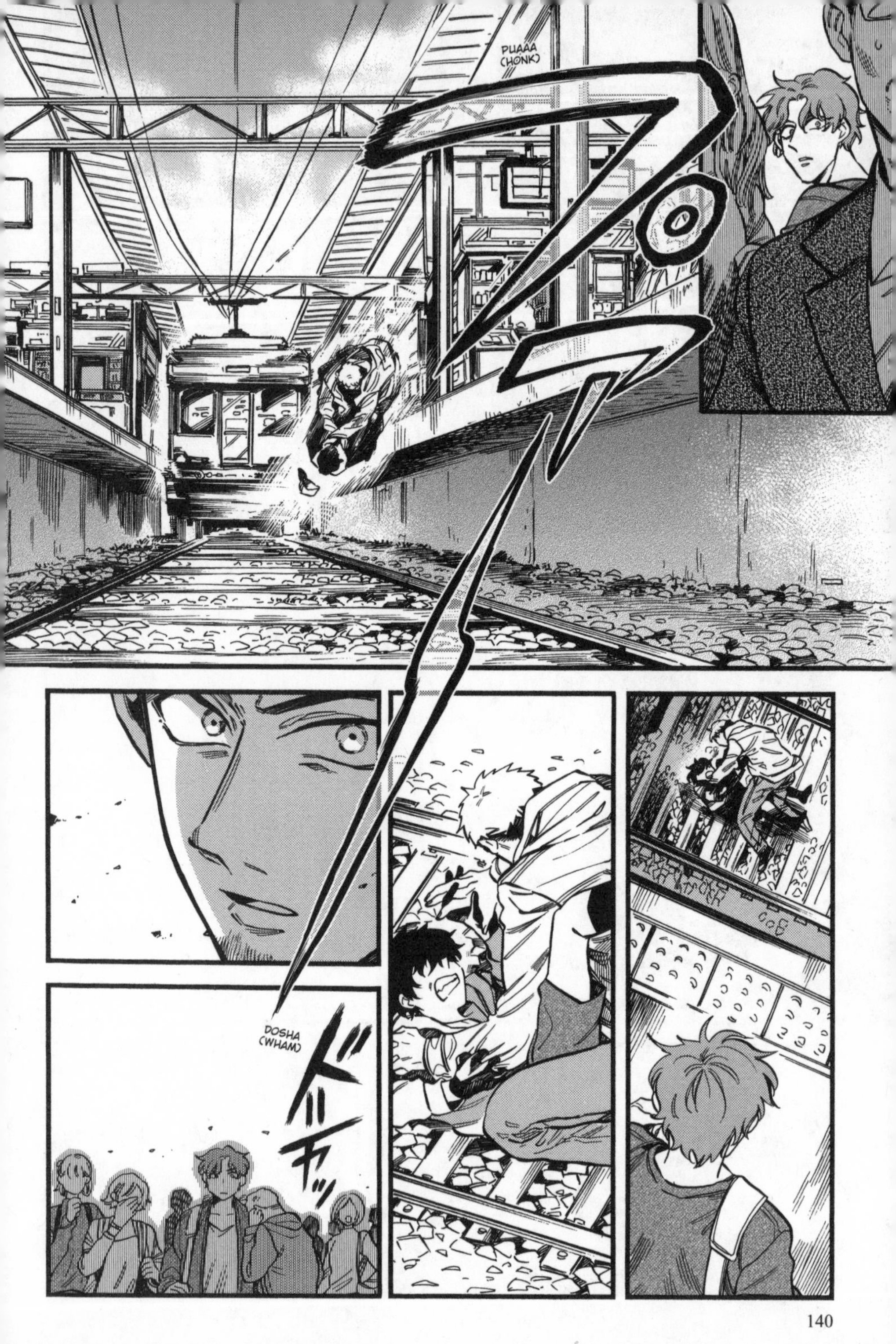
PUAAA (HONK)
DOSHA (WHAM)

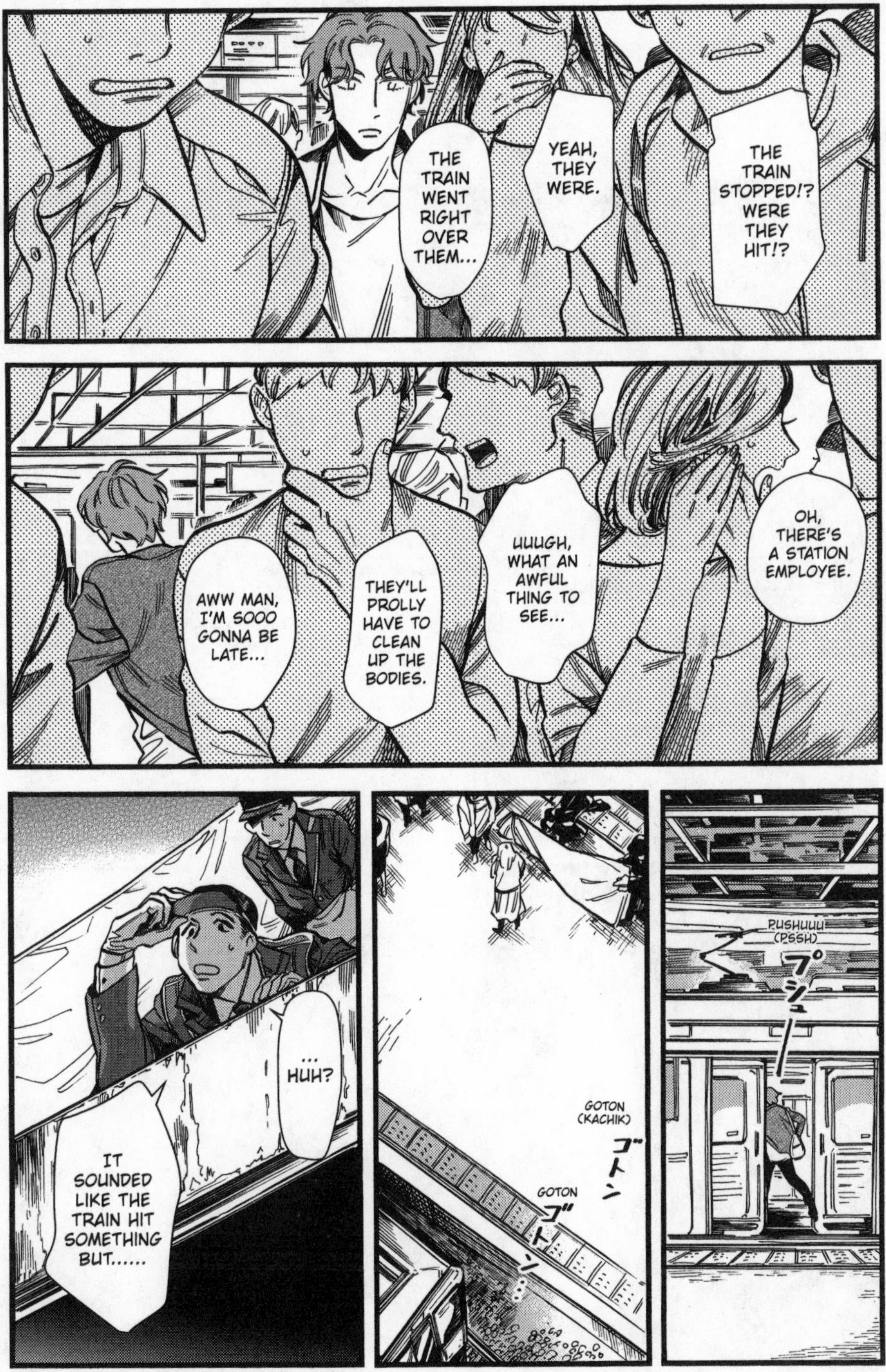
THE TRAIN STOPPED!? WERE THEY HIT!?
YEAH, THEY WERE.
THE TRAIN WENT RIGHT OVER THEM...
OH, THERE'S A STATION EMPLOYEE.
UUUGH, WHAT AN AWFUL THING TO SEE...
THEY'LL PROLLY HAVE TO CLEAN UP THE BODIES.
AWW MAN, I'M SOOO GONNA BE LATE...
PUSHUUU (PSSH)
プシュー
GOTON (KACHIK)
ゴトン
GOTON
ゴトン…
...HUH?
IT SOUNDED LIKE THE TRAIN HIT SOMETHING BUT......

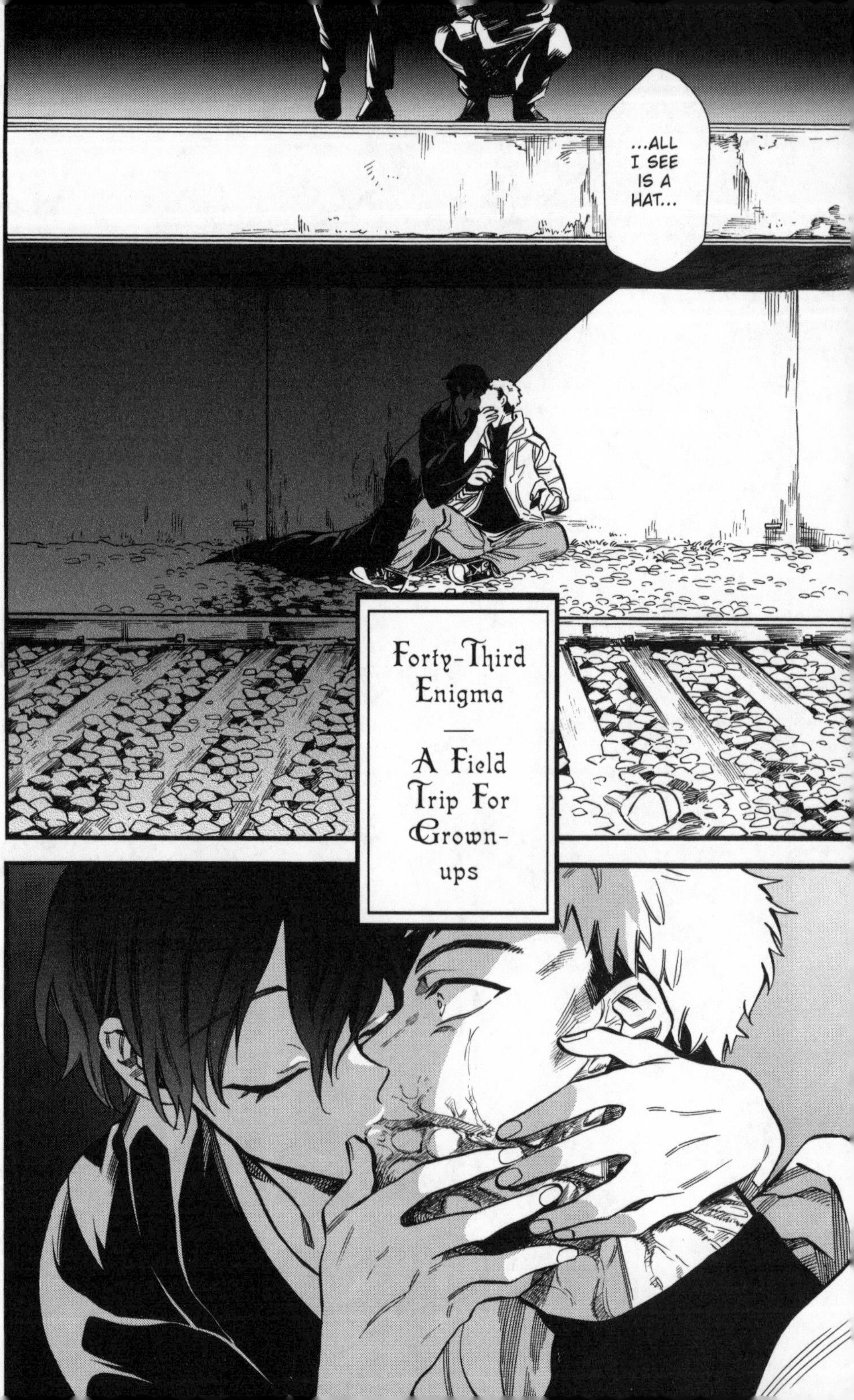
...ALL I SEE IS A HAT...
Forty-Third Enigma — A Field Trip For Grown-ups

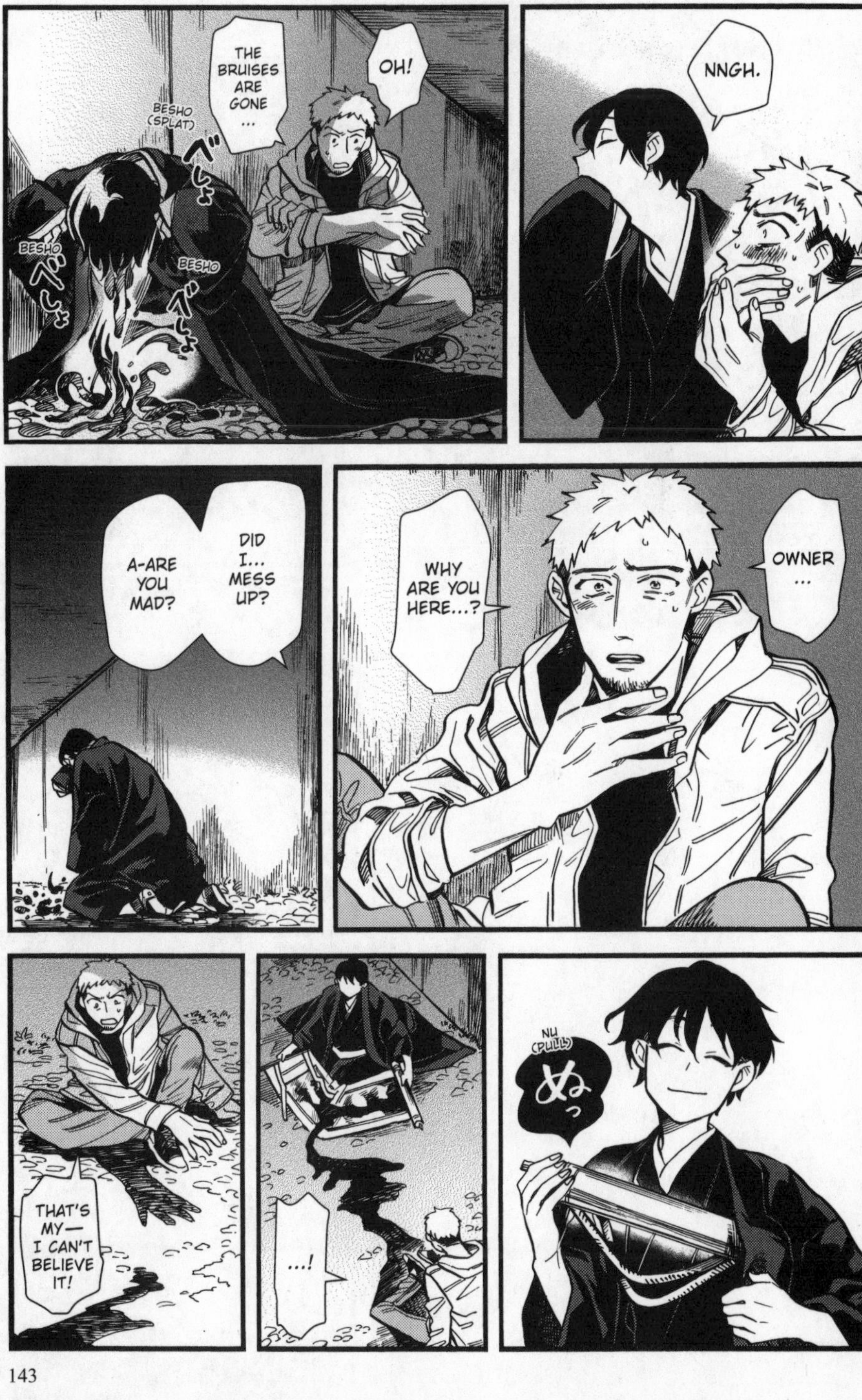
NNGH.
OH!
THE BRUISES ARE GONE...
BESHO (SPLAT) べしょ
BESHO べしょ
BESHO べしょ
OWNER...
WHY ARE YOU HERE...?
DID I... MESS UP?
A-ARE YOU MAD?
NU (PULL) ぬっ
...!
THAT'S MY— I CAN'T BELIEVE IT!

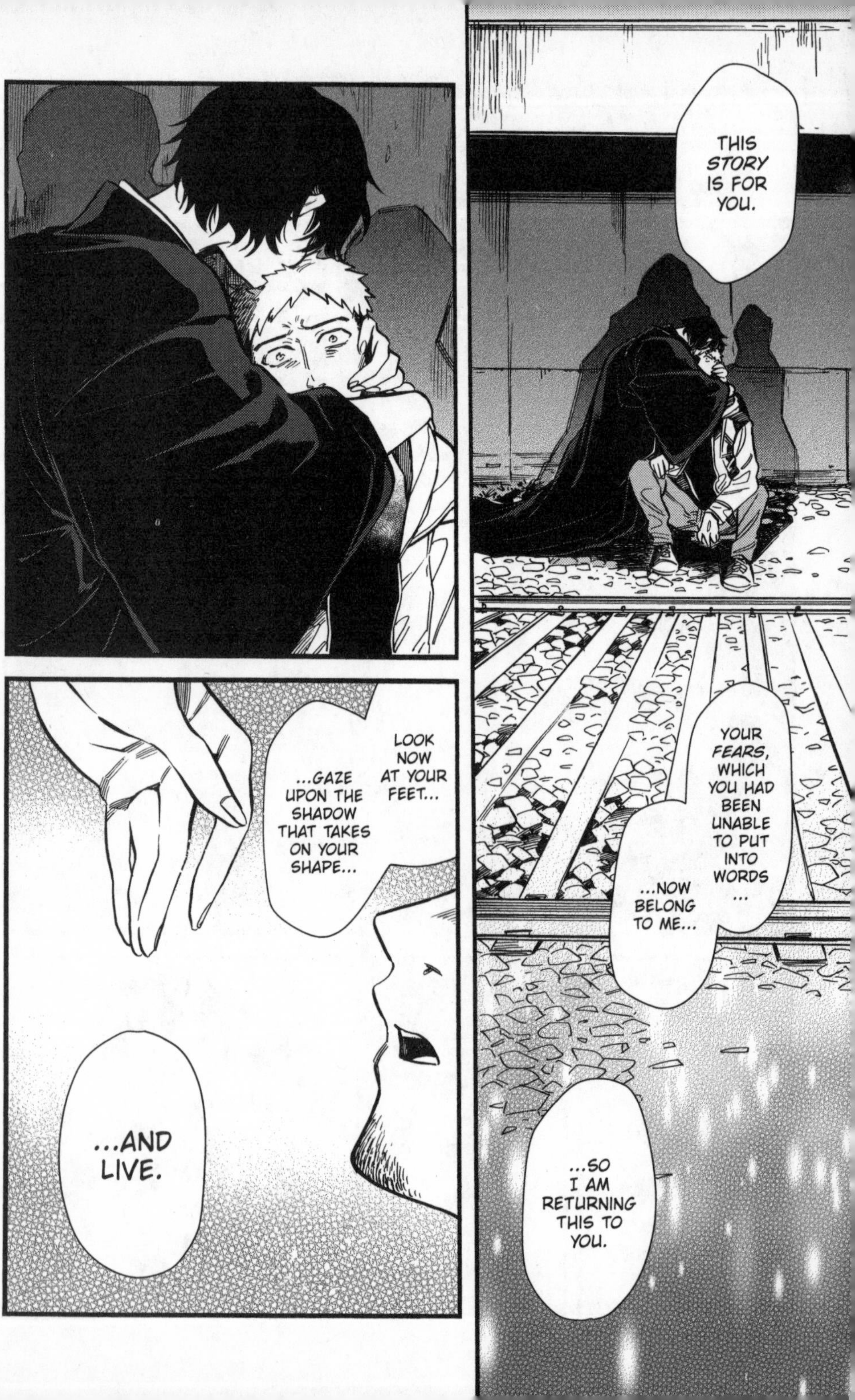
THIS STORY IS FOR YOU.
YOUR FEARS, WHICH YOU HAD BEEN UNABLE TO PUT INTO WORDS...
...NOW BELONG TO ME...
...SO I AM RETURNING THIS TO YOU.
LOOK NOW AT YOUR FEET...
...GAZE UPON THE SHADOW THAT TAKES ON YOUR SHAPE...
...AND LIVE.

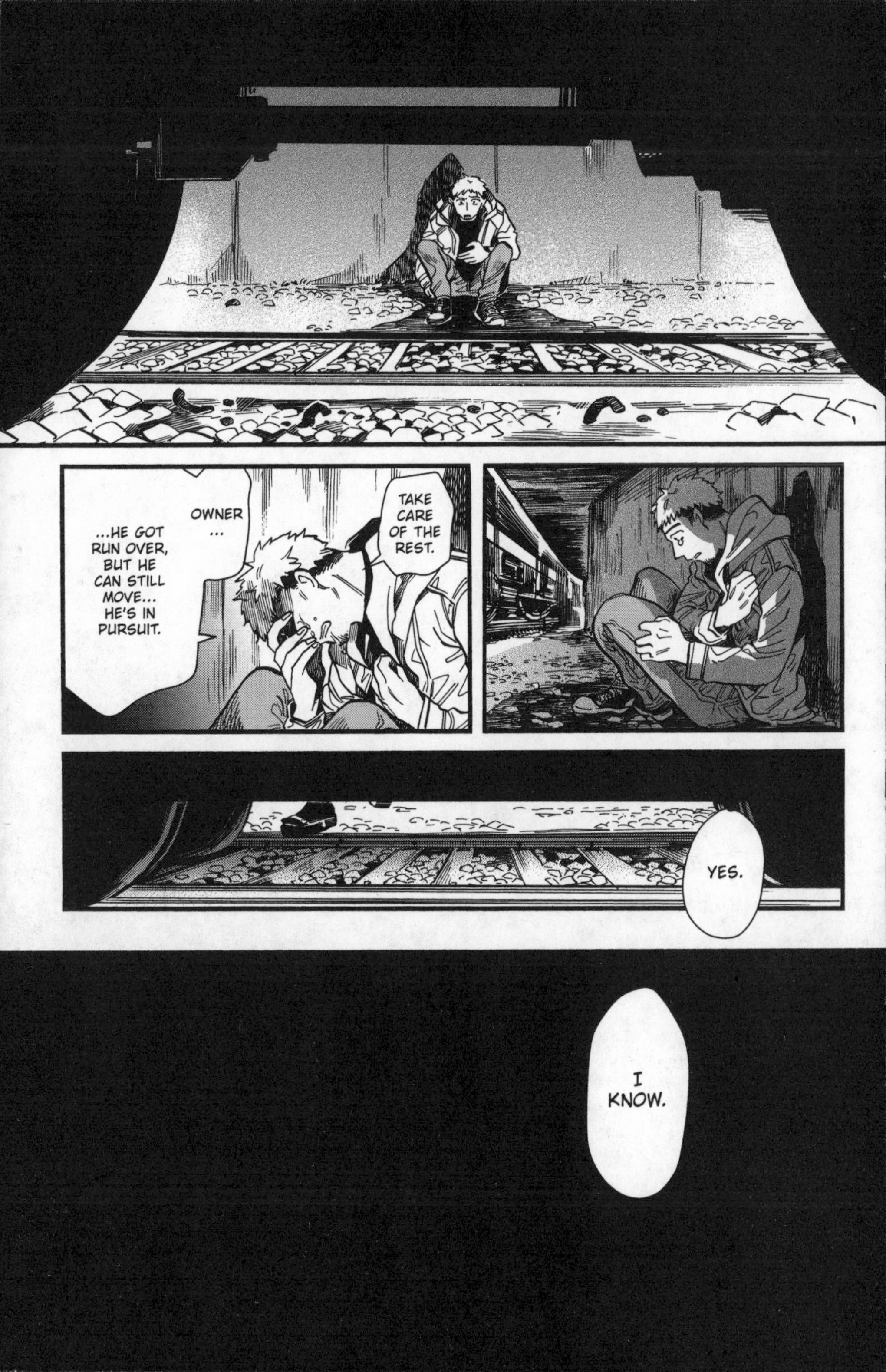
TAKE CARE OF THE REST.
OWNER ...
...HE GOT RUN OVER, BUT HE CAN STILL MOVE... HE'S IN PURSUIT.
YES.
I KNOW.

Phantom Tales of the Night

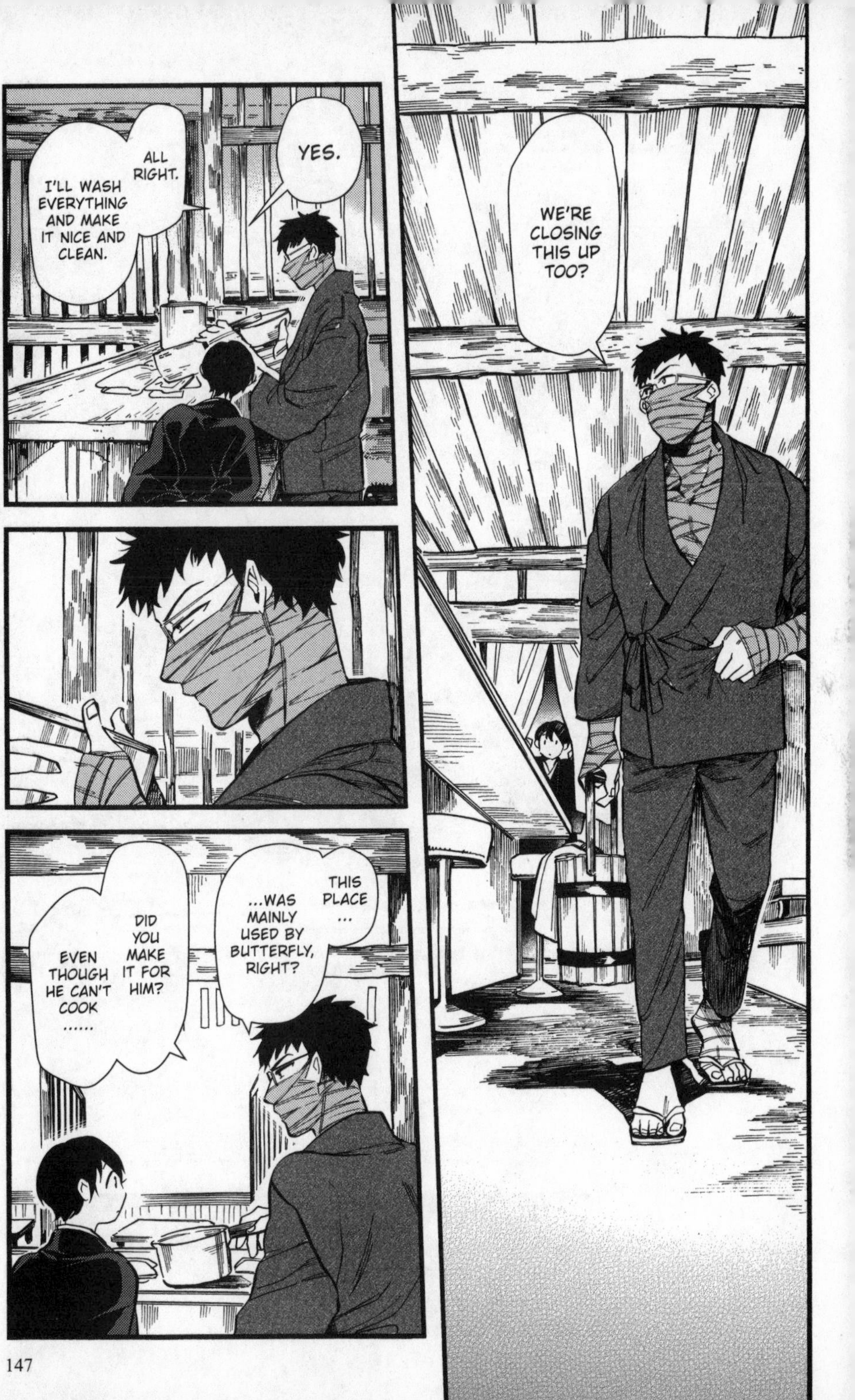
WE'RE CLOSING THIS UP TOO?
YES.
ALL RIGHT.
I'LL WASH EVERYTHING AND MAKE IT NICE AND CLEAN.
THIS PLACE ...
...WAS MAINLY USED BY BUTTERFLY, RIGHT?
DID YOU MAKE IT FOR HIM?
EVEN THOUGH HE CAN'T COOK ......

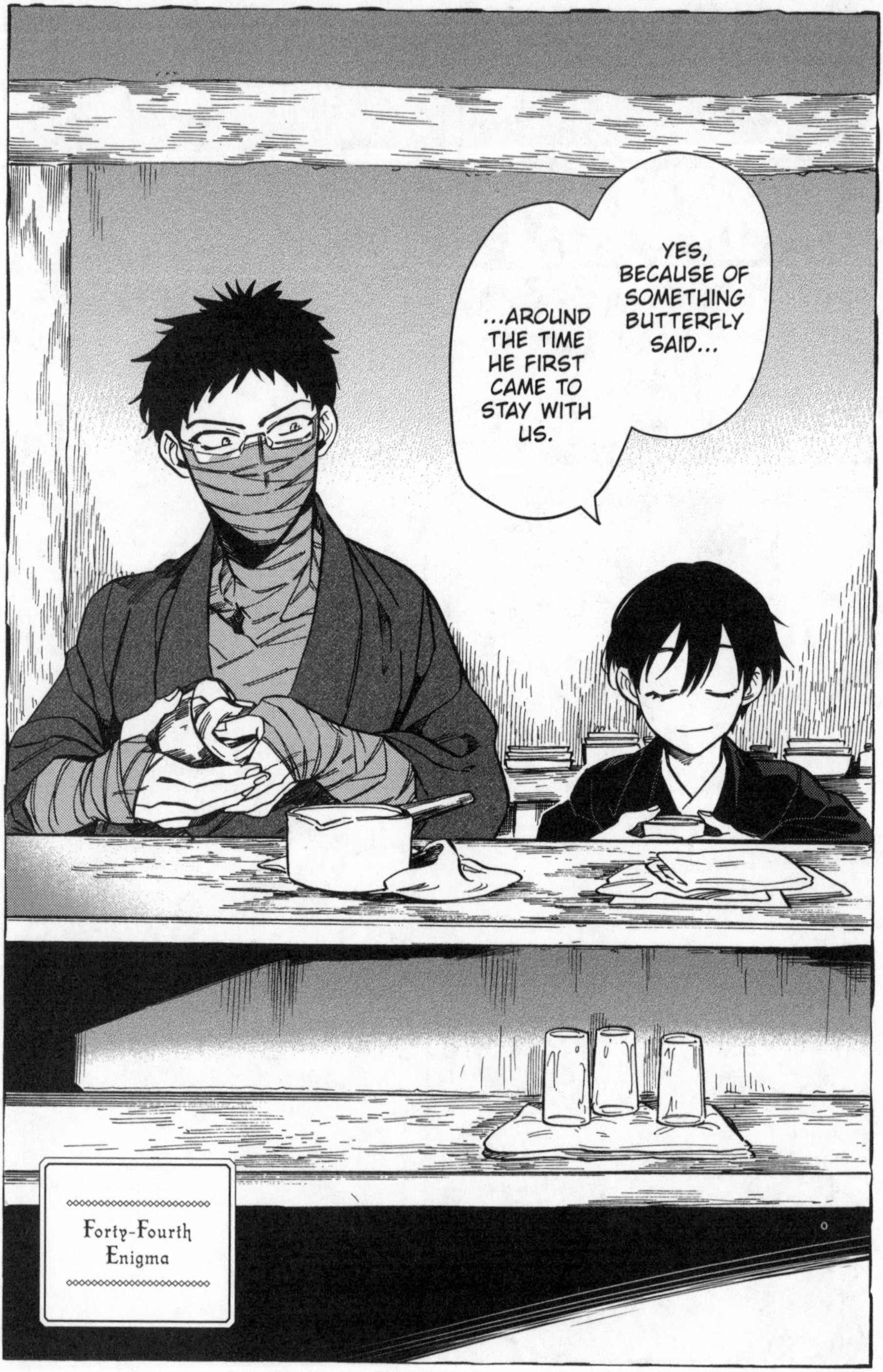
YES, BECAUSE OF SOMETHING BUTTERFLY SAID...
...AROUND THE TIME HE FIRST CAME TO STAY WITH US.
Forty-Fourth Enigma

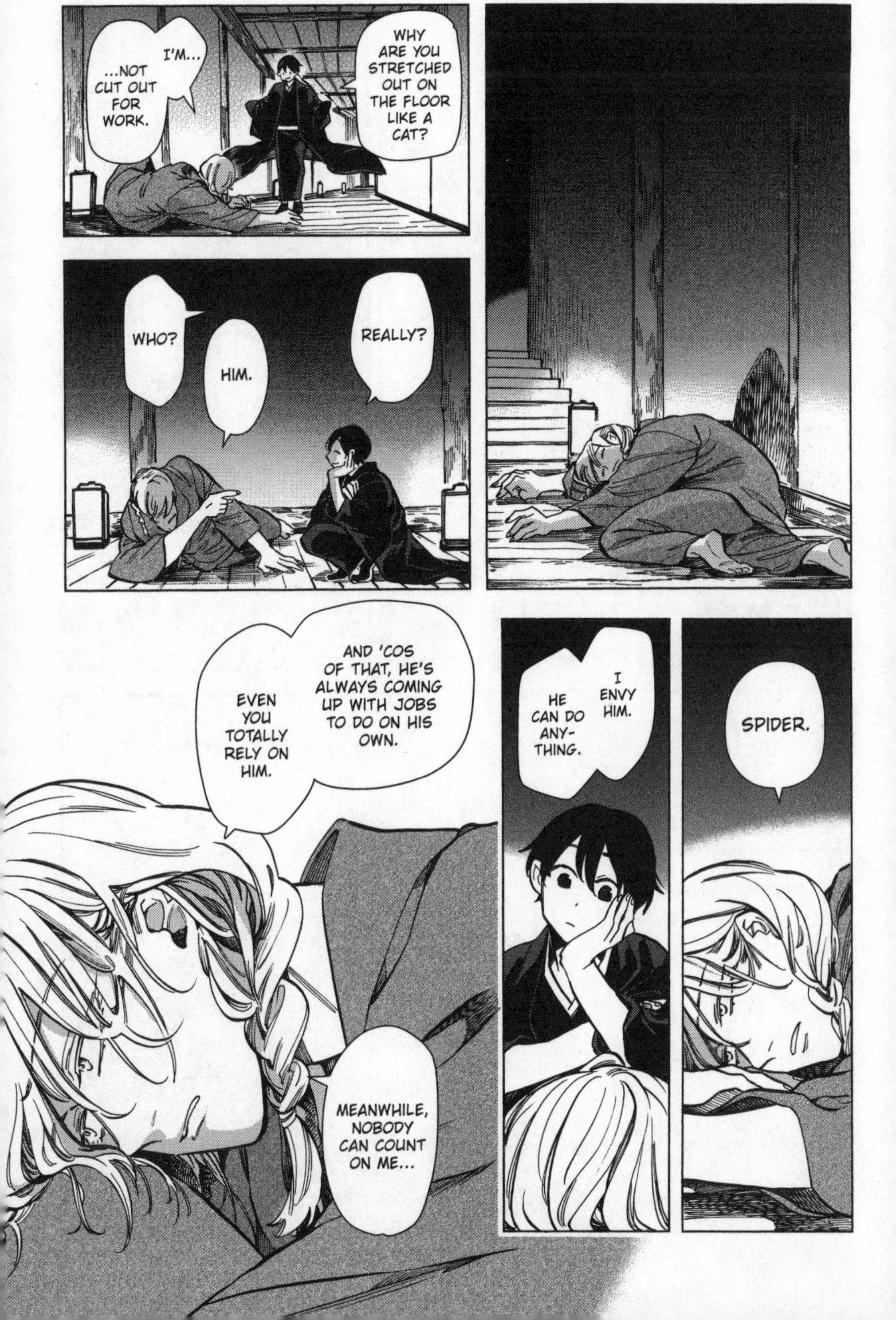
WHY ARE YOU STRETCHED OUT ON THE FLOOR LIKE A CAT?
I'M...
...NOT CUT OUT FOR WORK.
REALLY?
WHO?
HIM.
SPIDER.
I ENVY HIM.
HE CAN DO ANY-THING.
AND 'COS OF THAT, HE'S ALWAYS COMING UP WITH JOBS TO DO ON HIS OWN.
EVEN YOU TOTALLY RELY ON HIM.
MEANWHILE, NOBODY CAN COUNT ON ME...

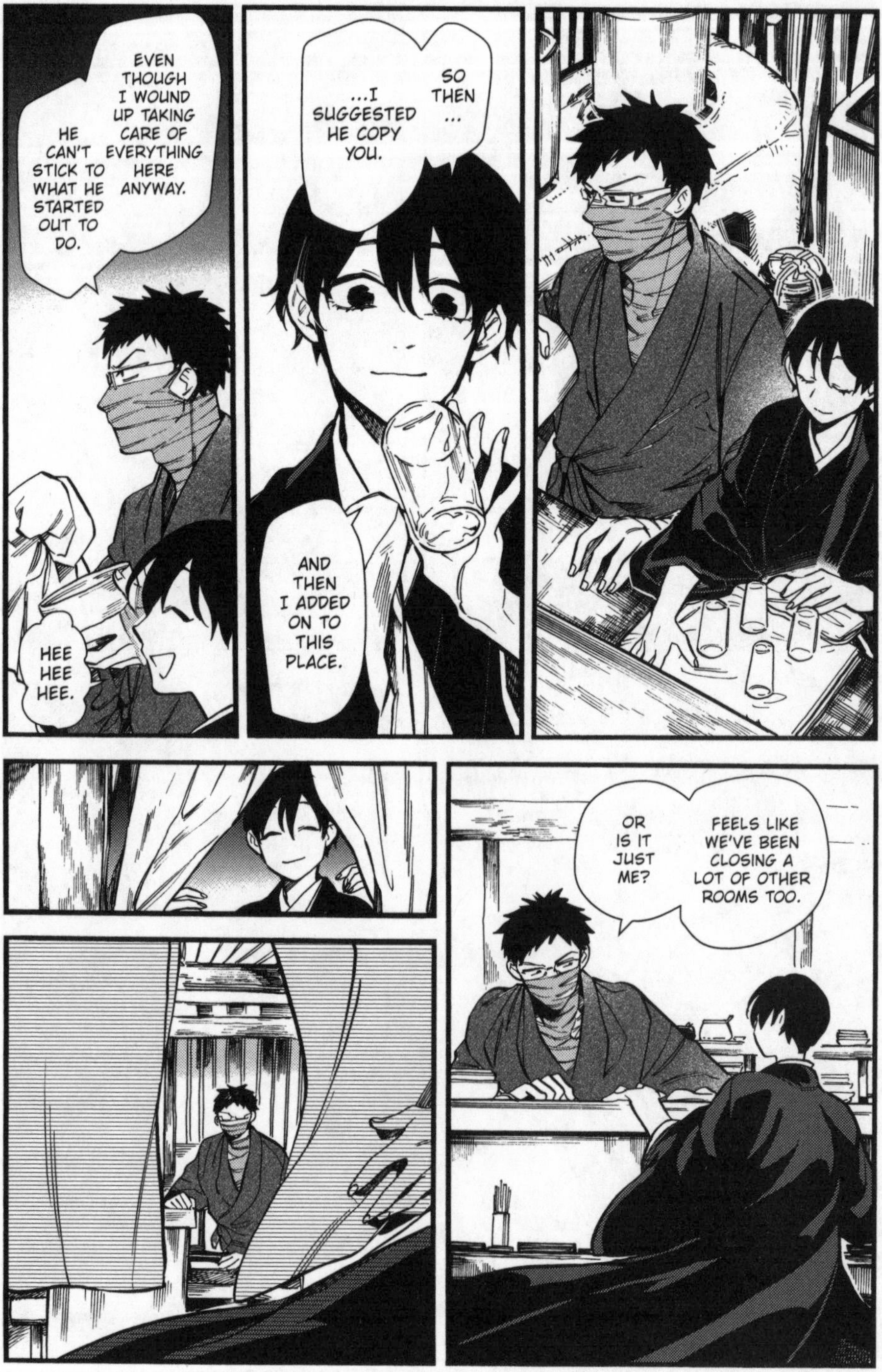
SO THEN ...
...I SUGGESTED HE COPY YOU.
AND THEN I ADDED ON TO THIS PLACE.
EVEN THOUGH I WOUND UP TAKING CARE OF EVERYTHING HERE ANYWAY.
HE CAN'T STICK TO WHAT HE STARTED OUT TO DO.
HEE HEE HEE.
FEELS LIKE WE'VE BEEN CLOSING A LOT OF OTHER ROOMS TOO.
OR IS IT JUST ME?

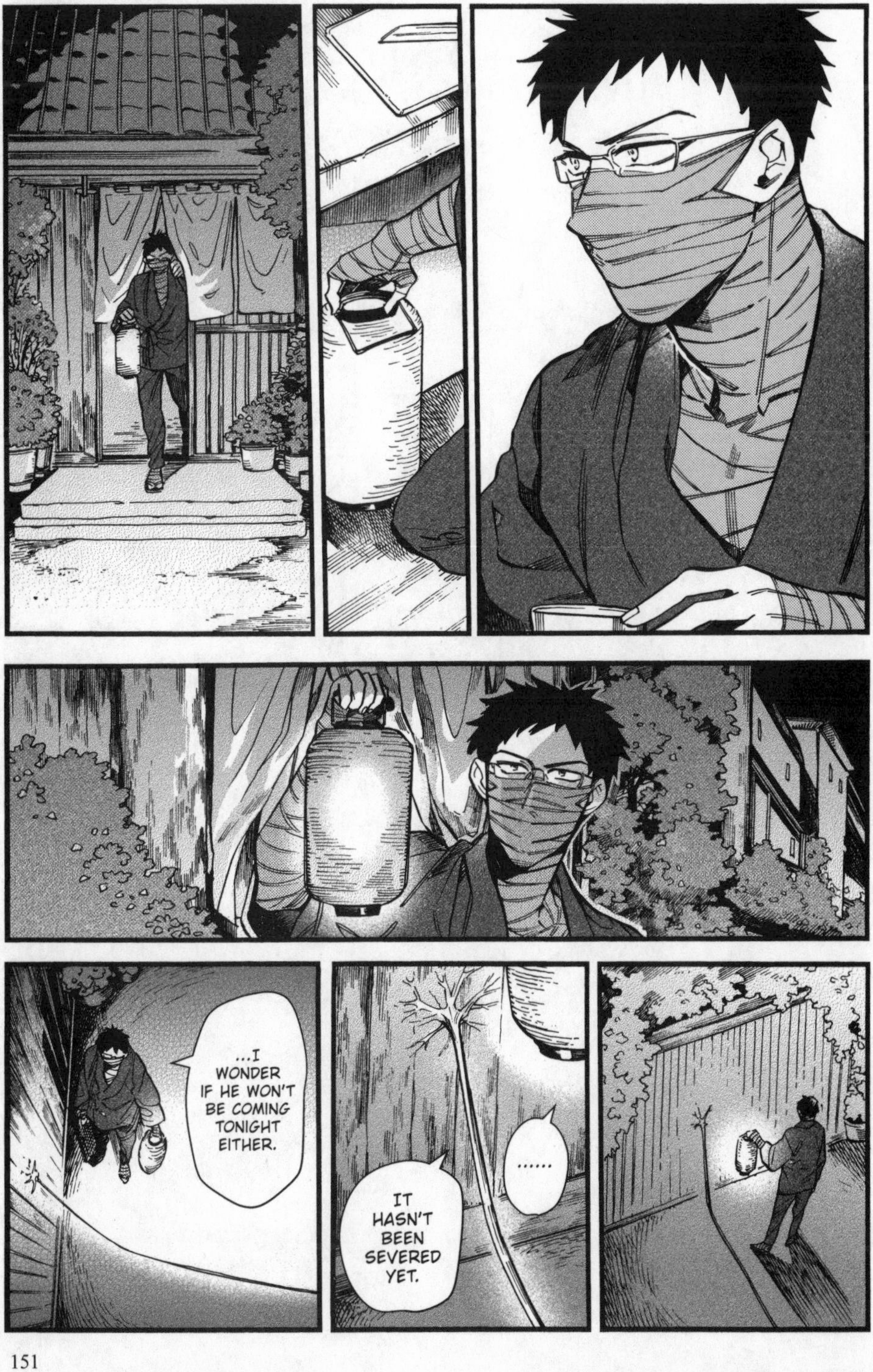
......
IT HASN'T BEEN SEVERED YET.
...I WONDER IF HE WON'T BE COMING TONIGHT EITHER.

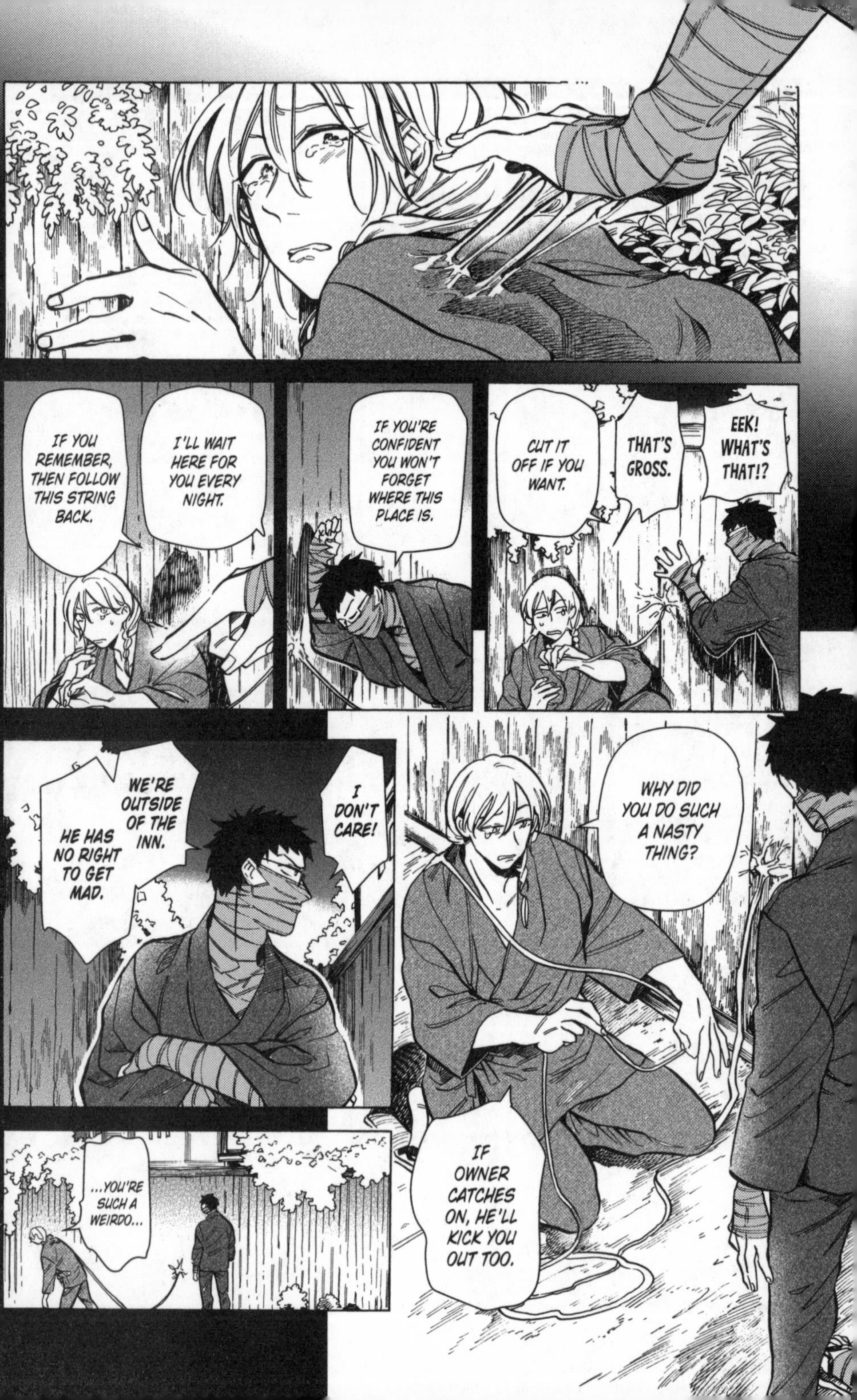
EEK! WHAT'S THAT!?
THAT'S GROSS.
CUT IT OFF IF YOU WANT.
IF YOU'RE CONFIDENT YOU WON'T FORGET WHERE THIS PLACE IS.
I'LL WAIT HERE FOR YOU EVERY NIGHT.
IF YOU REMEMBER, THEN FOLLOW THIS STRING BACK.
WHY DID YOU DO SUCH A NASTY THING?
IF OWNER CATCHES ON, HE'LL KICK YOU OUT TOO.
I DON'T CARE!
WE'RE OUTSIDE OF THE INN.
HE HAS NO RIGHT TO GET MAD.
...YOU'RE SUCH A WEIRDO...

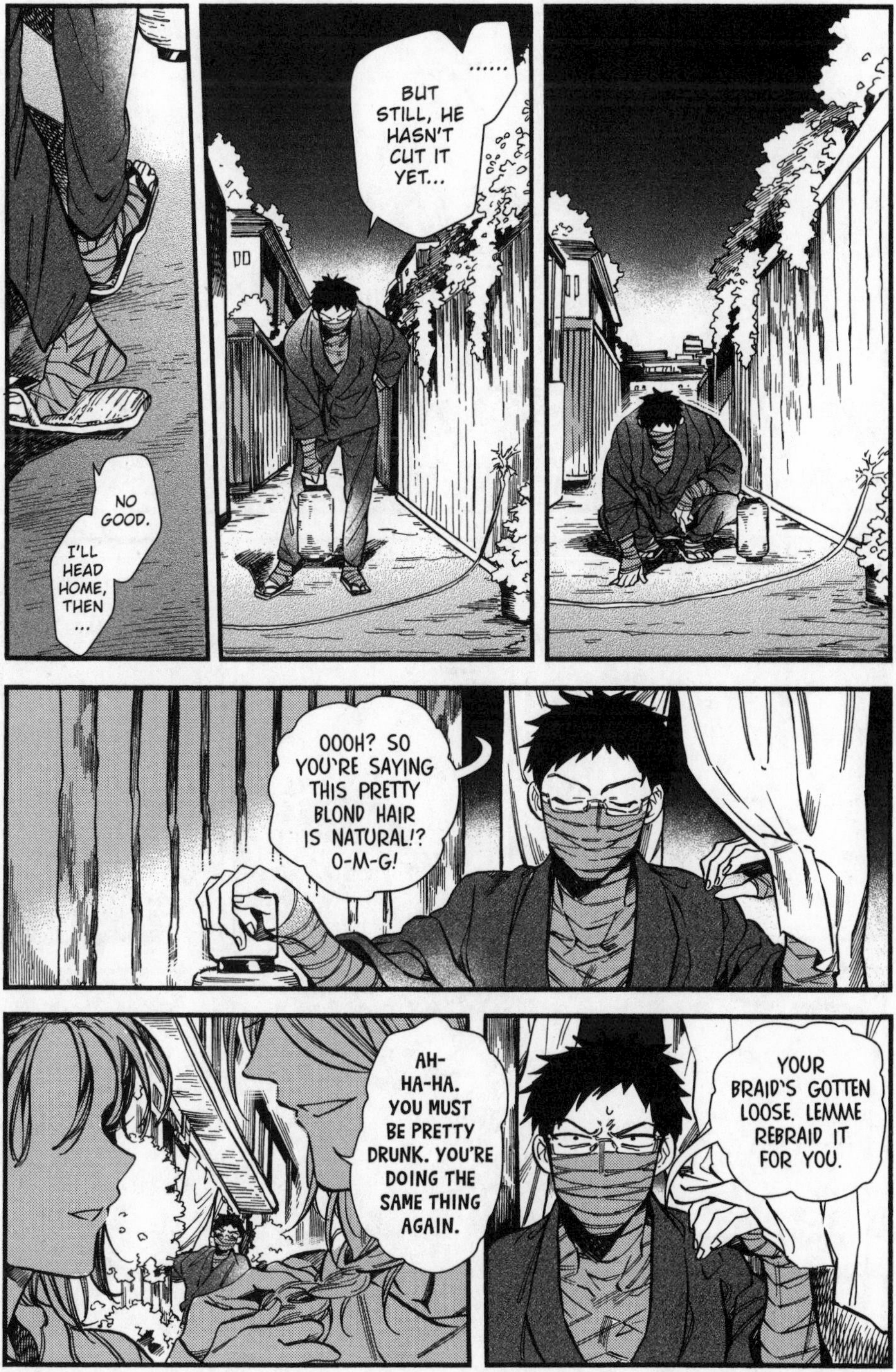
......
BUT STILL, HE HASN'T CUT IT YET...
NO GOOD.
I'LL HEAD HOME, THEN ...
OOOH? SO YOU'RE SAYING THIS PRETTY BLOND HAIR IS NATURAL!? O-M-G!
YOUR BRAID'S GOTTEN LOOSE. LEMME REBRAID IT FOR YOU.
AH-HA-HA. YOU MUST BE PRETTY DRUNK. YOU'RE DOING THE SAME THING AGAIN.

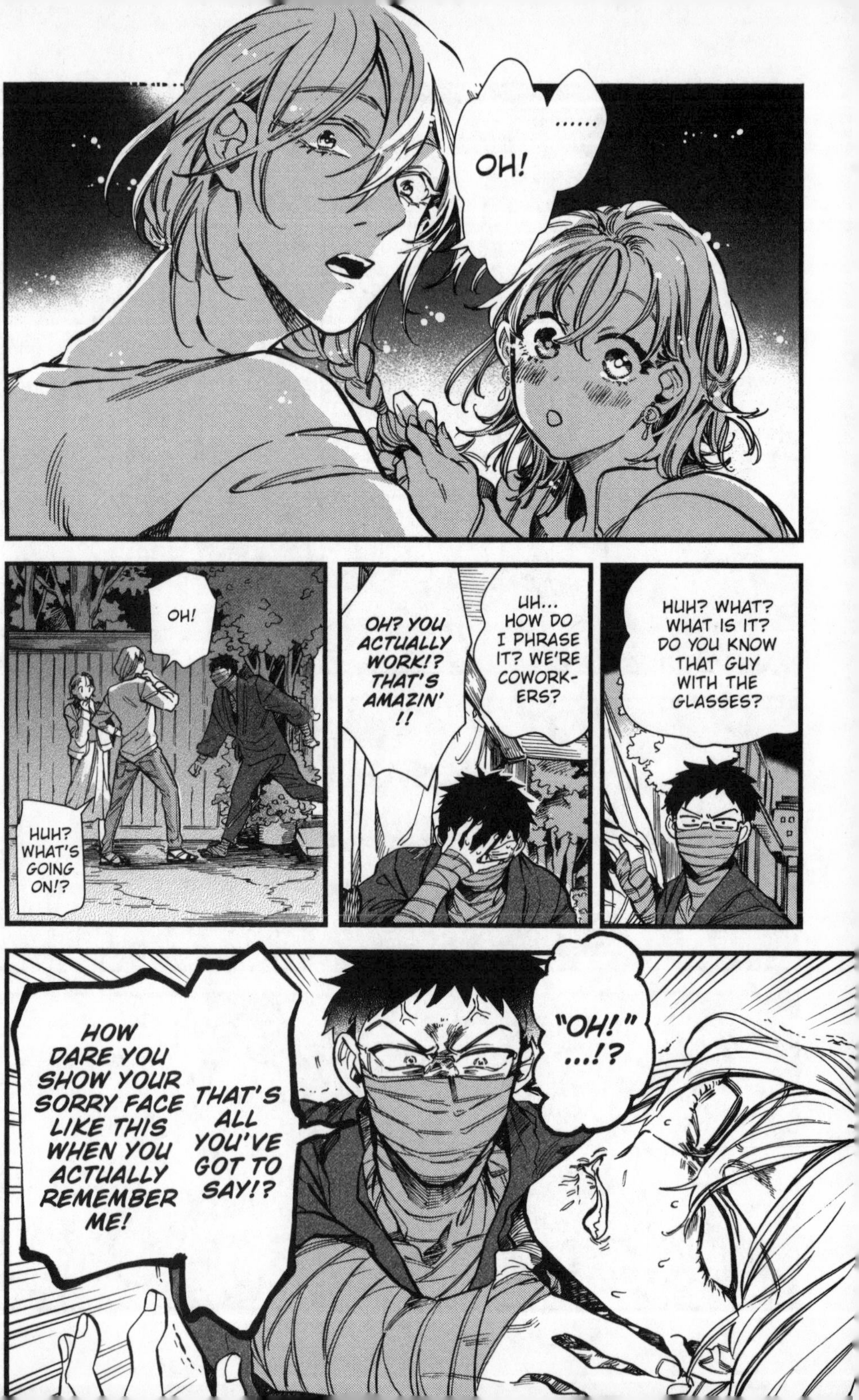
......
OH!
HUH? WHAT? WHAT IS IT? DO YOU KNOW THAT GUY WITH THE GLASSES?
UH... HOW DO I PHRASE IT? WE'RE COWORK-ERS?
OH? YOU ACTUALLY WORK!? THAT'S AMAZIN'!!
OH!
HUH? WHAT'S GOING ON!?
"OH!" ...!?
THAT'S ALL YOU'VE GOT TO SAY!?
HOW DARE YOU SHOW YOUR SORRY FACE LIKE THIS WHEN YOU ACTUALLY REMEMBER ME!

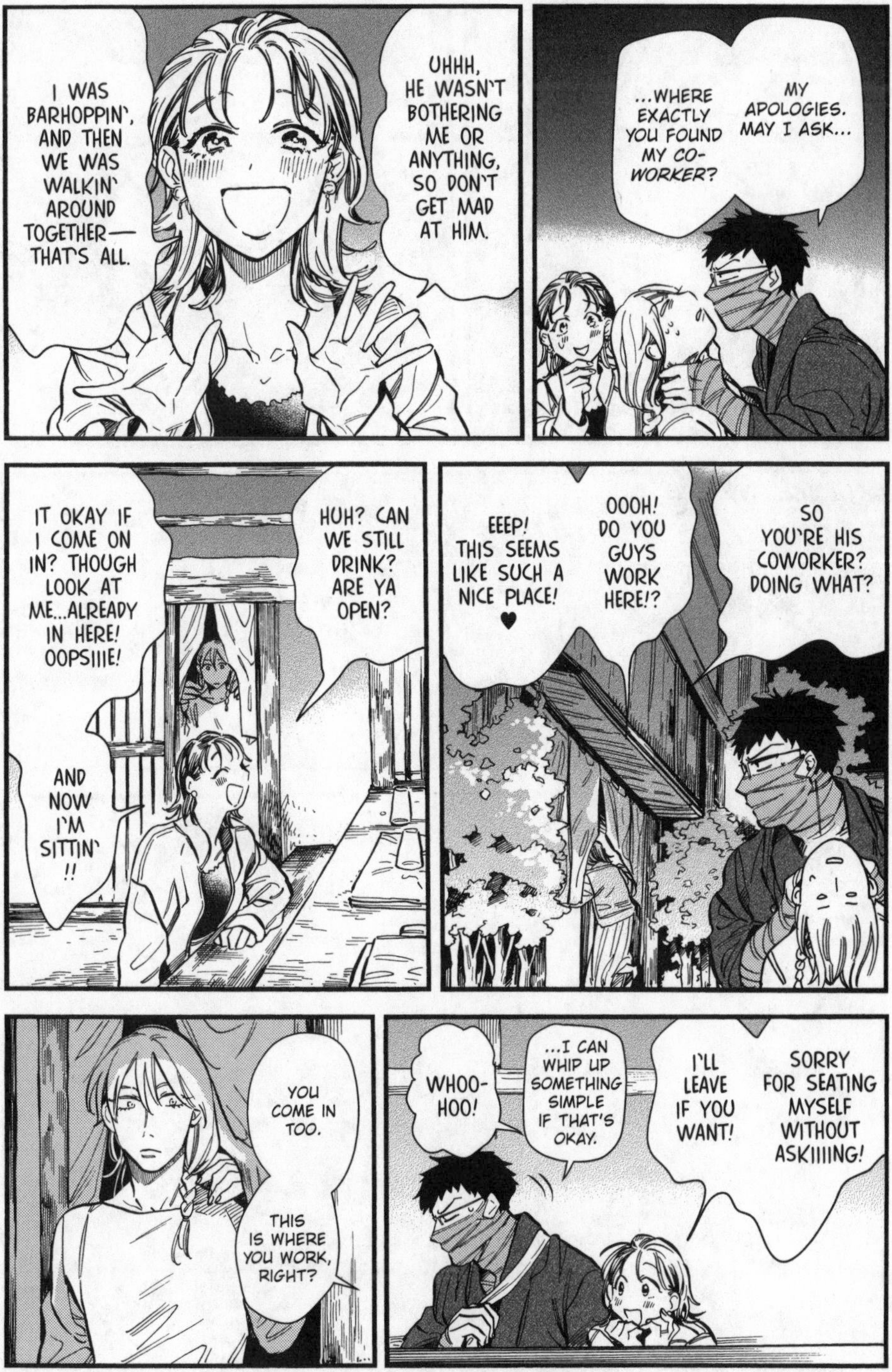
MY APOLOGIES. MAY I ASK...
...WHERE EXACTLY YOU FOUND MY CO-WORKER?
UHHH, HE WASN'T BOTHERING ME OR ANYTHING, SO DON'T GET MAD AT HIM.
I WAS BARHOPPIN', AND THEN WE WAS WALKIN' AROUND TOGETHER— THAT'S ALL.
SO YOU'RE HIS COWORKER? DOING WHAT?
OOOH! DO YOU GUYS WORK HERE!?
EEEP! THIS SEEMS LIKE SUCH A NICE PLACE! ♥
HUH? CAN WE STILL DRINK? ARE YA OPEN?
IT OKAY IF I COME ON IN? THOUGH LOOK AT ME...ALREADY IN HERE! OOPSIIIE!
AND NOW I'M SITTIN' !!
SORRY FOR SEATING MYSELF WITHOUT ASKIIIING!
I'LL LEAVE IF YOU WANT!
...I CAN WHIP UP SOMETHING SIMPLE IF THAT'S OKAY.
WHOO-HOO!
YOU COME IN TOO.
THIS IS WHERE YOU WORK, RIGHT?

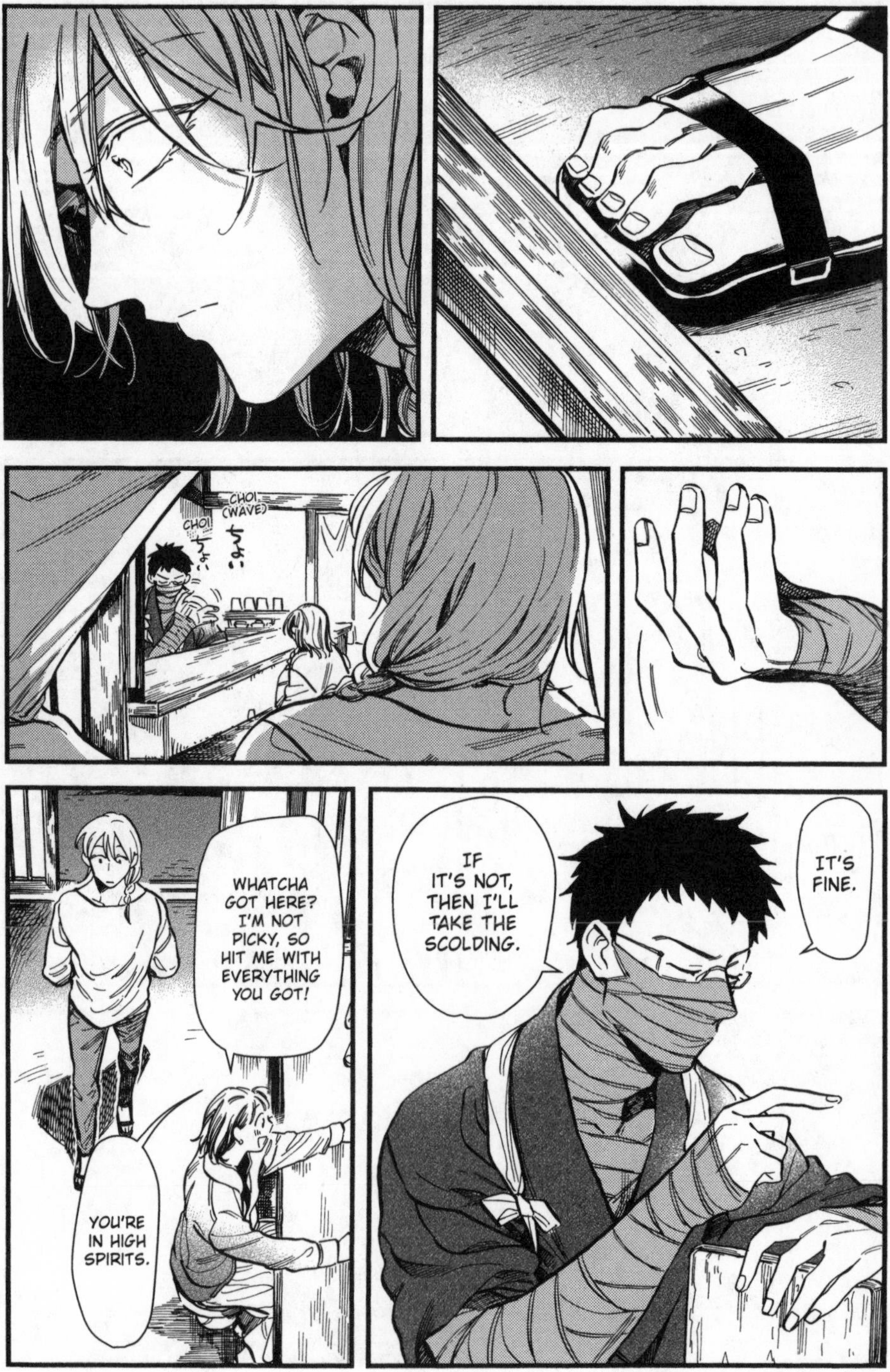
CHOI (WAVE) ちょい
CHOI ちょい
IT'S FINE.
IF IT'S NOT, THEN I'LL TAKE THE SCOLDING.
WHATCHA GOT HERE? I'M NOT PICKY, SO HIT ME WITH EVERYTHING YOU GOT!
YOU'RE IN HIGH SPIRITS.

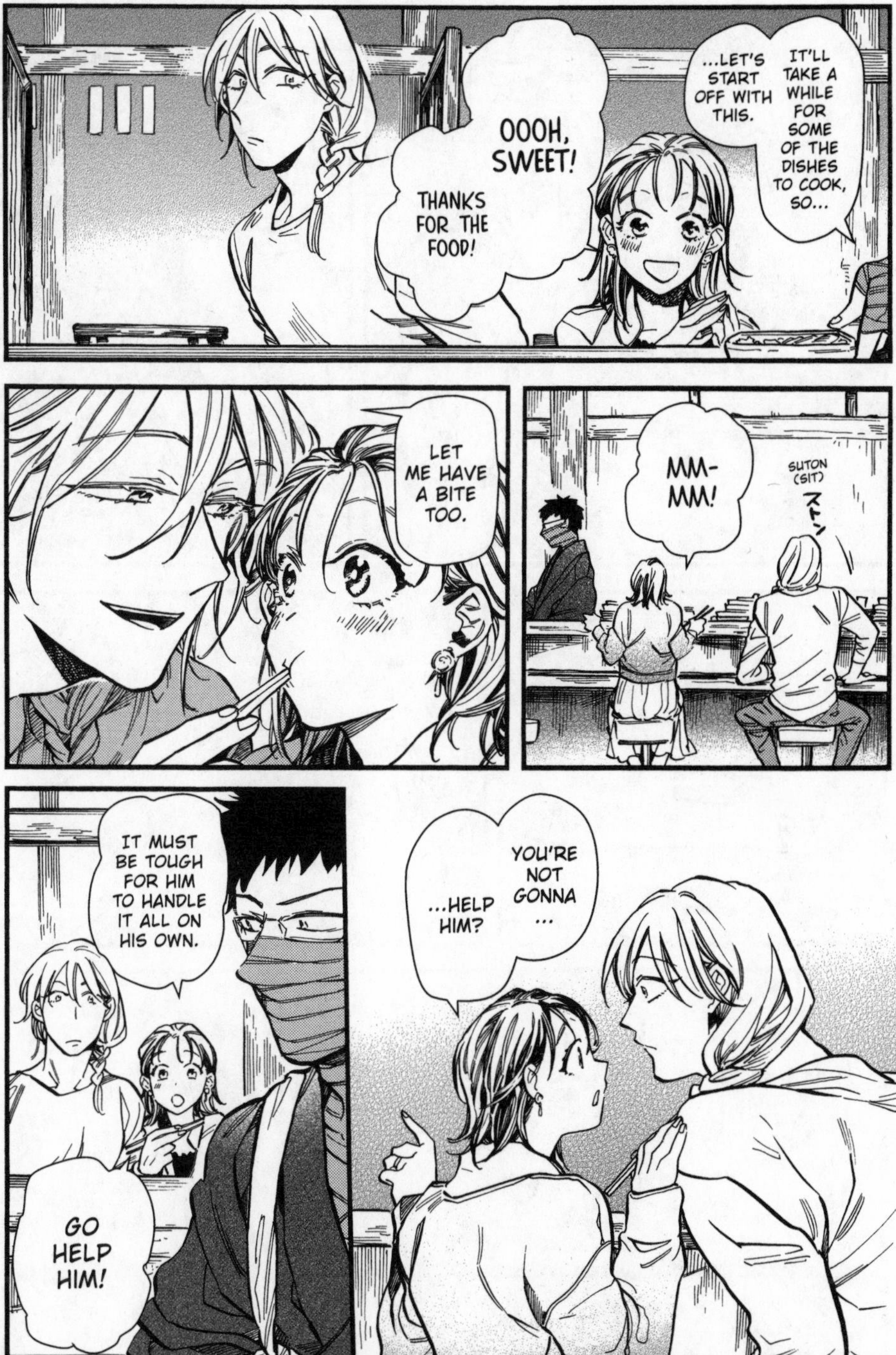
IT'LL TAKE A WHILE FOR SOME OF THE DISHES TO COOK, SO...
...LET'S START OFF WITH THIS.
OOOH, SWEET!
THANKS FOR THE FOOD!
MM-MM!
SUTON (SIT)
ストン
LET ME HAVE A BITE TOO.
YOU'RE NOT GONNA ...
...HELP HIM?
IT MUST BE TOUGH FOR HIM TO HANDLE IT ALL ON HIS OWN.
GO HELP HIM!

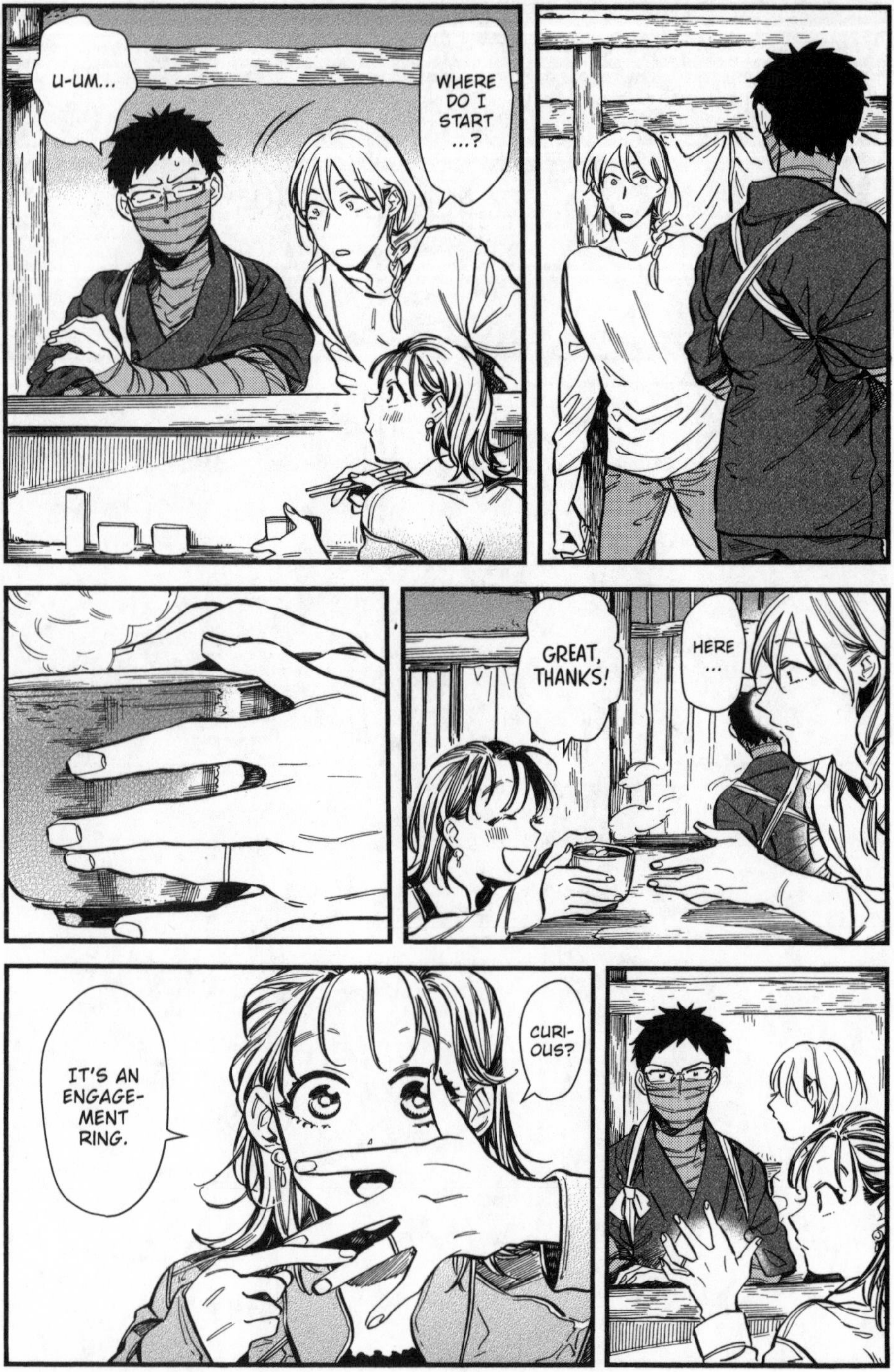
WHERE DO I START ...?
U-UM...
HERE ...
GREAT, THANKS!
CURI-OUS?
IT'S AN ENGAGE-MENT RING.

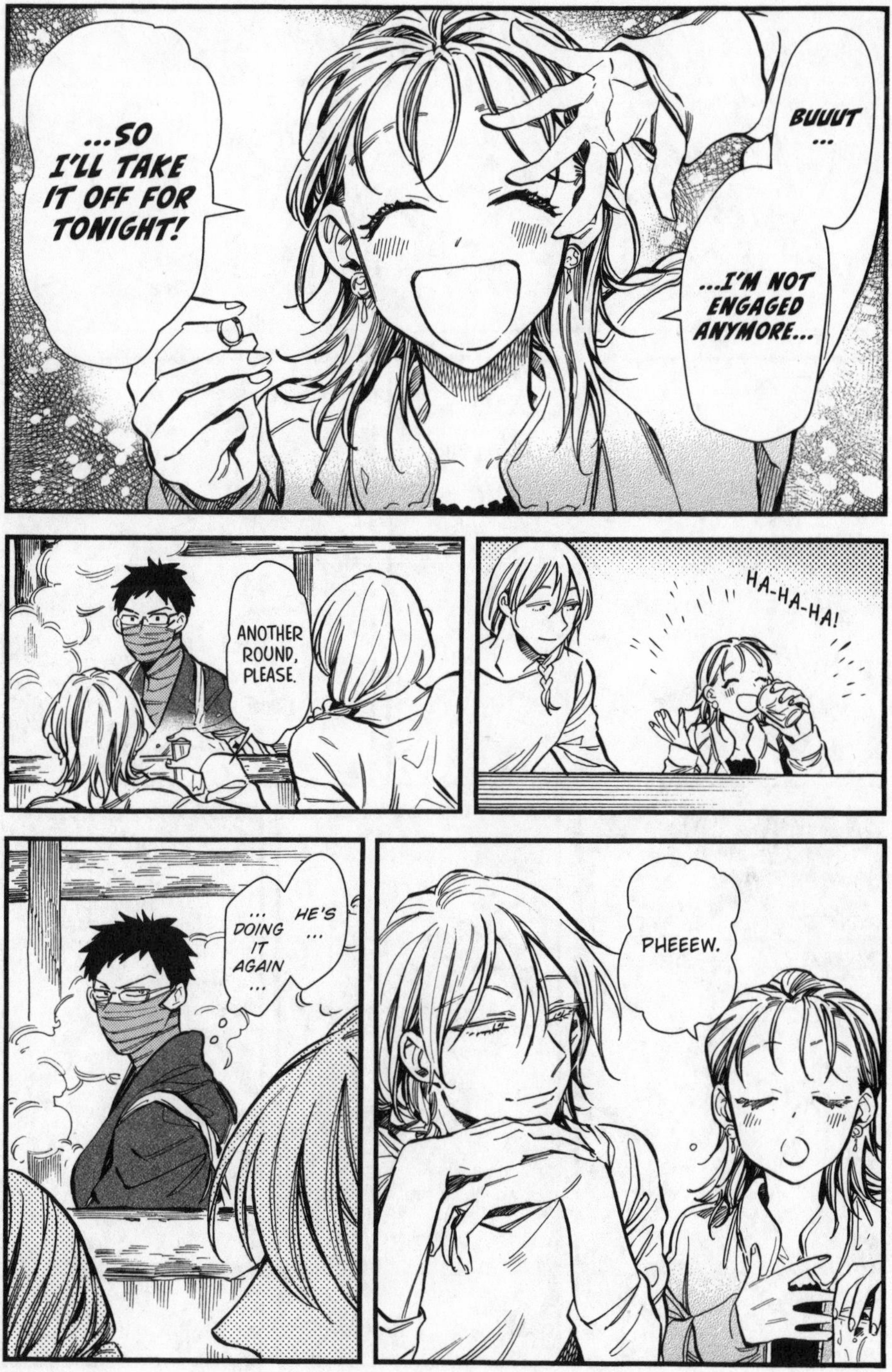
BUUUT ...
...I'M NOT ENGAGED ANYMORE...
...SO I'LL TAKE IT OFF FOR TONIGHT!
HA-HA-HA!
ANOTHER ROUND, PLEASE.
PHEEEW.
HE'S ... ... DOING IT AGAIN ...

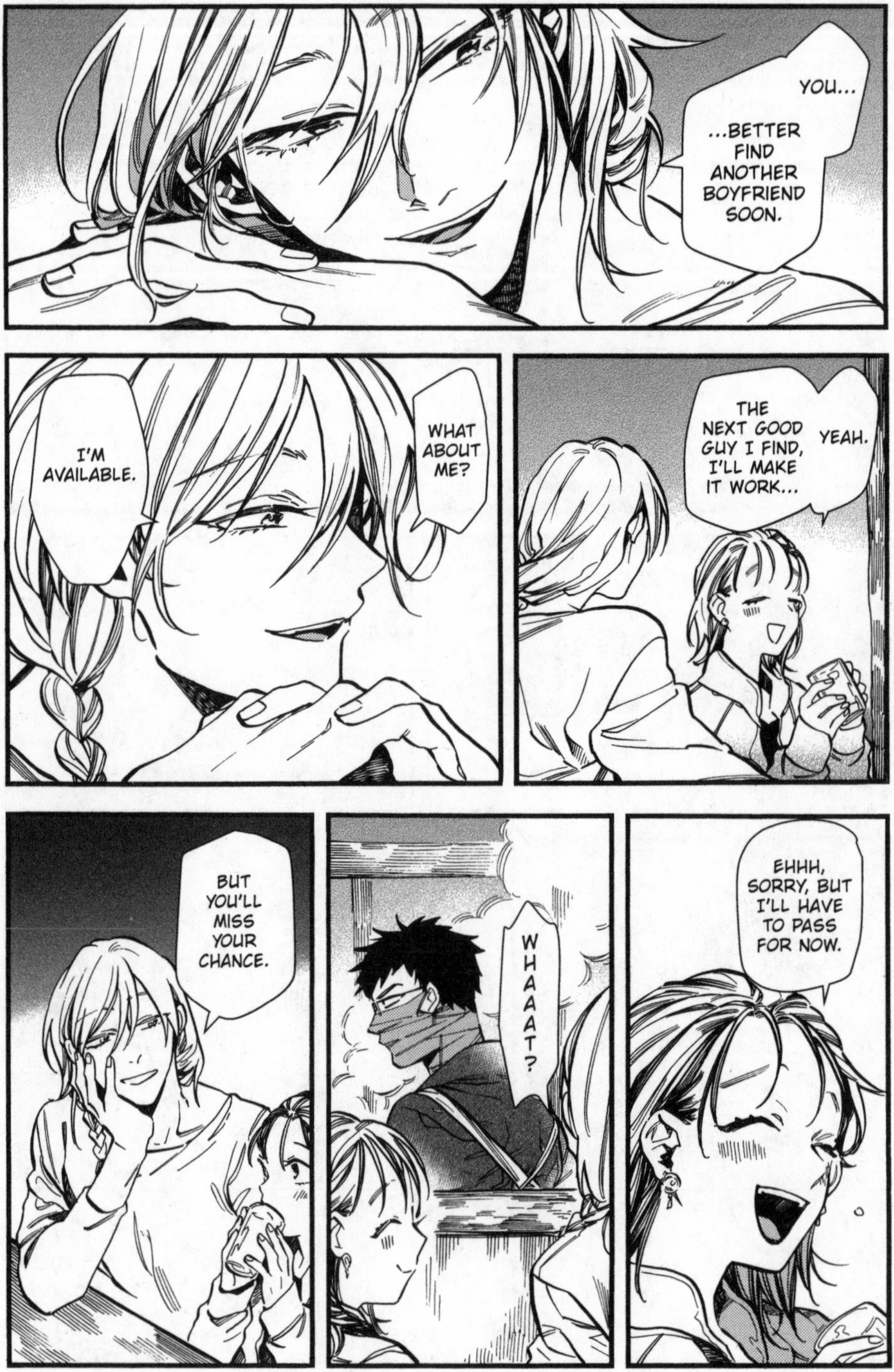
YOU...
...BETTER FIND ANOTHER BOYFRIEND SOON.
YEAH.
THE NEXT GOOD GUY I FIND, I'LL MAKE IT WORK...
WHAT ABOUT ME?
I'M AVAILABLE.
EHHH, SORRY, BUT I'LL HAVE TO PASS FOR NOW.
WHAAAAT?
BUT YOU'LL MISS YOUR CHANCE.

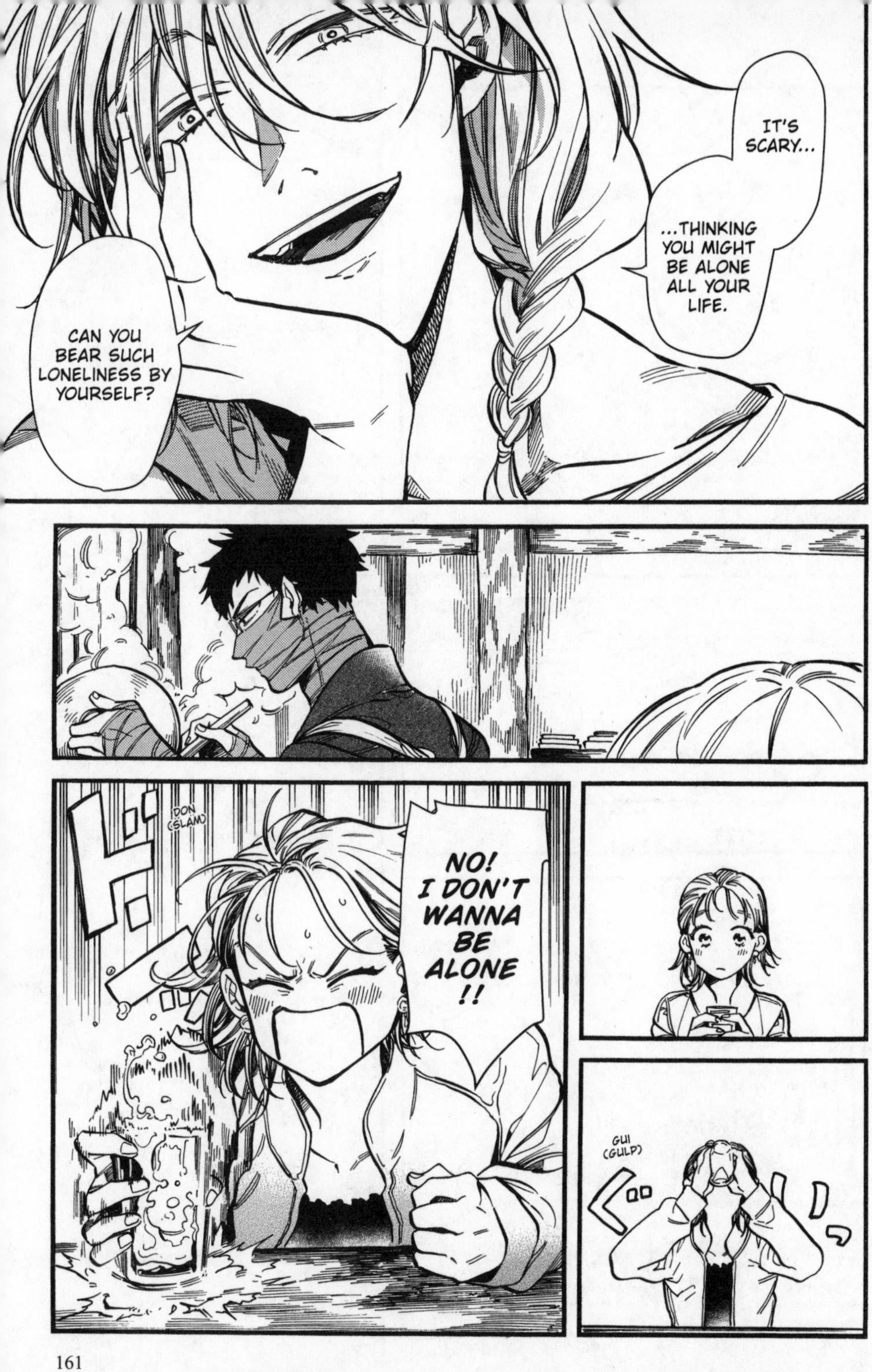
IT'S SCARY...
...THINKING YOU MIGHT BE ALONE ALL YOUR LIFE.
CAN YOU BEAR SUCH LONELINESS BY YOURSELF?
GUI (GULP)
DON (SLAM)
NO! I DON'T WANNA BE ALONE!!

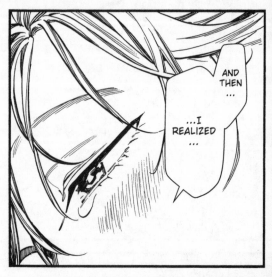

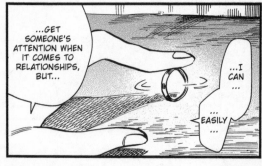

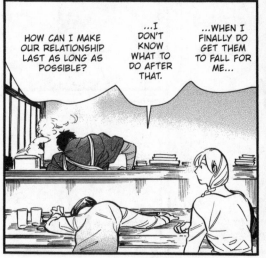

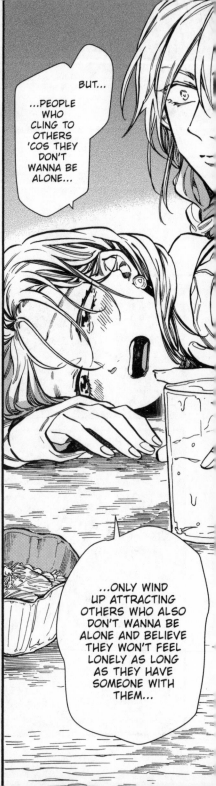

BUT...
...PEOPLE WHO CLING TO OTHERS 'COS THEY DON'T WANNA BE ALONE...
...ONLY WIND UP ATTRACTING OTHERS WHO ALSO DON'T WANNA BE ALONE AND BELIEVE THEY WON'T FEEL LONELY AS LONG AS THEY HAVE SOMEONE WITH THEM...
AND THEN...
...I REALIZED...
...I CAN...
...EASILY...
...GET SOMEONE'S ATTENTION WHEN IT COMES TO RELATIONSHIPS, BUT...
...WHEN I FINALLY DO GET THEM TO FALL FOR ME...
...I DON'T KNOW WHAT TO DO AFTER THAT.
HOW CAN I MAKE OUR RELATIONSHIP LAST AS LONG AS POSSIBLE?

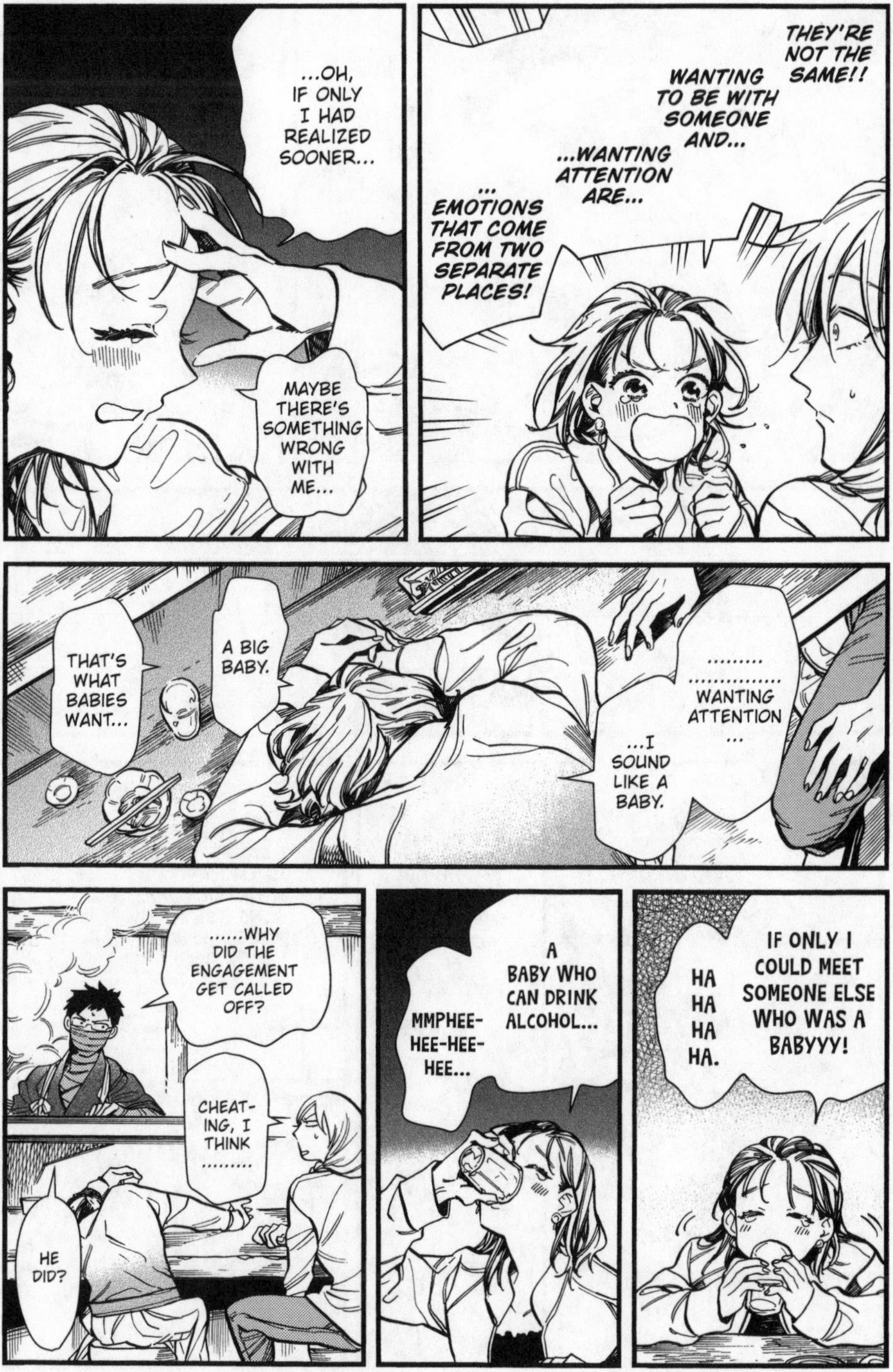
THEY'RE NOT THE SAME!!
WANTING TO BE WITH SOMEONE AND...
...WANTING ATTENTION ARE...
... EMOTIONS THAT COME FROM TWO SEPARATE PLACES!
...OH, IF ONLY I HAD REALIZED SOONER...
MAYBE THERE'S SOMETHING WRONG WITH ME...
.... WANTING ATTENTION ...
...I SOUND LIKE A BABY.
A BIG BABY.
THAT'S WHAT BABIES WANT...
IF ONLY I COULD MEET SOMEONE ELSE WHO WAS A BABYYY!
HA HA HA HA.
A BABY WHO CAN DRINK ALCOHOL...
MMPHEE-HEE-HEE-HEE...
......WHY DID THE ENGAGEMENT GET CALLED OFF?
CHEAT-ING, I THINK ....
HE DID?

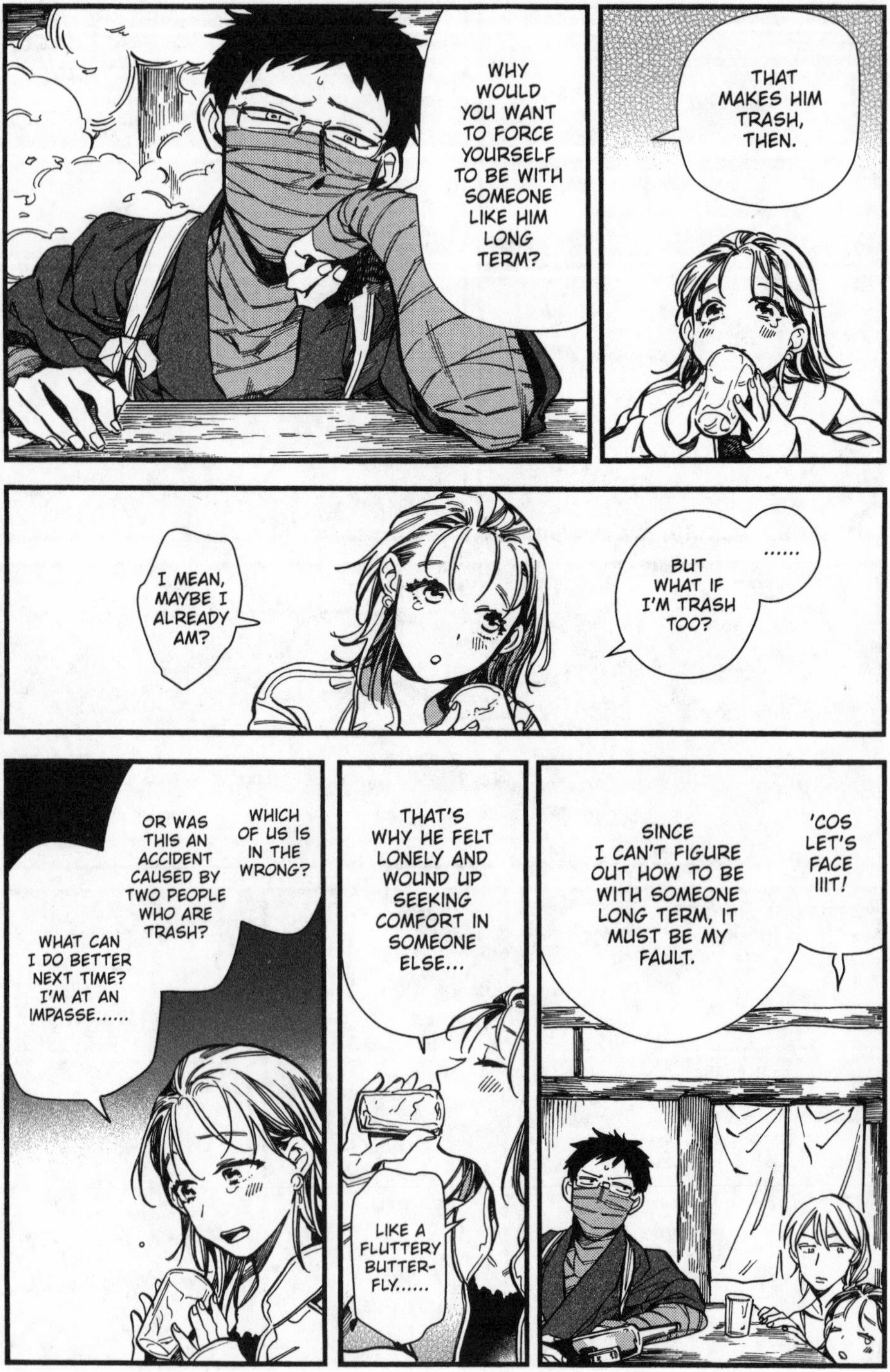
THAT MAKES HIM TRASH, THEN.
WHY WOULD YOU WANT TO FORCE YOURSELF TO BE WITH SOMEONE LIKE HIM LONG TERM?
...... BUT WHAT IF I'M TRASH TOO?
I MEAN, MAYBE I ALREADY AM?
'COS LET'S FACE IIIT!
SINCE I CAN'T FIGURE OUT HOW TO BE WITH SOMEONE LONG TERM, IT MUST BE MY FAULT.
THAT'S WHY HE FELT LONELY AND WOUND UP SEEKING COMFORT IN SOMEONE ELSE...
LIKE A FLUTTERY BUTTER-FLY......
WHICH OF US IS IN THE WRONG?
OR WAS THIS AN ACCIDENT CAUSED BY TWO PEOPLE WHO ARE TRASH?
WHAT CAN I DO BETTER NEXT TIME? I'M AT AN IMPASSE......

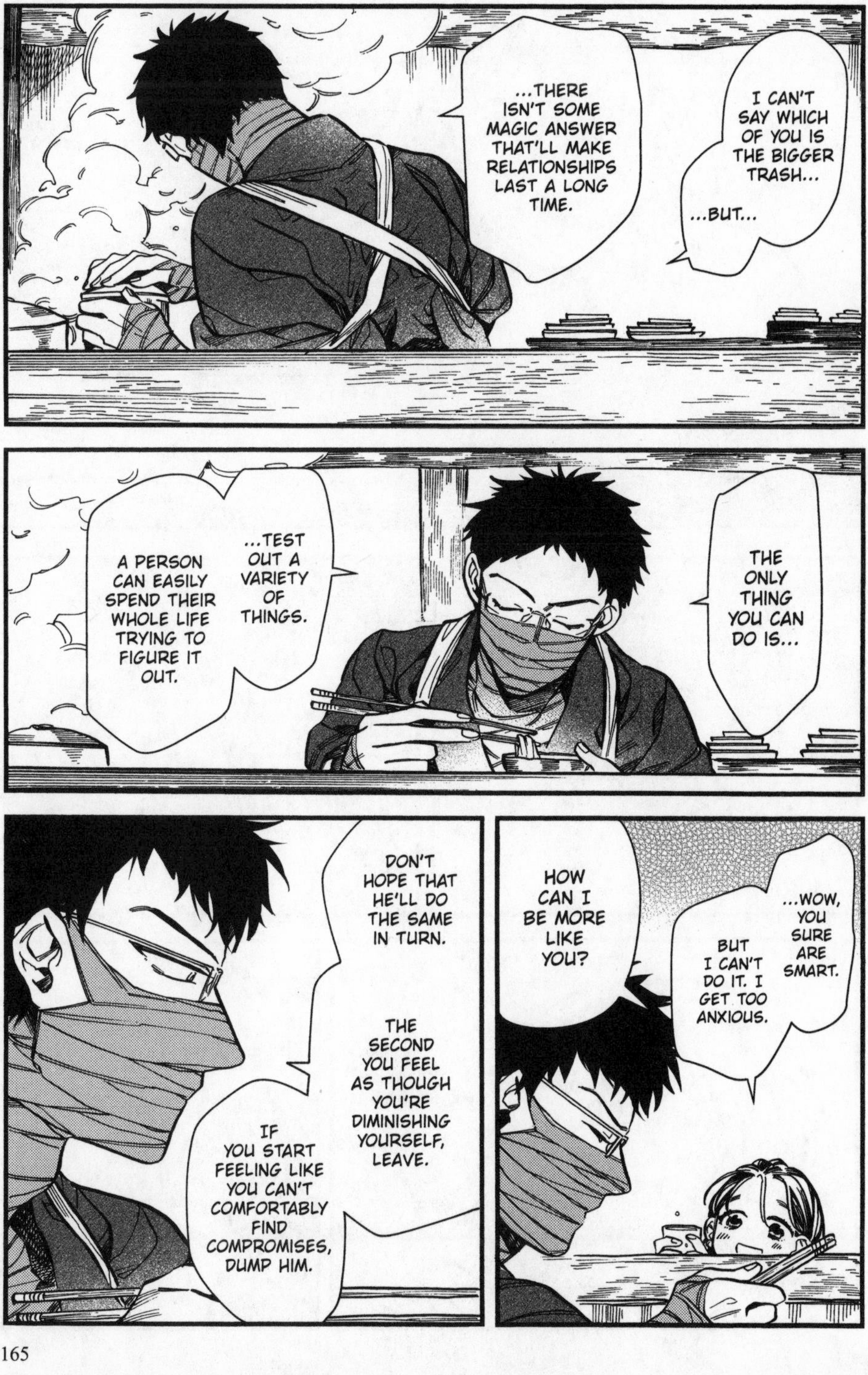
I CAN'T SAY WHICH OF YOU IS THE BIGGER TRASH...
...BUT...
...THERE ISN'T SOME MAGIC ANSWER THAT'LL MAKE RELATIONSHIPS LAST A LONG TIME.
THE ONLY THING YOU CAN DO IS...
...TEST OUT A VARIETY OF THINGS.
A PERSON CAN EASILY SPEND THEIR WHOLE LIFE TRYING TO FIGURE IT OUT.
...WOW, YOU SURE ARE SMART.
BUT I CAN'T DO IT. I GET TOO ANXIOUS.
HOW CAN I BE MORE LIKE YOU?
DON'T HOPE THAT HE'LL DO THE SAME IN TURN.
THE SECOND YOU FEEL AS THOUGH YOU'RE DIMINISHING YOURSELF, LEAVE.
IF YOU START FEELING LIKE YOU CAN'T COMFORTABLY FIND COMPROMISES, DUMP HIM.

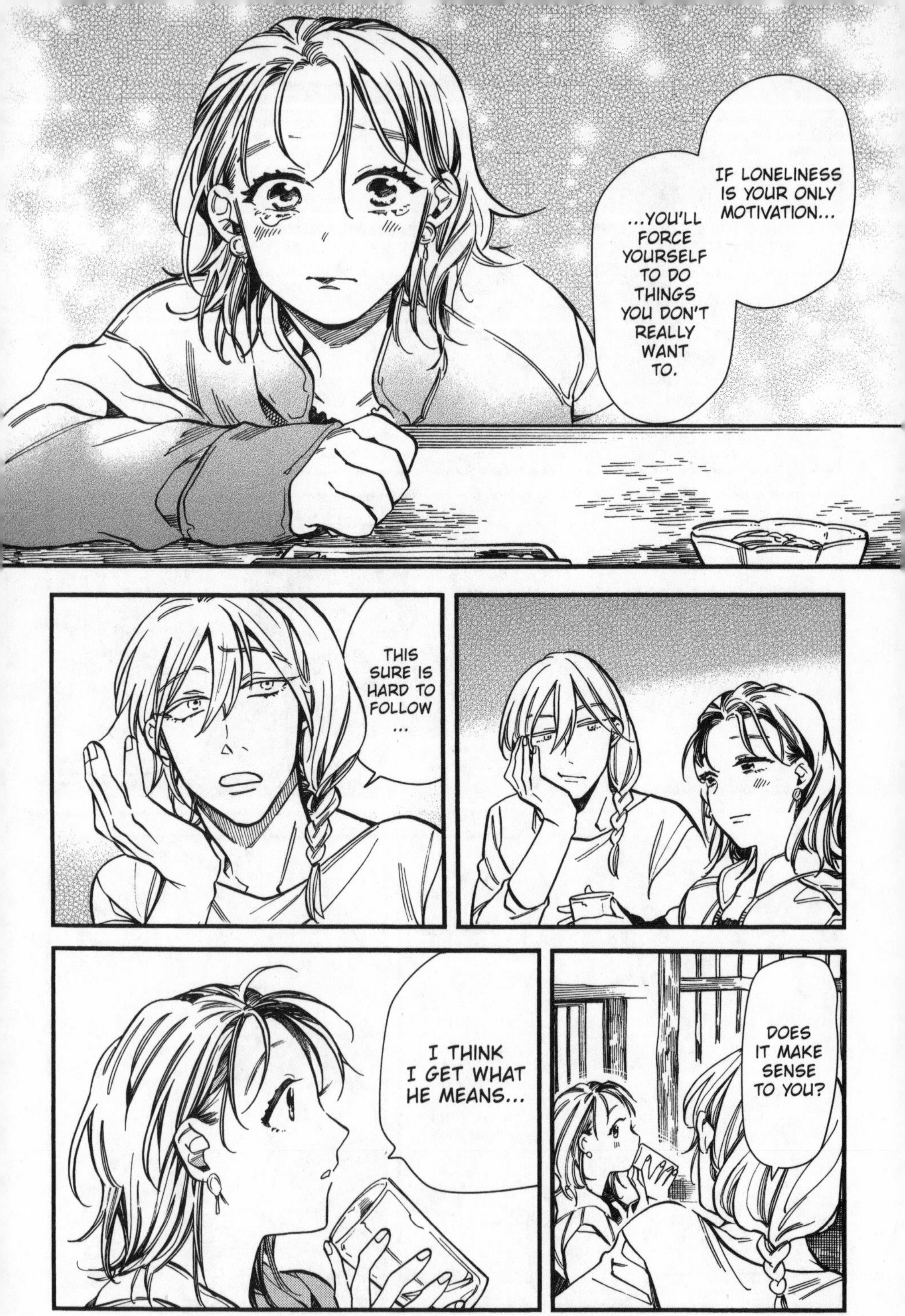
IF LONELINESS IS YOUR ONLY MOTIVATION...
...YOU'LL FORCE YOURSELF TO DO THINGS YOU DON'T REALLY WANT TO.
THIS SURE IS HARD TO FOLLOW...
DOES IT MAKE SENSE TO YOU?
I THINK I GET WHAT HE MEANS...

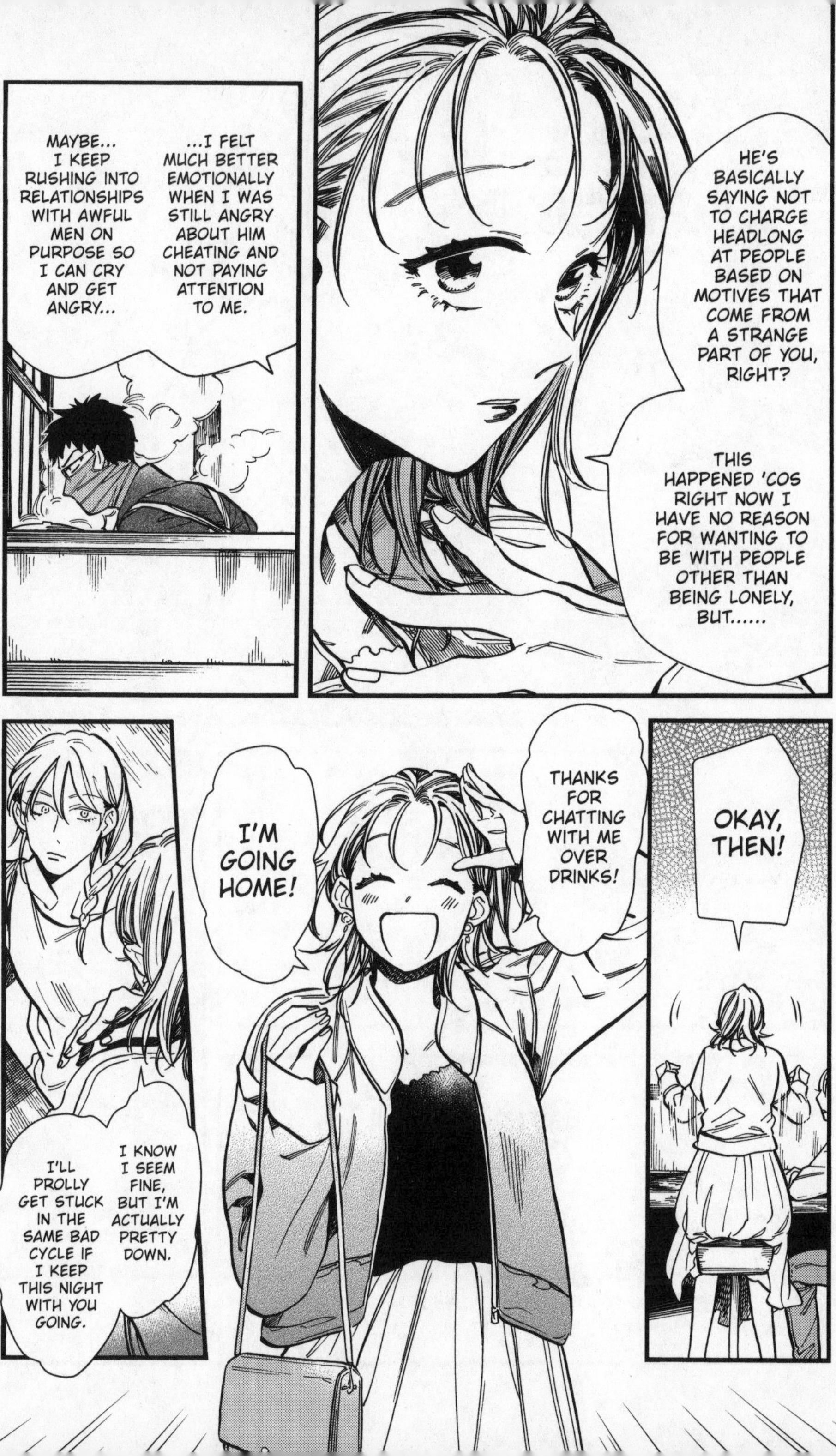
HE'S BASICALLY SAYING NOT TO CHARGE HEADLONG AT PEOPLE BASED ON MOTIVES THAT COME FROM A STRANGE PART OF YOU, RIGHT?
THIS HAPPENED 'COS RIGHT NOW I HAVE NO REASON FOR WANTING TO BE WITH PEOPLE OTHER THAN BEING LONELY, BUT......
...I FELT MUCH BETTER EMOTIONALLY WHEN I WAS STILL ANGRY ABOUT HIM CHEATING AND NOT PAYING ATTENTION TO ME.
MAYBE... I KEEP RUSHING INTO RELATIONSHIPS WITH AWFUL MEN ON PURPOSE SO I CAN CRY AND GET ANGRY...
OKAY, THEN!
THANKS FOR CHATTING WITH ME OVER DRINKS!
I'M GOING HOME!
I KNOW I SEEM FINE, BUT I'M ACTUALLY PRETTY DOWN.
I'LL PROLLY GET STUCK IN THE SAME BAD CYCLE IF I KEEP THIS NIGHT WITH YOU GOING.

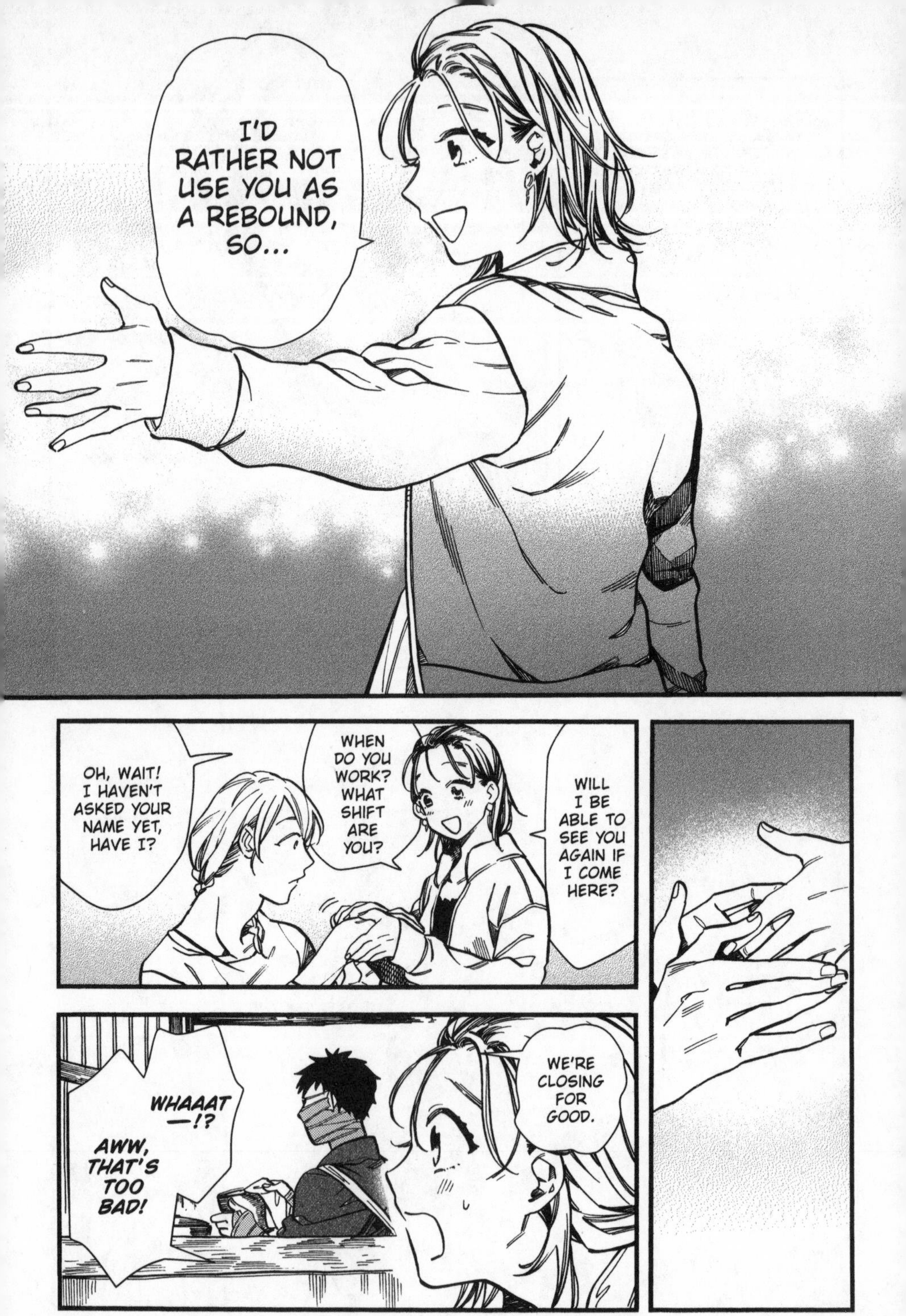

I'D RATHER NOT USE YOU AS A REBOUND, SO...
WILL I BE ABLE TO SEE YOU AGAIN IF I COME HERE?
WHEN DO YOU WORK? WHAT SHIFT ARE YOU?
OH, WAIT! I HAVEN'T ASKED YOUR NAME YET, HAVE I?
WE'RE CLOSING FOR GOOD.
WHAAAT—!?
AWW, THAT'S TOO BAD!

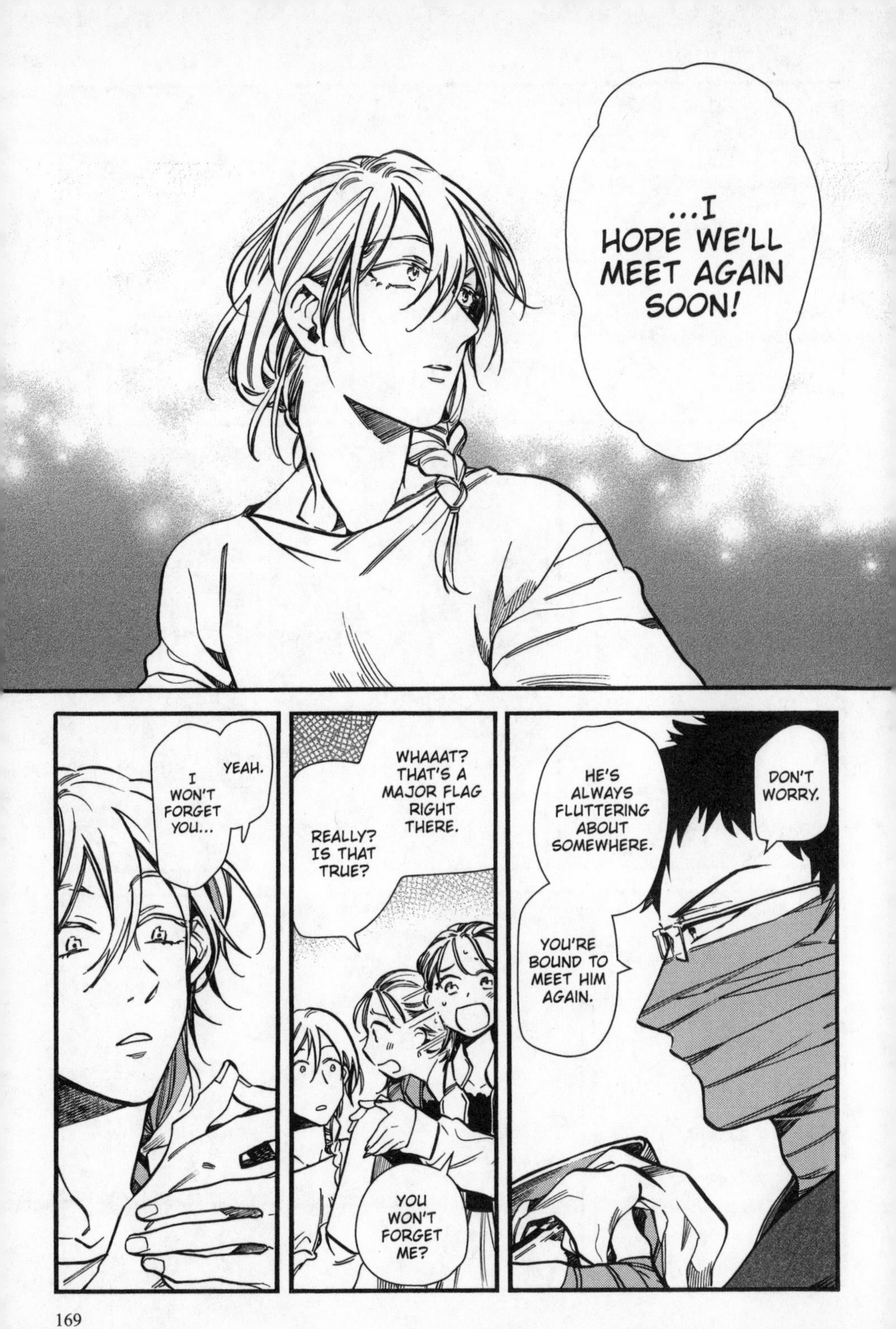
...I HOPE WE'LL MEET AGAIN SOON!
DON'T WORRY.
HE'S ALWAYS FLUTTERING ABOUT SOMEWHERE.
YOU'RE BOUND TO MEET HIM AGAIN.
WHAAAT? THAT'S A MAJOR FLAG RIGHT THERE.
REALLY? IS THAT TRUE?
YOU WON'T FORGET ME?
YEAH.
I WON'T FORGET YOU...

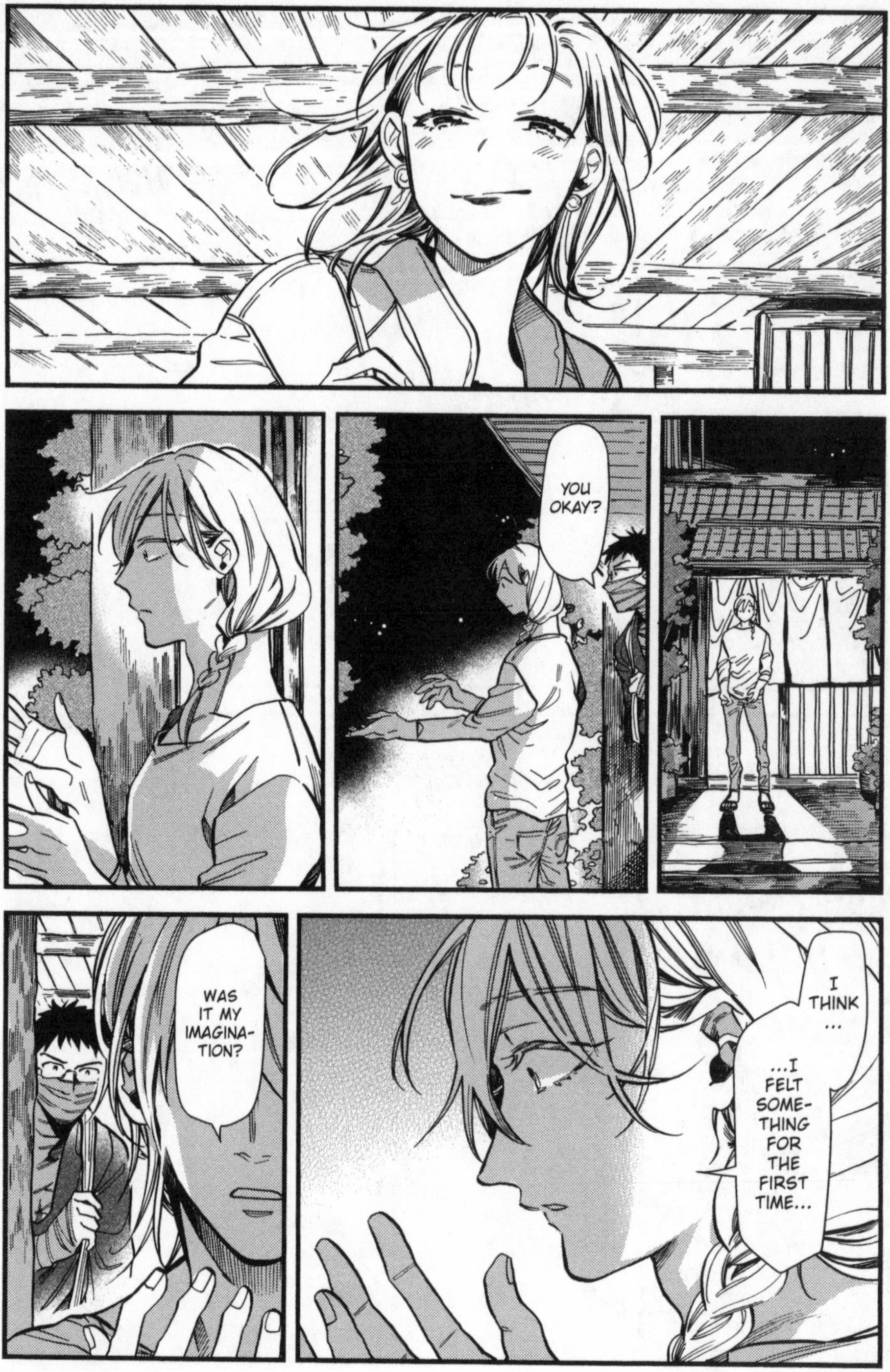
YOU OKAY?
I THINK...
...I FELT SOMETHING FOR THE FIRST TIME...
WAS IT MY IMAGINATION?

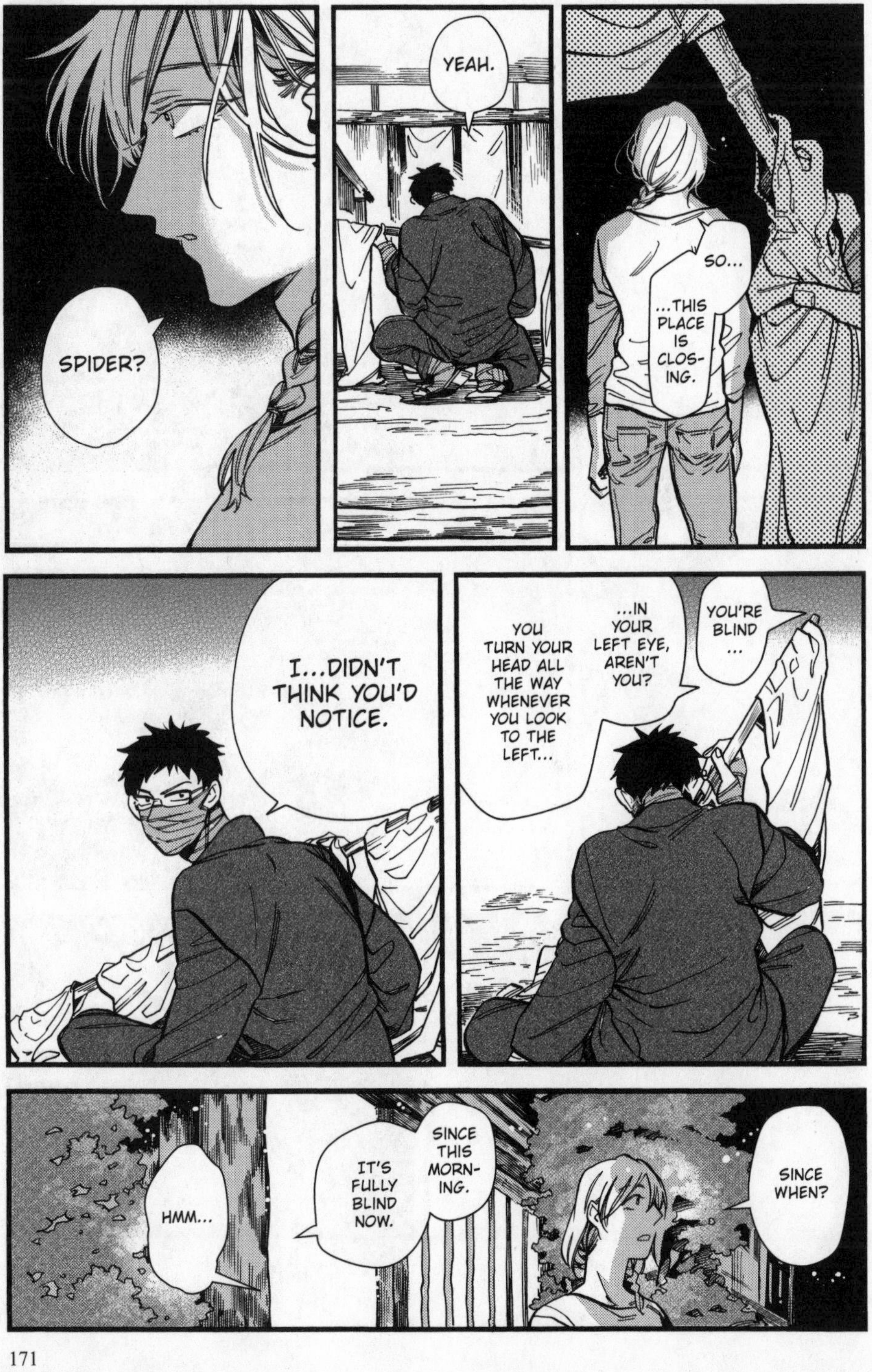
SO...
...THIS PLACE IS CLOSING.
YEAH.
SPIDER?
YOU'RE BLIND ...
...IN YOUR LEFT EYE, AREN'T YOU?
YOU TURN YOUR HEAD ALL THE WAY WHENEVER YOU LOOK TO THE LEFT...
I...DIDN'T THINK YOU'D NOTICE.
SINCE WHEN?
SINCE THIS MORNING.
IT'S FULLY BLIND NOW.
HMM...

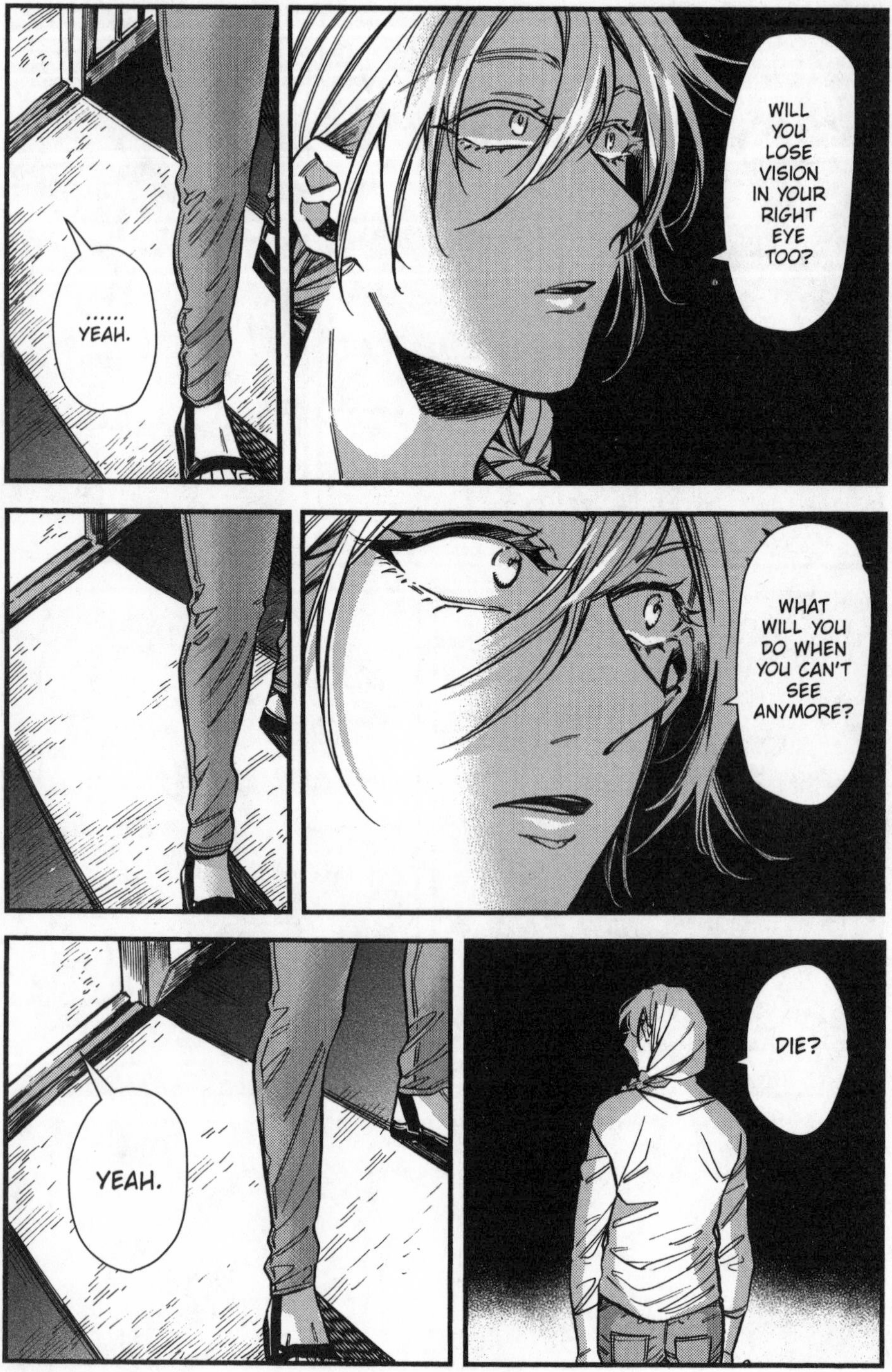
WILL YOU LOSE VISION IN YOUR RIGHT EYE TOO?
...... YEAH.
WHAT WILL YOU DO WHEN YOU CAN'T SEE ANYMORE?
DIE?
YEAH.

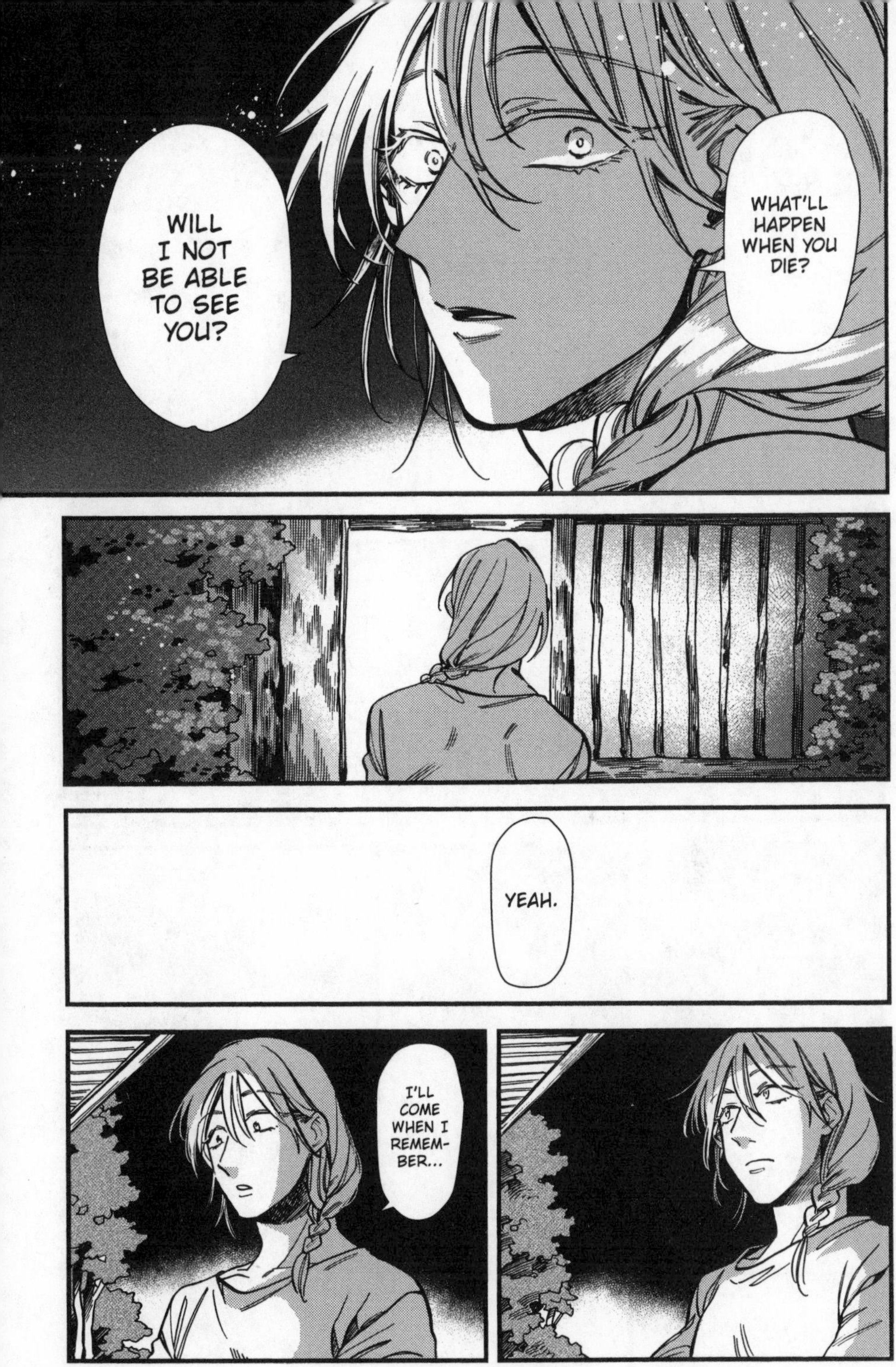
WHAT'LL HAPPEN WHEN YOU DIE?
WILL I NOT BE ABLE TO SEE YOU?
YEAH.
I'LL COME WHEN I REMEMBER...

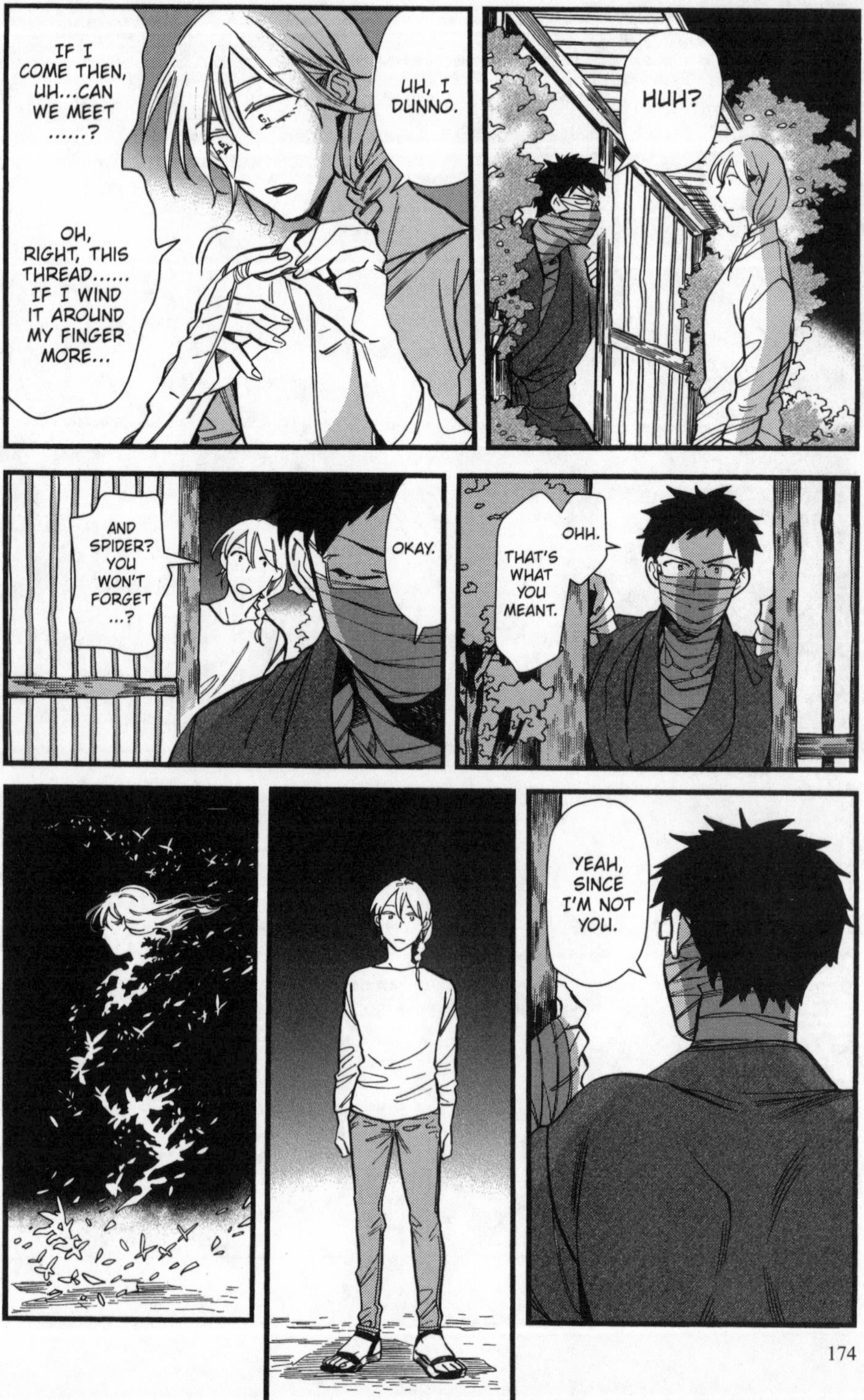
HUH?
UH, I DUNNO.
IF I COME THEN, UH...CAN WE MEET ......?
OH, RIGHT, THIS THREAD...... IF I WIND IT AROUND MY FINGER MORE...
OHH.
THAT'S WHAT YOU MEANT.
OKAY.
AND SPIDER? YOU WON'T FORGET ...?
YEAH, SINCE I'M NOT YOU.

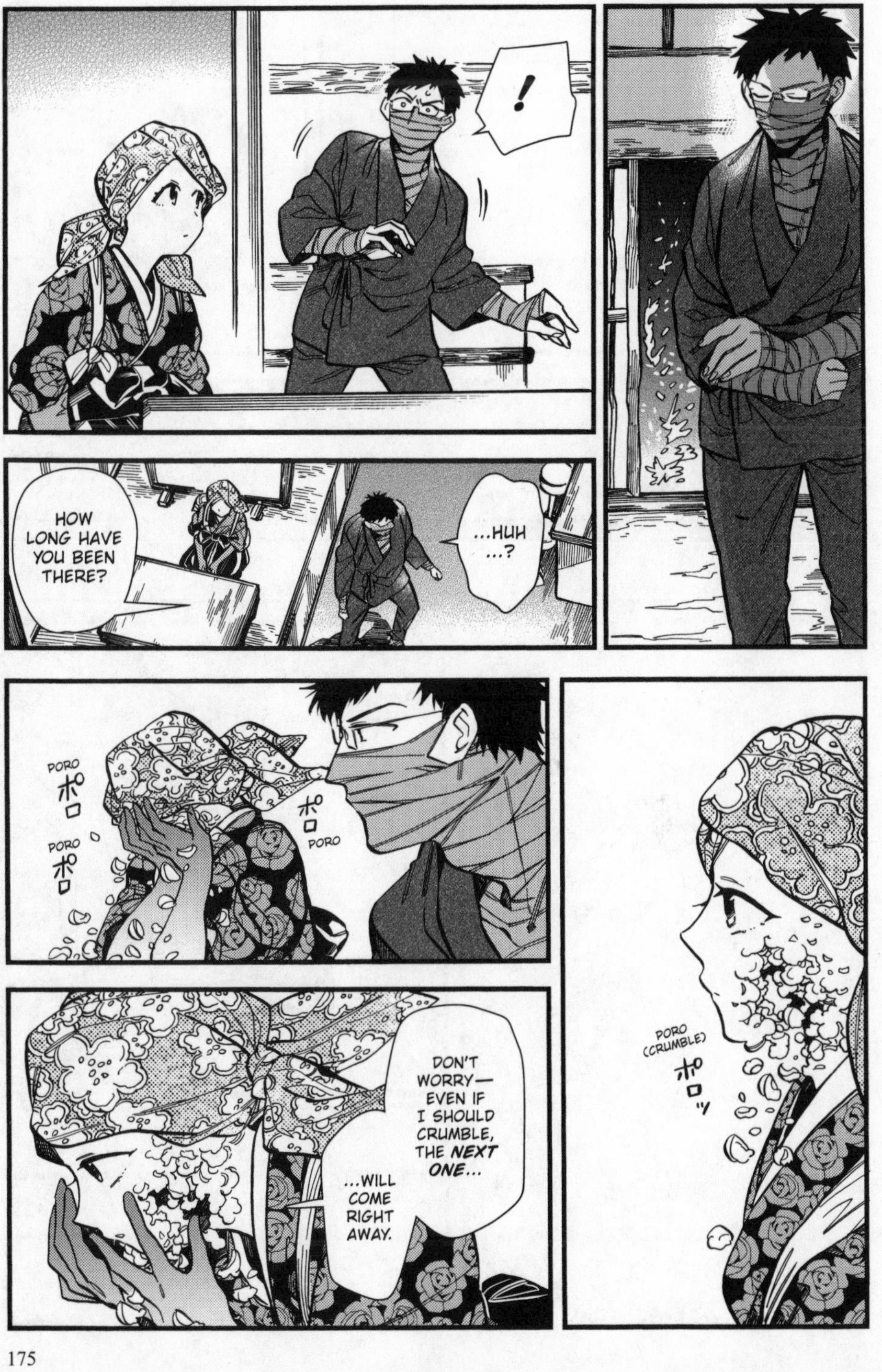
!
...HUH ...?
HOW LONG HAVE YOU BEEN THERE?
PORO (CRUMBLE) ポロッ
ポロ PORO
PORO ポロ
PORO ポロ
DON'T WORRY—EVEN IF I SHOULD CRUMBLE, THE ***NEXT ONE***...
...WILL COME RIGHT AWAY.

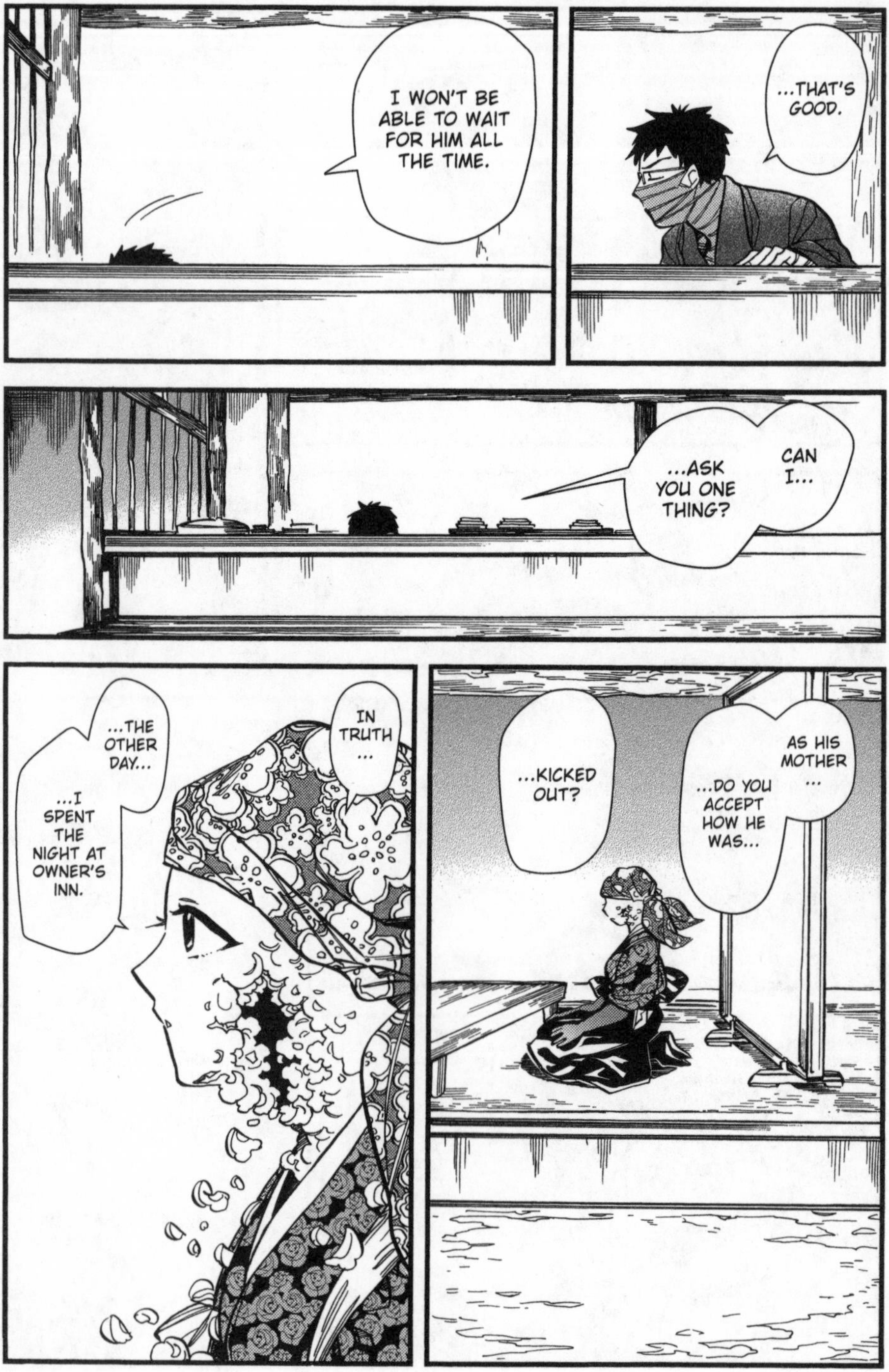
...THAT'S GOOD.
I WON'T BE ABLE TO WAIT FOR HIM ALL THE TIME.
CAN I...
...ASK YOU ONE THING?
AS HIS MOTHER ...
...DO YOU ACCEPT HOW HE WAS...
...KICKED OUT?
IN TRUTH ...
...THE OTHER DAY...
...I SPENT THE NIGHT AT OWNER'S INN.

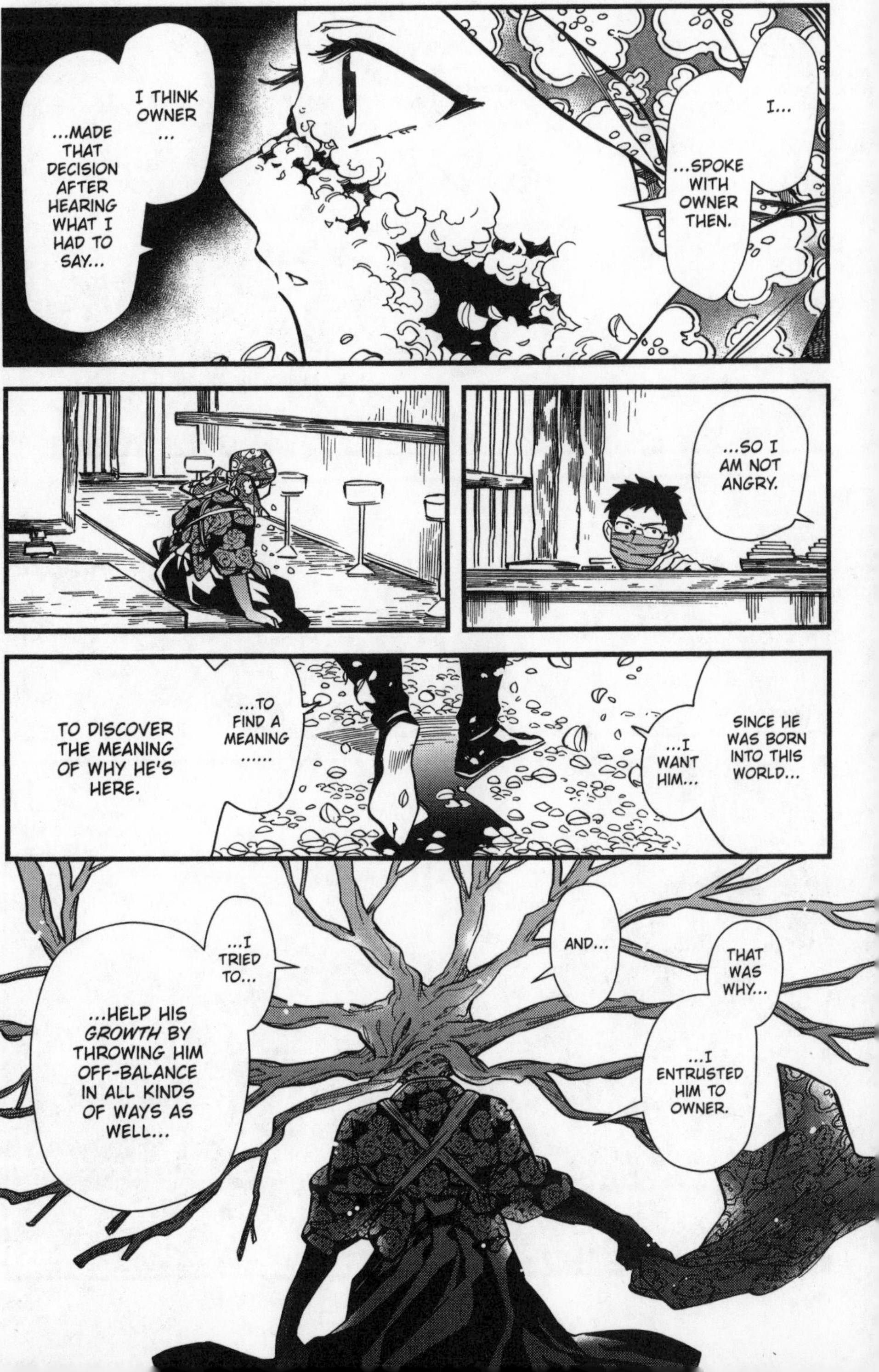
I...
...SPOKE WITH OWNER THEN.
I THINK OWNER...
...MADE THAT DECISION AFTER HEARING WHAT I HAD TO SAY...
...SO I AM NOT ANGRY.
SINCE HE WAS BORN INTO THIS WORLD...
...I WANT HIM...
...TO FIND A MEANING......
TO DISCOVER THE MEANING OF WHY HE'S HERE.
THAT WAS WHY...
...I ENTRUSTED HIM TO OWNER.
AND...
...I TRIED TO...
...HELP HIS *GROWTH* BY THROWING HIM OFF-BALANCE IN ALL KINDS OF WAYS AS WELL...

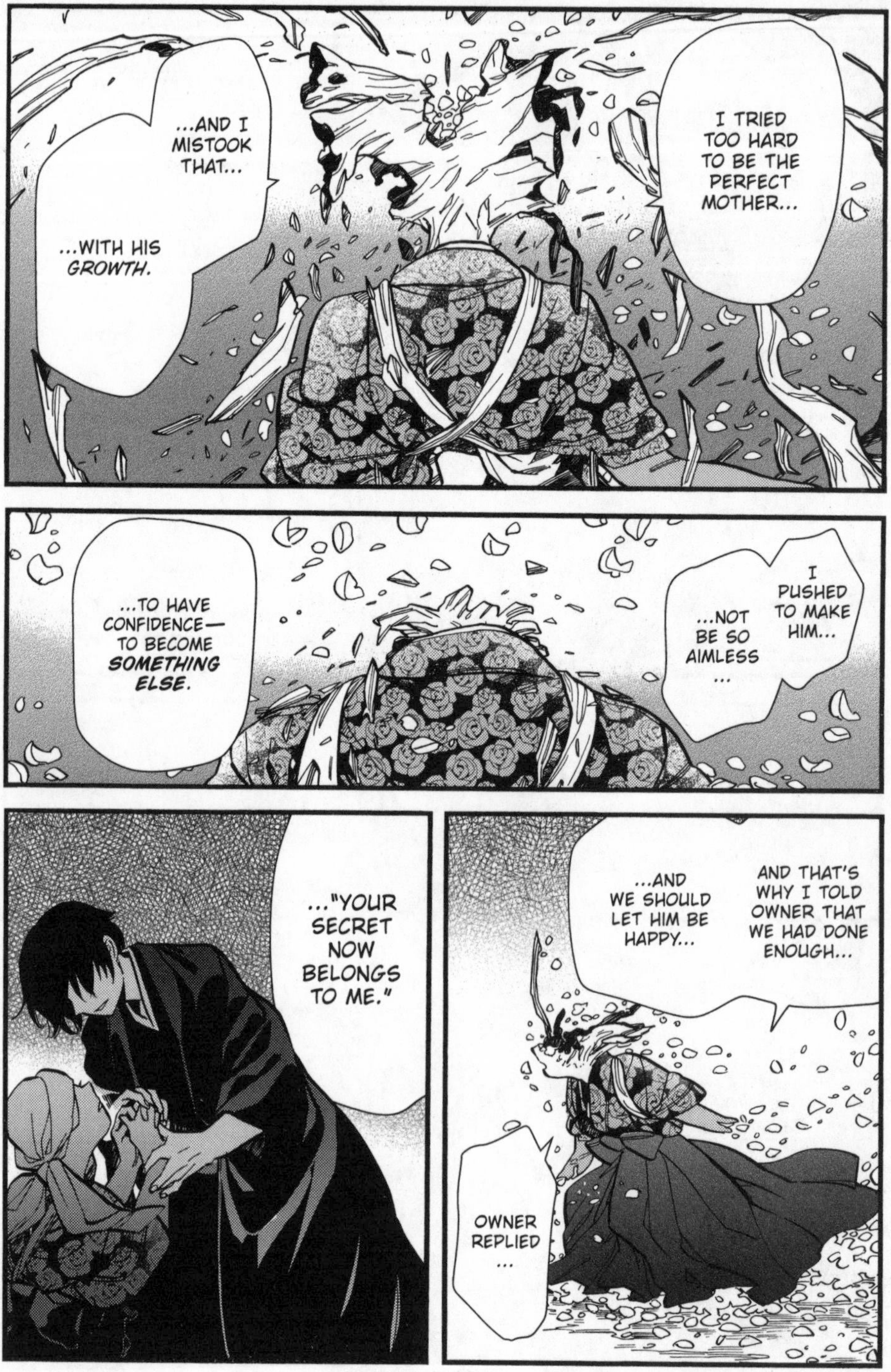
I TRIED TOO HARD TO BE THE PERFECT MOTHER...
...AND I MISTOOK THAT...
...WITH HIS *GROWTH*.
I PUSHED TO MAKE HIM...
...NOT BE SO AIMLESS ...
...TO HAVE CONFIDENCE— TO BECOME ***SOMETHING ELSE***.
AND THAT'S WHY I TOLD OWNER THAT WE HAD DONE ENOUGH...
...AND WE SHOULD LET HIM BE HAPPY...
OWNER REPLIED ...
..."YOUR SECRET NOW BELONGS TO ME."

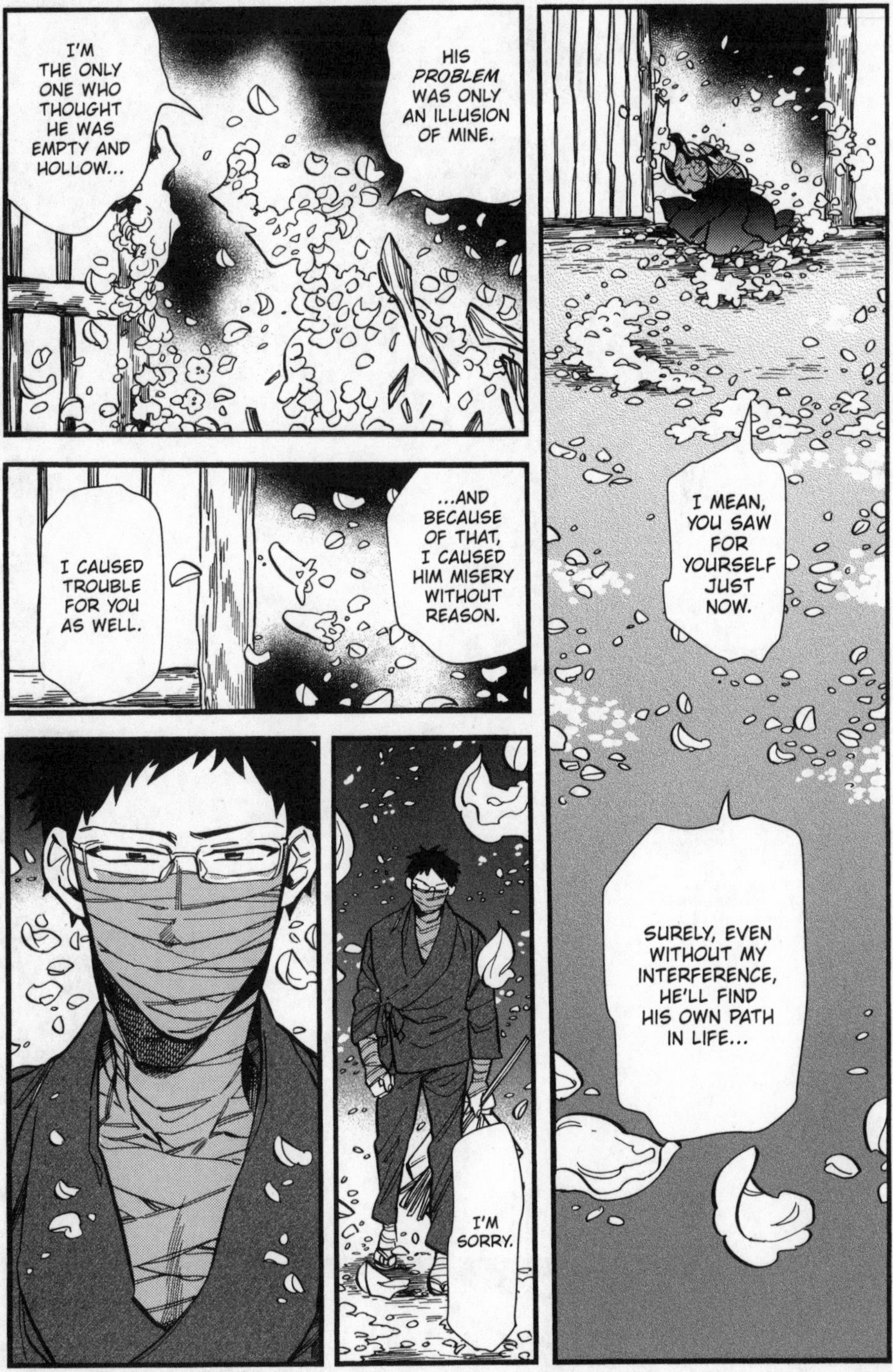
I MEAN, YOU SAW FOR YOURSELF JUST NOW.
SURELY, EVEN WITHOUT MY INTERFERENCE, HE'LL FIND HIS OWN PATH IN LIFE...
HIS *PROBLEM* WAS ONLY AN ILLUSION OF MINE.
I'M THE ONLY ONE WHO THOUGHT HE WAS EMPTY AND HOLLOW...
...AND BECAUSE OF THAT, I CAUSED HIM MISERY WITHOUT REASON.
I CAUSED TROUBLE FOR YOU AS WELL.
I'M SORRY.

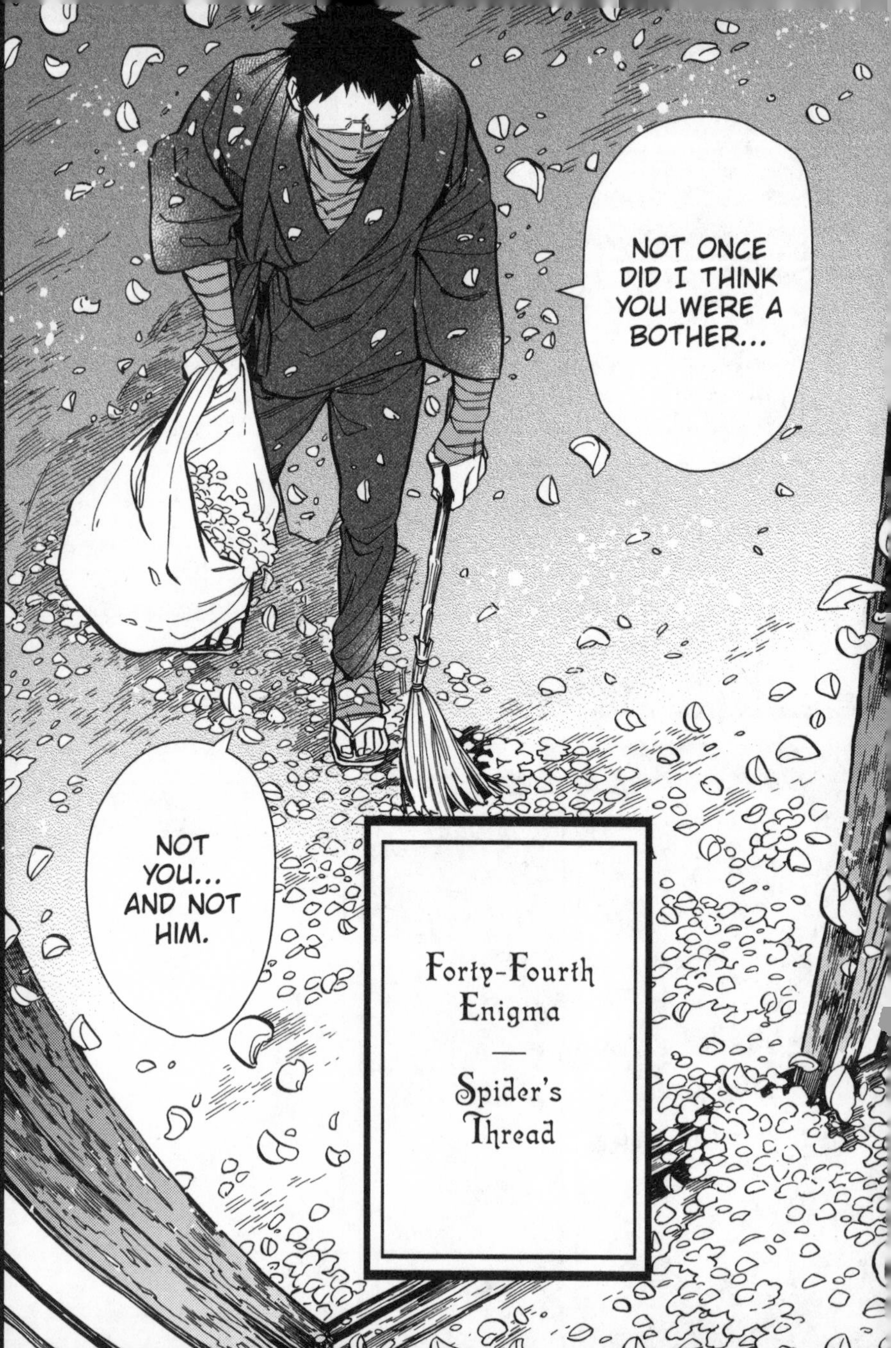
NOT ONCE DID I THINK YOU WERE A BOTHER...
NOT YOU... AND NOT HIM.
Forty-Fourth Enigma
—
Spider's Thread

Translation Notes

Common Honorifics

no honorific: Indicates familiarity or closeness; if used without permission or reason, addressing someone in this manner would constitute an insult.

-san: The Japanese equivalent of Mr./Mrs./Miss. If a situation calls for politeness, this is the fail-safe honorific.

-kun: Used most often when referring to boys, this indicates affection or familiarity. Occasionally used by older men among their peers, but it may also be used by anyone referring to a person of lower standing.

-chan: An affectionate honorific indicating familiarity used mostly in reference to girls; also used in reference to cute persons or animals of either gender.

-sensei: A respectful term for teachers, artists, or high-level professionals.

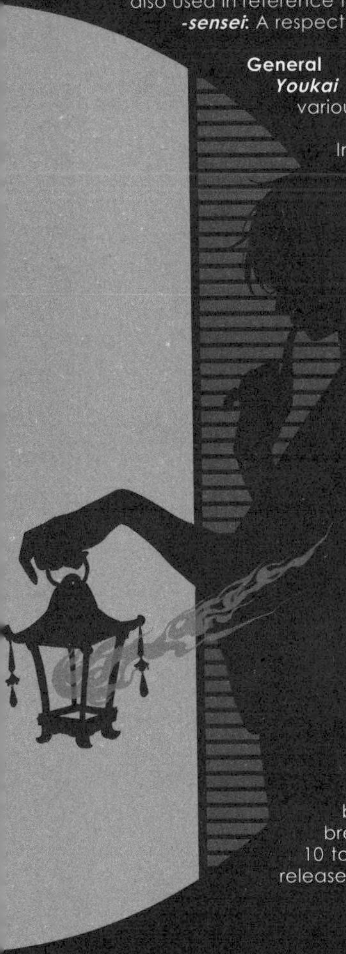

General

Youkai are a class of Japanese supernatural being, translated variously in English as "ghosts," "demons," "monsters," etc.

In Japanese, **Owner** is called *Taishou*, a term used to refer to the owners of traditional Japanese restaurants and inns. It generally means "boss" or "chief."

Spider in Japanese is *kumo*, and the character is referred to as such in Japanese. His full name, **Earth Spider**, is a translation of *tsuchigumo*, a *youkai* spider grown to gigantic size.

Butterfly in Japanese is *chou*, which is also the character's name in Japanese. His full name, **Incarnate Butterflies**, is a translation of *chou keshin*, a *youkai* consisting of butterflies merged with human souls.

Page 5

The **Meiji period** refers to the historical period from 1868 to 1912. The **Taisho period** came next during the years 1912 to 1926.

Page 10

Benten, also known as Benzaiten, is a Buddhist goddess associated with literature, music, wealth, femininity, and the sea. She is often depicted holding a kind of lute called a *biwa* while riding a dragon.

Page 118

Shochu is a type of alcohol made from distilled liquor. While closely related to sake, or rice wine, it actually can be made from a variety of materials like sweet potatoes or barley along with the rice. Also, since it is distilled instead of brewed, the alcohol percentage is higher than sake by about 10 to 15 percent. Sake should be consumed within a year of its release, while *shochu* ages well.

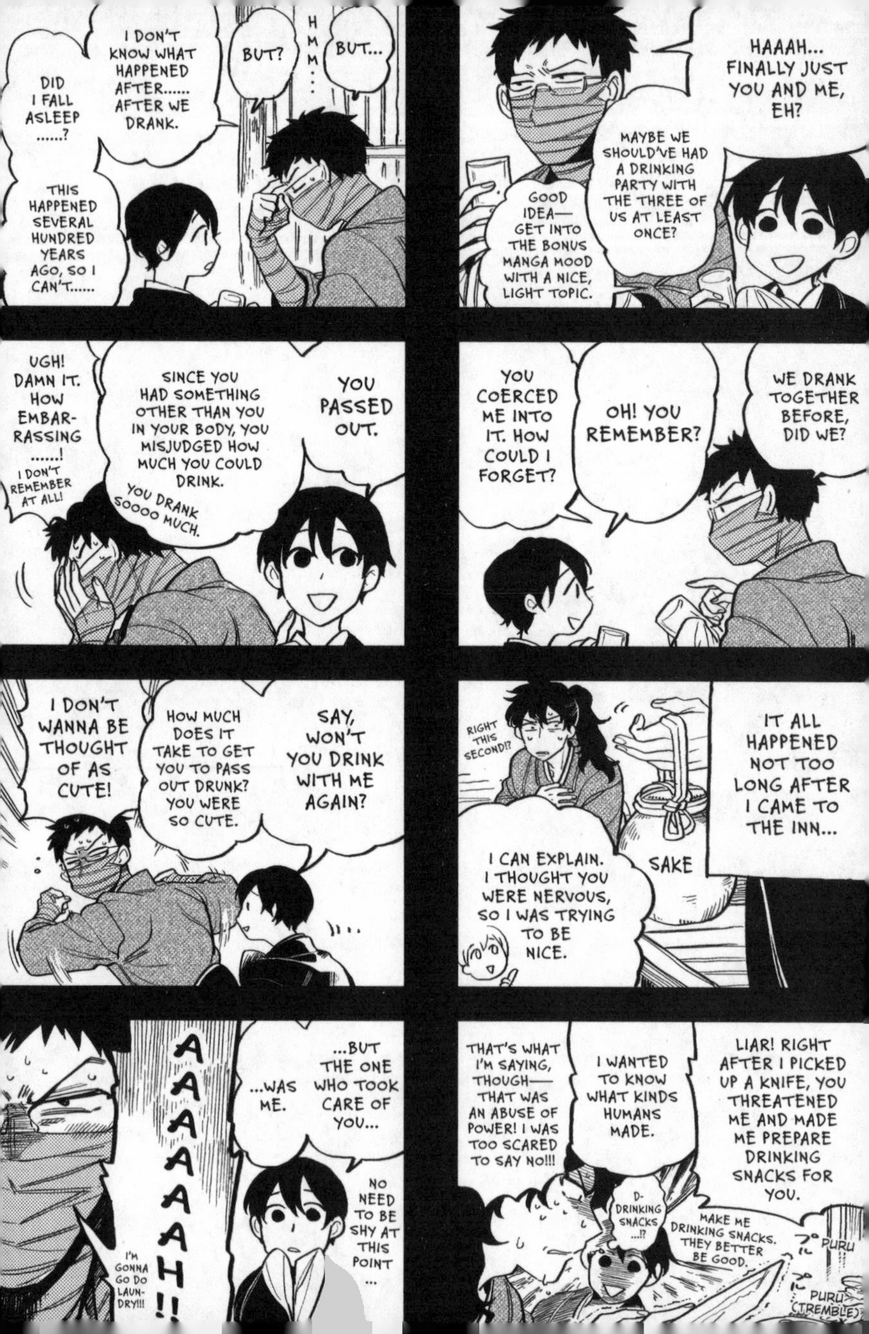
HAAAH... FINALLY JUST YOU AND ME, EH?
MAYBE WE SHOULD'VE HAD A DRINKING PARTY WITH THE THREE OF US AT LEAST ONCE?
GOOD IDEA—GET INTO THE BONUS MANGA MOOD WITH A NICE, LIGHT TOPIC.
BUT...
HMM...
BUT?
I DON'T KNOW WHAT HAPPENED AFTER...... AFTER WE DRANK.
DID I FALL ASLEEP ......?
THIS HAPPENED SEVERAL HUNDRED YEARS AGO, SO I CAN'T......
WE DRANK TOGETHER BEFORE, DID WE?
OH! YOU REMEMBER?
YOU COERCED ME INTO IT. HOW COULD I FORGET?
YOU PASSED OUT.
SINCE YOU HAD SOMETHING OTHER THAN YOU IN YOUR BODY, YOU MISJUDGED HOW MUCH YOU COULD DRINK.
YOU DRANK SOOOO MUCH.
UGH! DAMN IT. HOW EMBARRASSING ......!
I DON'T REMEMBER AT ALL!
IT ALL HAPPENED NOT TOO LONG AFTER I CAME TO THE INN...
SAKE
RIGHT THIS SECOND!?
I CAN EXPLAIN. I THOUGHT YOU WERE NERVOUS, SO I WAS TRYING TO BE NICE.
SAY, WON'T YOU DRINK WITH ME AGAIN?
HOW MUCH DOES IT TAKE TO GET YOU TO PASS OUT DRUNK? YOU WERE SO CUTE.
I DON'T WANNA BE THOUGHT OF AS CUTE!
LIAR! RIGHT AFTER I PICKED UP A KNIFE, YOU THREATENED ME AND MADE ME PREPARE DRINKING SNACKS FOR YOU.
I WANTED TO KNOW WHAT KINDS HUMANS MADE.
THAT'S WHAT I'M SAYING, THOUGH—THAT WAS AN ABUSE OF POWER! I WAS TOO SCARED TO SAY NO!!!
MAKE ME DRINKING SNACKS. THEY BETTER BE GOOD.
D-DRINKING SNACKS...!?
PURU
PURU (TREMBLE)
...BUT THE ONE WHO TOOK CARE OF YOU...
...WAS ME.
NO NEED TO BE SHY AT THIS POINT...
AAAAAAAH!!
I'M GONNA GO DO LAUNDRY!!!

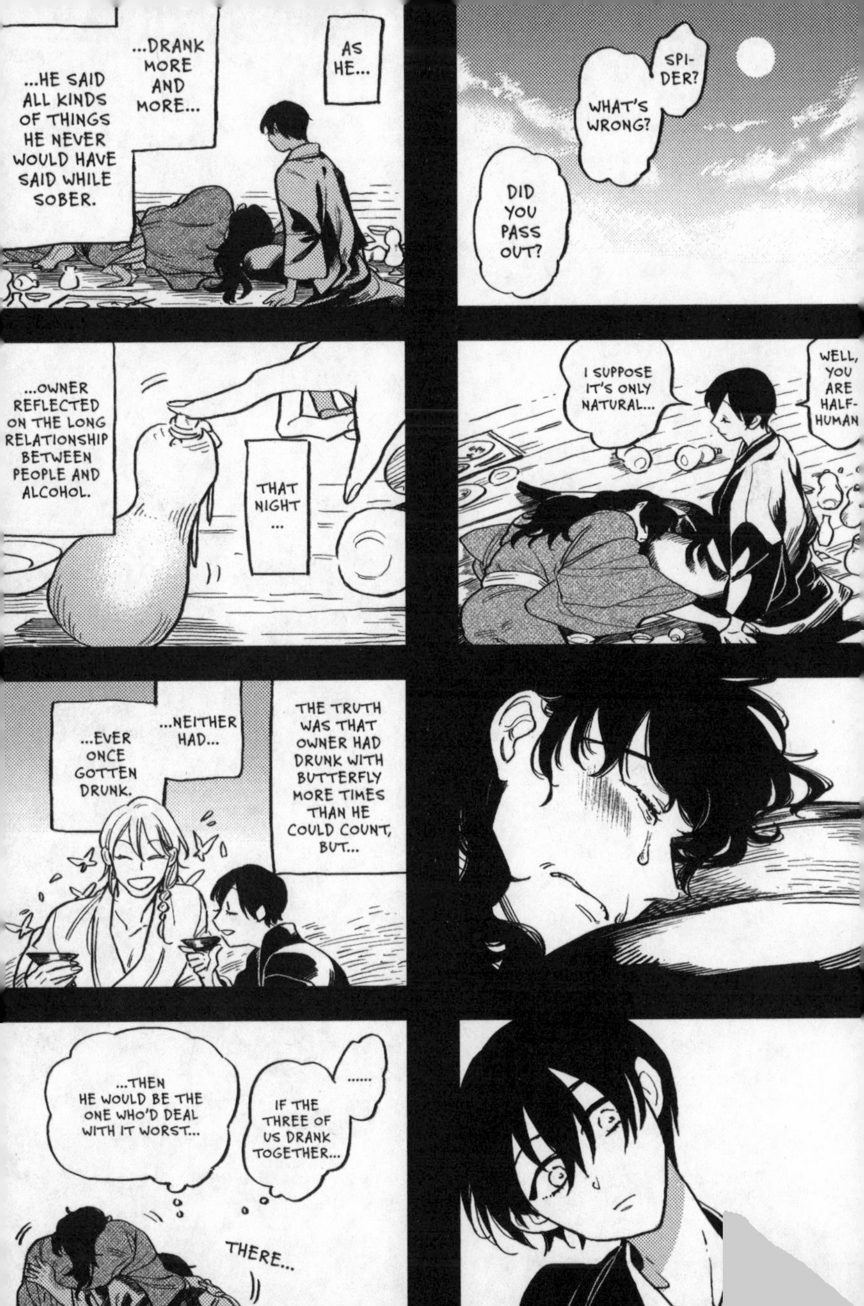
SPI-DER?
WHAT'S WRONG?
DID YOU PASS OUT?
AS HE...
...DRANK MORE AND MORE...
...HE SAID ALL KINDS OF THINGS HE NEVER WOULD HAVE SAID WHILE SOBER.
WELL, YOU ARE HALF-HUMAN
I SUPPOSE IT'S ONLY NATURAL...
THAT NIGHT...
...OWNER REFLECTED ON THE LONG RELATIONSHIP BETWEEN PEOPLE AND ALCOHOL.
THE TRUTH WAS THAT OWNER HAD DRUNK WITH BUTTERFLY MORE TIMES THAN HE COULD COUNT, BUT...
...NEITHER HAD...
...EVER ONCE GOTTEN DRUNK.
......
IF THE THREE OF US DRANK TOGETHER...
...THEN HE WOULD BE THE ONE WHO'D DEAL WITH IT WORST...
THERE...

Phantom Tales of the Night 9

Matsuri

Translation: Julie Goniwich

Lettering: Chiho Christie

BAKEMONO YAWA ZUKUSHI vol. 9
©Matsuri 2021
First published in Japan in 2021 by KADOKAWA CORPORATION, Tokyo. English translation rights arranged with KADOKAWA CORPORATION, Tokyo through TUTTLE-MORI AGENCY, INC., Tokyo.

Yen Press
150 West 30th Street, 19th Floor
New York, NY 10001

Visit us at yenpress.com
facebook.com/yenpress
twitter.com/yenpress
yenpress.tumblr.com
instagram.com/yenpress

First Yen Press Edition: July 2022
Edited by Yen Press Editorial: Danielle Niederkorn, Carl Li
Designed by Yen Press Design: Wendy Chan

Library of Congress Control Number: 2019942895

ISBNs: 978-1-9753-4528-0 (paperback)
       978-1-9753-4529-7 (ebook)

10 9 8 7 6 5 4 3 2 1

WOR

Printed in the United States of America